DAVIES

PRINCIPLES
OF
TAX LAW

AUSTRALIA
Law Book Co.
Sydney

CANADA and USA
Carswell
Toronto

HONG KONG
Sweet & Maxwell Asia

NEW ZEALAND
Brookers
Wellington

SINGAPORE and MALAYSIA
Sweet & Maxwell Asia
Singapore and Kuala Lumpur

DAVIES

PRINCIPLES OF TAX LAW

SIXTH EDITION

by

David W. Williams, LL.M., Ph.D., C.T.A.,
SOLICITOR
Social Security Commissioner and deputy Special Commissioner of Income Tax

Professor Geoffrey Morse, LL.B., BARRISTER
Professor of Corporate and Tax Law, University of Birmingham

LONDON
SWEET & MAXWELL
2008

First Edition (1980) Introduction to Revenue Law
by F.R. Davies
Second Edition (1985) Introduction to Revenue Law
by F.R. Davies, David Williams and Geoffrey Morse
Third Edition (1996) Davies: Principles of Tax Law
by Geoffrey Morse, David Williams and David Salter
Fourth Edition (2000) Davies: Principles of Tax Law
by Geoffrey Morse and David Williams
Fifth Edition (2004) Davies: Principles of Tax Law
by Geoffrey Morse and David Williams
Sixth Edition (2008) Davies: Principles of Tax Law
by Geoffrey Morse and David Williams

Published in 2008 by Sweet & Maxwell Limited of
100 Avenue Road, London, NW3 3PF
Typeset by YHT Ltd., London
Printed and bound in Great Britain
by Athenaeum Press Ltd., Gateshead, Tyne & Wear

ISBN 978 184 7033253

PREFACE TO THE SIXTH EDITION

Tax law as a subject for study at university or professional level provokes many different reactions. It is, after all, sometimes seen as a subject which consists of an almost impenetrable mass of very complex, detailed and often obscure provisions, many of a transitory nature—a subject for the specialist, (weird?) tax fanatic. It is also thought to involve the use of complex mathematical skills. To some extent, of course, at least part of that is true, but there is far more to the subject than that. Taxation is a cornerstone of this and every other civilisation—on the grand scale in the UK it has sparked a civil war, a war of independence, riots, rebellions and the fall of governments, but it is also a part of most people's everyday life and not just of non-domiciles, private equity groups or hedge funds. Above all, it is one of the principal relationships between the citizen and the state. As Lord Camden, speaking in the House of Lords, said in 1766:

> "Taxation and representation are inseparable ... whatever is a man's own, is absolutely his own; no man has a right to take it from him without his consent either expressed by himself or his representative."

Tax law is the foundation of taxation—it sets out the parameters of the subject and regulates that balance between the taxpayer and the government. Moreover, after peeling away the many layers of specialist provisions, detailed anti-avoidance sections and temporary rules, there is a clearly definable core or skeleton of tax law which is concerned with the basics of the subject. Further, this core is concerned with the very principles of tax law. Those do not require the mastery of complex factual matrices but instead require both an appreciation of the social and economic issues which underpin the tax system and an ability to define with some precision the meaning of such words as: emolument; wholly and exclusively; capital; income; dwelling house; gratuitous intent; supply etc. Students find that, far from worrying about some complex financial structure, they are concerned about such things as employee perks, the family home, even chocolate biscuits and the like.

This, the sixth edition of this book, is intended, as was the first, to explain that core or skeleton of tax law contained in the various statutes and as applied by the courts. We have concentrated on the two major revenue-raising taxes, income tax and value added tax, and the two direct taxes on capital, capital gains tax and inheritance tax, which are currently the subject of political debate. Since the last edition of the book the structure of tax law has changed in two major ways. In terms of legislative structure, the tax law rewrite project is now almost finished and income tax is now contained in a number of separate Acts, dealing with the subject in a sensible and orderly manner. In VAT, the many EC directives were consolidated into one in 2006. We would both like to record our thanks for the unsung, quiet and efficient work of the tax law rewrite team members. Their work will benefit generations of students to come.

In terms of the structure of the taxes themselves, there have been a number of upheavals in capital taxation—one in 2006 on the application of inheritance tax of trusts which was introduced with no warning or consultation and which gave trustees only a short time to limit the damage. The second, in 2008, changed the basic rate of capital gains tax, abolishing the system introduced by the same government 10 years earlier. Protests from businesses were loud and long and a new relief, based on the one abolished ten years earlier was introduced. That change was a hasty response to political pressure from the government's own back benchers. The third was also another knee-jerk reaction in the same year in the introduction of the transferable tax-free allowance for inheritance tax between spouses or civil partners. That was made in response to a very popular opposition proposal to raise the overall threshold and so allow those with modest houses south of the Wash to pass on the full value of those houses to their children. 2008 also saw an alteration in the rates of income tax, with the rather belatedly highly controversial abolition of the lower rate; and a revamp of the capital allowances and national insurance provisions.

Alongside those changes, there have been a number of important decisions by the courts, not least with regards to value added tax. The almost uniquely complicated system of that tax which operates in the UK continues to keep both domestic and the European courts in business. It is in that tax that many of the basic principles are still being honed by litigation.

For the future, one issue which will have to be resolved is how the new harmonised tribunal system in the UK will affect the Special Commissioners and VAT Tribunals and the subsequent hearings in the courts. Whatever else may be in store, and there will be an election, we will continue to keep this edition up to date by the use of a web-based supplement. In the preparation of this edition we have benefited as ever from the understanding and tolerance of both our publishers and our wives, Christine and Elisabeth, and we thank them for it.

The law in this edition is as known to the editors on July 8, 2008.

Geoffrey Morse
David Williams

Worcestershire and Gwynedd

CONTENTS

ix

CONTENTS

TABLE OF CASES

TABLE OF STATUTES

TABLE OF STATUTORY INSTRUMENTS

PART ONE

INTRODUCTION

CHAPTER 1

UNDERSTANDING TAX

Introduction

The question "What is a tax?" is surprisingly difficult to answer. **1–01**
It is tempting to rely on the well-known reply of the child who
was asked to define an elephant. "An elephant is large and grey,
and lives in a herd of elephants." Some payments are not clearly
one of the herd. This is so, for example, of the profits made on
postage stamps or the fees paid to government for the right to
operate independent television channels. Clarity is not helped
because some politicians find it convenient to say that things are
not tax when they certainly seem to look like taxes. An example
is national insurance contributions.

Defining taxes
So, as the elephant definition does not seem to work, we must **1–02**
try to define a tax. A tax has three characteristics. It is *a compulsory levy imposed by an organ of government for public purposes.* (For a rare judicial discussion of the meaning of "tax"
see *IRC v Oce van der Grinten* (2000) and, following a reference
to the European Court of Justice, ibid. (2003)). The legal essence
of this definition lies in the compulsion. Law requires that the
payment be made. The political essence lies in the public purposes for which the payments are made. Even the definition
reflects the disagreements that often take place about tax.

Another way to define taxes is by listing of levies that are,
beyond doubt, British taxes. Listing them all would be both
contentious and tedious. But here is a list of the ten principal
sources of tax revenue, in order of importance to government,
estimated for the year of writing (with the amounts estimated to
be received for 2007–08 in £billion): income tax (150), NI
contributions (97), VAT (81), corporation tax (46), fuel duties
(25), council tax (24), business rates (22), stamp duties (15),
with alcoholic drinks duties and tobacco duties coming a joint
tenth on £8 billion each. Capital gains tax (5) and inheritance
tax (4) do not even make this top ten. But they rank in the top
six in terms of complexity. Various other customs duties and
levies still rank above them (10 in total). But several of them are

3

not British taxes. Rather, the total is of the European taxes such as customs duties that are collected in the UK for the European authorities. Then there are others such as vehicle excise duty (6) and environmental taxes such as the climate change levy, and we could go on to add the lottery levy, the ports levy ... but then the list does get tedious.

Why do we tax?

1–03   Before we look in detail at the present United Kingdom tax system, it is valuable to spend a little time thinking about tax policy. Why do we tax the way we do? What are the political, economic, social and administrative pressures that have contributed to the shape of our tax system?

The primary purpose of taxation is to raise revenue for government expenditure. The government can raise revenue by borrowing, by "printing" money, and by selling things, but in practice it is unavoidable that taxation should raise most of the government's fiscal requirements. The government spends part of the money on services which private enterprise cannot provide, such as defence and law and order. It also pays for services that it is thought are better provided on a universal basis, such as social security benefits, and education. Attitudes to taxation depend to some extent on the views of taxpayers as to the merits of these items of government expenditure. Do you, for example, think it the job of government to provide a health service, or consumer protection laws, or pensions? If raising money to pay for these things was the only reason for taxes, however, we could have a much simpler system. If we raised the rate of income tax by two per cent, we could abolish inheritance tax and capital gains tax and still make money. Or we could raise the rate of value added tax and abolish most of income tax. Would that be fair? Would it be efficient?

1–04   Another purpose behind taxation is the redistribution of wealth and income. Certain aspects of this idea are generally agreed. It is generally—but not universally—agreed that income tax should be "progressive", and that some government revenue should be spent on welfare services. This was a major reason why the poll tax was so unpopular. People thought it unfair that everyone should pay *the same* tax, whether they were rich or poor, just because they lived in the same town. An unpopular tax is a failure—it loses politicians votes, and it proves too expensive to collect. Of course, for any tax the questions of rate and amount are of immense importance. *How* progressive should income tax be? *How much* should be spent on social services? Once upon a time it was considered right that income tax had a top rate of 98 per cent. Does anyone think that right now? Few do, but "once upon a time" was only 40 years ago. Fashions change in tax as in all else.

Taxes as means of control

Another purpose behind imposing taxes is control of the economy. Changes in taxation can and do affect the economy, but control is also exercised by adjusting the money supply and credit. A good example of using tax to control behaviour is the use of customs duties. There used to be a very high customs duty on imported leather. The aim was to protect the Scottish leather industry. This tax was successful because it collected no money! This also shows that taxes are not used only to raise money. That is an important point. One main way in which taxes are used to influence people is by what is *not* taxed. For instance, we put value added tax on most things that people buy, but we do not tax medicines. 1–05

eg Tax on leather

Taxes may also be used as a kind of social control. We see this idea concerning the taxing of alcohol and tobacco. More recently, politicians have decided that cars are less of a good thing, so they have been increasing the cost of taxes on them. 1–06

We can also use taxes to make sure people pay the full price for something. This is the idea of a pollution tax. When I buy goods, I pay the price the seller asks. That makes the seller a profit and meets the costs. What if the seller has polluted the local area while making the goods? Perhaps the seller has made something that I am going to dump untidily when I have finished with it (like car tyres or plastic bags)? Taxes can be used to impose the cost of destroying the tyre and collecting up the bags. This is a matter of debate at present. It is not widely used as a form of tax in Britain. There is an informal levy imposed by sellers on the price of every tyre and car battery to pay for its destruction. In 1996 a landfill tax was introduced and then a climate control levy and an aggregates levy.

Principles of Taxation

Choosing taxes, and the reasons for taxes, is a fascinating topic of academic analysis and discussion. It leads on to an easy question that it is almost impossible to answer: what is the best form of tax? That debate was started in this country by a former customs official, Adam Smith in *The Wealth of Nations* (first published in 1776). Smith set out four "canons" that, in his view, lead to better taxes. In modified form, they still influence official thinking today. The four axioms are: 1–07

5

- people should contribute taxes in proportion to their incomes and wealth;
- taxes should be certain, not arbitrary;
- taxes should be levied in the most convenient way;
- the costs of imposing and collecting taxes should be kept minimal.

To this we must add a modern canon: taxes should be both convenient and competitive internationally. We are a trading nation, and we trade in a global economy.

Taxation, then, can be used for several purposes other than collecting money. For a more detailed discussion, see Kay and King, *The British Tax System* (Oxford University Press). There is another side to the question of "better" taxes. If a tax operates in a certain way that they can sidestep (such as stamp duty taxing documents, but not oral transactions), people will change the way they do things to pay less tax. That is human nature. A tax that does not alter behaviour is said to be *neutral*. The aim of those designing taxes is to create neutral taxes, unless policy requires a tax to be non-neutral. In practice, taxes often have unintended side effects. The United Kingdom suffers, some allege, from this problem of non-neutral taxes.

Is *taxation fair?*

1–08   Let us look at the tax system from the point of view of justice. The current thinking on this matter concentrates on *equity*, which in this context means fairness. *Horizontal equity* is the idea that people in equal circumstances should pay an equal amount of tax. *Vertical equity* means that people in different circumstances should pay an appropriately different amount of tax.

1–09   Horizontal equity commands strong support. It was the reason that Adam Smith advocated an income tax, and it is a major reason for that form of tax today. Those with similar levels of income should pay similar levels of tax. Why should that be so? There are several ways of justifying the levels of tax paid by individuals. One economic view is the ability-to-pay argument. On that basis, those with equal ability to pay should pay equally. Another economic view is the benefit argument. Those who pay tax should do so according to the benefits they gain. Leaving aside personal circumstances (for example, that A needs more help than B because A is older/younger/less fit than B), again those with similar means should be paying similar taxes. The same result is achieved by taking the lawyer's view of fairness that "we are all equal before the law", or the democratic view that we are all members of the same society, and are equal within it.

Vertical equity is much more controversial. It is generally agreed that the richer should pay more tax than the poorer. That was why so many people did not like the poll tax, and found it "unfair". Incidentally, they effectively threw out the benefit argument in so doing, and dismissed the "equal before the law" view as insufficient. But how much more should the richer be paying? Even with a proportional tax the richer do pay more than the poorer. If there were an income tax at a flat rate of 30 per cent, someone with an income of £100,000 would pay £30,000 in tax. This is more than the £300 that someone with an income of £1,000 would pay. Should the person with £100,000 pay more tax than the person with £1,000 not merely absolutely but also proportionally? This is where a progressive tax comes in. Instead of paying at 30 per cent, those on £100,000 income should pay rather more (at least, on part of their income), and those with £1,000 rather less. Again the details become as important as the principle. Precisely what percentage? And on precisely what part of the income? Why?

1–10

An important aspect of the justice—or otherwise—of the tax system is the *tax base*. The base of a tax means the thing, transaction, or amount on which the tax is raised. All taxes have bases—whether the base is you (in the case of a poll tax), your income, your wealth, the number of shoes you buy, or whatever. This means the precise boundary of what is taxed as distinct from what is not taxed. Let us take an example. Hal has £200,000 in hand. He uses it to buy a house in which he then lives, paying no rent. Cher also has £200,000 in hand. She spends it on buying company shares. She lives in a rented house. Hal pays no tax on the use he has made of his £200,000 (the occupation of his house). Cher does pay tax on the use she has made of her £200,000 (the dividends). Is this fair?

1–11

As Adam Smith pointed out, another aspect of justice is certainty. The tax system should be clear, so that a taxpayer can see in advance how much tax must be paid. Secondly, enforcement should be consistent and universal. There is nothing more destructive of taxpayer morality than the suspicion that others are not paying. If you pay only half your income tax because of a trick, why should I pay more than that? Equally, if you get some form of special allowance, why should I not get one too? But if neither of us understands the law, we do not know if we are paying enough. So, certainty also requires rules that can be understood. This thought leads to another of the paradoxes of tax. The simpler the rules are, the less fair they are (because they ignore justified differences). But the fairer they are, the more complex they are. The more complex they are, the harder they are to understand and put into effect. Therefore they are less certain and, arguably, appear less fair. If both simplicity and complexity lead to unfairness, is there a happy medium?

Is taxation efficient?

1–12   The fourth Smithian canon is cost-effectiveness. The effectiveness of a tax system is partly a matter of success in enforcement, and partly a matter of the total cost of running it and complying with it. Some think that enforcement, in the case of income tax, is not showing a very high success rate. What we call the black economy has grown up, including moonlighting and other forms of tax evasion. Moonlighting is the practice of earning and paying tax on a source of income properly, but then undertaking a second job without declaring the tax. Then there are the ghosts—those who do not appear on any tax department records, and therefore pay no tax. Or do they? In practice, they may pay no direct income tax, but they would be hard put also to avoid all VAT.

Currently, the cost of collecting direct taxes is about two per cent of the total net yield, and the cost of collecting indirect taxes varies from tax to tax. But, of course, this deals only with the direct government costs. There are also hidden *compliance costs*, that is, the costs incurred by taxpayers in paying taxes. Two notable examples of these compliance costs are the costs of an employer for staff hours acting as an unpaid collector of income tax under the PAYE system, and the costs to a trader in complying with the VAT system. Both may also incur substantial costs for professional assistance and advice concerning tax affairs.

There is also an even more deeply hidden cost, a kind of social cost, which the community as a whole pays as part of the price of taxation. What we have in mind is the expenditure (one might almost say waste) of brain power. Some of the best brains in the country are exclusively devoted to tax matters; some on the official side, some on the other side. This brain power could be better employed in increasing the wealth, health or happiness of the community. In the past, this brain drain was closely linked to the immensity of the rates of tax. If someone is asked to pay 98 per cent income tax, or even 75 per cent tax, there is a high premium on good advice to avoid it. If income tax had a maximum rate of, say, 10 per cent, much less time and effort would be devoted to escaping the tax. But what would the state stop doing in return?

As for the effects of taxation, we are afraid that this is a topic where asking questions is easier than answering them. Does a high rate of income tax encourage people to work harder or does it discourage them? Most people would say that it discourages them, that it is a disincentive. But it is quite possible to argue that, on the contrary, it spurs people on to earn more, so that even when the tax is paid they will have enough left to live on. Does a high rate of tax on business raise prices? Does a high rate of tax on individuals raise wages and salaries? No one seems to know the answers. A high *average* rate of tax is probably an incentive to work, whereas high *marginal* rates are disincentives.

Tax Avoidance and Evasion

Of course, the ideal position for the taxpayer confronted with this dilemma is to ensure that whatever others pay, I pay no more tax than I must. In considering this, it is very important to emphasise the distinction between *tax avoidance* and *tax evasion*. Tax avoidance is arranging my affairs within the rules so that I pay the smallest tax bill that is possible. This is perfectly lawful. Tax evasion is when you escape tax by unlawful means. This usually involves some form of dishonesty, ranging from omitting to state some item of income in a tax return to forging a document to create untrue "facts". It is not easy to see (and keep to) the distinction between evasion and avoidance—if needed, evasion involves some crime where avoidance involves no crime. Two factors blur this distinction in practice. First, some quite honourable people think that a tax crime is not "really" a crime at all. What is "really" wrong with omitting to mention in a tax return some jobbing gardening or book-reviewing done at weekends? We tend to think that what we do ourselves is not really criminal at all. What others do is always bigger and badder. The second factor is that crime versus no crime is not the last word on the subject. Elaborate schemes of tax avoidance that have no other purpose may not be criminal, but they are distasteful to many taxpayers and to some judges.

Some taxes are more easily avoided than others. For example, income tax is more easily avoided than VAT. It is partly for this reason that governments have made a big switch from income tax to VAT. We did not have VAT as a tax in 1970. Just 40 years later it is one of our biggest taxes. Indeed, replacement of income tax by an expenditure tax is advocated in some quarters. The merits of this are said to be that it would be less easily avoided or evaded, it would encourage saving, and it would be cheaper to administer. (Remember that the cost of collecting

1–13

indirect taxes is less than the cost of collecting direct taxes.) On the other hand it contradicts the progressive principle. An expenditure tax hits the poor harder than it would hit the rich.

International aspects

1–14   We added a new principle to those of Adam Smith. It is that our rules have to work in the international arena. There are two aspects to this. First, we are now part of the European Union, and must comply with its rules. Secondly, there is strong tax competition between states. Tax systems are as much part of the global marketplace as any other aspect of a country. Both are extremely important in any overall view of current British tax policy. There is another dilemma here: we must both join them and beat them.

1–15   Say it softly, but Britain's entry into the EU limited the powers of the British Parliament and Government in respect of taxation. Certain articles of the EU Treaty prohibit rules of tax that would discriminate against persons in other Member States. Another article provides for Member States to work towards tax harmonisation, at least on indirect taxes—those on goods. This movement has progressed farthest in the field of VAT. It is partly why VAT is now so important as a British tax, but it is not the only reason. For most of British—and before it, English—history, the extraordinary revenues of the Crown (as taxes were called) came from customs duties on imports, and from excises. Excises have now been replaced by VAT—a European tax. Customs have now been replaced by the Community customs regime. So much so is this that to call the relevant collection department "Her Majesty's Customs" is a bit of a misnomer. It would be more accurate to call it "Her Majesty's VAT and Duties"—but it is nothing like as romantic. It would be even less romantic, and even more accurate, to call it "Her Majesty's part of the European VAT and Duties". But that might invoke the response given to Alice by the Queen of Hearts.

Our direct taxes have not been affected by the rising tide of EU law. Well, even that is not true, as we shall see. We might avoid the EU tide. We cannot avoid the currents caused by global tax competition. Ours is a world of offshore jurisdictions, tax havens (or tax heavens as French students consistently mistranslate "paradis fiscaux"), customs unions, free-trade zones, enterprise zones, special regimes, jurisdictions, tax holidays, free depreciation regimes ... in short, a highly competitive marketplace. This is the territory of international tax law, and the many thousands of double tax agreements entered into by states—fascinating, but beyond the scope of an introductory book. We must now begin at the beginning.

Introducing the Taxes

We want to finish this introduction, and start our detailed   1–16
analysis of tax, by introducing the taxes dealt with in this book and then by referring generally to the kinds of taxes that exist, and the issues that each tax must tackle. We want to try to state in a very few words what it is that each tax is taxing.

First, **income tax**. Why? Because it is in government terms the largest revenue raiser, and therefore the most important tax. And because, with corporation tax, it is the most complex tax, and the hardest to understand. And because it involves significant efforts by lawyers and accountants to ensure that their clients comply with the law, and avoid its excesses. What does it tax? In a famous aphorism in *London County Council v Attorney-General*, HL, Lord Macnaghten said: "Income tax, if I may be pardoned for saying so, is a tax on income." This is largely, but not absolutely, true. There are some items of income that are not taxed–for example, student grants. So income tax is not a tax on all income. On the other hand, there are some charges to income tax that are imposed on receipts that are not income tax receipts, but rather capital receipts. This is so, for example, of taxing premiums received on leasing land. Anyway, what is income? Such questions are why we wrote much of this book!

Second, social security contributions (or **NI contributions** as everyone and everything except the law itself terms them), which are the second source of government finance, and, for most people, a second income tax. The law is a little less complex and comprehensive than income tax law but is very similar to parts of income tax law, so it requires less extended treatment.

Third, **VAT** (which is what the Act imposing value added tax calls it, so we shall too). Why? Because it has become the most litigated of the taxes, and is gaining in complexity and practical importance each year.

Fourthly, **corporation tax**. This is simply income tax and capital gains tax imposed on companies. Well, not simply— parts are fiendishly complicated, although we avoid the worst of it!

Fifthly, **capital gains tax** (CGT). Its fiscal significance is trivial compared with the taxes so far listed. Nevertheless, its complexity—and therefore its nuisance value to lawyers—far outweighs its importance in filling a gap in the income tax. What it taxes is the gain represented by the difference between the price at which an item was acquired and the price at which it is sold. Since 1982 this taxes the *real* gain (taking account of inflation), not the *cash* gain.

Sixthly, **inheritance tax (IHT)** or, as it used to be called before they thought it fun to change its name, capital transfer tax. It is a tax on capital transfers, and has never been a tax on inheritances, but what does that matter? It is a tax on transfers of property by certain gifts, by transfers into trust, and by operation of law on someone's death from that person's estate. Although whether or not it is accurately named does not matter, accurate advice on where it may affect capital transfers is important. Again we must examine it in detail.

Collecting taxes

1–17   All these taxes, and all other taxes in Britain, can be grouped under three broad heads of taxation in terms of the way they are imposed and collected: withholding taxes, taxation related to particular transactions or their effects (called transactions taxes for short), and taxes based on profits or wealth of any kind (called assessed taxes, but normally now self-assessed). British taxes are of all these kinds, frequently muddled up together.

A withholding tax is a tax imposed on the payer of a sum so that the recipient receives less than would otherwise be received. For example, someone paying patent royalties to another person will be required to deduct from that sum an amount equal to the basic rate of income tax. If this is done, the recipient is treated as having paid tax on those royalties. The tax authorities are always on the lookout for ways of increasing the payment of taxes at source in this way. Most income tax and NI contributions are collected in this way through the PAYE system. Under most forms of withholding tax, the payer is liable to pay the tax to the tax authorities even though it was the *recipient* who is really paying the tax.

Transactions taxes are those based on particular transactions or their results. VAT is usually imposed on any supply of goods or services made by a business. Stamp duty is imposed whenever a document is used to transfer land. However, as electronic transfers take over, the stamp duty reserve tax and stamp duty land tax have been introduced to cover all transactions. Inheritance tax and capital gains tax can be regarded as being transactions taxes.

Assessed taxes are the most important taxes in Britain although most are now self-assessed by taxpayers. Income tax raises most of its money from the income of the employed, the self-employed and those with investment income. So does the National Insurance Fund through NI contributions. Then there are the special assessed taxes like petroleum revenue tax.

Anatomy of a tax

Whichever form of tax we adopt, and whatever the fiscal or 1–18 other reasons for its adoption, the lawyer's task is to identify when it is payable and when not. Tax law, or revenue law as many also call it, is there to define when taxes shall be charged. In respect of each tax this definition will contain the same elements:

- the tax base;
- the incidence (including the rate) of the tax; and
- the taxpayer, or person liable to pay.

The rate is often the most important point politically or commercially, but rarely detains the lawyer long. The other issues need further thought.

The tax base, as we have seen already, is the asset, transaction, profit or other thing which is liable to the tax. This may be anything from a television to the net profits of a year's trading. Each tax will have a limited tax base, the limits being of two kinds: the general limits on that kind of tax, and specific exceptions. Clearly, the wider the tax base of a tax, the more revenue it will collect. The more exceptions that are allowed, the smaller the return from the tax. Over the years, all our main taxes have become subject to important exceptions. This is partly because granting an exception is very easy politically, and votes are not easily won for removing it later. Nonetheless, in the last few years more attention has been turned to both the limits on the tax bases of our taxes and the width of exceptions. It has become common-place to regard exceptions as tax expenditures, that is, subsidies created by the tax not collected. The cost of these tax expenditures has often been worked out. As a result, some longstanding exceptions and reliefs from tax have been removed, such as the life assurance relief that lasted from 1842 to 1984.

The second issue is the identity of the taxpayer. Economists 1–19 talk of this as the incidence of the tax, distinguishing between the *formal incidence* of the tax (who is required by law to pay it) and the *effective incidence* (who ends up paying). Lawyers are concerned only with formal incidence. In most cases under modern laws different people can be made to pay in respect of some taxes, especially when withholding taxes are used to collect the tax. For example, if someone makes a gift of shares to someone else on which inheritance tax ought to be paid, the authorities can try to collect the tax from the donor, the recipient and most subsequent owners of the shares.

The Tax Authorities

Two departments into one
1–20   For centuries, our national taxes were administered by two government departments. They were the Inland Revenue Commissioners (known universally as "the Revenue") and Her Majesty's Customs and Excise (always proud of being "HM", but known by everyone else simply as "Customs"). They were unusual departments of state in that they were not headed by politicians. We have had no Ministers of Tax or Ministers of Finance. It was decided wisely a long time ago that politicians should not be involved in levying individual tax bills, because then they were directly responsible for them. Instead, both departments were headed by boards of Commissioners, individually appointed by the monarch. Further, the Commissioners were made responsible to the courts for all their decisions, but not to Parliament. High policy was left to the Treasury, but most policy decisions about the taxes themselves were taken by the two departments.

HMRC
1–21   The Commissioners for Revenue and Customs Act 2005 merged the two departments into one, Her Majesty's Commissioners for Revenue and Customs. At the same time there were two other changes. Most of the policy teams of the two departments were moved into HM Treasury. The Treasury and its ministers now have direct responsibility for almost all policy issues to do with any form of tax. And the prosecution functions of the two departments were hived off to become a separate tax prosecutions office.

The new department (under the standard abbreviation HMRC) has the same shape as its predecessors. It is headed by Commissioners appointed by The Queen, any two of whom can form the Board of Revenue and Customs. Below the Board, everyone else with authority to take individual decisions is now known as an officer of Revenue and Customs. All the old grades such as surveyor, inspector, or assessor have been combined into this one status. Further, HMRC has now insisted that all tax cases before the tribunals and courts be taken in its name. No longer can you tell indirect tax cases from direct tax cases by the name of the case ("Customs and Excise" not "IRC"). But you can also now always tell if a case is a tax case. The much-treasured prize of being the duty inspector of taxes who had his or her name immortalised by being the party to an income tax case has ended. And you can tell which are the new cases. All new tax appeals from 2006 are now "*v HMRC*".

The new department faced an enormous task in merging itself into a composite whole. The two separate departments had widely different cultures. For example, one was much more ready to challenge taxpayers through the criminal and civil courts and tribunals than the other. They also had widely different powers, even down to different time limits, under which to work. These are steadily being merged into a consistent set of powers. This happened with many time limits, powers and penalties in the Finance Act 2008. Further common ground will be established when the separate appeal routes from what are now parts of the same department are created, on current plans as we write, in 2009. 1–22

Another aspect to the merger is that of locations and internal structures. This has not been an easy process, not least because it is also combined with steps to automate considerable parts of the service provided by HMRC, and steps to transfer all appropriate areas to, or back to, taxpayers or their agents. Further, the department has also been expected to slim down. Nor should the scale of the operation be underestimated. HMRC is now responsible for all national taxes, including NI contributions, and all valuations for local taxes. It is also responsible for other earnings-linked activities: tax credits and some social security benefits, the national minimum wage and student loans repayments.

Controlling the tax authorities

It is important to note that the tax authorities are constrained to act only within the legislative powers at their disposal. As we explore in the next chapter, the United Kingdom has no constitution. It therefore has no constitutional limits on executive action. History is replete with examples of tax authorities being used to extract taxes for dubious official use. In most advanced states, there are therefore constitutional checks on such action. Lacking such limits in the United Kingdom, it has been left to judges to prevent the use of arbitrary power. They have been alert to ensure that a tax authority has clear legal authority both to collect a tax, and to carry out the procedures necessary to do this. Taxpayers have also been alert to ensure that any apparent 1–23 stepping beyond the limits is challenged. The result is a developed administrative law of taxation. If you look at any book on constitutional and administrative law, you will see a significant number of tax cases cited. It is precisely because it is only through such cases that the balance has been struck between the Executive and the taxpayer.

At the same time, the fair enforcement of a tax such as income tax depends heavily on taxpayers honestly providing information about what they are earning. Authorities need strong powers to obtain information and collect taxes from those who do not comply readily or who are dishonest. A balance has to be struck between giving powers to the tax authorities on the one side and respecting rights of taxpayers on the other. In particular, individual taxpayers do not expect their privacy to be invaded by tax officers, nor do businesses wish to sacrifice commercial confidentiality. Both will want to be inconvenienced to the minimum extent by the process of collecting and paying taxes.

The balance is struck in three ways. First, the powers of the tax authorities are limited by law and often subject to internal safeguards. These are found in the Taxes Management Act, the Customs and Excise Management Act and the Acts providing for individual taxes. Secondly, a dispute about either the law or the facts (and often also the procedure) can be referred to independent tribunals and courts. Thirdly, independent reviewers can check the fairness and efficacy of administrative issues.

Tax appeal tribunals

1–24   The bodies that determine tax appeals are another reminder of how old our tax systems are. Reform of them has been considered actively since at least 1993 but is still ongoing at the time of writing. The Tribunals, Courts and Enforcement Act 2007 provides the legislative structure for major reforms of administrative appeals, including tax appeals. And the Finance Act 2008 provides further powers for tax appeals. A new system is scheduled to apply to tax appeals in 2009. It is much needed now that there is only one central department of state dealing with all the national taxes. Until it happens, we need to outline both the current system and the proposed system.

If you want to appeal against a decision by HMRC about any main direct tax (income tax, NI contributions, corporation tax, CGT), you actually make your appeal to the HMRC officers responsible for the decision. There is a general right of appeal against any such decisions under s.31 of the Taxes Management Act.

Under new provisions in the Finance Act 2008, HMRC will respond to an appeal by reviewing the decision being challenged. In effect it will take a second decision. This allows it to look at any new factor introduced to the decision by the taxpayer.

The review may end the dispute. If not, the appeal continues. But HMRC will still try and settle most appeals with you even after looking at their own decision again. If they can reach agreement with you, then under s.54 of the Taxes Management Act they will seek to put that agreement into writing. If both sides agree, then that is the end of the appeal. And that is where most direct tax appeals end.

General and Special Commissioners

If a taxpayer will not agree, then HMRC must pass it on to one of two tribunals, at the choice of the taxpayer. There are local tax tribunals called the General Commissioners of Income Tax, and there is a central tax tribunal known as the Special Commissioners of Income Tax. The General Commissioners are based locally throughout the country. A tribunal will consist of two or more Commissioners sitting together with a clerk. The Commissioners are not lawyers or tax experts. The expert is the clerk. The Commissioners are local volunteers. They are chosen for their local knowledge of business.

1–25

The Special Commissioners are all tax specialist lawyers appointed for their professional expertise. They work from offices in London, Manchester and Edinburgh but sit in Cardiff, Belfast and the regions also. Unlike the General Commissioners, they have powers to award costs and impose penalties on the parties.

Appeals from the Commissioners to the Courts can only take place on a point of law. In practice a Special Commissioner always gives full reasons for a decision. General Commissioners do not give full reasons unless they are asked to do so by "stating a case". See ss.56-56A of the Taxes Management Act. The appeals are heard by the judges of the Chancery Division in England and Wales.

The VATD tribunal

Appeals on VAT, on customs duties matters and on excise duty decisions all go to the VAT and Duties Tribunal (VATDT). This is a single tribunal sitting locally throughout the United Kingdom. It consists of a chairman (always a lawyer) with one

1–26

or two wing members (paid tribunal members recruited with various areas of expertise).

The VATDT is now based in the same London, Manchester and Edinburgh offices as the Special Commissioners and most chairman are also deputy Special Commissioners. They have the same President at their head. But their procedures remain quite different. Appeals to the courts also go, in England and Wales, to the Chancery Division.

The new tribunals

1–27   In 2009 these three tribunals will be merged into a single tax chamber of the new multifunctional First Tier Tribunal. This will have a common team of tribunal judges to chair individual hearings, with a common team of members to sit as the wing members. Instead of the cases going to the courts, they will in Great Britain go to the tax chamber of the new Upper Tribunal. The ability to appeal will be limited. There is at present an open appeal on a VAT decision. Under the new rules the intending appellant will need permission from a first tier judge or an upper tribunal judge to appeal.

Tax reviews

1–28   There are two more informal ways in which taxpayers can get cases reviewed by independent assessors. The first is to refer matters to the Adjudicator. The office of adjudicator is informal, but provides a way in which a dissatisfied customer (as taxpayers are called in marketspeak) can get a file reopened and looked at afresh.

The Parliamentary Ombudsman provides a semi-formal method of reviewing complaints of taxpayers. The Parliamentary Ombudsman is an officer of parliament who has the specific job of investigating allegations that injustice has been caused to complainants by means of maladministration by a government department. Complaints to the Ombudsman are routed through the complainant's MP. Complaints can result in financial redress. This may be appropriate where no formal appeal is possible, or where the Revenue and Customs have applied a rule in a way that may strictly be correct, but has worked unfairly (for example, they have enforced the rule unevenly).

The tax professions

1–29   Our final introductory topic is that of the professional status of those who advise on tax matters. Taxpayers' advisers may belong to several professions or to none. Unlike the legal profession, but following the general approach taken to accountants in the country, the tax profession is an open profession not a closed profession. This means that a tax practitioner does not need a specific qualification to deal with tax affairs. Qualifications are only needed to represent a taxpayer before an appeal tribunal, and there the qualifications of both lawyers and accountants are recognised.

More generally, the complexity of tax makes a professional training advisable to any tax practitioner. There are, however, three separate routes to such status. The only specialist bodies covering the full range of taxation are the Chartered Institute of Taxation, whose members style themselves chartered tax practitioners, and the Association of Tax Technicians linked to it. Many tax practitioners are also lawyers (perhaps associated with the Revenue Bar or specialist solicitors), or accountants (where they may be associated with the Tax Faculty established by the Institute of Chartered Accountants of England and Wales). There is also the Institute of Indirect Tax Practitioners. A fourth source of private tax practitioners is former staff of the tax departments. However, as the profession is an open one, so that no qualification is needed to claim expertise in tax, there is also a range of less formally qualified advisers, and also limited companies, operating in the field. As this book shows, it is increasingly difficult to justify expertise in the field without a formal qualification. In Germany, for example, where tax is largely a closed profession, it has been stated that no individual can properly claim to be an expert in the whole field of taxation.

It may be for this reason that we are now starting to see reported cases about the (alleged) negligence of tax professionals: see *Palmer v Maloney* (1999), where the Court of Appeal could not agree.

Tax laws may be compared more with an iceberg than an elephant. They are certainly vast and often grey to the outsider. But they are also capable of sinking *The Titanic*! In practice, you will find that there is a lot more to the subject when you examine it closely than is seen by those who merely view it from a distance. Let us learn how to negotiate the ice flows.

1–30

CHAPTER 2

HANDLING TAX LAWS

Introduction

2–01   Tax is often regarded as being about numbers. Tax law is about words. It is an odd thing that many lawyers seem worried about studying tax, because they are worried about the numbers, while many others are worried about tax, because they are worried about the words! What needs to be understood by many lawyers is that you can be a completely sound tax lawyer yet leave the numbers for others to work out. That is the approach taken in this book. Any examples will be simple ones! At the same time, it is of the highest importance that a tax lawyer is fully competent at interpreting and applying the laws that impose taxes. This is because, quite simply, every tax case is a case about statutory interpretation and application.

2–02   The purpose of this chapter is to make an initial survey of the raw material of a tax lawyer's work—the statutes and other materials to be used in finding out what the relevant tax law for a particular matter is, what that law means, and how it is to be applied. To do this we must first reflect on the history of tax law. Despite Mr Ford's views on such things, it is not bunk. We must also examine the territorial extent of the tax laws. Having set the scene, we look at the forms of tax legislation, and current criticisms about those forms. Another point of importance is finding out about the current law. Tax law changes with extreme rapidity, and to be out of date is easy but useless. How are tax questions researched? That we must explore. We then look at how the laws are handled—the methods of interpretation and application, including some thoughts on the use of techniques to avoid the application of tax laws. Some of what we say is relevant to the study of any statute law. That does not make it any less important. On the contrary, the techniques involved are central to a lawyer's skills, and repetition of them is always justified.

History

It is no coincidence that some of the oldest documents in   2–03
existence are tax returns. We hold tax laws from over four
millennia ago in the British Museum archives. Wherever there is
social organisation there is also tax, unless there is almost total
slavery or serfdom. Even in the shorter history of England (and
the much shorter history of Great Britain) taxation played a
central role. It lay behind several rebellions (including, of course,
that of the American colonies) and the failure of governments,
both ancient and modern. We will not stray into those areas
now, fascinating as they are, just for their own sake. Happily,
others have chronicled the subject with care. Pre-eminent among
recent historians is Basil Sabine, whose *History of Income Tax*
and well-written contributions to the *British Tax Review* are of
considerable help. Stephen Dowell's *History of Taxation*, written at the beginning of last century, spans the previous 600
years, but is sadly found in too few libraries.

Is not the history of tax yet more clutter in the study of a
complex subject? We think not. We need to examine the back-
grounds of our taxes. This is because some of them are old and
understandable only in the context of their origins. Others of
our taxes may be new but there are lessons to be learnt from
previous experiments that are of continuing relevance.

The oldest regular taxes are the **stamp duties**. These were
introduced in 1694 by William of Orange. They were a direct
import from his home territories. The proceeds were exported,
in the shape of the English Navy, to fight the French. The taxes
changed little between 1694 and 2003, when some (but not yet
all) of the tax was modernised.

Income Tax

The next tax to be introduced was the **income tax**. Its pro-   2–04
ceeds were also exported to fight the French although, arguably,
the tax was the invention of a Frenchman, Colbert. It was
adopted in 1799 as a temporary tax to finance the war against
Napoleon. At the time, it replaced, and to some extent copied,
what were known as the assessed taxes and land tax that had
been used for over a century before. The need for new revenue
was desperate. The usual practice until then had to be to tax
things. In large part this was done by customs duties, the takings
from which were reduced sharply by the war at sea. In Britain
itself, the usual practice was to put excise taxes on things—
windows, servants, tea, wigs—but these were not enough. Pitt

introduced a "contribution on property, profits and income". It was based on a voluntary declaration that the sum of money paid was "not less than ten per centum" of the contributor's income. Not surprisingly, it did not raise much. In 1802, after a lull in the fighting, the tax was repealed. In 1803, it was reintroduced by Addington in a more efficient form. So efficient, indeed, was it that the tax still has much of the form given it by the 1803 Act. Addington's Act lasted to 1815, when peace finally arrived and the tax expired automatically. For 27 years, land taxes and trade taxes were again used, but they proved too weak a tax base for the emerging industrial economy. In 1842 the income tax, still much in its 1803 form, was reintroduced as a temporary measure. The need for revenues might again have had something to do with ships, as that year we seized Hong Kong. Income tax has been with us ever since, although it is still in form a temporary measure.

During its long history the details of the income tax have been chopped and changed by governments. For example, in 1910 we needed some more ships, so a higher rate of tax (in the guise of supertax) was proposed. That is one reason why the present tax is so difficult to understand. It is not the work of any one committee or team of drafters, but a patchwork of the efforts of innumerable minds with differing and often unstated aims. Every so often, someone has a go at sorting it out, but they have rarely succeeded in changing much.

2–05   It was always thus. Back in 1752, Lord Chesterfield and other "backbench" reformers wanted to change the calendar to get rid of the extra 11 days that had crept into the measurement of the year under the Julian calendar. In those days the official year started on March 25 (Lady Day). Lord Chesterfield and colleagues got their way and, despite rioting, the middle of September (mid-year) was removed in 1752. The end of the year was left as March 24, 1753—except for the Treasury. Then, as now, to lose 11 days from a financial year was just too expensive. So the tax year continued to April 5, 1753. For income tax, it still does, 250 years later. With the daily revenue from the tax exceeding £2 billion, it is unlikely to change.

2–06   There have been some spirited attempts to knock the income tax into shape. A Royal Commission on Income Tax had a go in 1920 (Cmd. 615). A few changes followed. More ambitious was a Codification Committee in 1936 (Cmd. 5131). This conducted the monumental task of sieving through our then tax laws to find the principles and the problems. It is a fascinating study which still repays the reading, but it was never implemented. There was another Royal Commission in the early 1950s, reporting in 1953 (Cmd. 8671), 1954 (Cmd. 9105) and 1955 (Cmd. 9474). It led to several changes but no substantial restructuring. There was an unofficial attempt by a committee on the structure and reform of direct taxation (and published by the Institute for Fiscal Studies under that name), chaired by Sir James Meade, a Nobel Laureate in economics. It advocated scrapping income tax to replace it by an expenditure tax. It didn't happen. But the work had some effect, in particular invigorating economic thought about our taxes and spawning work such as the brilliant summary by Kay and King, *The British Tax System* (para.1–03). If anything beyond black letter law interests you, read it.

None of these initiatives did anything to improve the shape of 2–07 the income tax. Finally (so far), a more serious attempt was started in 1995 when years of grumbling boiled up into a most unusual statutory requirement that something be done (see s.160 of the Finance Act 1995, passed against the wishes of the government). We discuss below what is being done. But even this is finding it difficult to break with the thinking imposed in 1803, and there is much caution in changing key terminology despite—or because of—the passage of two centuries. There is just a faint chance that now we don't need so many ships, the income tax (which was in essence always a war tax) may be allowed to fade away. But we still entered the new millennium with a law framed by those whose thinking pre-dated the French Empire. The inertia of a system that raises so much revenue is too great.

Some tidying took place over the years by the consolidation of the income tax. The 1842 Act did a bit of tidying, and some more was done in 1853. That was kept going until 1918 when, under the strains of yet another war, the laws were consolidated. The 1918 text was strengthened on several occasions (notably in 1936 and during the next war). It lasted until 1952 when a new consolidation changed the structure of the tax and attempted to give it a more modern appearance. It was given another structure and another consolidation in 1970, and yet another structure and yet another consolidation in 1988. But until the Tax Law Rewrite Project which started in 1995, it had never been simplified, just allowed to grow. For example, by 1999 the 1988 Act had grown from 845 sections to over 1,350, and 17 Schedules had been added to the original 31. Hidden at the heart of it was still the old flagship of the Napoleonic fleet, the 1803 Act, never codified and never reformed—at least, not until the 21st century. After years of patching, all political parties agreed that something had to be done. To do it involved changing parliamentary drafting techniques, the form and style of Acts of Parliament, parliamentary procedures and even the font in which Acts were printed and the page referencing of Bills. But in 2001 the changes were agreed and a full rewrite of our main direct tax laws started. By 2007, the structure of income tax had been completely reshaped and its laws nearly all rewritten, with progress being made on corporation tax. Income tax is now in the Income Tax Act 2007, the Income Tax (Earnings and Pensions) Act 2003, the Income Tax (Trading and Other Income) Act 2005 and the Capital Allowances Act 2001. A few provisions remain in the Income and Corporation Taxes Act 1988 and later Finance Acts. That is where the corporation tax law still is, although the main rewrite bill for that tax was published in 2008.

Later Taxes

2–08   Compared with the old taxes, the other taxes in this volume are comparatively modern. **Corporation tax** was introduced in the Finance Act 1965, as a modernisation of a profits tax on companies introduced in the last world war. It was, despite its name, devised as a parasite on the income tax and integrated into the 1970 Consolidation Act. It was reformed heavily in 1972, again in the 1980s, yet again in the 1990s and further reform is being planned. Only in the last few years do we see it emerging as a separate tax, with separate rules for calculating income, rather than something best described as "the same, but different".

2–09   **Capital gains tax** (CGT) also appeared in 1965. In reality, it was and is a device for plugging obvious gaps in the tax base of income tax. In some other countries it is part of the income tax. Maybe it should be here too.

2–10   **National Insurance contributions,** in their present form, came into being in 1973. The law was consolidated into a Social Security Act in 1975, and into a Social Security Contributions and Benefits Act in 1992. The idea of special contributions towards funding social insurance dates back to 1911, when the idea was adopted from Germany. It was modified in 1948, and again in 1973. Since 1973, contributions on both employees and the self-employed have been a second form of income tax, but only since 1999 have the two taxes both been collected by what is now HMRC.

2–11   **Value added tax** (VAT) also appeared in 1973, but for a very different reason. VAT is a peace tax. Several of our taxes were introduced in order to help us beat our European neighbours.

This one was introduced so we could join them. The adoption of VAT was a precondition of our entry into the European Community—now the European Union. It is the only permissible form of general indirect tax, or sales tax, in the Member States of the EU. This is because it proved to be the only major tax that could offer a neutral way of taxing production and consumption, and also handle international transactions neutrally. It was first introduced in the EC in 1967. Its main framework was established in 1977, and now applies not only in all EU states, but in practice throughout Europe.

Inheritance tax (IHT) has a shorter but odder (and in one way longer) history. It was introduced in 1974 and 1975 as a tax called capital transfer tax, to replace estate duty (dating from 1894) and to succeed to a tradition of taxing estates on death which predates even William of Orange. It had its name changed in 1984 to the present title, although it was not changed into an inheritance tax. It has been reformed since then, but now looks in some ways rather more like the 1894 Act than the 1974 Act! It has been threatened with abolition, but then so have most of the other taxes in this list. If it is abolished, it will only be the third time in our history that an estate duty has been abolished. Each time it has reappeared in a new guise, and with the same problems.

2–12

Old Ideas and New Forms

History therefore offers us a range of taxes, some a few years old and some over 300 years old. It confronts us with a range of approaches and a range of reasons for the form of tax used. More important to us as lawyers, it confronts us with a wide variety of language. Some is the product of the word processor, while some is only a little younger than the later plays of Shakespeare. It also confronts us with old ideas in new shapes—but we must remember that they are old ideas if we are to treat them correctly.

2–13

An annual tax

One old idea is that taxes are annual. Parliament still has to re-enact the income tax legislation every year. If it does not, then there would be no income tax next year. Read s.4 of the Income Tax Act 2007. You will see that it does not operate unless in any year there is a Finance Act imposing the income tax. Then read s.6 of the Income and Corporation Taxes Act 1988. You will see that no such provision is necessary for corporation tax. Nor is it a necessary approach for income tax, save for our history. Read

2–14

the preamble to any Finance Act. You will see that taxes are still granted annually to the Crown, not imposed by it. It is, we are supposed to believe, a voluntary offering. This fiction has the consequence that the income tax this year is different to the income tax last year. Further, a judge cannot assume that there will be an income tax next year. So any case about income tax can only look at what happens this year. If, for example, tax is imposed on a form of income, that form of income must exist this year to be taxed. It is not enough that it existed last year, or might exist next year.

The judicial reaction to the annual nature of income tax is called the source doctrine: see *Brown v National Provident Institution* (1921), HL. The doctrine means that if, say, a trader retires in one year, and receives income in the next, that income can be taxed in neither year. It was not received in the first year. There was no trade in the second year. It will not surprise you to learn that there are statutory provisions designed to prevent tax avoidance this way, but the doctrine still remains.

A schedular Tax

2–15 Another old approach that also haunts us still is the schedular nature of taxation. Old taxes like the income tax, customs duties, excise taxes and the stamp duties were drawn up as lists: so much to pay on this, and so much to pay on that. They are what is called schedular taxes. Modern taxes like VAT are comprehensive taxes. With a schedular tax, the tax authorities can only collect tax if they can show that what they are trying to tax appears in the list of things to be taxed. There was an extra reason for this in England. Our older taxes emerged at a time when the Stuart kings had developed a habit of raising taxes without asking for parliamentary help. (Like their successors, they needed to raise money for ships.) This was not too popular and led to a change of government and the Bill of Rights. This said that taxes could only be imposed by assent of parliament. For a tax to be imposed, therefore, it has to be shown that parliament has agreed to it. Without clear authority, a tax cannot be raised. This old idea still receives warm support from the judges. Lord Goff said in *Woolwich Building Society v IRC* (1992):

> "the retention by the state of taxes unlawfully exacted is particularly obnoxious, because it is one of the most fundamental principles of our law ... that taxes should not be levied without the authority of Parliament."

And, as we shall see, the income tax no longer has "schedules of charge" but it is still, nonetheless, a schedular tax. There is no single charge to tax but rather a whole series of separate charges.

Geography

Our diversions into the past have forced us to talk about   2–16 England and Britain as well as the United Kingdom. This is because taxes only apply to the territory whose government authorises them. This reflects international practice. One state will not enforce the direct tax laws of another state without express agreement. Our courts apply this rule: *Government of India v Taylor* (1955). They also operate on the basis that United Kingdom tax laws apply only in the United Kingdom: *Clark v Oceanic Contractors* (1983).

For this reason, tax laws need rules to decide who is, and who is not, "in" the United Kingdom. There is much detailed law on this, but broadly individuals are "here" if resident or ordinarily resident in the United Kingdom. Companies are taxable to corporation tax here if incorporated under United Kingdom law or if the central management and control of the company is here. Some UK-source income of foreign residents is also caught.

The United Kingdom
For tax purposes, the United Kingdom consists of its four   2–17 constituent countries together, since 1973, with the territorial sea and continental shelf. This includes, of course, the North Sea oilfields. They have their own tax, the petroleum revenue tax. This is imposed by the Oil Taxation Act 1983. But it is too specialist for a principles book like this.

Even defining the extent of the United Kingdom causes problems in modern tax practice. First, the United Kingdom is legally a union formed of states with a single tax system, but three different legal systems: those of Scotland and Northern Ireland cannot be ignored in the detail of our taxes. In addition, the Scots and Northern Irish have their own appeal systems, generating separate precedents. They are subject only to the unifying influence of the House of Lords—and the European Court of Justice.

For centuries, British governments have followed two key tax policies. First, all internal tax-collecting powers are centralised at national level. Second, our tax policies should support our national position as traders. But the wheels keep turning! We had just finished the final centralisation of all our taxes (by "capping" the powers of local councils to increase local tax rates), when we decided to recreate the Scottish Parliament and the Northern Ireland Assembly, and set up the Welsh Assembly. Much of *The Act of Union* with Scotland in 1701 is about tax and trade, and it sets up a customs union. But it leaves unstated the shift of taxing powers to London. Indeed, the main Scottish concern appears to be that the English should stop using taxes to block the import of Scotch beef—how things change! The Scotland Act 1998 gives little back. The Scottish Parliament can change the rate of income tax by up to 3p, and can decide its own limits on local taxes. And, at the time of writing, it was actively considering imposing a 3p income tax but abolishing council tax instead. But while it can alter the rates, it cannot alter the laws. Neither Northern Ireland nor Wales have any powers over their own national tax rates.

The problem of Scottish law is a real one. Its contract laws, property laws, divorce laws, trust laws and laws of succession are different to those of England. Yet the tax laws are supposed to be enforced throughout the kingdom in an even-handed way. Sometimes this results in separate Scottish terms, or separate Scottish sections. Often the problem is ignored, and the judges are left to do the best they can. This may mean generalising not just the Scottish law, but the English law too: for example *Kidson v MacDonald* (1974).

The European Union

2–18   Another aspect to the shifts of taxing powers is the un- avoidable fact that the United Kingdom is part of the EU. As a direct result, some of "our" taxes are European taxes, not British taxes at all. The United Kingdom is now part of a single customs union with the other members of the EU and the rather wider European Economic Area, together with Turkey and small states and territories such as Monaco and the Channel Isles. This is a vast single market with a single customs law. There is also a single form of VAT throughout the EU together with a legal prohibition against any Member State adopting a second VAT. As you will see in the discussion on VAT, most of the key VAT laws are European laws, and much of the case law is that of the European Court of Justice. For both reasons, a tax expert also has to be a European law expert! Repeatedly, we find that it is the European rule, not the British rule, which is to be followed.

The effect of European law on direct taxes is more sensitive politically and is still subject to national vetoes. But here also European law cannot be ignored, and precedence must be given to rights of free movement and establishment over national discriminatory direct tax laws. The recent law reports show the extent to which British legislation has been challenged for its alleged failure to comply with European requirements. These requirements involve the freedoms of movement that cannot be prevented by any fiscal measure. For VAT they also include the prevailing principles of European Union law such as legality and proportionality. For example, while the United Kingdom Parliament can legislate disproportionately and retrospectively about entirely internal taxation if that is its wish, it cannot do so for European Union tax law that is directly enforceable and applicable or in any way that brings United Kingdom taxes into conflict with the freedoms of movement protected by European Union law.

Recent examples of the limitations imposed by European   **2–19** Union law on United Kingdom law are the series of decisions that led to the decision of the House of Lords in *Fleming and Condé Nast v HMRC* (2008). This double appeal brought to an end a lengthy series of disputes about late claims for repayment of overpayments of value added tax. These claims arose when HM Customs and Excise tried to stop a growing number of back claims by shortening the time limit, and limiting the scope, for back claims by a provision in the Finance Act 1997. This was challenged successfully before the European Court in *Marks and Spencer Plc v Customs and Excise* (2002). Customs then tried imposing a transitional period to replace the one found at fault. This was rejected by the House of Lords in these decisions. The final answer (so far) came with a renewed time limit imposed under the Finance Act 2008. A comparison of the 1997 and 2008 legislation (removing any attempt to make the measure retrospective, and delaying the intended final time limit by over 12 years) brings home, in every sense, the curbs that European law now place on national tax authorities for VAT.

The curbs are also present for direct taxes, although the   **2–20** application can be less obvious. Nonetheless, the courts have also spent considerable time in the last decade dealing with a series of challenges, brought together as a series of group litigation cases, to the way in which groups of companies were treated for corporation tax purposes in the European Union. At the heart of the litigation was a contention that United Kingdom corporation tax laws discriminated between corporate groups involving subsidiary companies elsewhere in the European Union as compared with the subsidiaries that were in the United Kingdom. And when the European Court found the United Kingdom law to be inconsistent with the European requirements, group litigation was started to try and obtain compensation. For the latest round of another decade-long series of cases see *Pirelli v HMRC* (No.2) (2008).

The judgment of Moses L.J. in *Pirelli* does its best to get at the principles of what was going on. It is an illustration of just how complex the issues get when national law has to be read subject both to double tax agreements and European law. And, frankly, the detail is far beyond this book (though an appreciation of the incisive style of Moses L.J. is surely not). Nonetheless, it can be summarised as a cautionary tale about the limits of national sovereignty within the European Union on any tax question that has commercial implications.

Human Rights

2–21   The Human Rights Act 1998 adds another European dimension to our taxes. That Act introduces the principles of the European Convention of Human Rights internally into all aspects of our laws. It also imposes the duty on judges to ensure that human rights are protected, if necessary, by ruling that Acts of Parliament breach them. An early leading British case in the European Court of Human Rights is *National and Provincial Building Society v UK* (1997). The recent jurisprudence of the Human Rights Court has divided tax law between substance and procedure. In *Ferrazzini v Italy* (2001) the Grand Chamber of the Court, by a majority, ruled that taxpayers do not have any civil rights in respect of tax law. In other words, most of the protections of the European Convention on Human Rights do not apply to disputes about whether, or how much, tax is payable.

A series of cases including *King v UK* (No.2) (2004), and *King v UK* (No.3) (2005) have ruled that the penalty provisions in tax laws are to be treated as criminal cases. This requires the full rigour of the right to a fair hearing under Art.6 para.3 of the Convention to be applied by the tribunals and courts to these cases. Separately, individuals have challenged British tax laws as discriminatory, with mixed results. See *PM v UK* (2005) (is an unmarried father entitled to the same tax reliefs as a married father?) and in the local courts *R. v IRC* (2003) (is a widower of the same status as a widow?). Less obviously, the Human Rights Court has also rules that a failure by a national government to implement an EU VAT rule can be a breach of a taxpayer's human rights: *SA Dangeville v France* (2003).

"A Tax Shall Be Charged"

The key sections in any tax law are the charging sections. **2–22** These are the sections that actually impose the tax. Take them out, and the rest is mere verbiage. They are often signalled by the draftsman stating unambiguously that "a tax shall be charged". Look for this language in s.1 of the Value Added Tax Act 1994, of the Inheritance Tax Act 1984 or of the Income Tax Act 2007. But these are not the only charging sections in the Acts. Others are often found lurking in the more obscure parts of the Acts. The near-completion in 2007 of the rewrite of income tax has now removed the old structure of the income tax that dated back to 1803. The style of drafting two centuries ago was to put details in Schedules within an Act, and to divide Schedules into Cases. The income tax schedules and cases have now all gone (though not yet for corporation tax). However, it will be necessary for many years to come to know the historic pattern of the income tax in order to understand the cases. We list below the kinds of income within the scope of income tax, together with the details of the Schedules and Cases under which tax was imposed. For the record, however, we start with a short summary of the old schedules and cases:

Schedule A	Originally taxed the notional value of the ownership of land. Then became a tax on rents and profits from land.
Schedule B	Originally taxed the notional value of the occupation of land. Reduced to a tax on the commercial occupation of woodlands.
Schedule C	Taxed interest and other unearned income from government stock.
Schedule D	A collection of charges under a varying number of Cases:
	I profits of trades
	II profits of professions and vocations
	III interest, annuities and other annual payments
	IV income from foreign securities
	V income from foreign possessions (including foreign trades and foreign dividends)
	VI a "sweeper" case used to catch the tax under anti-avoidance provisions
	VII used for a period for a short terms gains tax before CGT was introduced

VIII used for some years as a charge on rents
before the old Sch.A was phased out

Schedule E   A tax on "offices and employments on emoluments therefrom". It was divided into Cases I, II
and III but these related only to where the
employee lived and worked

Schedule F   This taxed dividends from UK companies (which
originally were taxed under Sch.D).

The current kinds of income and the tax charges are:

- **Annual profits and gains** was the phrase used in Sch.D,
Case VI to catch the residue of forms of income that
should fall within the scope of income tax but did not fall
within any of the other schedules and cases. The Tax Law
Rewrite Project has moved them to more appropriate
parts of the legislation. Most have been moved to the
miscellaneous income charges in ITTOIA (the Income
Tax (Trading and Other Income) Act), save for those
properly moved to trading income (including income
from professions and vocations). Schedule D, Case VI
continues to apply to companies.
- **Annuities** were originally of considerable significance and
were subject to a specific charge under Sch.D, Case III.
The charge has been reassigned in part to the charge on
pension income in ITEPA (the Income Tax (Earnings and
Pensions) Act 2003), in part to one of the forms of savings and investment income in ITTOIA, and in part to the
category of miscellaneous income in ITTOIA, reflecting
the decline in the importance of this form of income.
- **Capital gains** were for a short time captured in income
tax as Sch.D, Case VII. Since 1965 the separate capital
gains tax applies to all chargeable gains. Income tax only
applies if there is a specific provision treating a capital
gain as income. The chargeable gains of companies are
charged as part of the corporation tax charge on the
company, not under a separate tax.
- **Dividends and other distributions** from UK companies
were originally charged under Sch.D, then Sch.F, but the
charge has been replaced by the charge on income from
savings and investments in ITTOIA. Dividends and other
payments from foreign companies were under Cases IV
and V of Sch.D, but are now also under the same ITTOIA
charge. This is also true of some linked anti-avoidance
provisions under Sch.D, Case VI. UK companies do not

pay tax on dividends and distributions received from other UK companies.

- **Employment income** was formerly charged to income tax under Sch.E. All earnings from employment are now charged together under the charging provisions of ITEPA. A company cannot in practice receive these forms of income. See also Class 1 of NI contribution liability.
- **Intellectual property royalties and receipts** are charged under provisions in ITTOIA.
- **Interest** from public revenue dividends was an extremely important form of income in 1803 and was taxed under a specific charge in Sch.C if it came from the UK government. Other forms of interest were caught by Sch.D, Case III—although for many years interest paid by a UK person was regarded as a "charge on income" and not directly charged to income tax on the recipient. If the interest came from a foreign source it was charged under Sch.D, Case IV. Schedule C was abolished in 1996. The remaining charges are being brought together as a form of the savings and investment income of individuals. Companies are charged to corporation tax under Sch.D, Case III on all forms of income from what are termed "loan relationships", and are not affected by ITTOIA.
- **Pension income** is subject to a separate charge under ITEPA. This reflects the growing importance of this form of income.
- **Property income** was charged to tax under Sch.A (receipts from a UK property business, known when first introduced as Sch.D, Case VIII), Sch.D, Case V (receipts from an overseas property business) and Sch.D, Case VI (income from lodgers). There is a combined charge in ITTOIA. These provisions do not apply for UK companies subject to corporation tax, and the Sch.A and D charges still continue for them.
- **Savings and investment income** brings together in ITTOIA several of the forms of unearned income previously taxed under a variety of different Schedules and Cases. It does not apply to UK companies.
- **Social security income** was charged under Sch.E in the same way as earnings. It is now subject to a separate charge under ITEPA, applying to both UK and foreign social security income. But social security pensions are charged as pension income. Most forms of social security income are exempt from income tax. See also Class 1 NI

contributions, from which most forms of social security income are exempt.

- **Trading income was** charged to tax under Sch.D, Case I (UK trades) and Case V (overseas trades), but is now subject to a combined charge under ITTOIA. This also includes income from professions and vocations. See also Class 2 and Class 4 NI contributions. But UK companies continue to be taxed under Sch.D, Cases I, V and VI.
- **Trust income and income from estates in administration.** Under ITTOIA there are provisions setting out the way in which trusts and settlements are taxed to income tax in an orderly mini-code.

It is clear from this list that corporation tax has both major similarities to and major differences from income tax. We deal with these in more detail in the chapter on taxation of companies.

What is not clear from this list is what is meant by "income". There is no one definition of the term, and its use changes from one context to another. Defining the precise forms of income that are subject to income tax is the essence of the study of the subject.

The Relationship Between Taxes and Charging Provisions

2–23 Faced with this battery of separate provisions, important questions arise. Can any form of income be charged under two charging sections, or even two taxes at the same time?

As regards income tax and corporation tax, only one can apply to any one taxpayer on any item of income. Corporation tax applies to companies (defined as bodies corporate by the Taxes Act 1988, s.832), and income tax to anyone or anything that is not a body corporate. Income tax therefore covers trusts and partnerships. For a fascinating case that decided that the Conservative Party under Mrs Thatcher was not a body corporate (because it consisted of Mrs Thatcher!) see *Conservative Central Office v Burrell* (1982). History does not record whether the tax inspector in that case was duly promoted.

There is also a clear ranking between income tax and capital gains tax (or the corporate equivalents). In every case, it must first be asked if income tax applies. Only if we conclude that it does not do we ask whether there is a charge to capital gains tax. A charge cannot arise to the two taxes at once. Case law establishes that the Revenue may raise alternative assessments under both taxes, but can only collect tax under one of them: *Bird v IRC* (1989).

This rule of mutual exclusivity also applies to the income tax 2–24 charging provisions. Whatever may be the theoretical possibilities, a form of income can be charged to income tax once only. If the legislation does not make clear which provision that should be, it will be for the judges to decide. The reason for this is that income tax is regarded as a single tax, not a series of taxes. It follows that only one set of provisions of that tax can apply to any taxable income at any one time.

These rules are necessary because it is not clear from the words of the legislation alone that there is no overlap between the taxes, or to charging provisions. Any other rule would, in principle, be unfair. Note that the rule does not apply to other kinds of taxes. A relationship between VAT and income tax, for example, does not exist. It is therefore irrelevant in law that something is or is not subject to income tax for VAT purposes. In other words, the mutual exclusion rule only applies to similar taxes.

Tax Legislation

As we have seen, one of the few clear principles that can be 2–25 said to be constitutional in the United Kingdom is the Bill of Rights of 1688/89 providing that taxes cannot be imposed save by consent of parliament. There is no common law of tax, nor any prerogative or other inherent rights to tax. Nor can taxes be imposed by treaty without parliamentary authority to recognise and collect them.

FINANCE ACTS For this reason, we must locate the express 2–26 authority of parliament to impose a tax on every occasion on which we wish to collect tax. If there is no authority, there is no liability to tax. Applying that approach to our tax laws may once have been a simple operation. Now it is enormously complicated. This is because there have been new tax provisions passed by parliament at least once a year for at least 130 years without any break. Since 1894 there has been at least one omnibus **Finance Act** each year. These have rarely shortened the extant law, even when taxes have been abolished.

The primary legislation imposing our main taxes is therefore of formidable dimensions. As a result, there is likely to be some provision covering most forms of income or transaction, and determining whether or not it comes within the tax. We cannot, however, assume this. Leaving aside, for the moment, the problems of interpreting tax laws, the rule remains that unless there is a provision that covers the income or transaction in point, no tax can be collected. At the heart of this process lies the simple fact that the purpose of a tax law is to impose tax on certain things, and not on other things. There may be a range of reasons why parliament has decided to do that. But, following the traditions of British legislation, the reasons why are normally left unstated. The question is always: "is this activity or thing within the scope of a taxing provision?"

2–27   DELEGATED LEGISLATION Traditionally, parliament has added extra levels of complexity to the process of imposing taxes by insisting that all major rules of tax are imposed by primary legislation. **Delegated legislation** is therefore limited. This means that any significant detail must be set out in a section of an Act, not in delegated legislation. This rule was in particular applied to the income tax. There were good democratic reasons for this. Every word of every section of a Finance Act is open for political and technical debate and may be the subject of a separate vote. This is restricted in the case of Schedules to the decision whether a Schedule "stand part". It is even more restricted in the case of statutory instruments to a vote whether the instrument be (or not be) made. Despite, or perhaps because of, these limitations, much greater use is made of Schedules and statutory instruments in the more modern taxes. Much of VAT is, for example, to be found in the VAT Regulations 1995, while many important aspects of National Insurance contribution law is found in the Social Security (Contributions) Regulations 2001.

2–28   Nonetheless, it is a pretence to claim that there is an open technical debate on every tax provision. Time does not allow it. A few selected provisions are subject to a high profile political debate on the floor of the House of Commons. Other selected provisions are subject to more technical debate in the Finance Bill committee. Other provisions pass without comment. All provisions pass without comment in the House of Lords, because they are (since the Parliament Acts were passed) effectively debarred from interfering in tax laws. The fact that this results in what some regard as our most important laws being subject to the least thorough scrutiny by parliament is of course justified by an appeal to history and democracy. Perhaps that is another of the principles of our constitution. If so, perhaps, now that the Queen also pays taxes, we should change it.

European Law Some of our tax laws receive even less 2–29
parliamentary scrutiny. These are the rules imposed by the
European Union Treaties, Regulations and Directives. Most
important is the Community Customs ·Code (reg.2913/92). By
virtue of the European Community Treaty (art.249) it is directly
effective in all Member States without further enactment. No
pretence was made to enact it in the United Kingdom. VAT is
also based on extensive EU law, although most of this is in the
form of directives. Many of the provisions of these directives
apply directly in the same way as provisions in regulations. This
is so, even though a Finance Act provision says otherwise. Why?
Because EU laws prevail over United Kingdom laws. Is that part
of our constitution?

Of course, as all readers know, we don't have a **constitution.** 2–30
In tax matters that is most important. Constitutions almost
always contain rules limiting aspects of the right to impose
taxes. We have no such rules. Even the simple rule in the Bill of
Rights is no longer right unless we amend it to include tax laws
imposed by the authority of the EU. More generally, we can
observe only that, constitutionally, parliament may choose to
tax anything it wishes in any way it wishes, and under any name
it wishes. Once it has so wished, we must pay. Or must we?

Before leaving the topic of tax legislation, we must notice 2–31
another curiosity. This is the collection of **extra-statutory concessions** (ESCs) issued alongside all our main tax laws. ESCs are
truly curious. They are not law, yet they prevail over the law in
practice. The courts cannot enforce them or interpret them,
because they have never been enacted, but yet they, arguably,
can ensure that others enforce them. They exist in a sort of
constitutional never-never land, supposedly authorised by ministers (who have no legal power to do it), and tolerated by a
parliament that has no time to enact them (except when it does
have time). In short, parliament, by an extrastatutory procedure,
allows us to ignore its enactments. Against that, it is said that
the system works. It is also argued that a lawyer who ignores
any ESCs would be negligent to the client. If so, it is a curious
law system indeed that holds a lawyer negligent for failing not to
observe the law! The approach of the Court of Appeal in *R.
(Wilkinson) v IRC* (2003) rightly put limits on the scope of such
"extras". But it was not until 2008 that the government got
round to recognising that laws are supposed to be legislated, not
conceded.

Even then, our list is not complete. The United Kingdom has 2–32
ratified over 100 **double taxation agreements.** These are given
formal effect as Orders in Council, each of which is then given

precedence over internal law by general enabling provisions in the primary legislation for dealings between taxpayers and the United Kingdom and the treaty partner. But they are beyond the scope of an introductory look at tax.

Finding the Law

2–33 The first rule in trying to find the current law imposing a tax is not to do so from the Acts of Parliament themselves. Even where there is a recent codification, this would be an excessively time-consuming occupation. It is also pointless, because there are splendid commercial consolidations of the law published annually by several publishers. One or other of these consolidations is indispensable for a proper study of tax law. They are also available on the internet as are official versions.

These commercial consolidations are particularly useful because they give the history of sections in the consolidation measures, and cross-reference texts to other relevant provisions. They also set out the SIs, the EU law, and the ESCs.

Using Tax Laws

2–34 There are traditionally two approaches to deciding how a tax law works. One is to try and determine its meaning. The other is to try and determine what the tax authorities think it means. These are often different things and require different techniques. For a professional adviser, which technique is appropriate depends on the client. One approach is to seek to establish with the maximum certainty whether the tax authorities will demand that a tax be levied on a transaction. The other approach is to form an independent view about whether tax applies, and be prepared to argue the point before the courts if necessary. But even the most law-abiding taxpayer is unlikely to do this to increase a personal tax bill. The first of these approaches is the process of *tax compliance*, that is, of ensuring that the law is obeyed at minimum cost and risk. The other is the process of *tax planning*, under which a taxpayer seeks to explore the law to mitigate a tax burden, or possibly to remove it altogether, within the terms of the law.

Self-assessment has caused these two traditional approaches to coalesce. The aim of self-assessment is to transfer to the taxpayer any decision about the extent to which something should be taxed. Decisions about the relevance of any tax provision to a set of facts, or of interpretation and application of the law to those facts, is for the taxpayer. Of course, tax officials check on the accuracy of the taxpayer's judgment. Self-assessment has also made it more important for the tax authorities to clarify their own views on what taxpayers should be doing. We will look at how they make their views known first, and then how tax laws are interpreted.

The Official View

In addition to the laws themselves, the tax authorities must in 2–35 a range of ways ensure that the laws actually work in practical terms. The Revenue and Customs have spent considerable time in recent years trying to do this. In part, they have been spurred on by the process of automation of our taxes. Computers demanding "yes or no" answers will not accept "perhaps", nor will they accept inconsistencies. In part, the shift to self-assessment has also forced a removal of issues previously left vague, such as transfer pricing.

HMRC produce guidance and information to assist taxpayers, or their own staff, in several forms. Together these add up to a substantial body of published statements. However, in every case it must be remembered that these express only the official view of the law. Save as noted below, the guidance is always general, and does not relate to individual taxpayers. The cumulated texts of these forms of guidance are published in the commercial compilations of tax material and are now on the internet.

Extra-statutory concessions. These were mentioned above 2–36 together with the statutes from which they purport to derogate. ESCs, as they are usually called, are a motley list of "fixes" of faulty procedures and minor gaps in the law, along with some generous interpretations of allowances. The Tax Law Rewrite has reduced a lengthy list of several hundred ESCs to a much shorter list of, often trivial points (except for the individuals who benefit from them).They are published in a kind of catalogue with individual reference numbers. For example, A61 helps lower paid clergy with their heating bills.

In 2008 it was accepted that this was not enough. In Finance Act 2008 s.157 Parliament finally gave way to criticisms. These date back to views of the House of Lords in *Vestey v IRC* in 1979, but were brought to a head by the further decision of the House of Lords in *R. (Wilkinson) v IRC* (2006). Parliament has now provided a compromise route to legislate, and thereby legalise, practices conducted as concessions. It remains to be seen how you make legislative provision for something extra-statutory. We assume these will now be called statutory concessions.

2–37 **Statements of practice.** SPs, as they are known, were first issued in a methodical way in 1978. They seek to apply the law (or ESCs), and can be quite lengthy. For example SP 5/96 on PAYE settlements is several pages long. Prior to 1978, these statements were often made through Parliament. SPs are published as press releases.

Revenue interpretations. This is a list of formal statements by (now) HMRC about the official practical approach to specific provisions or problems. Some, for example, are responses to decisions of the higher courts. Others are responses to recent developments in business or professional practice. Again, each has a reference number. RI 269 is about taxing the rights to use telecommunications cable systems.

2–38 **Press releases.** A steady stream of press releases are issued by HMRC, covering all changes to a Finance Bill, SPs, announcements of other publications and background information. They are also all on the internet on the HMRC websites.

The most important set of press releases are the huge bundle issued on the day of the Budget announcement. These often include details left out of the Chancellor's speech.

2–39 **Parliamentary proceedings.** Ministerial statements and planted parliamentary questions have long been used for making minor announcements about taxes. Since 1978, this practice is less common, although answers to other PQs may still reveal interesting points. Parliament rarely debates the tax affairs of an individual (and when it does, ministers rarely do more than give general answers). The Finance Bill debates have gained a new importance since the decisions in *Pepper v Hart* (1992), discussed under "Interpreting the Law" below. The adjudications of the Parliamentary Ombudsman on tax cases (published as House of Commons Papers), although also anonymous, give interesting insights to the otherwise mysterious workings of the tax authorities when things appear to have gone wrong.

The main parliamentary proceeding of relevance is the Budget speech and debate each year. Along with this the Treasury publishes a "red book": the Budget Statement and Financial Forecast for the year. It is important background reading to the budget process. It is also available on the internet.

Explanatory notes. All legislation is now accompanied on pub-   2–40
lication both in Bill form and then on enactment by Explanatory
Notes. These are particularly valuable and full with regard to
the Bills and Acts that have resulted from the Tax Law Rewrite
Project. They form a valuable detailed origin of any specific
provision not only in identifying previous legislation (including
secondary legislation) put in the new codes, but also provisions
derived from decisions of the courts, measures incorporating
previous ESCs or agreed practices, and corrections of technical
errors in previous legislation. The notes also reflect not only
drafting points but also the outcome of consultation with taxpayers and the professions. They are a valuable but often
neglected source of understanding of the new Acts.

Guidance leaflets. These have been published for many years,   2–41
but they have gained considerably in appearance and readability
since the Revenue started taking the Plain English Campaign
seriously, and they now regularly win praise for clarity. Guidance is issued with most standard forms (for example the
coding notices sent to most individuals, and the annual returns).
There are also a series of leaflets and booklets made generally
available on a wide variety of issues. For example, IR 20 deals
with questions of residence, and is important enough to be
referred to in context as the "Revenue code". These are also
available in full text on the Internet.

Instruction manuals. Open government appeared to take a step   2–42
forward when the Revenue agreed to publish all its volumes of
instruction manuals to staff. They are now available on the
HMRC website (although certain internal instructions are kept
secret).

Indirect guidance. HMRC also has the commendable habit of   2–43
reaching agreement with taxpayer representatives and professional associations about the operation of the taxes in its charge.
Agreements may be by way of a fairly formal statement of
agreement with appropriate groups, or by way of a letter sent to
a group in response to representations. These sometimes receive
restricted publication, but bodies such as the Tax Faculty of the
Institute of Chartered Accountants, the Chartered Institute of
Taxation and the Law Society's Revenue Law Committee regularly publish their own views, and exchanges with HMRC, on
points of law.

VAT and indirect tax guidance. The former Customs and Excise Commissioners issued their own sets of information about VAT. The programme of publication of guidance and other rulings has been unified both in print and on the internet since HMRC absorbed this department along with the Revenue. Much of what we have just outlined therefore has its direct equivalents for indirect taxes.

The most important Customs publications up to 2006 were its Business Briefs as businesses were expected to read and act on points made in these. And, less usually, some guidance about customs law and VAT has legal force, so is a form of tertiary legislation. This includes some of the practical points set out in Publication 700, *The VAT Guide*. This is because some parts of the procedure for collecting VAT demands detailed and specific rules to ensure that all traders do the same thing.

Interpreting the Law

2–44   This should be the easy bit. It is not. Consider the following provisions:

> "*Interest* means both annual and yearly interest and interest other than annual or yearly interest."
> "*Interest* includes dividends and any other return (however described) except a return consisting of an amount by which the amount payable on a security's redemption exceeds its issuing price."
> "*Interest and dividends* do not include any interest or dividend which is a distribution"
> "*Distribution* ... means ... any dividend payable by a company ..."
> "*Trade* includes any trade, manufacture, adventure or concern in the nature of trade"
> "*Trade* includes vocation and also includes an office or employment"
> "*Profits* means income and chargeable gains"
> "*Profits* or *gains* shall not include references to chargeable gains"
> "*Income* includes any amount on which a charge to tax is authorised to be made under any of the provisions of this Act".

Rule number one of interpreting legislation should be to note the meanings given to the language by parliament. In tax law, as the above illustrations (all drawn from the Tax Acts) show, this has to be modified by two reflections. The first is that the definitions may themselves add no extra meaning. The second is that words change their meaning from one part to another of the tax legislation. Or, as T.S. Eliot observed, "words strain, crack and sometimes break, under the burden." The job of the lawyer is to ensure that any words that do suffer in this way are patched back up again.

Words can have two kinds of meaning: a technical meaning given by the judges as a matter of law, or "the ordinary English meaning". Which kind of meaning is given to a word is itself a decision of law, but decisions about the language of the tax laws are not consistent on this point. The *Ensign Tankers* case discussed below (see "Escape to Victory?") illustrates this in the way it seeks to apply the simple word "trade". It also illustrates another dilemma of interpretation. If a word has an ordinary meaning, then it is for the tax authorities and the appeal tribunals to determine its meaning. It cannot be appealed to the higher courts, because it gives rise to no question of law. If, however, the word has a technical meaning, then that is a question of law and can be appealed to the courts. The *Ensign Tankers* case also illustrates this problem. How do we decide the meaning of a word?

Decisions on the meanings of words and the phrases in which   2–45
they appear are guided by the rules of statutory interpretation. For a long time, judicial thinking was that tax laws should be interpreted strictly. Judges justified this by references to analogies with the criminal law and by reference to the Bill of Rights. The result could be an excessively literal reading of the words of a tax provision in isolation from its context. More recently, judges have been seeking to establish the view that interpreting tax statutes is no different from interpreting other legislation, save that the words have to be clear before tax can be imposed. The judgment of Lord Wilberforce in the *Ramsay* case (1981) is formative:

> "A subject is only to be taxed on clear words, not on 'intendment' or on the 'equity' of an Act. Any taxing Act of Parliament is to be construed in accordance with this principle. What are 'clear words' is to be ascertained on normal principles; these do not confine the courts to literal interpretation. There may, indeed should be, considered the context and scheme of the relevant Act as a whole, and its purpose may, indeed should be, regarded..."

Unfortunately, this statement cannot be left without further comment. First, we must remind you that the Acts being interpreted are frequently codification or consolidation measures. An attempt to look at the purpose of a consolidation measure means looking at the purpose of the provisions lying behind it. In a real sense, what the drafters have stitched together for presentational purposes has to be unstitched to establish what is meant. For an example of the complexities that result from such unstitching, see the Court of Appeal decision in *IRC v Willoughby* (1995).

2–46   Part of the reason for the complexity in unstitching is the decision of the House of Lords in the tax case of *Pepper v Hart* (1992). This decided that in cases of ambiguous language, it was proper to look to the record of the House of Commons for any ministerial statements about the intention of parliament behind a specific provision. In the *Willoughby* case, the logic of this was to look through not only the 1988 Act, but also the 1970 Act and the 1952 Act back to original enactment of the provision in question in 1936. While this might help deal with ambiguities, the resulting need effectively to ignore the consolidation measure for interpretation purposes is not conducive to an easy operation of the law. It means that a "proper" consolidation should identify where each part of the consolidated provision comes from. This was also a problem for the Tax Law Rewrite Project.

2–47   A second reason for complexity is the constant adjustment in the precise terms of sections to deal with both the need to counter avoidance, and the need to avoid injustice in special cases. Some sections have therefore seen considerable amendment during their working lives, including reshaping during the consolidation process. Take the definition of "trade". In 1803, this was defined as including any trade, manufacture, art or mystery. The word was used in a phrase identical to that now in, but its statutory definition has changed. The words are the same as in 1803, but not the extended meaning. Had the relevant minister made its main meaning clear then, should we return to it now? Here again, we have the problem of some words and phrases being "ordinary" while others are "technical".

Because of the need to prevent avoidance, tax law is also at times aimed very widely. The sections in the *Willoughby* case are good examples. Another is s.776, which starts: "This section is enacted to prevent the avoidance of tax by persons concerned with land or the development of land." Does a statement like that make it easier to interpret a phrase such as "any arrangement ... effected as respects ... land which enables a gain to be realised by any indirect method ... by any person who is ... concerned in the arrangement"?

A further reason for complexity in interpretation is the influence of EU law. Some parts of our law are now subject to reference to the European Court of Justice (ECJ). It is their interpretation, and therefore their techniques of interpretation, that must prevail in these areas. This may lead to inconsistencies, as the approach taken by the ECJ is different to that in a purely national context. Given that VAT is a mixture of European and United Kingdom provisions, the result may be untidy. See, for an example, the House of Lords decision in *CEC v Robert Gordon's College* (1995). See also the full discussion of VAT at para.24–12.

Applying the Law

A reference to the ECJ emphasises another aspect of handling tax cases. The ECJ takes the view that it can interpret EU law, but it cannot apply the law to the facts. In the United Kingdom, these two stages in a case are often conflated. Take, for example, the child's definition of an elephant as something large and grey and living in a herd of elephants. The definition is that it is large, grey, and sociable. Whether the group of creatures is a herd of elephants is an application of the law to the facts. Application of law to facts in tax matters can be an issue of considerable complexity. If you wish to see how difficult, take a piece of paper and draw a diagram on it of the transactions described by the House of Lords in *Ramsay v IRC* (1981). Then try the same thing with the *Ensign Tankers* case discussed below.

Until the *Ramsay* case, judges would accept any series of transactions, however complicated, as something to be taken at face value. The underlying approach was one said to have been approved by the House of Lords in *IRC v Duke of Westminster* (1936). It was that the *form* of a transaction should be followed, not its *substance*. That doctrine has been modified by a series of cases including the *Ramsay* and *Ensign Tankers* cases but of which the most important is another House of Lords case, *Furniss v Dawson* (1984).

In *Furniss*, Lord Brightman, on behalf of the House, and following the lines already set out in *Ramsay*, propounded the rule that the court did not have to look at the form in isolation in certain series of transactions, or complex transactions. A broader view of the whole operation could be taken where the series was preordained, and where one or more steps in the series existed for no other purpose than tax avoidance. This broad view allowed the courts in both *Ramsay* and *Furniss* to look at what happened without getting caught up in the inter-stices of complex constructions which, in substance, had replaced much more straightforward transactions. A later House of Lords case, *Craven v White* (1988) emphasised that the new approach only applied where the conditions were strictly met. A further decision of the House in *Countess Fitzwilliam v IRC*

2–48

(1993), stressed that the courts could look through a series of artificial transactions to the real transaction underneath if the conditions were met. However, this had to be done to the transactions as a whole, and the Revenue could not pick and chose parts of the series to look through, while taking other parts at face value. However, in *Moodie v IRC* (1993), the House reaffirmed the underlying principle, and applied it notwithstanding an inconsistent decision of the House of an earlier date dealing with the transactions under question.

2–49   But the debate has not stopped there. Most important of several further judicial bites at the cherry of tax avoidance is the decision of the House of Lords in *MacNiven v Westmoreland Investments* (2001). The decision concerned now-abolished rules about the tax treatment of interest payments. But the issue could also have been, in the views of some, a straightforward application of the *Ramsay* principle. This approach was rejected unanimously by the House of Lords. The judgment of Lord Hoffmann, in particular, was seen as placing important limits on the doctrine. It applies only if the words of the legislation permit, and it does not override those words. The wider approach only applies to a transaction if the tax legislation has "a commercial meaning capable of transcending the juristic individuality of its component parts". In other words, it is back to the proper interpretation of the legislation. Or perhaps it all depends on how one sees the facts, as in the Court of Appeal's criticisms of those below in *Barclays Mercantile v Mawson* (2004).

That case also went to the House of Lords. On this occasion the House issued a single opinion. It is, and is intended to be, a most important statement of approach, and should therefore be read for itself. It categorised the decision in *Ramsay* as a decision that "liberated the construction of revenue statutes from being both literal and blinkered". This was not a new doctrine, but an attempt to rescue tax law from the excess of literal interpretation and put it back into the mainstream. What was needed was close analysis not sweeping generalisations about disregarding transactions. As a result, the Crown lost the appeal.

The following week the House, in a committee consisting of the same five law lords, heard another avoidance case as *IRC v Scottish Provident* (2005). In a short, almost peremptory, single opinion their lordships found for the Crown. On the facts:

"it would destroy the value of the *Ramsay* principle ... as referring to the effect of composite transactions if their composite effect had to be disregarded simply because the parties had deliberately included a commercially irrelevant contingency, creating an acceptable risk that the scheme might notwork as planned. We would be back in the realm of artificial schemes, now equipped with anti—*Ramsay* devices."

Unfortunately, this appears to mean that the only conclusion from this long line of cases is that there is no strong conclusion to be drawn. The courts clearly see both the danger of letting tax avoidance undermine the public revenues, and the danger of letting the public revenues undermine individual freedom of action of taxpayers under the law. Perhaps not surprisingly— they have come to no single clear view about where they as judges should strike the balance. But is that not the task of the United Kingdom legislature rather than its judiciary?

General Anti-avoidance Provisions

In many countries there are general statutory provisions dealing with avoidance either under general law or specifically for tax law. The French approach is the doctrine of *abus de droit*; in the Netherlands there is a principle of *fraus legis*. Put at its broadest, they require that any interpretation and application of the tax laws must be consistent with the purposes of those laws. In the United States, the judiciary have introduced rules of substance over form, while in other common law states such as Canada, Australia and Ireland, there are general anti-avoidance provisions in tax legislation.   2–50

The United Kingdom has a broad anti-avoidance provision for inheritance tax in s.268 of the Inheritance Tax Act (associated operations), but none for the main direct taxes. As noted above, the British approach has been the "hole and plug" approach. If a particular form of avoidance of tax is found to be unacceptable, then it is stopped by a specific legislative provision. This will often take effect from the date of its announcement but will rarely operate retrospectively. Much direct tax law was first enacted in this way.

When it was decided to rewrite direct tax law, consideration was also given to the introduction of a general anti-avoidance rule such as those adopted by Ireland or Australia. The Revenue published a useful discussion paper on this, *A General Anti-Avoidance Provision* (1998). This commented on a possible form of wording. The paper reached no particular conclusion, and the subsequent debate similarly stopped without any serious attempt being made to legislate a GAAR.

There are now signs of a broader approach by Government.   2–51

For example, the tonnage tax introduced in 2000 is subject to a GAAR: "It is a condition of remaining within tonnage tax that a company is not a party to any transaction or arrangement that is an abuse of the tonnage tax regime" Finance Act 2000, Sch.22, para.41.

In 2004 Parliament adopted a new approach for direct taxes, copying one used for the United States federal income tax. Anyone marketing a tax avoidance scheme is to be required to register it with the tax authorities, who will issue the plan with a registration number. Similarly, anyone adopting an in-house scheme must also register it. When the scheme is used, the taxpayer must notify the tax authorities of its use by number. This not only allows tax officials to keep fully abreast of the latest approaches of practitioners (and to block the ones they don't like) but also gives them a chance to rule that a scheme does not work before it is used. See Finance Act 2004, Part 7.

Part 7 of the Finance Act 2004 (ss.306 to 319) and the several sets of regulations that implement the Part establish a code of rules for reporting tax avoidance schemes. The Tax Avoidance Schemes (Prescribed Descriptions Etc) Regulations 2006 (SI 2006 No.1543) set out the current scope of the provisions. They list nine kinds of arrangement aimed at giving rise to a tax advantage with regard to income tax, corporation tax, CGT or capital allowances. If an arrangement is within the scope of the rules, then it must be notified to HMRC. HMRC allocate a reference number to each scheme. Anyone using the scheme must then disclose the number when completing a self-assessment tax return. But it is for HMRC to decide (subject to appeal rights) if a scheme is effective both generally and in any individual case.

Finance Act 2008 takes this further in two ways. It sets up a formal register of scheme numbers. It also contains a number of anti-avoidance provisions that Ministers explicitly acknowledge to be aimed at schemes notified to HMRC under this system.

Escape to Victory?

2–52   The tale of how a tax appeal is handled is best told by a case study. The case chosen here is formally known as *Ensign Tankers (Leasing) Ltd v Stokes (Inspector of Taxes)*. The reports of the case are at [1989] S.T.C. 705 (case stated by the Special Commissioners, and decision of Millet J.), [1991] S.T.C. 136, CA and [1992] S.T.C. 226, HL. It came to be a most important decision on the boundary between acceptable and unacceptable tax avoidance. A little less usually for a tax case, the plot involves

Michael Caine, Sylvester Stallone and Bobby Moore! How did they come to be involved with a tanker leasing company?

The story starts with an Inland Revenue Statement of Practice, SP 9/79. This announced the Revenue's view that the Revenue would accept claims for capital allowance for expenditure on plant in respect of the cost of master prints of films. In effect, this was a decision in favour of potential investors in the film industry, allowing them to write off against their profits (or claim losses) on the capital cost of producing the master print of any film for distribution. Ownership of the master print carries with it the rights to exploit and distribute the film.

A number of professional tax advisers were attracted by this statement of practice towards devising tax efficient ways of securing investment in the film industry. At the same time, the taxpayer company, previously a profitable leasing business, was finding it harder to make profits, and was looking to the film industry as a possible source of new business. As a result of complicated negotiations, the taxpayer company became a limited partner of a partnership known as the Victory Partnership with the intention of making a film called *Escape to Victory*. This was filmed in Hungary in 1980. (For the curious, it was about a football match that led to prisoners of war escaping: perhaps a sort of sporting equivalent to the concert at the end of *The Sound of Music*.) Commercially, it proved a failure.

A little after filming started, a meeting took place in London of the limited partners of the Victory partnership at which 17 documents were completed. These included the partnership agreement and a series of loan and financial agreements. Through them, in broad terms, the partnership put up capital of $3.25 million, of which Ensign put up $2.38 million. A further $9.75 million was lent to the partnership by the film production company, funded by an American bank. This was a non-recourse loan, that is, the film production company could not demand repayment of the loan from the partnership, only from the proceeds of the film. The partnership bought the partly completed film from the production company, and agreed to pay the production company a fixed amount to finish the film. Under other provisions, the partnership were to have 25 per cent of the proceeds from the film, while the production company were to receive 75 per cent towards repayment of the loan to the partnership. In other words, the partnership put up about $3 million of the $13 million that the film was budgeted to cost, but came to own the film outright subject to charges on the proceeds from the film. In tax terms, therefore, the partnership could claim an allowance for the cost of its master print of *Escape to Victory*, although it would in due course be subject to tax on the whole proceeds of the film.

2–53   The secret of the scheme lay partly in its cash-flow advantages, and partly in the fact that the taxpayer could not lose from its investment after taking account of tax. This was because it received the benefits of its share of the tax allowances for making the film in 1980 as offsets to the considerable profits being made by the group of companies of which it was a member. It would be taxed only later if profits were made. If they were not made, it still received an allowance against tax for a sum equal to about four times its actual investment. This was because the corporation tax rate was then 52 per cent, so the company received a right to claim a loss worth more in tax terms than its original investment. (The full details of how this happened are in the 1986 report of the case.) The film, unfortunately, did make a loss, so the company claimed the tax allowances (a setoff against profits of about £5 million) in its 1980 tax returns. The inspector refused them. Why?

2–54   To claim the tax relief, the company had to show that the partnership was a person "carrying on a trade". In the inspector's view, the partnership was not doing that. It was engaging in tax avoidance, not trading. This view was accepted by the Special Commissioners in a lengthy decision made after 18 days of hearings in 1986. They rejected evidence of one of the key witnesses that the scheme was a commercial scheme and held, as a matter of law, that the partnership was not trading. They were asked to consider also whether the case fell within the principles of the decision in *Furniss v Dawson*, and found on the facts that it did, but that this was not necessary to their decision.

2–55   The case went on appeal to the Chancery Division where it was heard by Millett J. (later, Lord Millett) for six days in 1989. He upheld the taxpayer's appeal on the ground that the Commissioners had reached a decision that no person acting judicially and properly instructed as to the law could have made. In particular, in his view the partnerships were trading. However, he could not make that finding of fact with authority, so the case had to go back to the Commissioners for a re-hearing. This is a good illustration of a judge not being able to change a decision on the facts, but only to see if the Commissioners took a decision that was correct in law. It reflects the limits on the judicial role in s.56 of the Taxes Management Act 1970. It means that the result of a successful appeal is that the process of appeal must start again.

2–56   The Revenue (usually referred to, as in this case, as the Crown) appealed to the Court of Appeal. The case was heard by the Vice-Chancellor and two Lords Justice of Appeal over four days at the end of 1991. Put shortly, they allowed the appeal by the Crown, but also found that the Commissioners had made an error of law (identified by Millett J.) in their decision, so referred it back for re-hearing. In the view of the Court of Appeal, Millett J. was wrong in saying that the only possible interpretation of the facts was different to the interpretation adopted by the Commissioners. So, in the view of the Court of Appeal, both lower levels of appeal had been wrong, and it was remitted to start again.

A little over a year later, the case was heard for a further six days before the House of Lords on an appeal and cross-appeal by both parties. The judgment of the House was given by Lord Templeman, a judge who earned during his judicial career a formidable reputation as a judge determined to see tax law applied with common sense and in the common interest. The other four members of the House agreed with his decision.   **2–57**

To Lord Templeman, the case was concerned about a tax avoidance scheme. His opinion on this issue should be read as a concise review of judicial thinking on tax avoidance (see pp.235 to 244 of the report). In forthright terms, Lord Templeman dismisses the operation of the scheme used by the taxpayer in this case as "play acting". Under his guidance, the House reached the decision that all three lower levels of appeal had been wrong. The case was therefore remitted to the Commissioners again, but this time with a direction to allow a claim for a loss equal to the actual amount put into the partnership (and lost) by the taxpayers—the sum of 2.38 million dollars, not the inflated sum the taxpayer had claimed, or the refusal of any claim by the inspector and Commissioners.

Thirty-four days of hearings therefore produced four different answers from the four levels of appeal, although three levels were merely, in the words of Lord Templeman, overseeing the task of the Commissioners to "find the facts and apply the law, subject to correction by the courts if they misapply the law." The answer, 12 years after the original taxable activity, was based to some extent on judicial decisions made after the deal was first incurred but equally was expressed as an interpretation of a simple word: *trade*. Who was right? Read the decisions for yourself and decide with which of the four levels of appeal you most agree. In one way, each of the four decisions could be said to be a permissible use of the accepted techniques of interpretation and application of the law (although, of course, the precedent system means that three are wrong, and only the last one is actually technically correct).   **2–58**

With which of the four decisions do you most readily sympathise? Why? That will tell you much about your own views on the taxing process. Whichever decision you do support, the story, which might be better entitled as *Escape To Where You Came From*, is also a comment on the weaknesses, as well as strengths, of a multi-layered system of tax appeals. What *does* the word "trade" mean? For a powerful discussion by a single judge see *Clarke v B.T. Pensions* (1998), disagreeing with the specials. Perhaps the 1803 Act was right in including mysteries in its definition of trade. Meanwhile provision of tax relief for films has resulted in a number of special legislative provisions in ITTOIA and elsewhere but beyond the scope of this book, and continuing disputes. See, for example, how the House of Lords was again divided (in its guise as the Privy Council) in dealing with an unsuccessful New Zealand film called *The Lie of the Land* in *Peterson v CIR* (2005).

A protected building or two

2–59   That case, and its difficulties are not unique. Similar disagreements and hard-fought litigation can apply to much simpler problems. The case of *Customs and Excise v Zielinski Baker* is an example of how such differences of view can arise in value added tax on a much more domestic level.

The problem, one might think, was simple. Owners of a house in a village in Northampton wanted to convert an old outbuilding next to the house into a games room and add a swimming pool alongside. Zielinski Baker were their project managers. ZB drew up plans that, they thought, would get the development zero-rated. This was because the house was a listed building, and "approved alterations" to a "protected building", including a listed building that is a dwelling, are zero-rated. Listed building consent was obtained, so the alterations were approved. Factually, very little else matters.

Customs and Excise did not agree with ZB. In their view the outbuilding was not part of the protected building. This is because a "protected building" could not include more than one structure.

The appeal was heard by the VAT Tribunal in Birmingham on May 18 and 19, 2000 (see VAT Tribunal decision 16722, but not fully reported). Lady Mitting, the chairman, decided in a short, clear decision that Customs and Excise were wrong.

They appealed. The case came before Etherton J. in the Chancery Division on February 20 and 21, 2007. The same representatives argued the case for both parties, but on this occasion counsel for Customs and Excise argued that Lady Mitting was wrong because she had not considered European Law. In a much longer decision, Etherton J. decided that a protected building had to be a single building, and that Customs and Excise were right.

ZB appealed. The case came before Aldous, Tuckey and Rix L.J.J. in the Court of Appeal on May 17, 2002. Aldous L.J. did not mention European law in his decision beyond saying that the points "are not directly relevant". He was more interested in the planning rules. He would dismiss the appeal. Rix L.J. thought otherwise, but again he was interested in the planning rules and not the European rules. He would allow the appeal. Tuckey L.J., in a judgement just six lines long, agreed with Rix L.J. So the appeal was allowed and ZB won.

Customs and Excise appealed. In the House of Lords, Lord   **2–60** Nicholls took the view that if the words in question were read literally then Customs' case was unanswerable. But he did not think that was the right approach, and he would dismiss the appeal. Lord Walker of Gestinghope gave the main opinion to allow the appeal. He noted how the arguments of the parties had changed as the appeal proceeded through the courts. For that reason, he did not need to consider the decisions of the tribunal or Etherton J. at all. After a careful exercise in statutory construction (all the more valuable in the general sense because it is also a critical analysis of varying interpretative techniques used in the Court of Appeal) he concluded that a building was a building, not two buildings. Lord Hoffmann thought Etherton J. was right and that "the language is too clear" to come to any other conclusion. Lord Hope did not think it so simple but nonetheless found that the ordinary meaning of the words used, in the order in which they were used, lead inevitably to the same view as that of Customs. Lord Brown considered that the plain fact was that the outbuilding was an outbuilding and it was that, not the house, which was being altered.

By a majority, but for different reasons, the House allowed the appeal. But what was the common reason, or ratio? In this case, even more than our other example, we see what look like superficially simple words changing meaning under the heavy scrutiny of tax lawyers and judges. And we have the decision about whether the development was to be zero-rated officially changing four times with each appeal, with both higher courts divided, and with four judicial views for one side and six for the other of the plain meaning of the ordinary words "protected building". Or was it a plain meaning and were they ordinary words? And do you think, in the words of the Interpretation Act (which no one mentioned) the singular should include the plural? With whom would you agree?

The continuing rewrite programme

2–61   Most of the income tax rewrite programme was completed by the enactment of the four re-written income tax bill as the Income Tax Act 2007. Even before the enactment of that measure the Rewrite's expert team of drafters and administrators had already started work on two bills to rewrite corporation tax. Bill 5, the main corporation tax bill, was published in draft in early 2008. The process will be completed by a seventh bill to cover the remaining areas—mainly common to both income tax and corporation tax in their international contexts. It is not clear at the time of writing whether the Project will move on to rewrite CGT, inheritance tax and NI contribution law, but it seems unlikely that the project (which started in 1998) will be funded to rewrite all direct tax.

The core of VAT is in the European legislation. If parliament makes rules inconsistent with the European Directives, or HMRC's practice is out of line with it, then any taxable person can appeal to the tax tribunals and the British courts about the conflict. In the most important cases the tax tribunals and courts, and also the European Commission, can seek a ruling of the European Court of Justice. Much UK legislation on VAT is therefore of secondary importance. The European Commission has recognised this by codifying the whole of European Community VAT legislation in a single Regulation in 2007. Although this emerged from a separate codification process and a different parliament, there are interesting common style and codification similarities between this law and the products of the Rewrite Project.

E-tax

2–62   When Ron Davies' first edition of this book was published in 1980, the idea that taxation would be assessed and imposed purely by electronic means was still in the realms of science fiction. It was about the time of the second edition that one of us witnessed a demonstration in Manchester of what may have been the first tax software programme written in Britain. The author was the teenage son of a partner in a major accounting firm. He had written a programme to calculate the inheritance tax payable on an estate. If that was Britain's first e-tax programme, then it was entirely appropriate that it was first shown in Manchester, as that was where the first computer in the world was programmed some four decades before.

Some three decades later, every aspect of taxation law and practice has been changed fundamentally by the availability of new information and communications technologies. You will recall that one of the basic principles of taxation is fairness. ICT has allowed previously impossible levels of information flow to and from not only taxpayers but also their agents and any payment agents. Full details of everyone's earnings are fed from employers' payroll computers to the HMRC computers. Full details of savings interest earned are also fed from banks' computers to HMRC computers.

At the same time, even the most complicated calculations can be standardised and checked automatically. But to do this all discretions and uncertainties must be removed from the legislation. As yet, computers are not trusted to exercise discretion so all rules must have any uncertainties or personal judgments removed from them.

So the rules have been rewritten to codify and simplify them and to remove such discretions. This has also enabled the transfer of responsibility for making tax assessments from the tax officials to the taxpayers (or their agents). And it is now a small step from making taxpayers undertake self-assessments to asking, then requiring, that this be done electronically on standard forms. Once the rules are stated in mandatory form, the availability of electronic communication also allows HMRC readily to provide all necessary information to ensure that taxpayers are properly briefed about the requirements of self-assessment.

E-finding the law

As you will be aware, the availability of ICT has also profoundly changed the study of tax law and similar topics. One of the perils of studying tax law in the past used to be the constant danger of being out of date. It was also a problem for writers of any book on tax law. And past students would sometimes have considerable difficulty in finding out the details of a specific area of tax law. 2–63

These are not now problems. The reverse is now the case. Put something such as "income tax" into a web search engine and you will be inundated with millions of references even if you ensure that you restrict your search to UK websites. Even the official site of HMRC (at *www.hmrc.gov.uk*) will inundate the unwary visitor with a flood of information. And anyone can have instant access on the web to (almost) all official material by way of primary and secondary legislation, official instructions by HMRC to its officers, and the various other kinds of publication summarised in this chapter. Then there are the private sites of major accounting and law firms together with those of the major professional organisations and the more specialist sites of various interest groups. In previous editions, we offered some help in identifying some of these sites. Search engines, including the search engines on individual sites, now find specific references on such sites so easily that any such guidance is now otiose.

The resulting problem is a danger that you can be too well informed about the detail. It used to be called the problem of not seeing the wood for the trees, or perhaps the undergrowth. There is now limitless undergrowth in the forest of tax information on the worldwide web, and there are many forms of weed running rampant in it. Do not lose sight, in entering that forest, of the underlying need to consider the legal and constitutional contexts within which individual rules are to be operated. But do not neglect the abundant resources to be found in that forest.

We draw your attention to just one—hidden away on the HMRC site. These are the detailed explanatory notes prepared by the Tax Law Rewrite Project about the rewritten tax laws and the provisions on which they were based. Tax law is, and in the UK will always be, a matter of what Parliament has laid down in legislation. So the best place to start a detailed study of any tax law topic that has been scrutinised by the Rewrite Project is with the informed discussion about the drafting of the specific provisions of that legislation. And the only easy way of finding that is on the web. See *www.hmrc.gov.uk/rewrite*.

For a suggested starting point for other sites, see our own page at *http://www.sweetandmaxwell.co.uk/academic*.

PART TWO

TAXATION OF INCOME

CHAPTER 3

ASSESSING INCOME TAX

Introduction

In this chapter we trace how an individual's tax liability is   3–01
determined both in straightforward and in contested cases. In
practice the most litigated rules of income tax are those dealing
with trades and professions. So let us look at the position of a
trader. Traditionally, assessment by the Revenue rather than
self-assessment by the taxpayer has been fundamental to the
initiation and development of an income tax case. Since 1996–
97, all individual taxpayers are required to make a full tax
return of income, and to "self-assess" what is taxable. However,
this does not apply to those whose only income is taxed by
PAYE.

Making a return

All individual taxpayers must make a return of income and   3–02
capital for each tax year. There are similar rules requiring
returns from all companies, trusts and other taxpayers. The
requirements are laid down in Part II of the Taxes Management
Act 1970 as amended by Finance Act 2007, s.88. All returns
must include a self-assessment return unless the taxpayer gets
the return to HMRC in good time. From 2008 all returns must
be in by October 31 in the calendar year in which the tax year
ends if made in non-electronic form, and by the following January 31 if in electronic form. These dates are known as the filing
dates. But if the taxpayer wants HMRC to work out the tax
payable, then the return must be in by August 31 of the calendar
year in which the tax year ends. And the income or other tax due
must be paid by the date a full return is due. Failure to make a
return by the final filing date incurs an automatic fixed penalty
of £100. And there are newly revised penalties for errors and
omissions made fraudulently or negligently. See para.3–07
below.

Where a business is carried on in partnership a partnership
return is required. This return requires details of the profits
made by the partnership and of the shares of profit allocated to
each partner. But no assessment will be made on the partnership

and therefore there will be no joint liability for the tax due on partnership profits. Instead, each partner is required to include his share of the partnership profit in his own return (and self-assessment) and will be liable for the tax due on that share.

If a taxpayer fails to file a return (and self-assessment) by the filing date a Revenue officer may make a determination of the tax due "to the best of his information and belief". This determination is then treated as the taxpayer's self-assessment for the relevant year until such time as the taxpayer actually files a return (and self-assessment). The determination is automatically replaced by the taxpayer's own self-assessment once filed.

Correction of errors and the power to make enquiries

3–03   HMRC may correct obvious errors in a taxpayer's self-assessment within nine months of the delivery of the return. Otherwise, HMRC may only conduct an investigation into a return if a notice in writing is given to the taxpayer indicating the intention "to make enquiries into the return". The notice must be served usually within 12 months of the filing date (s.9A(1) of the TMA 1970). If such enquiries are undertaken, a taxpayer may be required by notice in writing to produce documents and accounts which might reasonably be required for the purpose of determining the accuracy of the return. A self-assessment may be amended in the light of information unearthed during an enquiry, although there is a right of appeal to the tax tribunal against the amendment. On completion of an enquiry, no other enquiry into that return may be made, unless an officer "discovers" later an error in the return because of information not previously available or due to fraudulent or negligent conduct by the taxpayer. In such circumstances, HMRC may raise an "old-style" discovery assessment against which the taxpayer may appeal to the tax tribunals.

A taxpayer may amend a return within 12 months of the filing date, although this right is not exercisable during an HMRC enquiry.

Keeping records

3–04   Section 12B of the TMA 1970 requires a taxpayer to keep records which enable the taxpayer to deliver a correct and complete return in a given tax year. For a trader, this includes details of receipts and expenses of the trade and any supporting documentary evidence, e.g. accounts and books. Moreover, the taxpayer must preserve those records for five years from the filing date (a "non-trader" must preserve records for one year from the filing date). Failure to keep or preserve records in this way could lead to the imposition of a penalty not exceeding £3,000.

Appeals

If there is no agreement between the trader and the inspector the appeal goes to the tax tribunals (see para.1–24).

3–05

At the hearing of the appeal the onus is on the taxpayer. Section 50(6) of the TMA 1970 says:

> "If, on an appeal, it appears to the majority of the Commissioners present at the hearing, by examination of the appellant on oath or affirmation, or by other evidence, that the appellant is overcharged by any assessment, the assessment shall be reduced accordingly, but otherwise every such assessment shall stand good".

This is an enormously important point. It provides HMRC with a strong lever indeed with which to extract from the taxpayer all necessary information. The assessment is right unless it is shown by the taxpayer to be wrong. This is particularly important where HMRC raises an assessment based on "best of judgment" or a "discovery". It may be that HMRC can no more prove it right than the taxpayer can prove it wrong. It was emphasised in *Jonas v Bamford* (1973) that that did not matter. So, in practice, a taxpayer who is shown to have means well in excess of that declared for tax will have to proves he gained them from betting or Great Aunt Maud. Mere assertion is not enough.

The practice and procedure followed by tax tribunals is governed by regulations made under s.56B of the TMA 1970.

An appeal lies from the Commissioners to the court, but only on a point of law, not on fact.

Major reforms of the ways that tax appeals are conducted are scheduled for 2009. The enabling legislation is in the Finance Act 2008 but at the time of writing the necessary regulations have not been passed. However, it is clear that all direct and indirect tax cases will be heard by a special section of the First-tier Tribunal that is being introduced under the Courts, Tribunals and Enforcement Act 2007. It is assumed that there will be a common set of procedural rules for all tax cases.

An important difference that this will introduce will be that appeals go not to the courts but to the new Upper Tribunal. Further, both taxpayers and HMRC will need permission to appeal beyond the First-tier Tribunal, and they will be able to appeal only if they can show an arguable case that there is an error of law in the tribunal's decision. The most difficult cases will be permitted to start in the Upper Tribunal. This is because appeals from the Upper Tribunal will go, with leave, direct to the Court of Appeal in England and Wales. This will therefore cut out one level of appeal in these cases. It will also stop parties having a right to appeal at least once in every tax case, as is now the rule.

Law and Fact

3-06   It is very important to keep in mind the point made earlier that an appeal lies from the Commissioners to the court only on a point of law. The leading authority on this matter is *Edwards v Bairstow and Harrison* (1956), HL. The question at issue was whether certain transactions carried out by the respondents in relation to the buying and selling of textile machinery constituted an adventure in the nature of trade, in which case the profits were taxable, or whether they did not, in which case the profits were not taxable (though they would now be taxable as capital gains). The General Commissioners decided that there was no adventure in the nature of trade. The High Court and the Court of Appeal held that it was purely a question of fact and that the court could not interfere. But the House of Lords took a more robust stand. True, trade or no trade is a question of fact, but if the only reasonable conclusion to which the Commissioners could come on a consideration of all the facts contradicts the conclusion to which they did come, then their finding can be reversed by an appellate court. Naturally, this decision of the House of Lords greatly widened the scope for appealing from the Commissioners to the courts. But it still quite often happens that the court holds that it has no power to interfere with a decision of Commissioners because they are the sole judges of fact (see, for example, *Glantre v Goodhand* (1983)). It should be borne in mind that when this occurs the case is not much of an authority for the future. Where, on the other hand, the court does reverse a decision of Commissioners the judgment is of greater authority.

Penalties and Criminal Proceedings

3-07   So far the litigation that we have been considering has been purely civil litigation; the taxpayer and HMRC have been arguing as to which of them is right on the facts or on the law. But there can be criminal proceedings by HMRC and also proceedings for penalties. Proceedings for penalties usually arise out of "back duty cases", that is, instances where HMRC are investigating the possibility that a person has not paid all the tax in the past that should have been paid.

The enforcement powers of the Revenue were limited both by legislation and by practice. Traditionally, income tax was enforced not by the criminal law and by penalties but by persuasion, settlement and, if necessary, the use of the Revenue's powers to make best judgment assessments which imposed a burden of proof on the taxpayer to disprove.

The shift to self-assessment and the integration of the Revenue into HMRC, together with a need to make the whole system more effective have all put pressure on this. There were also a number of complaints at the time of the merger of the two departments into HMRC about the way that prosecutions were being handled in parts of the former departments.

The first shift from the traditional position came in the Commissioners for Revenue and Customs Act 2005. This created a new Revenue and Customs Prosecutions Office. This new office is established under a Director of Revenue and Customs Prosecutions appointed by the Attorney General. It is a separate government unit from HMRC, and answers to the Attorney General.

HMRC started to conduct a review of its powers and penalties shortly after its formation. A series of consultation papers have been produced under the general title *Modernising Powers, Deterrents and Safeguards*. They are all available (and some available only) on the HMRC website. Results of this ongoing review process are seen in the Finance Acts 20007 and 2008. These start a standardisation of penalties provisions. Behind the new provisions is an explicit aim of using initial penalties to encourage, but subsequent actions, both by way of imposing penalties and using prosecutions, of discouragement. As an HMRC note put it: "our aim, developed through consultation, is to support those who seek to comply but come down hard on those who seek an unfair advantage through non-compliance".

Penalties

HMRC has a range of powers to impose penalties on tax- 3–08
payers who fail to comply fully with various aspects of their obligations. The penalties, when imposed, are treated as an additional amount of tax payable, as are any surcharges or interest: s.69 Taxes Management Act 1970. The effect on a defaulting taxpayer of a penalty can be quite severe. The defaulter will, first, have to pay all the tax assessed for the period of default. That assessment itself may be a best judgment estimate so may be high. If the defaulter has no records, or is not

believed, then it may be hard to displace the HMRC officer's best guess with some other figure. To that will be added interest for the late payment of the tax that should have been paid. Then the penalties will be added to this, as extra tax. And, finally, the taxpayer will not be able to deduct any of this from any future tax bills either directly or even as an expense. In other words, interest and penalties must be paid out of taxed income.

The most common penalties are the automatic default penalties imposed if a taxpayer misses a deadline for making a return or paying tax. These are in s.93 of the Taxes Management Act 1970. There is an automatic penalty of £100. There is no discretion to reduce this. If the default continues for more than six months, another automatic £100 penalty is payable. If the delay is of more than a year, then the potential penalty may be increased to equal the amount of tax that should have been shown payable in the return. On appeal, a tax tribunal may discharge the fixed penalties if a reasonable excuse is shown for the delay, but otherwise must confirm it. Continuing default may also be penalised by a daily penalty of up to £60. This can only be imposed by a tax tribunal.

3–09   The Finance Acts 2007 and 2008 impose more severe penalties against taxpayers who submit documents to HMRC containing errors if the result is an understatement of liability to tax, a false or inflated statement of a loss or a false or inflated claim to repayment. These also apply to failures to correct assessment issued to a taxpayer by HMRC. The maximum penalty is a percentage of the potential lost revenue in respect of every separate error. The maximum is only payable if HMRC takes the view that the taxpayer's actions were both deliberate and concealed. If they were deliberate but not concealed, the maximum is 70 per cent of revenue lost. If they were careless, and not deliberate or concealed, then the percentage is 30 per cent. This can be reduced at HMRC discretion if the disclosure that leads to the recovery of lost revenue is unprompted or if there are special circumstances.

There are also penalties against taxpayers and others who fail to comply with taxpayer notices or notices to third parties requiring them to provide information or produce documents. A penalty of £300, plus a daily default penalty of up to £60 a day may be imposed. Concealing, destroying or otherwise disposing of a document after a notice is issued is subject, on conviction, to criminal penalties.

Time limits

How far back can HMRC go? And can the taxpayer go back   3–10
as well? The general time limit for ordinary assessments is that
they may be made not more than four years after the end of the
tax year to which they relate: s.34 of the 1970 Act as amended
in 2008. There is a parallel power for taxpayers to ask for errors
to be corrected, and this goes back a similar length of time: s.33.
However, in cases where the tax loss is deliberate or to a failure
by the taxpayer to notify HMRC of a liability to tax, then
HMRC can take assessments back 20 years. If the action is
careless rather than deliberate, then it can go back five years.

Criminal proceedings

The Revenue tradition over many years has been to accept   3–11
cash settlements in most cases of evasion, rather than to prosecute. Consequently, criminal prosecutions for tax offences
were rare. Most evaders had the sense to pay-up and avoid the
publicity. More recently, this approach has given way to a more
aggressive stance. In *R. v W* (1998) the Court of Appeal agreed
that the Crown Prosecution Service could pursue a prosecution
against an evader although HMRC had declined to do so
because a settlement had been reached. In *R. v Barton* (1999)
the Revenue and Customs mounted a successful joint prosecution using elaborate information technology resources to
marshall evidence totalling 60,000 pages. Most significantly, in
R. v Dimsey (1999) the Court of Appeal upheld convictions for
the common law offence of "cheating the public revenue"
against taxpayers and advisers engaged in what some considered
as avoidance not evasion. Parliament strengthened this approach
by enacting a general criminal offence of fraudulent evasion of
income tax in section 141 of the Finance Act 2000. It is left to
the criminal courts to define "evasion".

Following this, in *R. v Faggon* (2003) the Court of Appeal
confirmed that compensation orders could be used to seize assets
following conviction for cheating the public revenue. In that
case over £1 million was seized from bank accounts of an
individual, in addition to a sentence of two years in prison.

Tax laws are also being used to reinforce other attempts to
seize assets from those convicted or suspected from profiting in
crime, or money laundering, or of holding funds for terrorist
activities. The Proceeds of Crime Act 2002 allows, from 2004,
an assessment to income tax (but not to any particular taxing
provision) to be imposed on those with untaxed and unex-
plained sources of income.

From 2007, the Revenue and Customs Prosecutions Office has   3–12 taken over sole responsibility for decisions to prosecute in tax cases. For details of this, and of the conduct of prosecutions and asset seizures by the Office, see the separate website at *www.rcpo.gov.uk*.

CHAPTER 4

TRADING INCOME AND LOSSES

Introduction

We now begin a study of each particular kind of income. It is **4–01** convenient to begin with trading income.

The rules about trading income have been codified by the Tax Law Rewrite Project in the Income Tax (Trading and Other Income) Act 2005 (or ITTOIA), Part 2 (ss.5 to 259). The basic provision is in s.5 which states simply that: "Income tax is charged on the profits of a trade, profession or vocation." With equal simplicity, s.7(1) imposes the charge on the full amounts of the profits of the tax year. And s.8 provides that the person liable for any tax charged under these provisions is the person receiving or entitled to the profits.

We must define "trade" and "profession or vocation". Each **4–02** of these definitions presents in practice a major problem requiring considerable thought in drawing the lines around activities caught within the words. But the operation of the tax rules on trades and on professions is broadly the same, although we will note a few differences. We will therefore follow ITTOIA in assuming trading income includes professional income unless stated otherwise.

The key "trade" problem is this: Is a given sum a trading profit or a capital gain? In the good old days a capital gain was entirely free of tax; since 1965 it has been subject to capital gains tax. Capital gains tax is distinct from income tax (this is unaffected by the rates of capital gains tax and income tax). Each tax has its own regime for the computation of gains/losses, and the characterisation of a particular gain/loss can have important repercussions for a taxpayer.

The key "profession" problem is this: Is a given person's exercise of a profession (or vocation) carried on within an office or employment, in which case he is to be taxed on employment income or is it carried on outside any office or employment, in which case he is to be taxed as trading? The issue is between trading and employment income. It is nowadays accepted that the distinction falls to be made on the same principles as in the law of tort, and also employment law. In tort the distinction is important in connection with vicarious liability, and it is generally described as the distinction between a servant (or employee) and an independent contractor.

Employed or Self-employed

4–03   In employment law the same distinction has led to considerable case law, especially on the questions of unfair dismissal and redundancy payments. In tax law it is described as the distinction between employees and the self-employed. In all contexts it is the distinction between a contract of service and a contract for services. For example, a solicitor in private practice, either as sole principal or as a partner, is self-employed and is taxed as if trading. A solicitor engaged in local government or in, say, BT Plc, is employed and has employment income. So does an employed solicitor in private practice; that is, a person qualified as a solicitor who works otherwise than as a partner in a firm of solicitors. And, of course, the same person can be employed and self-employed at the same time.

Is there any importance in this distinction? Yes, there is. The tax rules are different as between trading income and employment income. In particular, an employment income earner is subject to PAYE and the rules governing expenses are less generous.

Although the advantages are not all one way, most people would rather be taxed on trading income than on employment income. It is not surprising to find that Parliament has intervened to determine whether liability to tax should be trading income or employment income. One such instance concerns what is called "The Lump". The Lump means those in the construction industry who, though performing the functions of employed persons, claim the status of self-employed persons by means of "labour only" sub-contracting. Several attempts at dealing with this situation have been made, and currently the position is governed by ss.57–77 of the Finance Act 2004. Except where a sub-contractor holds an "exemption certificate," the contractor must deduct from each payment that it makes to the sub-contractor a sum equal to the basic rate of tax, after allowing for the sub-contractor's expenditure on materials. So a sub-contractor, though nominally remaining self-employed, is to suffer deductions as though employment income. That is the theory of the thing: in practice it does not always work very well.

4–04   Attention has also been directed towards "workers supplied by agencies." They are taxed as employees of their agencies.

Examples of workers caught by this provision are secretaries, typists and nurses.

A third group of workers have been dealt with differently. These are "divers" and "diving supervisors". Section 15 of ITTOIA provides that the Income Tax Acts shall have effect as if the performance by a diver or a diving supervisor of his duties constituted the carrying on by him of a trade. This is the reverse of the treatment meted out to "The Lump" and to agency workers; it is a case of treating employed persons as self-employed. One gathers that the reason for this generous treatment is the political or economic reason that if it were not done these divers and diving supervisors would leave the North Sea for sunnier places; sunnier fiscally speaking as well as climatically.

ITEPA contains general powers to treat those trying to reduce tax by working through a partnership or "pocket book company" or by other means trying to avoid being an employee, as caught by the employment income charge in any event. We shall return to these new rules and the distinction between "employed" and "self-employed" when we come to deal with employment income.

We want to discuss more fully the problem: Is a given sum a trading profit or a capital gain? Another way of putting the same question is, What is trading?

What is Trading?

There is a kind of definition of "trade" in s.832 of the Taxes Act. We say a "kind of definition" because it is one of those so-called definitions, common in tax legislation, which merely expand a word without defining it. "Trade", we are told, "includes every trade, manufacture, adventure or concern in the nature of trade." Notice that the last few words are "nature of trade", not "nature of *a* trade." Even so, this is little better than defining an elephant as being either an elephant or something which looks and behaves like an elephant.

Judges have also resisted giving an exhaustive definition to "trade", as widened by s.832. There is a useful discussion of the concept, and its problems, in the anti-avoidance case of *Ransom v Higgs* (1974), HL. This concludes that it is possible for something to be a trade even though no one can actually give the trade a name; see also the consideration of *Ensign Tankers (Leasing) Ltd v Stokes* in Ch.2.

One other point to watch is that the same person may be carrying on two or more separate trades at the same time,

4–05

possibly in the same place. If so, it may be necessary for the trades to be taxed separately.

4–06   The question whether a particular person is or is not trading is a question of fact. It was neatly described in one case as "a compound fact made up of a variety of things": *Erichsen v Last* (1881). We look in a moment at the variety of things that may bear on the decision, but first we draw attention again to the point that an appeal lies from the tax tribunals only on a point of law. At first sight, it would seem that a finding that a person is trading (or is not trading) can never be reversed by the court. This is not so. Following the decision of the House of Lords in the case of *Edwards v Bairstow and Harrison* (1956), the court can and will reverse a tribunal decision if it is of the opinion that (per Lord Radcliffe) "the facts found are such that no person acting judicially and properly instructed as to the relevant law could have come to the determination under appeal." His judgment in that case, with that of Viscount Simonds, repays close study.

The Badges of Trade

4–07   The factors which bear on the question "Trade or No Trade" were graphically described by the 1954 Royal Commission on Taxation as "badges of trade". The Commission listed six badges of trade and though subsequent cases have indicated others those six are still the dominant factors. Quite a useful approach to the problem is to ask oneself, when considering a transaction or series of transactions, if it is not trading, what is it? The rival candidate is usually, though not always, investment. To purchase and then sell an investment is not in itself trading. Another candidate is a hobby, or private and non-commercial activities.

4–08   The first point to consider is **what is sold**. Generally, if the subject-matter is such that the purchaser cannot either use it personally or derive an income from it or derive pleasure from it that points towards trading. Thus in *Rutledge v IRC* (1929) the taxpayer, while in Berlin in connection with a cinema business, bought a million rolls of toilet paper for £1,000. Shortly after his return to England, he sold the whole lot to one purchaser at a profit of over £10,000. It was held that this was an adventure in the nature of trade. Notice that in this case, as in many others, the fact that there was only one transaction (a one-off as the saying is) did not prevent its being held to be trading.[1] Contrast the case of *Salt v Chamberlain* (1979). Mr Salt was smitten by computers. He thought he had hit the jackpot by inventing a fool-proof method of investing in shares. He didn't and it wasn't. He lost a lot of money and tried to claim it as a trading loss. The court held that the shares were bought as investments. One test was whether the subject-matter itself produces income. Subsequently, however, in *Marson v Morton* (1986) it was suggested that land could constitute an investment even though it was not income producing.

The second point is **length of ownership**. This is not a compelling consideration, but there is something in it. A quick re-sale points towards trading but see also the fifth point, below.   4–09

The third point is **repetition**. Although, as we have seen, a single transaction can amount to trading, there are situations where a single transaction would not be trading but that kind of transaction repeated several times would be trading. In *Pickford v Quirke* (1927) a director of a spinning company formed a syndicate which bought the shares of a mill-owning company and then sold the assets of that company at a profit. He then took part in three similar transactions, although the members of the syndicate were not always the same people. The Court of Appeal held that he was carrying on a trade, even though each transaction considered by itself was not an adventure in the nature of trade.   4–10

The fourth point is **supplementary work** in connection with the realised property. In *Martin v Lowry* (1927), HL the taxpayer (who had had nothing to do with the linen trade) purchased from the Government its entire surplus stock of aeroplane linen, about 44 million yards. He found difficulty in selling it, and so he had to advertise extensively, rent offices and engage a manager and staff. He sold the linen to more than a thousand purchasers over a period of about 12 months and made a profit of nearly £2 million. It was held that the operations constituted trading. In *Martin v Lowry* there was a definite sales organisation, but there are cases where simple supplementary work has been held to make the transaction of buying and selling into trading. Thus in *IRC v Livingston* (1927) three   4–11

---

[1] There was a rumour that this case should really be called the case of the *imaginary* toilet rolls. It is said that the taxpayer invented the story of the toilet rolls to explain an increase in wealth, in the same way as many taxpayers claim that their wealth has arisen from betting-winnings (which are not taxable). It is said that this taxpayer thought that the toilet roll story would not be taxable. It is the tax law equivalent of the alleged non-existent snail in the ginger beer bottle.

individuals, a ship-repairer, a blacksmith and a fish salesman's employee, who had not previously been connected with each other in business, bought a cargo steamer, converted it (partly by their own labour) into a steam drifter, and sold it at a profit. The Court of Session overruled a finding of no trade, and held that this was a trade.

4–12   The fifth point is **why the sale took place**. There may be some explanation why something is sold which negatives the idea of trading. In *West v Phillips* (1958) a builder built some houses to hold as an investment and some for resale. Later on he decided to sell the investment houses, and he did so through the same organisation that sold his trading houses. The Special Commissioners held that there was trading, but the Court of Appeal reversed them, holding that the taxpayer decided to sell his investment houses because of rent control and the rising cost of repairs and higher taxation, and that in respect of the investment houses he was not trading.

4–13   The sixth point is **motive**. Although a trade may be held to exist even where there is no intention to make a profit, the absence of such an intention points against trading, whereas where there is such an intention that points towards trading. It is an important factor in a borderline case. Just such a case was *Taylor v Good* (1973) where the taxpayer bought a house at an auction without really intending to, in the hope that he might live there. He later sold it, making a profit, but the Court of Appeal held he did not intend to trade when he bought it, and had not traded with it (see also *Kirkham v Williams* (1991)).

So much for the case law on trading. Some activities have been declared by statute to be trading. The most important are farming and market gardening. Section 9 of ITTOIA states that "All farming and market gardening in the United Kingdom shall be treated as the carrying on of a trade ..." There are also "statutory trades" listed in s.12. Finally, other provisions give priority to trading income over other charges where, for example, interest is earned on balances outstanding from customer or on current trading accounts, where a dividend is received as trading income, or where certain property income is received as trading income.

What is a Profession?

4–14   We must now turn to Case II, professions and vocations. Neither term is defined by the statutes, so the judges have done the job instead. In *IRC v Maxse* it was said that the hallmark of a profession is the use of intellectual skill, with or without manual skills. In individual cases it will be a matter of fact whether, on balance, say a photographer running a shop is a professional photographer taxable under Case II, or a trader taxable under Case I, or possibly both at the same time, because the trade is separate from the profession.

"Vocation" is a calling, the way in which someone spends his life. In ordinary speech it carries a rather starry-eyed idea of nurses or others dedicated to their work. This seems to mean that they carry on their work without worrying about mundane things like pay. It is somewhat ironic to find that the leading case on vocations is a case about a bookmaker. The case is *Partridge v Mallandane* (1886). But, although the work of a bookmaker, a jockey and a racing tipster have all been held to be vocations, a full-time gambler is not! This was decided in *Graham v Greene* (1925), for the sensible reason (if illogical) that the Revenue would stand to lose far more than it gained from such people, because of loss claims! Anyway, betting and gaming taxes ensure such people contribute their share to the Exchequer. Having noted this, ITTOIA has now removed almost all the differences in treatment between traders and professionals. So these are usually distinctions without a difference.

The Computation of Profits

The importance of accounts
What we have said so far may suggest that the charge to tax is concerned with individual items of income. This is true of value added tax, and in individual tricky cases for income tax, but not in the vast majority of income tax cases. Remember that there is a charge not on receipts, but on annual profits.

The fundamental point about an assessment on this basis is that taxpayers need to produce accounts to find out for themselves if they have made a profit and for self-assessment purposes.

It is the professional task of accountants to produce accounts of profits and losses, or income and expenditures, over a set period, usually a year. Professional accountants do this in accordance with generally accepted accounting practice.

Companies' accounts are limited by guidelines. Most companies must produce and publish annual accounts which follow the forms and formats laid down in the Companies Acts. Furthermore, the accounts must be independently audited by professional auditors who must certify that the accounts comply with legal requirements, and also reflect a "true and fair view" of the company's profits for the period.

4–15

As the prestige of the accounting professions and their role in tax matters grew so the question of relationship between tax law and accounting practices and principles became sharper. The underlying question of the relationship is whether evidence that proper principles of accounting practice requires that an item be dealt with in a certain way should be decisive of its treatment in tax law. For example, if accountancy principles treat an item as revenue expenditure, to be included in the profit and loss accounts, can the item be treated as a capital expense for tax purposes?

Courts will now readily accept more than in the past that accounts prepared in accordance with accepted principles of commercial accountancy are adequate for tax purposes as a true statement of the taxpayer's profits, etc. However, such accounts will not be acceptable for tax purposes to the extent that they or particular items contained within them conflict with any express or implied statutory rule or are contrary to principles established by case law. It is noteworthy in the latter respect that Sir Thomas Bingham M.R. in *Gallagher v Jones* (1993), CA said:

> "I find it hard to understand how any judge-made rule could override the application of a generally accepted rule of commercial accountancy which (a) applied to the situation in question, (b) was not one of two or more rules applicable to the situation in question and (c) was not shown to be inconsistent with the true facts or otherwise inapt to determine the true profits or losses of the business."

4–16   For many years, the view was taken that "profits" for tax purposes were not the same thing as the profits of a business. A major difference was the treatment of capital and the consequent distinction between income and capital. But there were a series of other differences. For example, there was much concern about when income was received. So it was standard practice to accompany the accounts of a business with a series of adjustments converting the business profit from the accounts into the taxable profit on which tax was payable.

There has been a fundamental shift in official thinking about this in recent years. It is increasingly the case that—aside from two issues—the taxable profits are expected to be the same as the business profits. One of those two major differences remains the treatment of capital expenditure, and we discuss this in the chapter on capital allowances below. Another is the limitation on expenses that can be deducted from gross profits to produce the net profit for tax purposes, and we must also look at those rules in more detail. And for another, see the discussion on trading stock below.

Aside from those rules, and some specific rules of lesser importance, the general rule is now that professionally prepared accounts produced for a business or a company will provide the basis for assessing the tax due. See the decision of the House of Lords in *HMRC v William Grant & Sons Distillers Ltd* (2007) also discussed below.

The important point here is the recognition that properly prepared accounts must meet international and national standards of accounting practice. This started with the requirement in company law that all company accounts take a "true and fair view" of the company's finances. But there is now a detailed regime of international standard approaches to accounting issues such as the basis on which both income and expenditure are recognised as relevant to one year rather than another. Further, this applies to all accounts, not merely company accounts.

Section 42 of the Income and Corporation Taxes Act 1988 introduced a rule requiring all accounts to reflect a true and fair view. But as accounting standards developed, this was modified from 2002 to be a requirement that they be computed in accordance with generally accepted accounting practice. Tax was further aligned with accounting practices by the Finance Act 2005, s.84 and Sch.4. See now the same rules rewritten for income tax in ITTOIA, ss.25 and following. These set out the main rule and variations between accounting practice and the income tax rules. Of particular importance is s.27. This provides that references to receipts and expenses are "to any items brought into account as credits of debits in calculating profits". And subsection (2) sternly warns: "There is no implication that an amount has been actually received or paid."

If two or more principles of commercial accountancy, either or any of which is generally accepted, are pertinent in a particular case it is for the court, taking into account the professional evidence submitted to it, to determine what is the correct principle of commercial accountancy to apply—see, for example, *Johnston v Britannia Airways Ltd* (1994) and, for a review of the cases, *Herbert Smith v Honour* (1999).

In the more workaday world of tax offices, if sensible-looking accounts are produced by respected accountants, they will usually be accepted without much problem, even if they do "try it on" from time to time.

Profit and loss accounts must follow a basic form, whatever precise rules deal with individual items. They must show the

4–17

totals of relevant forms of income for the period and, against that, the totals of relevant expenditures. They must also show the opening and closing balances of trading stock (or opening and closing values of work in progress). The profit is the excess of income over expenditure, adjusted to reflect any increase or decrease in stock or work in progress between the start and end of the accounts period. But if gross profits are under £15,000, a simple three-line account is usually enough:

Gross profit	*10,000*
Expenses and allowances	*6,000*
Net profit	**4,000**

Those are the general rules. But *HMRC v William Grant & Sons Distillers Ltd* (2007) emphasises that it is now accounting practices that prevail. The case involved the way whisky distillers account for their stocks at each year end. Alongside it was a case involving Mars Ltd and raising the same point about foodstocks. Lord Hoffmann in the leading judgment emphasised where the courts, and therefore HMRC, now start:

> "Although the requirement that the initial computation shall give a true and fair view involves the application of a legal standard, the courts are guided as to it content by the expert opinions of accountants as to what the best current accounting practice requires. The experts will in turn be guided by authoritative statements of accounting practice issued or adopted by the Accounting Standards Board, which is given statutory recognition ..."

Their Lordships took a detailed look at the Financial Reporting Standards and Statements of Standard Accounting Practice relevant to the task of carrying forward stocks of whisky (as distillers are required to do). They decided that depreciation carried in stock in accordance with these principles was a permissible deduction from profits even if this involved depreciation being carried forward from one year to the next, if that gave a true and fair view of the profits.

The case is also an example of how British systems are brought together for tax purposes. The *William Grant* case was (of course) a Scotch case, while the *Mars* case was an English case. Both started life as a joint case before the Special Commissioners. One then went to the English courts, and the other to the Scots courts, before they cam back together again. The Court of Session and High Court both overturned the decisions of the Special Commissioners, but the House of Lords agreed with them and overturned the decisions of both courts.

We will now examine the income tax rules determining what should be included as a trading receipt, how trading stock is handled, what expenditures are allowable as deductions and how losses are handled. Broadly, these rules also apply where a trade is carried on by a company (see para.13–16). In addition, for corporation tax purposes, the profit, losses and expenses relating to loan relationships entered into by companies for the purposes of a trade are treated as receipts or expenses of that trade.

Trading receipts

The first question to be asked about any receipt is, is it a trading receipt or is it a capital receipt?

In some circumstances the answer to the question is perfectly plain. Thus, if a manufacturer sells a factory because a more up-to-date one was built it is clear that the proceeds of the sale constitute a capital receipt, which consequently does not enter into the computation of profits for income tax purposes. It is equally plain that if the same manufacturer sells a widget which has been made in the factory the proceeds of that sale constitute an income receipt which becomes an item in the income tax computation.

In other circumstances, the question "trading receipt or capital receipt?" is quite difficult to answer. This is particularly so where compensation is paid to a trader, and in cases of voluntary payments to traders.

Compensation

There is a mass of decided cases on this matter. We will look at three. In *Van den Berghs Ltd v Clark* (1935), HL the appellant English company entered into agreements with a competing Dutch company under which each company agreed to conduct its business on certain lines. After a dispute it was settled that the agreements should be terminated on condition that the Dutch company paid £450,000 to the English company. It was held that this was a capital receipt, and thus was not taxable. Lord Macmillan said that "... the cancelled agreements related to the whole structure of the appellant's profit-making apparatus."

In *Kelsall Parsons & Co v IRC* (1938) the appellants were manufacturers' agents; they held contracts with several manufacturers under which they sold their products for a commission. One of these manufacturers wished to terminate its agency contract and it did so about 16 months before it was due to

4–18

4–19

expire, paying Kelsall Parsons & Co £1,500 as compensation. This sum was held to be an income receipt, and hence taxable. The loss of this one agency clearly did not relate to the whole structure of the appellants' profit-making apparatus. Lord Normand said (in the Court of Session): "The agency agreements, so far from being a fixed framework, are rather to be regarded as temporary and variable elements of the profit-making enterprise."

In *London and Thames Haven Oil Wharves Ltd v Attwooll* (1967), CA the taxpayer company owned a jetty which was seriously damaged by a tanker when it was coming alongside. The owners of the tanker paid a sum of money to the taxpayer of which part was apportioned to physical damage to the jetty and part to consequential damage, namely loss of use of the jetty during the 380 days taken up in repairing it. The Revenue did not seek to tax that part of the payment which was apportioned to physical damage, but it did seek to tax the part apportioned to consequential damage. The assessment was upheld by the Court of Appeal. Diplock L.J. gave a limpidly clear judgment. He said:

> "Where, pursuant to a legal right, a trader receives from another person compensation for the trader's failure to receive a sum of money which, if it had been received, would have been credited to the amount of profits (if any) arising in any year from the trade carried on by him at the time when the compensation is so received, the compensation is to be treated for income tax purposes in the same way as that sum of money would have been treated if it had been received instead of the compensation."

The Lord Justice went on to say that two questions have to be asked. First, was the compensation paid for the failure of the trader to receive a sum of money? If the answer to that is yes, there arises a second question: If that sum of money had been received by the trader would it have been credited to the amount of profits of the trader? The same question can be put more shortly, namely, would it have been an income receipt of the trade (and not a capital receipt)? If the answer to that question is yes, the compensation is taxable; if the answer is no, the compensation is not assessable to income tax. In the instant case that part of the compensation which had been apportioned to loss of use of the jetty (1) was paid for the failure of the trader to receive a sum of money, and (2) represented the profit (surplus of receipts over expenses) which would have followed from the use of the jetty during 380 days. So the assessment was correct.

Voluntary payments

A problem which has vexed the courts considerably is the   4–20
status of a payment made to a trader voluntarily, without a
contractual requirement that it be paid. When should such
receipts be treated as trading receipts?

It was established by the Privy Council in *Taxation Commissioner of Australia v Squatting Investment Co Ltd* (1954), an
Australian case, that the mere fact that a payment was voluntary
did not prevent it being a trading receipt. Equally the Court of
Appeal in *Simpson v John Reynolds & Co (Insurances) Ltd*
(1975) confirmed that not all voluntary payments were taxable.
That case concerned a payment of £5,000 by clients of the
insurance brokers following the discontinuance of use by the
clients of the broker's services following a change in control of
the clients, a company. Important factors in the decision were
that the payment was unsolicited and of an amount not tied to
possible future sales, and that the trading relationship between
broker and client had ceased. The payment could not relate to
future performance. A different Court of Appeal working on
different facts, reached a similar conclusion in *Murray v
Goodhews* (1978).

The *Simpson* case was, however, distinguished by another
Court of Appeal in *Rolfe v Nagel* (1982), a case concerning
voluntary payments to a diamond broker. It was held that here
the sums were compensation for otherwise unremunerated work
and were not unsolicited, and were trading receipts. Similar
thoughts lay behind *McGowan v Brown and Cousins* (1977).

Trading stock

It is important to grasp that trading stock (stock-in-trade) is   4–21
an essential item in a trader's account—for tax purposes no less
than for commercial purposes. Let us take a simple trading
account as it is usually presented.

	£	£
Sales for the year		85,000
Opening stock	3,000	
Purchases	40,000	
	43,000	
Less Closing stock	5,000	
Cost of goods sold		38,000
Trading profit		47,000

Notice that in the account we have used the phrase "trading
profit". This account does not deal with expenses such as wages,

rent, rates, heating, lighting, telephone, postage. Those matters would be dealt with in a further account, so reducing the trading profit to a taxable profit.

Trading profit is the amount by which the proceeds of the goods sold (£85,000) exceed the cost of those goods (£43,000).

If one omitted stock—both opening and closing—from the trading account one would get a different result. One would get sales £85,000, less purchases £40,000 = profit £45,000. But that would be unreal. This trader has not only made a profit of £45,000 on sales during the year compared with purchases during the year; he has also improved his position by having increased his stock during the year from £3,000 at the beginning of the year to £5,000 at the end of the year, an increase of £2,000.

The closing stock figure for one year becomes the opening stock figure for the next year.

As closing stock represents expenditure on goods not yet sold, that expenditure is credited to the current year and carried forward to be charged in the subsequent year—as opening stock—in which the stock is to be sold.

4–22   In *IRC v Cock, Russell & Co Ltd* (1949) the court gave its approval to the accountancy practice of permitting a trader to value stock at its cost price or its market price, whichever is the lower, and to treat each item of stock separately. So, when any item of stock is expected to fetch less than its cost, its market value (or "net realisable value") (instead of its cost) is included in the total of closing stock. The effect is to charge immediately in the current year that part of its cost which is considered to be irrecoverable. This is now a question of whether the business has accounted for its stock values in a generally accepted way, as judged by accounting standards and not the courts.

4–23   WORK IN PROGRESS   "Work in progress" is the phrase used to cover such things as goods in the process of manufacture. A manufacturer, at the end of a particular accounting period, will have some items in his factory which are partially but not wholly constructed. Such items are brought into account in the same way (broadly) as is closing stock, although this may not be a simple exercise (see *Duple Motor Bodies v Ostime* (1961), HL). And the same principle applies to many other things besides partially manufactured goods; it applies for example to partially performed contracts of a professional person.

4–24   THE RULE IN SHARKEY V WERNHER   This case established the rule that if you transfer an asset from a taxable activity of yours to a non-taxable activity you must bring in to your accounts the market value of the asset which you have transferred just as though you had sold it. *Sharkey v Wernher* (1956), HL concerned Lady Zia Wernher. Lady Zia carried on a stud farm, the profits of which were assessable to income tax under Case I. She also owned horses and ran them at race meetings as a recreation, in respect of which activity no liability to tax arose. In one year she transferred five horses from the stud farm to her racing stables. The House of Lords held that the horses must be treated as having been disposed of by way of trade, and the sum which should be regarded as having been received on their disposal must be a sum equivalent to their market value. Lord Simonds neatly observed that the same point arises when "the owner of a stud farm diverts the produce of his farm to his own enjoyment or a diamond merchant, neglecting profitable sales, uses his choicest jewels for the adornment of his wife, or a caterer provides lavish entertainment for a daughter's wedding breakfast. Are the horses, the jewels, the cakes and ale to be treated for the purpose of income tax as disposed of for nothing or for their market value or for the cost of their production?" And the House of Lords (with one dissentient) answered "Market value."

FA 2008 codifies this law in new ss.172A–F of ITTOIA. But it will be the same rule—just harder to remember!

TRANSFER PRICING The rule in *Sharkey v Wernher* is a **4–25** common law rule, but there is a similar statutory rule in s.770A of the Taxes Act and Sch.28AA. Where the buyer and the seller are under common control ("associated") HMRC may substitute in the accounts of either party the notional market price of the thing sold for the price in fact charged, thus counteracting a transaction at an over-value or an under-value. The section does not apply where the under-value or over-value will be reflected anyway in the accounts of the benefitted party, which is the case where he (or it) is taxable as a United Kingdom trader. The section is clearly aimed at "transfer pricing" between the United Kingdom and overseas. But measures in the Finance Act 2004 widen the scope of the provisions beyond that limit. Bear in mind that where the section does not apply, the rule in *Sharkey v Wernher* may apply.

Trading expenses

The rules about deduction of trading expenses for individuals **4–26** used to be a legislative mess: see s.74 of the Income and Corporation Taxes Act 1988, which still applies to companies. The codification of the law into ITTOIA gave drafters an opportunity to clear away the debris of two centuries of lawmaking on the subject and restructure the legislation. This they have done with considerable skill. As a result, we can now present these rules relatively simply by following the pattern of the code.

We have already seen the core basic rules for calculating trading income. These are set out in chapter 3 of Part 2 of ITTOIA, under the title "trade profits: basic rules". And we have noted the key basic rules. We now need to note one more. Section 31 provides that if one provision in this Part of ITTOIA provides for a deduction from profits for tax purposes, and another prohibits it, then the permissive rules has priority over the prohibitive rule.

That introduces us to chapter 4 of the Part (rules restricting deductions) and chapter 5 (rules allowing deductions).

Chapter 4 starts with three key rules. First, no deduction is allowed for items of a capital nature (s.33). Read this with s.28 which directs that we read this with the provisions of the Capital Allowances Act which treat allowances and charges made under that Act as receipts or expenses of a trade. The second rule is that no deduction is allowed for expenses not incurred wholly and exclusively for the purposes of the trade or for losses not connected with or arising out of the trade. See s.34. The third rule is that no debts may be deducted as expenses unless the debts are either bad or are estimated to be bad. See s.35.

There are then a series of rules of much narrower importance. But we must first look at the first two rules in greater detail.

Revenue, not capital, expenditure

4–27   The same distinction falls to be made in regard to expenditure as in regard to receipts. It is not an easy distinction to make. In one case Lord Greene M.R. remarked, "... in many cases it is almost true to say that the spin of a coin would decide the matter almost as satisfactorily as an attempt to find reasons." (*British Salmson Aero Engines Ltd v IRC* (1938), CA). But judges do not toss coins, at least not visibly. So we must look at some reasoning.

The first point to be clear about is that a payment which is a revenue receipt in the hands of the payee is not necessarily an item of revenue expenditure by the payer. Equally a payment which in the hands of the recipient is a capital item may be a revenue expenditure on the part of the payer. The two things have to be looked at separately. The principles, however, are the same whether one is considering receipts or expenses.

In some cases of expenditure the matter is perfectly clear. If a manufacturer expends money on a new factory, that is capital expenditure; if he spends money on raw materials, that is revenue expenditure. Adam Smith's distinction between fixed capital and circulating capital is of some help here.

However, in cases where the matter has been less clear–cut reliance has been placed often on the classic statement to be found in the speech of Lord Cave in *British Insulated and Helsby Cables Ltd v Atherton* (1926), HL: "When an expenditure is made, not only once and for all, but with a view to bringing into existence an asset or an advantage for the enduring benefit of a trade. I think that there is very good reason ... for treating such an expenditure as properly attributable not to revenue but to capital." There is no doubt that this is a helpful general statement, but some qualification is needed. First, it is clear from later cases that "enduring benefit of a trade" must be taken as meaning "a thing which endures in the same way that fixed capital endures": see per Rowlatt J. in *Anglo-Persian Oil Co Ltd v Dale* (1931), approved and adopted by Lord Wilberforce in *Tucker v Granada Motorway Services Ltd* (1979), HL. Secondly, there may be expenditure which has an enduring effect, but which, nevertheless, is not deemed to be capital in nature. Thirdly, the identification of an "asset or advantage for the enduring benefit of a trade" may not be easy. For example, if a taxpayer borrows money for a term, is he to be treated as only receiving cash to be used in his business or is he effectively securing a continuance of his trade [and hence an advantage for his trade] for the duration of the loan?

Probably four main factors emerge from the welter of decided **4–28** cases on the point: the nature of the benefit acquired in exchange for the payment; the manner in which that benefit is to be used; the means by which it is obtained (periodical payments or lump-sum payment); and, more recently, how the expenditure is treated in standard accounting practice. Different weights are to be attached to these four factors in different circumstances. In *Regent Oil Co Ltd v Strick* (1966), HL Lord Reid said:

"Whether a particular outlay by a trader can be set against income, or must be regarded as a capital outlay, has proved to be a difficult question. It may be possible to reconcile all the decisions, but it is certainly not possible to reconcile all the reasons given for them ... The question is ultimately a question of law for the Court, but it is a question which must be answered in light of all the circumstances which it is reasonable to take into account, and the weight which must be given to a particular circumstance in a particular case must depend rather on commonsense than on a strict application of any single legal principle."

Wholly and exclusively for the purposes of the trade

4–29   The rule about expenses in s.34(1) is a rule of primary importance, and overrides any rule of accounting practice. It imposes a prohibition on expenses of any kind unless those expenses are shown to meet all three of the tests laid down in the subsection:

(a)   the expenses must be wholly incurred in the trade; and
(b)   they must be incurred exclusively in the trade; and
(c)   they must be incurred for the purposes of the trade.

Although this rule is newly drafted, these tests are of long standing, and there has been much case law about them. And those cases have perhaps added a test that is not in the statute.

"WHOLLY"   It seems that the word "wholly" relates to *quantum*. The whole amount of the expenditure must be laid out for the purposes of the trade, or rather the expense is only allowable up to the amount of it which is laid out for the purposes of the trade.

"EXCLUSIVELY"   The word "exclusively" has proved difficult to apply. The classic statement of the law is in the judgment of Romer L.J. in *Bentleys Stokes & Lowless v Beeson* (1952), CA. This case was concerned with business entertainment expenditure. At the time of the case there was no special rule relating to such expenditure; there is such a rule now (in s.356 of ITEPA and s.577 of the Taxes Act) disallowing it save in the case of a very limited number of exceptions. Romer L.J. said:

"It is . . . a question of fact. And it is quite clear that the purpose must be the sole purpose. The paragraph says so in clear terms. If the activity be undertaken with the object both of promoting business and also with some other purpose, for example, with the object of indulging an independent wish of entertaining a friend or stranger or of supporting a charitable or benevolent object, then the paragraph is not satisfied though in the mind of the actor the business motive may predominate. For the statute so prescribes. *Per contra*, if in truth the sole object is business promotion, the expenditure is not disqualified because the nature of the activity necessarily involves some other result, or the attainment or furtherance of some other objective, since the latter result or objective is necessarily inherent in the act."

And so the Court of Appeal allowed the expenditure which had been incurred in entertaining clients.

Lord Justice Romer made it all sound very easy, but in practice it has not proved easy to separate sole purpose cases from dual purpose cases, and one is sometimes left with the feeling that honesty is not the best policy. In *Bowden v Russell & Russell* (1965) the sole principal of a firm of solicitors visited America and Canada with his wife to attend the annual meeting of the American Bar Association in Washington and the Commonwealth and Empire Law Conference in Ottawa. It was his intention to have also a holiday with his wife. The court held that the expenses incurred in connection with the conferences were not deductible, because they were incurred for a dual purpose, the advancement of his profession and the enjoyment of a holiday.

Can there be apportionment?

These rules and the doctrine of "dual purpose" have been applied somewhat unhappily for many years. Unhappily because of the point already made and because they do not allow sums incurred for two purposes (such as telephone rentals and car expenses) to be apportioned. But in practice every accountant knows that they can be apportioned, as long as one is not too greedy, whatever the strict provisions of the law. Take, for example, *Lucas v Cattell* (1972). This was actually a Sch.E case but, as we shall see, these parts of the deductions rules are the same for both Schedules. Lucas was required by his employers to have a telephone at home, but they refused to meet the expense of the telephone rental. For several years the Revenue allowed Lucas to deduct a small part of the rental. One year he demanded more! One is reminded of Lionel Bart's famous song from *Oliver*. The result was predictable. Lucas ended up with nothing. His payment was not wholly and exclusively for his employment; and the rental payment could not be severed so that part could be said to be deductible. Section 34(2) allows an identifiable part or proportion of an expense to be deducted where only that part or proportion is incurred for the trade.

4–30

The "object" test

Then Ann (now Lady) Mallalieu, a barrister, gave the courts a chance to make some sense of the rules. They tried, but they found it difficult to resolve the issues and by a four-to-one majority the House of Lords overruled the Court of Appeal and Chancery Division and left the law in as much a muddle as ever: *Mallalieu v Drummond* (1983), HL.

4–31

The facts could not be simpler. Mallalieu claimed £500 for replacement items of court dress, their laundering and cleaning. This was revenue expenditure which she incurred to comply with the official guidance to barristers on dress in court. It was undisputed evidence that, at the time she bought the clothes, her only conscious motive was to comply with these professional requirements.

The judgment of Lord Brightman (for the majority) made clear that there was another source of unease about the rules in his mind. It is often felt that the expenses rules are over-generous to the self-employed as compared with employees. So his Lordship observed, the case was really about "the right of any self-employed person to maintain ... partly at the expense of the general body of taxpayers, a wardrobe of everyday clothes which are reserved for work."

After reciting the dual purpose rule, Lord Brightman reminded himself that the "object" of the expenditure was the decisive factor in applying the dual purpose rule. But, he said, the object of expenditure must be distinguished from its effect. Further, the conscious motive of the taxpayer in making the expenditure was not the deciding factor in establishing the "object". "It is inescapable that one object, though not a conscious motive, was the provision of the clothing that she needed as a human being." He adopted the judgment of Goulding J. in *Hillyer v Leeke* (1976), which, in effect, rested its conclusion on the "self-evident truth" approach to the question.

Implicitly, this seems to overrule the test laid down in the *Bentleys* case (and cited by Lord Elwyn-Jones in his short, powerful dissent) without mentioning it. So we must now judge the object of an expense objectively, distinguishing its effect. But how do you judge the object of a British medical consultant's flight to the South of France to see a patient (or was it partly to have a holiday?) objectively? Further, for an example of the anomalies to which the application of this test may give rise, see *Watkins v Ashford Sparkes and Harward* (1985). In *McKnight v Sheppard* (1999) the House of Lords returned to the subject. The case concerned the deductibility of a fine incurred under a professional disciplinary procedure. Pragmatically, their Lordships decided the issue was one of policy and that taxpayers generally should not be required to help pay the fine.

"For the purposes of"

4–32   Returning to the words of the section, note that it says that the expenditure must be "for the purposes of" the trade. This has been held to mean: "for the purpose of earning the profits":

Strong & Co Ltd v Woodfield (1906), HL, per Lord Davey. Damages that were paid by the owners of a licensed house to a guest who was injured when one of the chimneys fell on him were held not to be deductible. Despite criticism, this case and its test were approved by the majority in the *Mallalieu* case.

Specific expenses

We want now to make special mention of certain types of expenditure.   4–33

TRAVEL TO WORK AND AT WORK   There are no special rules in the Acts governing the deduction of travel expenses by traders, so the general rules apply. However, there seems to be a lot of misunderstanding about expenditure on travel from home to work and from work to home. Some people think that home to work (and return) travel is not allowable for employment income taxpayers but is allowable for traders. This is not correct. It is quite true that there is a big difference in the rules relating to expenditure from employment income and from trading income, and we shall be looking at the difference in the next chapter. But in practice the courts have reached, albeit by different routes, similar conclusions about the allowability or otherwise of travel expenses under both provisions. This is because the phrase in ITEPA, "travelling in the performance of the duties", more or less balances the phrase in ITTOIA, "wholly and exclusively for the purposes of the trade" (as applied to travel).

In *Newsom v Robertson* (1953), CA a barrister who had chambers in Lincoln's Inn and lived at Whipsnade was held not entitled to deduct the expenses of travelling between the two places. This was so even though he had at his home a library of law books, and worked at home in the evenings and at weekends. On the other hand, in *Horton v Young* (1972), CA a self-employed bricklayer was held entitled to deduct the expenses of travelling from his home to the various sites on which he worked. At first glance this may seem to be inconsistent with *Newsom's* case. But this is not so. Mr Horton kept at his home his tools and account books and made his contracts there. It was held that his home was his base, whereas in Mr Newsom's case it was held that his chambers were his base. If your home is your base, travel to work and back home is wholly and exclusively for the purposes of your trade or profession. If your home is not your base then such travel is not wholly and exclusively for the purposes of your trade or profession; it is partly because you choose to live at, e.g. Whipsnade.

A later case caused some consternation. This is *Sargent v Barnes* (1978). A self-employed dental surgeon had a dental laboratory which was on the route between his home and his surgery. He called at the laboratory on his morning and evening journeys for the purpose of collecting dentures and discussing work with his technician. He claimed to deduct the expenses of travel between the laboratory and his surgery. His claim failed, the judge holding that the expenditure was not wholly and exclusively for the purposes of the taxpayer's profession. The journey did not "cease to be a journey for the purpose of getting to or from the place where the taxpayer chose to live". There is another interesting point in this case—because of a mistake. The General Commissioners were muddled when they heard the appeal, and thought the Sch.E rules applied, and that the travel was necessary.

4–34   LEGAL AND ACCOUNTANCY CHARGES   The professional costs incurred in a tax appeal are not allowable. This is because the tax is not an expense in earning a profit—it is the way the profits are spent: *Smith's Potato Estates Ltd v Bolland* (1948), HL. But as a matter of practice the fees paid to an accountant for preparing self-assessment returns are allowed, and so are fees paid for advice on tax liability.

4–35   INTEREST   Section 29 of ITTOIA provides that interest is always income not capital. Interest is quite capable of being wholly and exclusively laid out for the purposes of the trade and, if it is, it is a deductible expense. This is immensely important in practice. But dividends are never deductible expenses for companies, and nor are the profit shares paid to partners of a partnership.

4–36   REPAIRS AND IMPROVEMENTS   Expenditure on repair is allowable, whereas expenditure on improvements is not. In a famous passage Buckley L.J. (in *Lurcott v Wakely & Wheeler* (1911), CA said:

> "Repair is restoration by renewal or replacement of subsidiary parts of a whole. Renewal, as distinguished from repair, is reconstruction of the entirety, meaning by the entirety not necessarily the whole but substantially the whole subject-matter under discussion."

In subsequent cases the distinction made by Lord Justice Buckley between repair and renewal has been taken to be the same as the statutory distinction between repair and improvements. His idea of "the entirety" seems attractive, but of course it means that everything depends on what the court regards, in any particular case, as the entirety. In *O'Grady v Bullcroft Main Collieries Ltd* (1932) the expense of replacing a chimney by another on a different site was held to be not deductible. But in *Samuel Jones & Co (Devondale) Ltd v IRC* (1951) the expense of replacing a factory chimney was held to be deductible. In the first case the court regarded the chimney itself as the entirety; in the second case the court regarded the chimney as part of a larger entirety, namely the factory.

The distinction between repair and improvements runs into (in some circumstances it is virtually the same as) the distinction between revenue and capital expenditure. In *Law Shipping Co Ltd v IRC* (1924) a trader bought a ship in a state of disrepair. The periodical survey of the ship was overdue, but she was ready to sail, with freight booked, and she did sail. When that voyage was over, the ship underwent survey, and the owners had to spend some £50,000 on repairs, of which some four-fifths was attributable to the disrepair of the ship at the time of purchase. It was held by the Court of Session that that latter expenditure was in the nature of capital expenditure and was therefore not deductible. In *Odeon Associated Theatres Ltd v Jones* (1973), CA the appellant company bought a large number of cinemas which had not been kept in repair. Some years later they carried out repairs which had been outstanding at the time of purchase. The cinemas were usable in their unrepaired state, but they were not up to the standard set by the new owners. The Special Commissioners made a finding of fact that on the principles of sound commercial accountancy these deferred repairs would be dealt with as a charge to revenue in the accounts of the company. The Court of Appeal held that the cost of the repairs was deductible as revenue expenditure. The *Law Shipping* case (above) was distinguished on three grounds: (1) in that case, but not in this case, the purchase price was less by reason of the disrepair; (2) in that case but not in this case the asset could not (except temporarily) earn profits until it had been repaired; and (3) in that case there was no evidence of accountancy practice, whereas in this case there was such evidence and it pointed towards deductibility.

Rules allowing deductions

Part 2, chapter 5 of ITTOIA sets out the rules that expressly allow deductions against profits that would fail under the rules prohibiting deductions. There are nearly 40 of these specific rules. Most are focussed on specific trades or activities, but a few

4–37

are of general importance. There are also a few further rules allowing deductions as exceptions to the rules prohibiting deductions in Ch.4. Several of the items allow expenditure on employees and ex-employees that would not otherwise be allowed. Another item of general importance is in s.87. This allows a trader to deduct expenses of research and development if it is "related to" a trade—a wider test than expenses for the purposes of a trade. And s.88 allows a deduction for payments made to others, such as a university, for research—but in the fields of natural or applied science only.

The Treatment of Losses

4–38　　What happens with losses arising in a trade or profession? These losses can be set off against taxable income from other sources. The tax position of a trade or profession is calculated by subtracting from the income the relevant expenses. If that calculation leaves a credit balance there is a taxable profit. But if it leaves a minus quantity there is a loss. Thus far, a loss is calculated in just the same way as a profit is calculated. In particular a trader cannot claim for tax purposes to have made a loss merely because a loss is made on one transaction. For example, if a builder undertakes to build a house extension for £75,000 and in the event it costs him £80,000 to build it, he cannot claim to have made a loss of £5,000. What matters is the overall relationship of trading income and expenses throughout a whole year's operation of the trade.

There are four main ways in which relief for losses may be given: set-off against general income and capital gains; carry-forward against subsequent profits; carry-back of terminal losses; and a special mode of relief for losses in the early years of a trade. These rules have now been re-written as Part 4 of the Income Tax Act 2007 (ITA). We will look at these in turn.

Set-off against general income and capital gains

4–39　　By ss.61 to 66 of ITA a person who sustains a loss in any trade or profession carried on by him either solely or in partnership may make a claim for relief. The relief works by way of setting off the loss in the trade, etc., against profits in some other trade or indeed against any income of the claimant in the same year. If the claimant's income of that same year is not sufficient to absorb the whole of the loss then the balance may be set off against the claimant's income of the preceding year.

The amount of the loss for the purposes of these sections

generally includes capital allowances which are *treated* as trading expenses.

By s.66 a loss is not available for relief unless it is shown that the trade was being carried on on a commercial basis and with a view to the realisation of profits. And by ss.67 to 70 an even more stringent rule applies to farming and market gardening, namely that a loss cannot be relieved if in each of the prior five years a loss was incurred. The point of these sections is to exclude from loss relief against other income "hobby-trading" and particularly "hobby-farming". Hobby-farming is a pretty popular activity. It arises in this way: a person with a substantial income (say a stockbroker) buys a farm and spends a great deal of money on building it up as a capital asset. If he could contrive to have no farming profits because of capital expenditure and set the farming losses against his stockbroking profits he could lay a gigantic nest-egg largely at the expense of HMRC. HMRC has disobliged.

A claim for relief under these sections against general income may be extended to the claimant's capital gains of the same year. However, the loss must be set off against the general income before relief can be given against capital gains. If the claimant's capital gains of that year are not sufficient to absorb the whole of the loss then the balance may be set off against the claimant's capital gains of the preceding year (this also applies to existing businesses during the transitional year).

Carry-forward against subsequent profits

Section 83 provides for the carrying forward of a loss in one year against the profits in a subsequent year of the same trade or profession. Notice that it must be the *same* trade, etc. In that respect this relief is totally different from immediate relief. A loss can be carried forward under s.83 indefinitely, but it must be set off against the first subsequent assessment and then, so far as it remains not fully relieved, against the next assessment, and so on. If a loss has been partially relieved under some other provision, the unrelieved amount may be carried forward. Or a trader can ignore immediate relief and go straight for s.83 relief. **4–40**

It may happen that the profits of a particular year are not big enough to absorb a loss which is being carried forward into that year. In that case, interest or dividends (if there are any) arising to the trader will be treated as though they were trading profits. This point needs a bit of explanation. If interest or dividends which have borne tax by deduction are received by a trader they are not included in the computation of his trading profits. The present point is that those receipts can nevertheless be *treated as* **4–41** profits, and a carried-forward loss can be relieved against them by means of a repayment of tax.

Another point on s.83 concerns interest, meaning payments of interest outwards. If a trader makes a payment of interest that will, prima facie, be an expense of his trading. But if he has an overall loss the interest will not get relieved. But the amount of the interest payment may be carried forward under s.85 "as if it were a loss."

4–42   The general rules for s.83 relief are that not only must the prior loss and the subsequent profit be incurred in the same trade, but also the claimant must be the person who incurred the loss. However, there is an important exception to these general rules in s.86 which provides that where a business carried on by an individual (or individuals) is transferred to a company, the individual may claim to set off any losses which he incurred before the transfer against income derived by him from the company after the transfer. The consideration for the transfer of the business must consist solely or mainly of the allotment of shares in the company. The income from the company may take the form of director's remuneration or salary or dividends. Further, a partner does not usually lose the relief available when there is a change in the membership of a partnership, e.g. when a partner joins or leaves the partnership. This is so because a partner is deemed to be a sole trader/professional in respect of his share of the partnership profit or loss. Therefore, his ability to carry forward his share of any such loss against his share of the partnership profits from the same trade or profession in subsequent years is normally unaffected by a change within the partnership (save where the actual trade/profession is subsequently carried on by him alone, see below).

Carry-back of terminal losses

4–43   By s.89 terminal losses (meaning losses outstanding at the termination of a business) may be set off against the profits of a trade or profession in the year of cessation and for the three years of assessment preceding the year in which the cessation or discontinuance occurs.

If the business is carried on by a partnership the position is as follows. A partner may claim relief for terminal losses when his deemed sole and separate trade, etc. is discontinued. Broadly, this occurs when he ceases to be a partner, where the actual trade or profession is subsequently carried on by him alone, or when the actual trade or profession ceases. Also on what one might call a statutory discontinuance caused by a change of partners. In the latter case the retiring partner can have relief but the continuing partners cannot. This is fair, because (as we have just seen) they can, despite the discontinuance, have relief against subsequent profits.

Losses in the early years

The three heads we have so far looked at provide for relief for 4–44 losses by set-off against any income or capital gains of the same or the preceding year; against profits of the same trade, etc. in any following year; and (for terminal losses) against profits of the same trade in the year of cessation and for three previous years. This relief, which is provided for in s.72, works by way of a set-off of losses in the year of commencement of a trade or profession and/or in the next three years of assessment against any income of the taxpayer for the three years of assessment preceding that in which the loss is sustained. The relief applies to sole individuals and to partners. It does not apply to companies. Of course, a new company would not have any previous income, so the possibility of this relief could not arise. But an existing company sometimes sets up a new trade; it will not qualify for this relief. There is a provision to exclude hobby-trading from the relief. This seems a wise precaution on the part of HMRC. In genuine cases, however, s.72, in effect, provides a subsidy to a loss-making new business.

The Basis of Assessment

Thankfully, the complex rules that used to determine which 4–45 income related to which year have been swept away recently. All trading income is computed on a current year basis. This means that the income taxed in any year is the income earned in that year. For everyone's convenience, the income of the year is taken to be the income of the accounting year of the trade that ends in the current tax year. For example, if Pru Trader keeps accounts on a calendar year basis, then Pru Trader's accounts of the calendar year 2003 are treated as being Pru Trader's taxable trading income for the tax year 2003–04. Special rules apply in the first two years of a business and in the final year, to stop both double counting and avoidance. Other rules deal with cases where the accounts are drawn up for periods that are longer or shorter than 12 months, and adjustments can also be made to deal with pre-trading expenses and post-trading income (known as "post-cessation receipts").

Post-cessation Receipts

4–46   A post-cessation receipt is a sum received after the end of a trade, for example for items sold or services rendered before the trade ended. Almost all trades are now taxes on what is called the earnings basis. This means that income is taken into the accounts when it accrues to the trade, not when it is (later) received. So the accounts will usually include all sums earned by the trader even though they are received after the end of the final accounts period.

Some trades are taxed on a cash basis. This applies to many writers. This is because writers often do not know how much they will earn by way of royalties or similar payments. The same is true of barristers, at least when they start in the profession. So a barrister or writer who receives income after the trade ends will not have accounted for tax on the income. That used to lead to such people "retiring" several times in order to avoid tax. It does not work now. There are anti-avoidance provisions, now to be found in ss.241 to 257 of ITTOIA that catch all such sums and ensure they are added back into a year during which the trade was still continuing.

NI contributions for traders

4–47   The self-employed are required to pay two kinds of National Insurance contribution. There is a flat-rate contribution called Class 2, payable for each week in which an individual is ordinarily self-employed, and which entitled the payer to a limited range of social security benefits. There is also a Class 4 contribution which earns no benefit entitlement and is, in effect, an additional rate of income tax on some self-employed.

Class 2

4–48   Class 2 is payable by those who are ordinarily self-employed and more than 16. There is no definition of "ordinarily", but it is clear that individuals do not cease to be ordinarily self-employed just because they go on holiday for a week. For contributions purposes someone is self-employed if employed gainfully in employment other than employed earner's employment. The distinction between the employed and the self-employed is as important here as anywhere. This is not just because of the very considerable difference in the contributions paid by the employed compared with the self-employed, but because of the differing benefits the two categories can receive.

Categorisation is the only real problem with Class 2. Note,

however, that an employee can also be self-employed at the same time, and pay Class 2 contributions as well as Class 1 contributions, subject to a maximum annual limit (see below). The Class 2 contribution is a flat-rate weekly amount of £2.30 for 2008–09. Those whose earnings from self-employment are lower than that year's exception level £9,825 for 2008–09, need not pay the contributions if they wish. This is a voluntary limit. Someone not paying contributions cannot receive benefits either.

Class 3

Next, we ought to deal with Class 3. This class is a class of voluntary contributions that may be paid by anyone not paying Class 1 or Class 2 contributions. It is therefore not a tax. It may be a good idea to pay them sometimes, but this is the individual's choice.

4–49

Class 4

Class 4 is payable by many of the people who pay Class 2 contributions. Class 4 is entirely separate in law from Class 2, and is entirely parasitic on the tax charge on trading income. The rate for 2008–09 is 8.0 per cent from £5,435 (lower profits limit) to £40,040 (upper profits limit) with 1 per cent on all profits above the upper profits limit.

4–50

Tax credits

Applying the income tax rules on trading income to the calculation of income for tax credits claims purposes is relatively straightforward. The income for income tax as assessed under the standard rules is also the income for tax credits purposes.

4–51

CHAPTER 5

PROPERTY INCOME

Introduction

5–01　"Land", observed Anthony Trollope, "is about the only thing that can't fly away." This is a thought that has occurred to landowners, would-be landowners and the Revenue. The taxation of land has a long and tangled history. Income from land in the United Kingdom is now taxed under ITTOIA Part 3 by reference to the "profits of a property business." This requires some explanation. This had its origins in the Finance Act 1963. However, before our attention is directed towards these provisions we should look briefly at some history, with a view to, hopefully, throwing some light upon the present position. And it must therefore look at what was Sch.A.

History

5–02　Originally, Sch.A was a tax on the *ownership* of land. From that it followed that it caught not only landowners who let out their land but also owner-occupiers. It was based on annual values (that is, a notional annual rent for the land). These annual values were supposed to be revised every five years, but they became hopelessly out-of-date and absurdly low. The Finance Act 1940 then introduced a system of taxing landlords (under what was then Case VI of Sch.D) on what were called "excess rents", that is on rents received to the extent that they exceeded the annual values fixed under Sch.A.

5–03　Then the Finance Act 1963 re-modelled the whole system. Tax on owner-occupiers was abolished. They had, after all, only been subjected to income tax on the basis of a notional income (equal to the annual value) not a real income. And in practice many owner-occupiers had been able to eliminate any tax charge by making a "maintenance claim" in respect of repairs, insurance, etc. So far as non-occupiers were concerned the Finance Act 1963 combined the Sch.A and excess rents provisions into a new taxing code which was labelled Case VIII of Sch.D.

　　For the next six years there was no Sch.A; that label was

vacant. Then by the Finance Act 1969 Case VIII was re-named "Sch.A". The remodelled Sch.A, which, in essence, taxed the annual profits or gains derived from certain rents and other receipts arising from the ownership of land or an interest in land, then held sway until it was superseded for income tax purposes by a new Sch.A which was introduced by the Finance Act 1995. The Schedule was again rewritten with effect from 1998 for both companies and individuals. Schedule 5 to the Finance Act 1998 is one of the first enacted examples of the "rewrite approach" to amendments.

Tax on profits from worldwide property

ITTOIA completed the process of rewriting the tax by con- 5–04
verting the old Sch.A into a tax on the profits not of land but of a property business. And it also broke new ground (if the metaphor is excused) by imposing the same charge both on land in the UK and overseas land. Previously there had been entirely different charges on land outside the UK and UK land. Section 269 of ITTOIA now charges UK residents on their profits from a property business anywhere in the world.

For the sake of completeness, it should be mentioned that 5–05
there was a Sch.B tax until it was abolished by the Finance Act 1988. Originally, this was a tax on *occupiers* of land which was payable in addition to any Sch.A liability. So an owner-occupier paid both with the important exception that dwelling-houses and trade premises were exempted from Sch.B. However, from 1963 until its abolition, Sch.B was confined to taxing the occupation of woodlands "managed on a commercial basis and with a view to the realisation of profits".

The council tax and council tax benefit

We should also mention the council tax. This has in practice 5–06
replaced the old form of Sch.A, though it superficially looks very different. At first sight council tax appears to be a simple tax imposed on anyone living in his or her home by reference to the level of the tax in the local authority area where the house is and the valuation band applying to the house. And it applies to the occupiers, not the owners. For example, if you own or rent, and live in, a house that is valued as a Band D house, and the local council sets a tax of £1,000 on Band D houses, then that is what you pay. And it is the joint responsibility of every adult living in the house. It is even simpler for students, because they are exempt. The tax is imposed under the Local Government Finance Act 1992. And, as might be expected of a local tax, the

rules vary between England, Scotland, Wales and Northern Ireland (but not the student exemption).

5–07   Council tax is more complicated for most others on small incomes because alongside the council tax is a council tax benefit. This reduces the amount of council tax payable by up to the full amount of the tax if the occupier's income is below a set level. And no less than 64 kinds of unearned income, and 16 kinds of earnings, are excluded from the totals taken into account in calculating the income of a council tax benefit claimant. But his or her capital is taken into account (with 62 exclusions including the value of the house in which the claimant lives). An occupier living only on means-tested state benefits will have the whole council tax bill removed. The result is that in some local authority areas less than half of all council tax payers are paying the full council tax. See for the details the Council Tax Benefit Regulations 2006 (SI 2006 No.215).

So council tax is a disguised form of income tax and there are, in reality, two income taxes applying to property. One applies to profits from property and is payable to HMRC for the Treasury. The other applies to the notional value of occupying your home and is payable to the local council. The council tax benefit is complicated because it is a sort of negative income tax. You have to pay the full flat rate council tax unless your income is below a certain level. The lower your income, the higher the level at which the benefit is credited to you to offset and reduce what you must pay. But how much you pay also depends on the levels of council tax locally and on the value of your house. The marginal rate of council tax benefit (in other words the negative rate of tax) is one of the clumsiest statements of a tax rate in UK law:

> "The prescribed percentage for the purposes of subsection (5)(c)(ii) of section 131 of the [Social Security Contributions and Benefits] Act [1992] as it applies to council tax benefit shall be 2 6/7 per cent."

The reason for this is that council tax benefit is calculated on a daily basis. Income is usually calculated on a weekly basis, so the amount is 7 times 2 6/7, or a more understandable 20 per cent. In other words, if your income exceeds a weekly minimum level you lose council tax benefit of 20 per cent of that excess. That rate should be factored into any consideration of overall rates of tax as we discuss in Ch.12.

The business rate

There is another local tax applying to businesses alongside income tax and council tax. It is the national business rate. This applies to the commercial value of the property occupied by any business. Again, it appears a simple tax in that it is levied at a set rate in each local council area by reference to the rateable value of each commercial property. But it is also a major tax on businesses that occupy expensive sites such as city centre shops or offices.

5–08

Discussions of tax law tend to pay little attention to council tax, council tax benefit and the business rates because there is little law in them. Much of the difficulty lies in the factual question of checking the value of the house or land. But do not be misled. In 2007-08 the council tax and business rate between them raised nearly £50 billion—slightly more than was raised from corporation tax, and more than all the excise taxes added together.

5–09

ITTOIA thus ends a strand of income tax law from the original Act in 1803—and indeed, in the form of the land tax, many years before. Just before the latest version of Sch.A followed Sch.B into oblivion, the Finance Act 2004 reintroduced a form of the original Sch.B (by imposing an income tax charge on gifts of land subject to reservations). (See para.5–29.) And then there's the council tax! As Alphonse Karr nearly observed in 1849, *"plus ça change, plus c'est la même taxe."*

5–10

The charge on property income

The repeated rewrites of the law imposing income tax on land, or the profits from land, evolved finally in 2005 into the rules codified into Part 3 of ITTOIA. As already noted, they bring together for the first time a source-based income tax on the profits of land in the UK and a residence-based income tax on UK residents who make profits from land anywhere. For example, if you live in the UK and own a second home in, say, Spain, and you let it out for much of the year, then your profits from letting the house out will be taxable in the UK. (They will also be taxable in Spain but that is another story). And for most purposes the way in which profits from foreign land are taxed is the same as for UK land, so we can ignore where the land is for the rest of this introduction.

5–11

Section 268 charges income tax on "the profits of a property business". And s.270 imposes the tax on the full amount of the profits arising in the tax year. But this wording is somewhat

5–12

deceptive. This is because the "business" need not be a business. Section 264 states that a UK property business consists of:

> "(a) every business which the person carries on for generating income from land in the UK, and
> (b) every transaction which the person enters into for that purpose otherwise than in the course of such a business."

5–13 "Generating income from land" is then defined by s.266 to meant exploiting an estate, interest or right in or over land as a source of rents or other receipts. This is further elaborated by s.267. That removes the charge on income from farming and market gardening, and also from most other forms of exploitation of the natural resources found in the soil or land covered in water such as mines, quarries and canals to the charge to trading income.

Hidden behind this is a distinction between what lawyers refer to as land and what the general public calls land. Hence the label "property income" rather than income from land. What these provisions tax is the benefit that arises from exploiting a legal interest in land, not the land itself. The distinction was discussed, by reference to the former income tax rules, in *Lowe v Ashmore* (1971) and *McClure v Petre* (1988). These cases also make the point that the income tax charge is on income and not capital receipts. Capital receipts are caught by capital gains tax.

In the latter, the taxpayer received a payment in return for the grant of a licence to dump waste on his land. It was held that the payment was a capital receipt and, therefore, not taxable under Sch.A. By granting the licence, the taxpayer deprived himself of a right, namely, the right to dump, which he could otherwise have enjoyed over his land. The payment was the consideration for the disposal of that right. The taxpayer had realised part of the value of his freehold.

5–14 Under these rules, each source of income, e.g. each letting where the individual has granted a number of leases is treated as part of a single business, and the taxation of the individual in respect of that business is determined by taking into account the income generated and pertinent expenses incurred by such sources as a whole.

Calculating the profits

5–15 The rewrite of the new basis of taxing income from interests in law was also used to rebase the way in which the profits were to be calculated for income tax purposes. The old Sch.A had its own rules for the income and expenses that could be allowed.

The new, and much simpler, approach is to start with the assumption that the rules for calculating trading income also apply to property income. Section 272(1) provides that "the profits of a property business are calculated in the same way as the profits of a trade." Section 272 then specified which of the rules about trading income are to be applied. However, these include the most important provisions such as that applying generally accepted accounting principles (s.26) and excluding expenses not wholly and exclusively for the purposes of the trade (s.34) and capital expenditure (s.33). Some capital allowances can be claimed for capital expenditure on land and buildings. See Ch.10.

Specific rules about taxing land

The significant simplification achieved by these rules has removed much of the need for a lengthy discussion about the way profits from land are taxed to income tax. But we must take note of several special sets of rules that apply to particular kinds of income from land. These include special tax exemptions that apply to some forms of such income and also rules that treat capital receipts from land as being income.

5–16

Rent-a-room

A "rent-a-room" letting arises where an individual rents out a spare furnished room in his only or main residence. See Part 7 of ITTOIA. This is not a step which an individual would necessarily take without encouragement. That encouragement is provided by a tax incentive. An individual is eligible for relief from income tax if the income from a "rent-a-room" letting or lettings in a particular year of assessment does not exceed £4,250. If the income exceeds this amount, the individual may choose either to be taxed on the excess over £4,250 or to be taxed on the actual profit made (i.e. gross receipts less actual expenses). The value of the "rent-a-room" exemption is increased for tax credits claimants, as the income is also ignored for that purpose.

5–17

Alongside that relief in Part 7 is another that is partly a relief for the use of land and partly for personal care services. It is a relief from income tax for those who receive income (often from a local authority or charity) for providing accommodation and maintenance for a child as a foster carer. While this sounds simple, and has an obvious social purpose behind it, it is also a generous allowance and therefore requires strict rules to target and limit the relief. In broad terms it allows a foster carer a personal limit of up to £10,000 a year, plus up to £250 a week for each child, after taking certain expenses into account, before income tax is payable.

5–18   There is additional help behind these reliefs because exclusion of these sums from income tax also applies to tax credits. And some payments to those looking after children, plus a small amount of the income from boarders and lodgers, are also ignored for council tax benefit purposes. If account is also taken of those exclusions, the total combined values of the exemptions and benefits can have a considerable effect on lower earnings.

Premiums

5–19   The next section may be regarded, with hindsight, as perhaps a well-meant mistake. It is common form with commercial lettings in some areas for the consideration payable by the tenant to come in two forms. The first is the annual rent. The second is a lump sum, usually paid at or before the beginning of the lease. In principle, the lump sum is capital. Nowadays it is liable to capital gains tax. But in 1963 when the first fundamental revision of Sch.A occurred there was no capital gains tax, so such sums went tax-free. If premiums were not taxable there would be an obvious and simple tax-avoidance device—don't charge a rent, just take a premium, which, being a capital sum, would not be subject to income tax because it is not an *annual* profit or gain.

The normal meaning of "premium" in relation to land is a lump sum paid for the granting of a lease. But for income tax purposes "premium" has an extended meaning. The broad principle is that certain premiums are deemed to be income and are charged to income tax. The detailed provisions in ss.276 to 307 of ITTOIA are concerned to stop up various tax-avoidance devices which would otherwise be open. This is an excellent field in which to observe the battle between tax avoiders and HMRC.

5–20   A premium (or part of a premium) which is not caught for income tax may be caught for capital gains tax. Conversely, that part of a premium which is caught for income tax is not chargeable to capital gains tax.

There are three main heads of charge on premium income: (1) under s.277, premiums and like sums are chargeable; (2) under s.282, where a lease is granted at an undervalue the "amount foregone" may be chargeable on a subsequent assignment of the lease; (3) under s.284, where land is sold with a right to reconveyance the difference between the selling price and the reconveyance price may be chargeable to tax.

Let us look first at s.277. Section 277(1) applies the section whenever a premium is required to be paid under a short term lease (defined as 50 years or less). In such cases the landlord is regarded as being involved in a property business and as receiving as income from that business and amount calculated by a standard formula. The formula, in s.277(4) is:

$$\text{``}P - \frac{(P \times Y)}{50}$$

where P is the premium and Y is the number of complete periods of 12 months (other than the first) comprised in the effective duration of the lease."

Notice that the way the section taxes a premium is to treat the landlord as being in receipt of rent which is then part of the profits of the Sch.A business. Notice also that a lease for more than 50 years is not caught, and that the nearer a lease gets to being for 50 years the less income tax is payable. Thus a premium on a lease for 49 years is reduced by 48/50, or 96 per cent, leaving only 4 per cent taxable. A lease for nine years is reduced by eight-fiftieths (or 16 per cent), leaving 84 per cent taxable. A lease for one year enjoys no reduction at all. But remember also that the part of the premium not caught by income tax *is* liable to tax in so far as a chargeable gain arises. Because of this sliding scale there are detailed rules (in ss.303–4) for ascertaining the duration of leases.

We now come to some extended meanings of the word "premium". Section 278 treats as a premium a requirement on the tenant to carry out works on the premises (beyond mere maintenance and repairs). The deemed premium is of an amount equal to the increase that the requirement makes in the value of the landlord's reversionary interest. So the premium provisions cannot be avoided by requiring works rather than a cash payment. 5–21

Section 279 also deals with other kinds of disguised premium. It deems a sum to be a premium if it becomes payable by the tenant in lieu of rent or as consideration for the surrender of the lease. Section 281 deems a sum to be a premium if it becomes payable by the tenant as consideration for the variation or waiver of any of the terms of the lease.

Where a premium (or a deemed premium, as above) is payable by instalments the tax may be paid in corresponding instalments spread over a maximum of eight years. Before that there was no time-limit, and ingenious leases appeared under which a premium was to be paid over a period of, say 250 years, with the bulk becoming payable in the 250th year.

5–22   Section 282 deals with another possible avoidance device. A premium paid on the *grant* of a lease is taxable (as we have seen), but a premium paid on the *assignment* of a lease is not taxable under the provisions we have so far looked at. Therefore, if it were not for this, a simple avoidance would be for A to grant a lease to B (a relative, say, or a friendly company) at a very small premium or without any premium at all and then for B to assign the lease to C (a stranger) at a premium. Section 282 catches this situation. Suppose the market is such that A could have required a premium of £10,000 on the grant of the lease to B, whereas in fact he took a premium of only £2,000, then £8,000 is said to be "the amount foregone". If B later assigns the premises for £14,000 he is charged to tax on the excess of £14,000 over the amount of the original premium (£2,000), except that the chargeable amount cannot exceed the amount foregone. So on these figures the chargeable amount would have been £14,000 less £2,000, but the upper limit is £8,000, and so the chargeable amount is £8,000. If B had assigned the premises to C for a premium of £5,000 the chargeable amount would have been £3,000. In that circumstance HMRC would not have collected tax on the whole of the amount foregone, but they would be able to pick up the balance on subsequent assignments by C, D, E, etc.

5–23   Section 284 deals with yet another avoidance device, namely selling land subject to a right of reconveyance. If A, a landowner, is minded to take a premium of, say, £7,000, on granting a lease to B, he could, instead, sell the land to B on terms that he, A, could buy back the land from B for the sale price minus £7,000. Section 284 ensures that on such a transaction A is charged to tax on £7,000. If the sale contains a right for A to take a lease back of the premises from B, the lease back counts as a reconveyance. This lease back procedure is very common in practice, because it is a neat way of solving a liquidity problem or a cash-flow problem, and, as it is not very wicked, the section contains a proviso excepting such a transaction from the tax charge if the lease back is granted, and begins to run, within one month after the sale. That seems a very arbitrary way of marking out the exception, but it does enable (as it is intended to do) a genuine lease back arrangement to be free of the tax charge. But capital gains tax may be chargeable on the transaction; also if the lease back is at more than a commercial rent, only the commercial rent will be an allowable business expense; also in certain circumstances a proportion of the sale price may be taxed as though it were income (s.780 of the Taxes Act). This is one of the few ICTA income tax provisions still waiting to be rewritten.

Artificial Transactions in Land

We must finally turn to some anti-avoidance provisions in the Income Tax Act 2007 and not in ITTOIA. Part 13 of ITA is devoted to tax avoidance or, rather, stopping tax avoidance. And Ch.3 is entitled "transactions in land" (not, notice, transactions in interests in land). Section 752 heads the chapter with a bold set of statements:

5–24

> "(1) This Chapter has effect for the purpose of preventing the avoidance of income tax by persons concerned with land or the development of land.
>
> (2) This Chapter imposes a charge to income tax in some circumstances where gains of a capital nature are obtained from disposing of land."

This is achieved by treating certain capital gains (see below) arising on the disposal of land as income. The rationale of this can be best understood if one looks at its history and antecedents. One must bear in mind that the provisions date from before there was a capital gains tax. In those days an owner of land who sold the land could make a tax-free profit, unless he was a dealer in land. If he was a dealer in land he was taxed on the gain as an item in his trading profit (and still is: see, for example, *Pilkington v Randall* (1966) and compare *Marson v Morton* (1986)). He could avoid this tax by forming a company to hold the land and then selling the shares, rather than selling the land as such.

These sections seek to block this device by a very wide-ranging provision. At first it was little used. However, a series of largely successful Revenue contests in the courts in the 1980s indicated that it might be potentially a very wide section indeed: see *Yuill v Wilson* (1980) in the House of Lords, and *Page v Lowther* (1983) and *Yuill v Fletcher* (1984) in the Court of Appeal. These decisions must be read in the light of two developments. First, it may be questioned whether the section is needed in view of the approach adopted by the courts in cases such as *Furniss v Dawson* (1984), HL, (see above, para.2–48). Secondly, the importance of the section reduced since 1988 with the unification of the rates of tax for capital gains tax and income tax. Will it come back with the split of rates in 2008? The section may apply wherever:

5–25

(1) land, or property deriving value from land, is acquired solely or mainly to realise a gain on its disposal; *or*
(2) land is held as trading stock; *or*
(3) land is developed solely or mainly to realise a gain on disposal when developed,

and a disposal of the land gives rise to a capital gain. The whole of the gain is treated as taxable income for the year in which the gain is realised. For this purpose, "disposal" includes disposal of control over land, so covers the case of land owned through companies, where the companies' shares, rather then the land itself, are transferred.

Even more broadly, the gains can be treated as the income of any person by whom the gain is realised or who provides directly or indirectly an opportunity to realise it. This is wide enough to catch a "mastermind" who has taken no actual part in the process of making a gain, as was illustrated in the two *Yuill* cases mentioned above.

Section 752 is unusual even in tax-avoidance law, and almost unprecedented in general statute law, in containing a statement of its purpose in subs.(1). But it is not clear whether this provision adds anything to the operation of the section.

Tax credits

5–26   Property income (and losses) both from a UK property business and an overseas property business are to be taken fully into account in calculating a claimant's income for tax credit purposes. However, the rent-a-room provisions apply to exclude income from lodgers. This makes the rent-a-room exemption particularly valuable to those entitled to tax credits. Not only do they save the income tax (and there are no NI contributions on rental income) but also they can in effect save a further 39 per cent of the rent because there is no decrease in the tax credits payable. Put another way, those getting £10 of taxable employment income will pay income tax and NI contributions (as will the employer) through PAYE on it, and will lose a further £3.90 tax credit entitlement. Those getting £10 rent-a-room income get £10.

Some Tailpieces

Capital Gains Tax
5–27   In considering the taxation of receipts from land, one should bear in mind that as well as income tax (in connection with rents

and premiums and s.752 gains) a transaction in land may attract capital gains tax. Aside from the important exemption for principal private residences, this is of importance to individuals as well as companies. This, of course, applies when land is sold.

Stamp duties

Of considerable more practical importance to individuals are the taxes to be paid when land and buildings are bought. Purchases of land have been liable to stamp duties for centuries. But the Finance Act 2003 completely rewrote the laws on the duty, converting it into separate stamp duty land tax. This is a levy of up to four per cent of the capital value of any land transaction, payable by the buyer. It is now of far more practical importance to the Treasury than capital gains tax. And it can be of far more importance to potential purchases of houses, not least for a principal private residence. But it is specific to, and should be studied as part of, conveyancing.

5–28

An occupation tax returns?

Chapter 4 of Part 13 of ITA contains provisions that bring back a form of income tax on the occupation of property as an anti-avoidance measure. A practice developed of seeking to avoid inheritance tax by an older person passing his or her ownership of the family home (and often its contents) to younger members of the family, subject to a right to continue living in it. Section 776 of ITA 2007 seeks to impose income tax on the taxable amount that accrues from the continuing benefit to the donor of such a transfer. Where the property was transferred since March 1986, the donor becomes liable to income tax on the rental value of the property. In other words, the donor is assumed for income tax purposes to be receiving the value of the rent that would be paid to live in the house. This is a clear echo of the old Sch.B, which was in its heyday a tax on the value of occupying property, based on the rental value.

5–29

CHAPTER 6

INTELLECTUAL PROPERTY AND OTHER INCOME

Introduction

6–01   This is the area of tax law that has benefitted most in recent years from a combination of specific reform and the attentions of the Tax Law Rewrite Project. What we are concerned with here are the untidy bits of tax law that seek to tax individuals and companies on income that was not earnings, nor trading income, nor property income, nor savings and investment income. The topic is untidy because there is no one definition of "income" on which tax is imposed, nor has there ever been. If the government wishes to impose tax on a form of income, then it must ask Parliament to pass laws to catch that form of income. If we had a single definition of income, as for example is found in the US federal and other income tax laws, then it tends to be left to the judges to draw the line. But in the UK the absence of any general provision available to tax the miscellaneous kinds of income that fall outside the main charging provisions means that those forms of income do not get taxed save by specific additional provisions.

So we need a "sweeper" provision (or series of provisions) to catch and impose tax on these various other forms of income. Under the pre-Rewrite tax law this was Case VI of Sch.D. And there were a long list of individual sections added over many years that treated various forms of income (or sometimes capital, or even deemed income) to be taxable under that case.

6–02   The rewritten laws, as they apply to individuals, must therefore contain a code dealing with these forms of income. And somewhere in that code, or at least in the laws generally, there must be a fall-back provision. Because the line must be drawn somewhere whether or not we have a general definition of income. You will find most of these provisions in the "other income" parts of ITTOIA. Part 5 of ITTOIA is headed "Miscellaneous Income". It is unfortunate that it could not be given a more pleasing title, but it is accurate. Part 5 deals with:

- Receipts from intellectual property (Ch.2)
- Non-trade receipts from films and sound recordings (Ch.3)
- Non-trading income from communications rights (Ch.4)
- Settlements (Ch.5)
- Income from estates in administration (Ch.6)
- Annual payments (Ch.7)
- Income not otherwise charged (Ch.8)

We also need to look at Part 6 (exemptions) with Part 5. Chapter 8 of part 6 (other annual payments) needs to be read with Ch.7 of Part 5, and Ch.9 of part 6 (other income) with Ch.8 of Part 5.

We do not agree, however, that it is right to deal with set-   6–03
tlements and estates in administration as "miscellaneous income" in this work. Those topics raise important issues for lawyers about the structures through which income is received, and are not simply a matter of deciding what is to be taxed. We need to consider how and when income tax is applied to these important legal structures and situations. So we deal with them in a separate chapter. But we do not need to spend time on some of the more specific forms of miscellaneous income. So in this chapter we will look at the increasingly important issue of taxing intellectual property income, and then at annual payments and other income.

Receipts from intellectual property

Before we get into the details of the specific provisions about   6–04
intellectual property, we must note s.575 of ITTOIA. This sets out the rules giving priority between different sets of charging provisions where one of them is to be found in Part 5. Section 575(1) gives priority as between Part 2 and Part 5 to Part 2. In other words, if the income can be treated both as intellectual property income and as trading income (including income from a profession) then it is to be treated as trading income. So an author who receives royalty payments for her work will be taxed on the payments as trading income and not as royalties. If she gives the rights to her mother, then her mother receives the payments as intellectual property income. But if she sells them to someone who trades in such rights, then again it is trading income. Note that it is therefore the reason why the individual has the rights that dictates how it is taxed.

Section 575 also gives priority where appropriate over the rules in Part 5 to Parts 3 (property income) and 4 (savings income), and also to ITEPA parts 2 (employment income), 9 (pension income) and 10 (social security income). So for example someone may receive income from rights as part of his employment, in which case the rules about employment income apply.

In all these cases, there is a need to examine any link between the income and any of the prioritised activities of a taxpayer. These rules are also important when we look at the "other income" provisions. The important point to remember is that the rules about intellectual property income and other kinds of "other income" only apply if the main rules about earned income and savings and property income do not apply. So we are concerned in this chapter about income received from these sources, for example, by people who have purchased or been given intellectual property rights, not by the original inventors, creators or authors.

6–05   The concept of intellectual property as a general category of property rights is of course relatively new. It is therefore no surprise to find that the Income Tax Acts had no simple answer to the problem of taxing receipts from this kind of property. The problems were solved (if at all) by an accretion of separate answers produced by Parliament and the courts as separate kinds of intellectual property gave rise to a scope for taxation and a need for tax relief. Even the Revenue described the eventual result as "complex, inconsistent and out of date" with "no overarching rationale". This was in a technical note produced in 2000, "*Reform of the Taxation of Intellectual Property, goodwill and other intangible assets*". That description was more than justified. Income from varying forms of intangibles was taxable under several different income tax provisions and under capital gains tax (and its corporate equivalent) with some forms of capital receipt being deemed to be income, and some forms of income being subjected to deduction of income tax at source.

What followed was a partial reform. The taxation of receipts from intangibles and related revenue expenditure for companies was subjected to a new code in the Finance Act 2002, but this does not yet apply to individuals. It was also made clear that where the property or goodwill was held as part of a trade, the receipts would be taxed as trading income, and relevant expenditure allowed accordingly. Measures were also taken to sort out the varying time limits over which different forms of receipt and expenditure were taxed or allowed.

6–06   The result has been tidied by the Tax Law Rewrite Project. This brings together in a short code within ITTOIA a series of provisions dealing with "intellectual property". The concept of IP is defined widely as including "any patent, trade mark, registered design, copyright, design right, performer's right or plant breeder's right"; any foreign equivalent of any of these; and "any information or technique not protected by" any of those rights.

While that sounds like an all-embracing title, what follows still reflects the patchwork of provisions on which it is based historically. Provisions still discriminate between royalties (chargeable as annual payments); income other than annual payments; profits arising from the disclosure of know-how; and profits from the sale or licensing of patent rights. The consequence is that an agreement that encompasses several forms of intellectual property and goodwill in a single transaction has to be broken up for tax purposes into its constituent parts. Each element of the capital and income changing hands then has to be assessed separately.

The following is a brief guide to the rules in Part 5 dealing with IP income of non-trading individuals.   6–07

PATENTS Perhaps most important of these rules are those applying to patents. The receipt of a royalty payment for a patent is taxable income. Sums paid as royalties will usually fall within ss.597 and 598 of ITTOIA. This applies to patents, but not to sums not paid as royalties, in the sense that they are not annual payments. Where someone in the UK sells a patent right otherwise than in the course of a trade, the net profit received is treated as income received in instalments over the year of receipt and the next five years. A patent licence is treated as a sale and purchase of those rights. There are also special rules allowing inventors to deduct the expenses of devising a patented invention although the inventor is not a trader. Those rules are important because the individual who thinks up a new invention in his or her spare time may not be trading while doing so. Because of that, under the usual rules for non-trading income, no expenses would be allowed. Yet both the invention itself and the cost of patenting may cost considerable sums. The special rules prevent those costs being ignored as pre-trading expenses. The rules for deduction of the expenses of buying patent rights are, by contrast, treated as capital and are dealt with by capital allowances under the Capital Allowances Act 2001, Part 8.   6–08

KNOWHOW By contrast, profits from the disclosure of know-how are normally charged to income tax as profits when the sums are received otherwise than as part of a trade or the   6–09 receipts are treated as royalties. This is charged by specific provisions in ITTOIA (see s.583), for otherwise the receipts might fall outside the scope of income tax. This reflects the fact that much "knowhow" is in every sense intangible and cannot even be a form of property. This rule applies even though the disclosure is part of a non-enforceable agreement (that is, there is no contract). Receipts will usually be regarded as capital only if the sale is part of the sale of the business to which the knowhow is linked. Expenditure on knowhow acquisition, whether by purchase or internally to the business, is normally revenue expenditure.

6–10   COPYRIGHT Leaving aside for the moment computer software, any income generated from copyrights (payments usually being in the form of royalties or sums paid in advance of or in lieu of royalties) is taxable as trading income, of a copyright held as an investment under Part 5. Lump sums are accordingly usually regarded as income, not capital. There will only be a capital receipt where the full copyright interest is sold as an investment, in which case capital gains tax will apply. There are no capital allowances for acquiring copyright. Special rules apply to software, and capital allowance may be available.

6–11   TRADE MARKS Royalties from a trade mark will be taxed as trading income, while lump sums received will normally be treated as capital receipts. The costs of buying a trade mark will be regarded as capital, but no specific capital allowance is available. The costs of creating a trade mark will usually be revenue costs deductible against profits. Much the same rules apply to design rights, and other similar rights.

6–12   GOODWILL This is not a form of property, and has long presented both lawyers and accountants—and therefore tax authorities—with problems. "Goodwill" is often the description given to the unidentifiable extra part of a sale or purchase beyond the identified assets. As such any payment for it is capital. There are no specific capital allowances for acquiring goodwill, but capital gains tax will apply to sale proceeds attributable to it.

6–13   OTHER INCOME Anything left over, such as a one-off receipt for the provision of intangibles that is not capital and not trading income, will in principle be caught as "other income" not IP income. This will apply, for example, to a fee for the use of a single article written for a journal or newspaper. This reflects the rule we have seen that single payments received from an activity of a trading nature will be trading income, while single payments for the disposal of something are usually capital. If the payment is not capital and not from a trading activity, then it is either caught in this way or falls outside the scope of the direct taxes. It is for this reason that there are special rules bringing into charge to income tax the receipt of sums for the provision of knowhow or other information. Other relevant items of expenditure can be deducted under the "R and D tax credit" provisions of capital allowances, noted in Ch.7.

This complex of rules means that licensing agreements involving a number of different kinds of intellectual property rights may need unpicking to identify (a) what is capital and what is income, (b) when that capital or income is received or treated as being received, (c) when income tax has to be deducted at source on any payments made, and (d) what deductions for expenses or capital allowances are available. And there may be plenty of scope for argument if the buyer, the seller and the Revenue all conclude that their optimal approaches to the agreement are different. This can also give rise to arguments between tax experts and intellectual property experts. One particular reason is the application of the rules about deduction of tax at source to some forms of royalty, rules to which we now turn. **6–14**

Annual payments

Why do we talk about income tax on "annual payments"? Surely, we are not concerned with the nature of a payment, but the nature of income as received by a taxpayer? Yes, we are. But "annual payments" is a phrase from the old tax law of the nineteenth century that has defeated the attempts of drafters to modernise it effectively. We can reduce the difficulty only by referring to the history of the words. **6–15**

While we cannot change the name, the nature and importance for income tax purposes of annual payments have decreased hugely in recent years. When the income tax was first introduced, an annual payment was regarded as a way that income was transferred from one taxpayer to another. For example, I must pay you an annual payment under a covenant, or a sum by way of annual interest on a loan by you to me. In the original pattern of the income tax that was regarded as transferring or alienating that income from me to you. So you were taxable on that income and not me. But that raised other issues. How did I get tax relief because I reduced my income in that way? And how did the tax authorities find out that I had done this so they could collect the tax from you?

How was this done? Conceptually the answer was ingenious, and the approach was disarmingly simple. I deducted income from the payment when I made it, and paid you only what was left. This was because I was transferring the income to you after tax. I was entitled to keep the income tax I had paid in receiving it, so only paid you what was left. For instance, I have to pay you £100 as income when the tax rate is 20 per cent. I pay you £80 and give you a piece of paper saying that I have deducted £20 from the original £100. That gives me tax relief on the £100 reduction in my income resulting from the payment of it to you, but without me having to claim it from the HMRC. You have in effect paid tax at 20 per cent on the £100 income you have received so you do not have to declare it. This approach was called "charges on income". That is, the £100 was a charge on my income, reducing my income by £100.

6–16   When higher rates of income tax came in, the effect was more dramatic. If the tax rate I had to pay was, say, 60 per cent, and I could claim full relief for a charge on income, then it would cost me £40 after tax to pay you £100, in the form of £70 plus the piece of paper for a further £30. If you did not pay tax at all then you would want the £30 back, while I would want to keep the full tax relief. On my example, it would then cost me £40 to give you £100, with other taxpayers footing the difference. That by any definition is a good deal for the taxpayer, and it gave rise to very widespread use of, for example, covenants to student children (who were adults but not earning enough to pay tax) and charities (which were never taxpayers). It was also used as a way of minimising the cost of making maintenance payments from a high earning ex-husband to a poorer ex-wife and children. It will not surprise you to know that such generosity at the public expense has now been stopped. This is subject to a major exception for payments to charities. But there also the way the help is given has changed. See para.11–28.

The charge to tax

6–17   Despite the best efforts of the drafters of the Tax Law Rewrite, the law on this question remains both conceptually unsatisfactory and untidy in detail. It is conceptually untidy because, try as the drafters and others would, no one could come up with a satisfactory form of wording which removed "payment" from this phrase to replace it with "income" or "receipt" or some other form of wording that reflected the fact that income tax taxes income not payments. This is in part because of the difficulty of turning the case law about annual payments into sensible statutory provisions. And the detailed untidiness is because the lack of any coherent pattern to taxing annual payments leaves the code provisions about annual payments stranded across Parts 5 and 6 of ITTOIA.

The drafters were left recommending the following sweep-up   6–18
provision, to be found in s.683 of ITTOIA:

"(1) Income tax is charged under this Chapter on annual payments that are not charged to income tax under or as a result of any other provision of this Act or any other Act.

(2) Subsection (1) does not apply to annual payments that would be charged to income tax under or as a result of another provision but for an exemption."

The section then signposts nine forms of exempt annual payment, all to be found detailed in Part 6.

This curious wording hints at, but hides, a significant amount   6–19
of legislative and judicial history. You will notice that the section carefully avoids any attempt at defining what is meant by an annual payment. Well, not quite. Subsection (3) gives some help:

"(3) The frequency with which payments are made is ignored in determining whether they are annual payments for the purposes of this Act."

Well, not quite to that too. If there is only one payment, then it is probably not an annual payment. And there may be questions over totally irregular payments where there is no pattern to the payments. These may be capital payments, not income payments. If so, they will be received as capital receipts and not income.

A clearer picture starts to emerge if we turn at the same time   6–20
to Part 6, and we also think about what other provisions in the Taxes Acts can catch annual payments of one kind or another.

Historically, the most important kind of annual payment for many people was a payment of annual interest. A typical example used to be the interest paid on a mortgage on a house. That was a long term loan in almost all cases. So the interest paid to the mortgagee was annual interest, and therefore an annual payment. It is for this reason that for many years the income tax system had provisions in it allowing mortgage interest relief. But that is now entirely history. And we have seen that interest is charged to income tax under Part 4 of ITTOIA as savings or investment income. So it is not charged any longer as an annual payment even if that it what it also is.

6–21   Once interest was removed from the scope of annual payments, the approach taken was to deal with the problem by generally exempting other forms of annual payment from income tax while making specific kinds of annual payment liable to tax. That sounds more generous than it is. The main use of annual payments, aside from interest payments, was in transferring income from someone liable to pay a higher rate of tax to someone liable to pay a lower rate of tax. In the long distant past when the authors were students, this allowed wealthy parents to transfer income to their broke student children. The students paid no tax, but the parents were no longer liable to pay income tax on the income transferred so might save, say, 50 per cent of the cost. Wealthy ex-husbands could support their ex-wives and children in this way with a generous subsidy from the Treasury thrown in.

The direct effect of exempting the receipt of an annual payment is the removal of any reason for that payment to be deductible when paid by the payer. That is confirmed by s.727 of ITTOIA. Subject to two major exceptions only, s.727(1) exempts from income tax any annual payment made by an individual (as against a trust or company) if the payment arises in the United Kingdom. The two exceptions follow.

Section 728 removes from exemption any payment made by an individual for commercial reasons in connection with the individual's trade, profession or vocation. An example of this is a payment by a continuing partner in a partnership of an annual payment to a retired or former partner as part of the arrangement under which the partnership interest was passed to the new partner. These payments may not, as receipts, be income from a trade or be a pension, so they will fall within s.683(1).

Section 729 removes from exemption payments for non-taxable consideration. This is an anti-avoidance provision. You will find the other half of the provision in s.904 of ITA 2007. Subject to limited exceptions, the sections catch any arrangement under which the annual payment is made under a liability incurred for consideration. The mischief occurs where all or some of that consideration is non-taxable for some reason (for example, it is itself exempt). This stops a clever device where exempt transfers can take place both ways by stopping the exemption. It is one of the better anti-avoidance provisions in that it is effective, so is rarely called into question. Again, these payments, as received, would not readily fall under another charging provision, so also fall into s.683(1).

The nature of annual payments

The above discussion gives an insight into annual payments, nevertheless it begs the question what *is* an annual payment? The courts have identified the following five characteristics of an annual payment.

6-22

First, the *ejusdem generis* rule of interpretation applies. The context is highly important. The charging provision used to say: "Case III—tax in respect of—. . . any interest of money, whether yearly or otherwise, or any annuity or other annual payment . . .". A payment, to be an "other annual payment", must be the same kind of payment as those payments. It remains to be seen how this will be handled after the Rewrite. Secondly, the payment must be made under a **binding legal obligation**. A gift, even if it be in money and even if it be one of a series, is not an annual payment. But it is important to appreciate that a payment under a covenant is an annual payment. How can this be, since a covenanted payment is (most commonly) given for no consideration? The answer is that a covenant is a promise under seal, and the seal creates a legal obligation.

6-23

Thirdly, the payment must have the quality of **recurrence**. But this requirement is not very exacting. Payments which are variable or contingent are not prevented from being recurrent. This is reflected in the s.683(3), which in part is a codification of previous practice.

6-24

Fourthly, the payment must be, in the hands of the recipient, **pure profit income** and not a receipt which enters into the computation of profit. In *IRC v National Book League* (1957), CA, the League (a charity) decided to raise the membership subscription except that those members who entered into seven-year covenants could continue to pay their subscriptions at the existing rate. Over 2,000 members executed deeds of covenant, and deducted tax in making the covenanted payments. The League claimed repayment of the tax from the Revenue, arguing that the payments were annual payments within Case III. The argument was not upheld. The subscriptions were not pure profit income of the League, because the League had to provide benefits, such as the amenities of a club, in return for the subscriptions. *The National Book League* case left a few questions unresolved because the judges propounded alternative tests for deciding what was pure profit income. However, in *Campbell v IRC* (1970), HL, the House of Lords (although *obiter*) had another look at the question. They adopted the phrase "pure profit income" to describe Case III, but were at pains to emphasise that non-commercial benefits resulting from a pay-

6-25

ment, such as having one's name printed in an advertisement or receiving a copy of an annual report, did not count.

6–26   Fifthly, the payment must be of the nature of **income, and not capital**, in the hands of the recipient. The point arises when A sells property to B in return for instalment payments. Are the instalments income or capital? A payment may be of a revenue nature from the point of view of the payer and yet may be of a capital nature in the hands of the payee. If it is of a capital nature in the hands of the payee it cannot be an "annual payment" even from the point of view of the payer. If it is of an income nature in the hands of the payee it may or may not be of a revenue nature from the point of view of the payer. In *Vestey v IRC* (1962) Lord Vestey sold a block of shares valued at £2 million for the sum of £5.5 million payable without interest by 125 yearly instalments of £44,000. It was held that the instalments should be dissected into capital and interest, and that the interest element was taxable income of the payee.

6–27   In *IRC v Church Commissioners for England* (1977), HL the Church Commissioners sold to their tenant the reversion on a lease in consideration of rent charges payable annually for 10 years and totalling £96,000 a year. The tenant was not willing to buy for a single lump sum. The House of Lords held that these payments were pure income in the hands of the payee and were not to be dissected into capital and interest elements. The church commissioners, being a charity, were entitled to repayment of the tax which had been deducted by the payer from each payment. (The same rent-charges had previously been held—also by the House of Lords—to be capital payments from the point of view of the payer: *IRC v Land Securities Investment Trust Ltd* (1969), HL.)

Why worry about annual payments?

6–28   We have spent a considerable time on the complexities of annual payments and collection of tax at source for several reasons. It illustrates some fundamental issues about levying income tax in Britain. First, the system must deal fairly with transfers of income under trusts and covenants but must also seek for that reason to curb avoidance. Secondly, the aim is to collect tax at source where possible, but that is not always easy given the flexibility of British trust laws. Third, there is no general statutory provision to curb abuse of the tax law. The case of *IRC v Duke of Westminster* (1936) shows that a valid covenant can transfer income effectively from anyone to anyone for income tax purposes in the absence of statutory provisions.

Deducting income tax from annual payments

As we have already seen, the old way of dealing with annual **6–29** payments was to exempt the payer from tax and tax the recipient. But the tax was collected by the payer and taken in place of the relief to which the payer was entitled from making the payment. This avoided the need to allow the payer to have a reclaim against income tax paid for the payment.

The provisions dealing with deduction of tax used to be a pair of provisions in the Taxes Act. One allowed deduction of tax and permitted the payer to keep the tax. That happened when the payer had paid the annual payment from his or her own taxes income. The other required the payer to deduct tax and pay it to the tax authorities. That happened when the annual payment was not made out of taxable income. The process of rewriting these provisions has now split what were two sections sitting beside each other in the Taxes Act (the former ss.348 and 349) into a series of separate provisions in ITTOIA to be read alongside several provisions in ITA 2007, and in particular Chs 6 to 8 of Part 15 of ITA 2007. That might sound like making things complicated, but you need only look at the lengthy commentary to those former sections in any of the standard works to realise that splitting the provisions into many constituent parts is in practical terms a great simplification. It only looks complicated when, as here, we try and take an overview of the system.

The starting point is now in ss.898 and 899 of ITA 2007. This **6–30** is the signposting provision to the sections requiring deduction of income tax from annual payments, and with them patent royalties (which are a specific form of annual payment). It also signposts the main exceptions.

Section 899 defines "qualifying annual payments". These are various kinds of annual payment including those caught under s.683 of ITTOIA. They are caught if they arise in the United Kingdom. Different lists of payments apply to companies and to other taxpayers (including individuals). Just as important are the payments that are not qualifying annual payments under s.899(5). This cuts out payments of interest, payments that qualify for other tax relief as payments to charities, and also the payments caught by the anti-avoidance provisions in s.904 of ITA and s.729 of ITTOIA.

If an individual makes a qualifying annual payment, and the **6–31** payment is made for genuine commercial reasons, then the payer *must* deduct tax from the payment when making it at the basic rate in force for that tax year. We emphasise the *must*. There is no option about this. If the payer does not deduct the tax, then it merely means that the payer has to pay HMRC as well as having paid the recipient. So ignoring the provision is not a good idea. Similar duties are imposed separately on companies and other entities making payments (for example, a local council). There are also provisions requiring deduction of tax when patent royalties are paid.

The most common way in which individuals come across these provisions under the new rules is when United Kingdom banks or building societies deduct income tax at the basic rate from payments of interest made to individuals.

As a result, the recipient of several forms of annual payment will receive the payments net of tax. If that happens, then the payments are not subject to any further income tax in the hands of the recipient. And the series of provisions noted above prevent the recipient demanding the income tax payment from the payer. There may however be further adjustments at the end of the year if the payer or recipient are subject to higher rate tax, or the recipient is not liable to tax.

Other income

6–32   Somewhere in every comprehensive code there must be the final fallback provision. All taxes levied under the rule of law, like history, must come to a. For income tax, this is it.

The provision of last resort may be designed to ensure that the code is truly all-inclusive, or it may be designed to draw the line between what at the margin is in the code and what is outside. In the 1803 form of the income tax—that lasted until the Income Tax (Trading and Other Income) Act replaced Schs A and D— that final fallback position is Sch.D, Case VI. It is necessary because "income" is not defined in the Acts, and it is also clear that the tax on income tax is not a universal tax on all possible forms of income. But drawing this line was never easy.

6–33   In the brave new world of the rewrite, the final provision that draws the line between taxable income of individuals and receipts that are not taxable to income tax is to be found right in the middle of the new code. Specifically it is in Ch.8 of Part 5 of ITTOIA, which is of course the end of the fifth of the ten chapters in the fourth of the seven rewrite Acts. Where else would you expect to find it—surely not at the end?

The key provision is s.687 of ITTOIA: the charge to tax on income not otherwise charged to tax. Section 687 carefully ensures that the section does not apply to annual payments (caught under s.683 discussed above). With that exception subs.(1) provides:

> "Income tax is charged under this Chapter on income from any source that is not charged to income tax under or as a result of any other provision of this Act or any other Act."

And just to be careful, subs.(3) adds:

> "Subsection (1) does not apply to income that would be charged to income tax under or as a result of another provision but for an exemption."

That wording deliberately echoes s.683. What emerges from this is that there are in effect two parallel provisions of last resort in the rewritten income tax code. One applies to annual payments, and the other to any other form of income. The only trouble with this is that in addition to the absence of any definition of annual payment we also find no clue in this section of its real scope. "Income" is not defined.

In the pre-rewrite language of the old Case VI, the central wording of the sweeper provision was "annual profits and gains". It was generally agreed that this did not help much, as no one really knew what that meant, and the term "income" has replaced it.

6–34

At some point the courts are likely to get asked what "income" means in this section. The only help we can give you at the present about this is to go back and look at the scope of the old Case VI, with the suggestion that it is at least the intention of the rewrite legislation that the line between what is taxable to income tax and what is not should not have moved.

The scope of income

So what *was* caught by the general aspect of Case VI? In *Scott v Ricketts* (1967), CA, Lord Denning said that what is caught includes "remuneration for work done, services rendered, or facilities provided". A good example of a Case VI profit was in *Leader v Counsel* (1942). A group of racehorse owners purchased a stallion. If any member of the group did not have a mare which required the services of the stallion he could sell his nomination to anyone else. It was held that there was not a trade, but that these receipts from the user of property were income receipts and were taxable under Case VI.

6–35

Similarly, income from activities which do not form part of a profession or vocation, but would do so if repeated, may be

121

charged to tax under Case VI. For example, writing one newspaper article does not make someone into a writer. Case VI also catches income made by selling one's story to the newspapers. The wife of one of the Great Train Robbers sold her story to the *News of the World*. In *Alloway v Phillips* (1980), CA, the court held that the £39,000 she received derived from her contract with the newspaper, and that her rights under that contract were "property", so that she was liable under Case VI.

Gifts, betting winnings and "winnings" by finding are not assessable under here any more than they are as trading income.

There are three final points to be made about assessment under these provisions.

First, assessment is on a current year basis, and income tax is computed on the full amount of the profits or gains arising in the year of assessment. Secondly, "arising" has been held to mean "received": *Grey v Tiley* (1932), CA. So assessment is on the cash basis rather than the earnings basis. Thirdly, losses are not so favourably treated as losses of trading income, because a loss of this kind can only be set off against similar profits, not against other kinds of income.

CHAPTER 7

CAPITAL ALLOWANCES

Introduction

When we were considering the computation of trading profits,   7–01
we saw that the cost and depreciation of capital assets are
regarded as being of a capital not of a revenue character. But
this does not mean that no relief is given for tax purposes in
respect of such capital expenditure. It is given by a separate
system of "capital allowances". We consider the manner in
which such relief is given later in this chapter. Initially, however,
we must determine when capital allowances are available.

The law on capital allowances was rewritten into a separate   7–02
Act some years ago. It was then further rewritten to form the
first of the Tax Law Rewrite Project Acts. This was enacted as
the Capital Allowances Act 2001. The Rewrite Project reviewed
the success of the new Act after the first year. It found general
satisfaction among many users and professionals at the changes.
Lawyers, however, greeted it with some suspicion. It was
assumed that because the precise order of words in the new Act
was new, there could be some changes in the law. They were not
reassured that—or were unaware that—both the Rewrite Project's consultees and Parliament's lawyers had looked for, and
not found, any changes. They were also largely unaware of the
valuable full commentaries issued by the Rewrite Project about
its drafts. Any detailed study of the Act should bear both those
points firmly in mind. So far, the courts have had no occasion to
look at the new rules. The downside of the Rewrite is that it
shows graphically how complex the law is becoming. The last
re-enactment was in 1990, when the Act started life with 165
sections. The 2001 Act had over 620 sections on enactment. But,
following the FA 2008, the 2001 Act has started to lose the tidy
look of a rewrite Act. That Act, for example, repeals both Part 3
and Part 4 of the 2001 Act, while leaving Parts 3A and 4A in
place. Sections 40 to 46 also have an odd look. Sections 40 to 45
have gone, leaving in place ss. 45A to 45J! This reflects both the
political sensitivities and the economic usefulness of trimming
capital allowances on a regular basis.

Capital allowances are available as follows: 7–03

- plant and machinery allowances (in Part 2);
- business premises renovation allowances (Part 3A);
- flat conversion allowances (Part 4A);
- mineral extraction allowances (Part 5);
- research and development allowances (Part 6);
- know-how allowances (Part 7);
- patent allowances (Part 8);
- dredging allowances (Part 9);
- assured tenancy allowances (Part 10).

It can be seen from the list that many items of capital expenditure do *not* attract any allowance. Also, the allowances are broadly confined to income taxable as trading income. One exception is the allowances for machinery and plant, which are available to persons carrying on a profession (or vocation) or to persons in employment, as well as to traders: CAA, s.20.

Before looking at aspects of the substantive law two important questions must be addressed—first, what is the rationale for capital allowances and, secondly, the distinct but interrelated question of the rate(s) at which capital allowances should be available?

Why capital allowances?

7–04   It is implicit in the opening remarks in this chapter that the availability of capital allowances should in some measure be an acknowledgement of the need to take account of the depreciation in value or obsolescence of capital assets acquired by a business. However, for many years, successive governments perceived capital allowances principally as a means of encouraging businesses to invest, and a system of generous allowances developed which enabled a business to write off capital expenditure markedly in advance of any actual depreciation or obsolescence. Thus, by 1984, a business, if it wished, could set the whole of the cost of buying machinery and plant against its taxable profits for the year of purchase, together with most (and sometimes all) of the cost of industrial buildings. In many instances it was not the desire to invest per se which prompted expenditure by a business, but the prospect of claiming these allowances with a view to cutting down taxable profits in the year the expenditure was incurred. Such practices, which were intended to exploit the generosity of the system, brought forth the following lament by Chancellor of the Exchequer Nigel Lawson in his Budget Speech in 1984. He said:

"... Over virtually the whole of the post-war period there have been incentives for investment in both plant and machinery and industrial, although not commercial, buildings. But there is little evidence that these incentives have strengthened the economy or improved the quality of investment. Indeed, quite the contrary ... too much of British investment has been made because the tax allowances make it look profitable rather than because it would be truly productive. We need investment decisions based on future market assessments not future tax assessments."

However, it was a lament which acted as a prelude for a fundamental restructuring of the capital allowances system. The general policy was to phase out first year and initial allowances and to provide, thereafter, for the writing down of such capital expenditure solely on the basis of writing-down allowances applicable over a number of years and at rates which bore some resemblance to actual depreciation. But over the following two decades the first year allowances and other special provisions started creeping back in again. Another axe was taken to the system by Chancellor Darling in the 2008 Finance Act. His measures remove entirely the longstanding allowances for expenditure on industrial buildings and agricultural buildings, and cut all allowances on plant and machinery. They also remove most remaining first year allowances, for example for smaller businesses. All go by 2011. **7–05**

We will now look at allowances on plant and machinery, and then (much more briefly) at some other allowances. **7–06**

Plant and machinery allowances

What is plant and machinery?
Neither machinery nor plant are defined in the tax legislation, and it is often a matter of some difficulty to decide whether a particular item is entitled to an allowance. The meaning to be given to the word plant has been particularly problematic and no attempt was made to codify it in CAA 2001. This is typified by Parliament's enactment in 1994 of a rule that buildings and structures *cannot* qualify as plant (subject to the proviso that buildings and structures already so qualifying would continue to do so). CAA ss.21 to 23 sets out those individual items or assets which fall with these expressions and which *cannot* qualify as plant. But, interestingly, it also lists items or assets which although within the definition of these words may nevertheless qualify as plant. In respect of an item in the latter category, it is open to the taxpayer to establish in the light of the meaning **7–07**

given to plant by the courts that it does in fact qualify. It is to the approach of the courts that we now look.

It is an interesting fact that the case most often cited as a starting point for judicial statements about the meaning of plant is not a tax case at all, but a tort case. The case is *Yarmouth v France* (1887), DC. A workman brought a claim under the Employers' Liability Act 1880 for damages for injuries caused by a defect in his employer's "plant", namely a vicious horse. Lindley L.J. (in holding that the horse was plant) said:

> "... in its ordinary sense [plant] includes whatever apparatus is used by a business man for carrying on his business—not his stock-in-trade, which he buys or makes for sale; but all goods and chattels, fixed or movable, live or dead, which he keeps for permanent employment in his business."

7–08   From that beginning a huge structure of case law has been built up as to what may constitute plant. The item must be a good or chattel; it must have some degree of durability; it must be an item *with* which a trade is carried on as distinct from an item which comprises part of the premises or setting *in* which it is carried on.

It is this latter distinction which has often been difficult to draw, although it is established that an item which becomes part of the premises in which the trade is carried on cannot be plant (except in those cases where the premises are themselves plant for example, *IRC Barclay, Curle & Co Ltd* (1969), HL), and that this will be so even if the item also has a distinct business purpose, e.g. to embellish the premises with a view to pleasing and attracting customers. The determination of whether an item has become part of the premises depends on whether it is more appropriate to describe the item as having become part of the premises as opposed to having retained a separate identity. This is a matter of fact and degree, and a court may take into account whether the item retains visually a separate identity, the degree of permanence with which it is affixed, the incompleteness of the premises without it and the extent to which it was intended to be permanent.

7–09   In *Wimpey v Warland* (1989), CA, the court was concerned with whether various improvements including tiling on floors and walls, glass shop fronts, raised and mezzanine floors, staircases and false ceilings which were undertaken at the taxpayer's fast food restaurants were plant. It was conceded that the improvements were designed to attract potential customers and to provide a particular atmosphere which the taxpayer considered conducive to the meals served. Nevertheless, the Court of Appeal decided that the improvements were not plant as they had become part of the premises. In circumstances where items have not become part of the premises, it has been accepted by the courts that they may be plant if the taxpayer's business includes the provision of atmosphere and the items are designed to create that atmosphere (see *IRC v Scottish and Newcastle Breweries* (1982), HL).

It is obviously easier to apply the ideas inherent in Lindley L.J.'s statement in *Yarmouth v France* to a trade than to a profession, and in *Daphne v Shaw* (1926) it was held that law books bought by a solicitor and used in his practice were not plant. However, 50 years later, in *Munby v Furlong* (1977), CA, *Daphne v Shaw* was overruled by the Court of Appeal. Mr Munby, a barrister, won his claim for capital allowances in respect of law reports and textbooks bought in his first year of practice. Lord Denning said:

> "Counsel for the Crown ... would confine a professional man's 'plant' to things used physically like a dentist's chair or an architect's table or, I suppose, the typewriter in a barrister's chambers; but, for myself, I do not think 'plant' should be confined to things which are used physically. It seems to me that on principle it extends to the intellectual storehouse which a barrister or a solicitor or any other professional man has in the course of carrying on his profession."

Lord Denning divided what he called "a lawyer's library" into three parts: first, a set of law reports; secondly, textbooks; thirdly, periodicals, including current issues of law reports. Expenditure on this last group was, said Lord Denning, revenue expenditure; expenditure on the first two groups was capital expenditure, and qualified for capital allowances. And another 30 years later, the list would have to include IT equipment and software. Section 71 of CAA makes provision for capital expenditure on this.

Claiming allowances

If an item constitutes either machinery or plant, capital allowances may be available to a trader who has incurred capital expenditure on acquiring that item wholly and exclusively for the purposes of his trade and where as a result of that expenditure the item belongs to the trader. The meaning of the phrase "wholly and exclusively" was considered in Ch.4, although it might be useful to add that where capital expenditure is incurred for the acquisition of plant or machinery to be

7–10

7–11

used partly for trade and partly for other purposes a system of apportionment may be applied. The word "belongs" has an extended meaning for these purposes. Thus, an item of machinery or plant may be deemed to belong to a person even though technically it belongs to another! This is best explained by the following example. Where a lessee of a building incurs capital expenditure on the provision of machinery or plant, which is required to be provided under the terms of the lease, for the purposes of a trade (in circumstances where that machinery or plant is not installed or fixed so as to become part of the building or land) then the machinery or plant will be deemed to belong to the trader and in respect of which capital allowances may be claimed.

Using allowances

7–12   Finally, before we look at how allowances for expenditure on machinery or plant work, we must mention the methods of using the allowances.

When income tax was first introduced, no thought was given to capital expenditure. And in the nineteenth century the courts ruled that no deductions could be made against income tax for capital costs. This meant that the standard deductions from profits of a business for depreciation were not allowed to be set off against taxable profits. But both fairness and expediency prompted the introduction of specific allowances for some kinds of capital expenditure, while continuing to disallow deductions for depreciation. The reason for that was that at that time the way in which depreciation was set against profits was largely a matter of individual choice. There were no equivalents to the standard accounting practices that now exist.

The approach taken was therefore to create allowances that could be set off against taxable profits. They were deductions after profits had been calculated, rather than deductions to be made when calculating profits.

As commercial profits became steadily more standardised, and income tax profits became steadily more aligned with them, this approach gave way to the more realistic approach of treating capital allowances as deductions from gross profits to be made when calculating taxable profits. But the perceived need to retain objectivity and so prevent those deductions being left to individual businesses meant that the refusal to accept traders' own views of their capital depreciation were still not accepted.

7–13   The current scheme therefore requires all trading and property business accounts to be adjusted with respect to capital expenditure. Any provision in the accounts for depreciation of capital expenditure must be removed. In its place the trader may claim up to the maximum of any capital allowances allowable in respect of capital expenditure of that or past trading years.

The key provisions giving effect to this are not in CAA but in ITTOIA. Section 28 of ITTOIA provides the link:

> "The rules for calculating the profits of a trade need to be read with—
> (a) the provisions of CAA 2001 which treat charges as receipts of a trade, and
> (b) the provisions of CAA 2001 which treat allowances as expenses of a trade."

This must be read with s.33 of ITTOIA:

> "In calculating the profits of a trade, no deduction is allowed for items of a capital nature."

We discussed the nature of those items also in Ch.4. Section 272 of ITTOIA also applies these rules to property businesses, covered by Ch.5. And s.574 of ITTOIA ensures that these rules also apply in respect of intellectual property and similar expenditure incurred as part of a trade or property business, rather than the special rules in Ch.6.

First-year allowances

7–14

Throughout the twentieth century encouragement to businesses to invest was provided by allowing deductions of varying degrees of generosity against the profits of the year in which the expenditure was incurred. This could apply even though the profits being taxed were earned in the previous year. From 2008, only the most limited forms of such allowances remain.

Section 39 of CAA limits the allowances to qualifying expenditure. And from 2008 few kinds of expenditure qualify. The list runs from s.45A. It covers only certain kinds of environmentally positive expenditure. But most of those forms of expenditure entitle the taxpayer to an enhanced capital allowance of 100 per cent of the capital cost. This will apply for example to environmentally beneficial plant or machinery. (See s.45H of CAA to see how this is defined.)

First-year tax credits

7–15

The FA 2008 adds a new approach to the remaining first year allowances, but only for companies. Where a company makes a loss in the same year as it invests in items on which it incurs qualifying expenditure, then it may claim immediate relief for the amount by which its allowances exceed its profits. So a company that invests in environmentally beneficial plant in the same year as it makes a loss will qualify. There is a central list of the equipment that qualifies for this treatment.

A company wishing to claim the credit must first set off the allowances against any available profits. Having done this, it may surrender any available losses to HMRC. If a loss is surrendered, then HMRC is required to pay the company in cash an amount equal to 19 per cent of the losses surrendered. (This ties in with the corporation tax rate on small companies.) It is an unusual example of using the tax system to provide direct cash subsidies to business, and is clearly analogous to the personal tax credits discussed in Ch.12.

Writing-down allowances

7–16   Where a person carrying on a trade incurs capital expenditure on the provision of an item of machinery or plant wholly and exclusively for the purposes of the trade and in consequence of that expenditure the item belongs to him a writing-down allowance may be available on a 20 per cent per annum reducing balance basis. A writing-down allowance may also be claimed by a person who is exercising a profession and by the holder of an office or employment who purchases an item of machinery or plant "necessarily provided for use in the performance of his duties".

EXAMPLE   Suppose trader T buys equipment costing £100,000 in year one. There is no first year allowance on the equipment. T cannot include anything for this expenditure in the business accounts other than the standard writing-down allowance. This is allowed at 20 per cent annually on a reducing balance basis, in this way. In year one T claims 20 per cent of £100,000 or £20,000. In year two T has £80,000 unallowed expenditure and can claim 20 per cent of that, or £16,000. So in year three T has £64,000 so far unallowed. The maximum for that year is 20 per cent of that total, or £12,800. That leaves £51,200 to be carried forward to year five, and so on. However, if T claims the annual investment allowance for the first £50,000 of this equipment, the writing-down allowance will apply only to the remaining £50,000.

Annual investment allowance

7–17   From 2008 another new feature of the capital allowances system for plant and machinery is an annual investment allowance.

This applies to all businesses regardless of size including individual traders and professionals. It will be of particular value to smaller businesses. But there will be a few exceptions including (big surprise) cars.

Any business will be able to claim the annual investment allowance on all relevant expenditure in that year up to £50,000. This will deal with all small claims. The standard writing-down allowance only applies to expenditure in excess of the £50,000.

Pooling

All items of machinery and plant belonging to a trader are treated as being in one "pool", except where the item is expressly excluded, e.g. certain cars costing more than £12,000, or where at the election of the taxpayer a short-life asset is not pooled in order to allow it to be written down over the period of its prospective useful life (for up to four years). There is also a separate pool for "long-life assets". These are assets with likely useful economic lives of over 25 years: CAA, s.91.

7–18

Where there is a pool, the 20 per cent is calculated on the qualifying expenditure of the pool as a whole. Each new expenditure increases the qualifying expenditure in the pool.

Balancing allowances and charges

As each new item of equipment is purchased, the allowances for it are added to the pool of that kind of expenditure. And the unallowed amounts of each item of expenditure are carried forward from one year to another. So the previous expenditure in the pool steadily gets worth less, while being topped up by new expenditure in any year.

7–19

The pools will need other kinds of adjustment during the life of a business in addition to reductions for the annual setting off of writing down allowances against profits and increases for new expenditure.

First, capital items may be sold off at a profit. If this happens, then the amount by which the price received for the asset exceeds the value of the allowance for the equipment in the pool must be deducted from the pool. If the amount received exceeds the amount in the pool then this must be corrected by what is called a balancing charge. This is a direct offset to reflect the fact that the trader has received more for the equipment than the unallowed capital expenditure, so is making a profit against the capital allowances received. The idea is that after the balancing charge is made, the trader will have received a capital allowance equal to, but no more than, the actual cost to the business of the equipment. Section 55 of CAA provides for this. It does so by reference to the formula that the charge is TDR – AQE. In words, that means that the total disposal receipts from items in the pool exceed the available qualifying expenditure in the pool. But if AQE exceeds TDR, then the difference is available for a writing down allowance.

The reverse applies if equipment is written off or scrapped. For example, machinery becomes obsolete or breaks down and is not worth repairing. When this happens, the value of the equipment will be next to nothing. But there may still be a significant unallowed capital expenditure in the pool for it. In that case, the trader can claim a balancing allowance to ensure that the full capital cost is available for allowances. This has the reverse effect to a balancing charge.

If a business comes to an end, then there will probably be a series of both balancing charges and balancing allowances that need to be made to close the pools at the correct values.

7–20   EXAMPLE In year seven T has pooled expenditure of £200,000 carried forward from year six. T will receive an allowance of 20 per cent, or £40,000 on this. But T sells an item of specialist equipment for £60,000. So AQE in year seven is £200,000, while TDR is £60,000. So the amount available for allowances is £140,000. The allowance of 20 per cent of that, or £28,000, is deductible against the profits for that year. The AQE for year eight then starts at £112,000. In that year T spends only £20,000 on new capital but is able to sell an asset that has gone up in value for £120,000. T can claim the AIA for the £20,000, but that leaves a TDR of £120,000 and an AQE of £112,000. So there will be a balancing charge of the difference, £8,000, added as additional income to the trading profits, and the initial AQE for year nine will be zero.

Industrial and agricultural buildings

7–21   For most of the twentieth century there were capital allowances also available for both industrial buildings and agricultural buildings. For some of those years there were also especially generous allowances for new buildings erected in enterprise zones. These are all being phased out from 2008, and will have gone by 2012. For most building the allowance was a long term one of 4 per cent of the capital cost each year for 25 years. In enterprise zones the allowance could be up to 100 per cent.

As these forms of allowance will already have stopped

influencing decisions about investment in property, we need not spend any more time on them. But they make the distinction between different kinds of expenditure particularly sensitive. For example, if you look around an office, what parts of the office are plant and machinery, and what parts are the building? What about the ceiling lights, or the semi-mobile partitions or bookshelves?

A practical answer is given to this question to help deal with the problem of the absence of any allowance for buildings. Provision is made for allowances for plant and machinery for what are referred to as integral features of a building, in addition to the allowances that are noted above for such things as energy efficient heating systems. For example, heating and air conditioning systems, and fire alarms, are covered by this provision. But the writing down allowance for these forms of expenditure are limited to 10 per cent a year. See CAA s.23.

Other Capital Expenditure

The other kinds of capital allowance listed at the beginning of this chapter are merely noted here. But it is, perhaps, apposite to add in passing that, notwithstanding the generally diminished importance of first year allowances since the middle of the 1980s, it is still possible, in some instances, to enjoy capital allowances which write off capital expenditure in one year (see, for example, the 100 per cent capital allowance available for research and development). 7–22

CHAPTER 8

EMPLOYMENT INCOME

Introduction

8–01   By far the most important part of income tax is the part that imposes tax on earnings from employment. Most of us earn most of our money as employees, directors, or office holders. And HMRC collect not one but two taxes on those earnings: income tax and NI contributions.

The marginal rates at which we pay are rather higher than many people realise. The "marginal rate" is the rate we pay at the margin, that is, on the last pound we earn. So, for example, if I was already earning £25,000, and I earn an extra £1 from my employment, how much tax is paid? The answer is 20p income tax and 11p NI contribution (slightly less if I also pay a pension contribution on the £1), plus my employer also pays an 11.8p contribution. That is, the employer and I pay 22.8p NI contributions while I also pay 20p income tax. So, what's my marginal rate? That depends on how you define things. But the fact we both pay between us 42.8p to HMRC for the extra £1 my employer pays me does suggest we need to pay close attention to employee taxation.

Since 2003 there's a further twist. In some cases if I gain an extra £1 in earnings, I lose 39p from my tax credit entitlement. In those cases that extra £1 could cost me 70p in deductions and lost credits—and my employer still has to pay its bit. Not much left. That is why in this chapter we look closely at income tax on earnings, then at NI contributions, then at tax credit income calculation.

8–02   The importance of being earners may also explain why this is the first part of the main income tax laws to benefit from a complete rewrite. Whole generations of practitioners and students had to learn something called "Schedule E", which was a tax on something known as "emoluments". Mercifully, Sch.E was put out of its misery in April 2003 by the ITEPA—the Income Tax (Earnings and Pensions) Act 2003. We now have a codified set of income tax laws on earnings. So all the references in this chapter are to sections in that Act. Well—not quite.

ITEPA was only 10 days old when irrepressible legislators got at it in the Finance Act 2003. They returned again in 2004.

Both old and new laws require us to deal with two central questions. In plain English they are: what is employment, and what are earnings?

Employment

"Employment" is not defined in ITEPA beyond a few pointers. Section 4 tells us that it includes any employment under a contract of service, a contract of apprenticeship, or in the service of the Crown. Section 5 adds that the employment income rules apply equally to office holders. "Office" is defined as including any position that has an existence independent of the person who holds it and may be filled by successive holders. Section 5 is a rare modern example of codification. It enacts the conclusions of the courts in *GWR v Bater* (1920) and *Edwards v Clinch*, a House of Lords decision in 1982. Office-holders include company directors, trustees, elected officers such as MPs and independent officials such as judges. But an office holder such as a director can also be an employee if there is a contract of service.

"Employment" is a far more difficult word to define, and attempts to define it for ITEPA were abandoned at an early stage. The difficulties arise both in law and in fact. This is in part because of the importance of the distinction between someone being employed and being self-employed. The question of drawing that line is considered as part of our discussion of trading income. It is worth noting how important it is. It is not only important in deciding if Sch.D applies to the income instead of the charge to tax on employment income. It is also directly relevant to whether there is VAT to be paid to the earner, and whether Class 1 NI contributions have to be paid by the earner and employer rather than the lower Class 2 and 4 rates by the self-employed earner alone. Then there may be differences for tax credits and the social security benefits to which the contributions count.

Much recent case law is in the field of employment law. One important case is *Young and Woods Ltd v West* (1980). In that case the Court of Appeal drew attention to the need to keep the tax and contributions rules in line with the entitlement rules that give employees the right to challenge unfair dismissals and demand redundancy payments, and also to gain the benefits of

8–03

8–04

health and safety laws. To those we would add the more recent rights to holidays and statutory pay.

In another employment case, *O'Kelly v Trusthouse Forte* (1983), CA, the Court emphasised that the decision whether someone was employed or self-employed was a question of fact to be decided by the competent body. But HMRC will also often ask for documents such as the obligatory contract of employment in doubtful cases—and interpreting documents is a question of law.

8–05   The multiple importance of drawing the line gave rise to confusion, and sometimes contradictions, in practice because at one time the income tax, social security and VAT authorities all took their decisions separately about what was or was not employment. That has now been stopped. The power to decide on all employment questions not only for income tax and contributions, but also most social security purposes, was transferred to the Revenue by s.8 of the Social Security (Transfer of Functions) Act 1999. Since their merger, the Inland Revenue and Customs and Excise Departments now work as one in deciding these questions.

The borderline also occurs between professionals and employees and officer holders. Many doctors are both employees at their hospitals and self-employed in their private practices. In *Mitchell and Edon v Ross* (1960) CA, the Court confirmed that in such cases the employment income and professional income should be taxed separately. The case went on to the House of Lords on the related point that employment expenses of a doctor not allowed as deductions from employment income could not be set off against the doctor's professional income.

8–06   Someone cannot hold an office or employment as part of a profession. This is because the charge to tax on professions is mutually exclusive to that on employment income. This was made clear in the House of Lords decision in *IRC v Brander and Cruickshank* (1971). It was much criticised, and is not always strictly observed in practice, but remains another part of the borderline.

Personal service companies

8–07   A common borderline problem is that of the one-man or one-woman company. E sets up a small company, Ecoltd, of which she owns all the shares and is the director. Ecoltd contracts with various customers to supply E's services to them. The customers pay Ecoltd. Ecoltd then pays, or does not pay, E. That payment could come as employment income for a contract of employment between Ecoltd and E, or as fees to E as director, or as dividends on E's share, or by way of loans or benefits. That kind of arrangement was queried in the courts in *Cooke v Blacklaws* (1984) but held valid for tax purposes.

A determined effort to squeeze out these personal service or "pocket book" companies was launched in 2000. They became known as IR35 companies as that was the number of the Revenue leaflet about the new rules. Attempts, by reply, to squeeze out the IR35 rules by political means and by challenges on human rights grounds both failed. The rules are now in ss.48–61 of ITEPA under the heading "Application of Provisions to Workers under Arrangements Made by Intermediaries".

The rules apply where someone (the worker) personally performs or is under an obligation personally to perform services for someone else, but where the services are provided under a contract between that person and an intermediary rather than directly with the worker, and the circumstances are such that if the services were provided under a contract directly with the worker the worker would be regarded for income tax purposes as an employee of that person (s.49(1)). The intermediary is often a company but can be a partnership or a third party individual.

If a worker falls within these rules, then the intermediary is treated as paying a sum known as the "deemed employment payment" to the worker as earnings. That sum is based on 95 per cent of the sums received by the intermediary together with any sums received by the worker from the customers but not charged to tax as employment income less expenses and taxed employment income (s.54). The deemed employment payment is then caught—subject to some limits—by the PAYE rules (below) and fully taxed as employment income, with NI Class 1 contributions also due.

Another squeeze on these personal companies takes full effect in 2009. This takes the form of a tax-rate rise on small companies. Where once these companies paid little corporation tax and individuals paid a lower rate of income tax, now the company pays 21 per cent before the dividend is paid out. See Ch.13.   8–08

Earnings

The charge to tax on employment income is a charge to tax on general earnings and specific employment income (s.6(1)). "General earnings" comprise both "earnings" and "any amount treated as earnings" (we shall return to these). "Earnings" are defined by s.62(2) as meaning—   8–09

(a) any salary, wage or fee;
(b) any gratuity or other profit or incidental benefit of any kind obtained by the employee if it is money or money's worth; or
(c) anything else that constitutes an emolument of an employment.

This odd definition is where the tax law rewrite procedure broke down on rewriting the old (1803) rules into modern English. It did so because there are conflicting political imperatives on any rewrite measure neither to expand nor to contract the tax base. So ITEPA had to catch everything within the old Sch.E. That Schedule was defined in grand terms as charging tax "in respect of any office or employment on emoluments therefrom". These grand terms, it has to be said, informed few and helped even fewer in recent years. At least the rewriters have put the easy bits at the beginning!

8–10   The reference to "emoluments" keeps in being the decisions of the judges that stressed how wide the catch of employment income was and is. The test set out by Lord Templeman in *Shilton v Wilmshurst* (1991), HL, is therefore still relevant. He said that the phrase "on emoluments therefrom":

> "... is not confined to 'emoluments from the employer' but embraces all 'emoluments from employment'; the section must therefore comprehend an emolument provided by a third party, a person who is not the employer. [The charge] is not limited to emoluments provided in the course of employment; the section must therefore apply first to an emolument that is paid as a reward for past services and as an inducement to continue to perform services and, second, to an emolument that is paid as an inducement to enter into a contract of employment and to perform services in the future. The result is that an emolument 'from employment' means an emolument 'from being or becoming an employee'."

In that case Peter Shilton (then England goalkeeper) was paid what would now seem the trifling sum of £75,000 for a transfer to Southampton from Nottingham Forest. The sum was paid by the team he was leaving, but was held by the House of Lords to be an inducement for signing for the new team, Southampton. It was therefore an emolument for working for Southampton and taxable accordingly. At the same time Lord Templeman interpreted the wording as covering past services, so emphasising that the maxim "past consideration is no consideration" does not apply to emoluments.

Lord Templeman also indicated that a payment would not be

caught as an emolument under this general rule if it were paid for something other than being or becoming an employee, for example if it were paid to relieve distress. This view was endorsed in *Mairs v Haughey* (1993) HL in which it was held that a payment to employees to relinquish contingent rights under a non-statutory redundancy scheme was not taxable. Payments such as these take their character from the payments they replace, which in this case would be a redundancy payment that was not taxable if made. However, most redundancy payments are now taxed, save for a £30,000 threshold, by ss.401–416 of ITEPA.

Wide as the test is, it must be shown that the payment is a **8–11** "reward for services". Of course, this can be widened further by statute, and many ITEPA provisions do this. Section 6(1) of ITEPA applies the term "employment income" both to earnings and to "specific employment income". Section 7(6) defines this as bringing into charge both the various forms of income that are neither earnings nor share-related but are set out in Part 6 of the Act, and sums caught by Part 7, which applies to income and exemptions relating to securities. Part 6 includes the redundancy payment provisions just mentioned along with provisions dealing with non-approved pension schemes (see pension income).

Even then, payments can still be caught under the general rules beyond the reach of those special provisions. An example is *Hamblett v Godfrey* (1987), CA. In that case the Court decided that sums of £1,000 paid to employees of GCHQ Cheltenham who agreed to give up their rights to belong to trade unions was taxable. There is a good review of the case laws in *EMI Group Electronics v Caldicott* (1999), CA.

Gifts

The most difficult area in which to draw the line between **8–12** emoluments and non-emoluments is in the field of gifts. There is a mass of decided cases on this matter, and it is not easy to discern in them any clear-cut principle. It is tempting to say that if a payment is made by an employer it must be an emolument and if it is made by other persons it is not an emolument. But the cases do not bear that out; the most one can say is that a payment made by an employer is *likely* to be held to be assessable. In *Ball v Johnson* (1971) a bank clerk who was paid £130 by the bank which employed him for having passed the examinations of the Institute of Bankers was held not to be assessable on that amount. In *Calvert v Wainwright* (1947) a taxi-driver was assessed on the tips paid to him by his "fares", who could not be considered to be his employers. Again, it is tempting to say that if a payment is made in pursuance of a term of the contract of employment it must be assessable and if it is made without legal obligation it cannot be assessable. But that again is not borne out by the cases.

In *Ball v Johnson* (above) the £130 was almost paid under a contractual obligation; a term of his employment required him to sit for the examinations, and it was stated in the bank's handbook that it was the usual practice to make such a payment. But perhaps *Ball v Johnson* is rather an exceptional case. We think one can assert that a payment made in pursuance of the contract of employment is almost, but not quite, bound to be assessable. After all, because it is obligatory it is not a gift, so what is it? But the converse is definitely not true; it is not true to say that if a payment is not in pursuance of a contractual obligation it cannot be assessable. In *Wright v Boyce* (1958), CA, a huntsman was held to be rightly assessed on Christmas presents of cash received from followers of the hunt even though his contract of service conferred no right to the gifts. The payments were made in pursuance of a custom. Custom seems to be a very important factor in this area of the law.

8–13   The world of sport has produced some interesting cases in this field. In *Seymour v Reed* (1927), HL, where a benefit match was held for a professional cricketer on his retirement, the gate money was held not to be assessable. But in *Moorhouse v Dooland* (1955), CA, money collected from the crowd for a professional cricketer for outstanding performances was held to be taxable. A cynic might think that the distinction between these cases is the distinction between county cricket and Lancashire League cricket, but the Court of Appeal were able to make more orthodox distinctions: in *Dooland's* case there was a contractual right to have a collection made whenever his performance was outstanding; and collections had been made for him not once but several times.

The case of *Moore v Griffiths* (1972) arose out of England's winning the World Cup in 1966. The Football Association paid £1,000 to each member of the squad. These payments were held not to be taxable. Brightman J. held that the payments had the quality of a testimonial or accolade rather than the quality of remuneration for services rendered, and he set out a number of factors which pointed to that conclusion. One factor was that "the payment had no foreseeable element of recurrence" (on which one might comment "You can say that again"). Another factor was that "each member of the team, regardless of the number of times that he played or whether he was a player or reserve, received precisely the same sum of £1,000. The sum therefore was not in any way linked with the quantum of any services rendered."

That last factor raises an important and constant theme in these cases. A payment may be unconnected with services rendered, either (as in the *Bobby Moore* case above) because it is given to more than one person without measuring their separate merits, or (more commonly) because it is given to one person precisely as an appreciation of his merits, but his merits as a human being rather than as an employee. There is a flavour of this latter idea in *Seymour v Reed* (above) and in *Calvert v Wainwright* (above), where Atkinson J. said:

> "Suppose somebody who has the same taxi every day, which comes in the morning as a matter of course to take him to his work, and then takes him home at night. The ordinary tip given in those circumstances would be something which would be assessable, but supposing at Christmas, or when the man is going for a holiday, the hirer says: 'You have been very attentive to me, here is a 10-shilling note,' he would be making a present, and I should say it would not be assessable because it has been given to the man because of his qualities, his faithfulness and the way he has stuck to the passenger."

Non-cash payments

So far we have looked at the rules applying to payments made to an employee in cash. But it was long ago ruled that payments "in kind"—or non-cash form—were also within the scope of emoluments. The old language used the word "perquisites", long ago shortened to "perks" but only removed from the statute in 2003. The most obvious example of a perk until recently was "the company car", but there are many ways in which it was sought to reduce the income tax liability of an employee (and the NI contributions of the employer too) by converting cash into non-cash forms. You must therefore study the many provisions that bring these non-cash payments within the tax charge.

To do this, legislation must provide two rules for each kind of payment: a rule that makes the payment taxable, and another rule that gives the payment a value. The second rule is normally necessary because a little ingenuity can reduce or even remove value from a benefit. If there are no special rules then the underlying rule is that in *Tennant v Smith* (1892) HL. The House of Lords blocked early attempts to avoid employment income by providing, in the words of Lord Halsbury, that a

8–14

benefit was taxable if it was "capable of being turned into money". Or, in the words of Lord Watson, the Revenue could tax "that which can be turned into pecuniary account." That is relatively easy to apply, say, to a payment in the form of the ownership of a car. You can resell it. But how do you value the non-assignable exclusive right to *use* the car subject to certain further conditions? It cannot legally be turned into pecuniary account. In some cases a third rule is also necessary. That provides when the value is to be applied to the benefit. For example, the long term loan of a car would be expected to, and does, give rise to a charge each year.

These special rules accumulated over many years. ITEPA gave all concerned the opportunity to tidy the rules up into a convenient form. It was used, and the result is:

The benefits code

8–15   The benefits code is set out in Part 3 of ITEPA, after Ch.1 (which comprises only s.62 noted above). Chapter 2 defines the code as being the provisions in Chs 2–7, 10 and 11 of that Part. Chapters 8 and 9 list some exemptions. The benefits code applies to anyone liable to be taxed on employment income. However, those in lower-paid employments are left outside the scope of parts of the code. We return to them later. There are two more general exclusions from the code. Section 64 excludes from the code anything already caught under the general rules. This stops double taxation of benefits. Section 65 authorises dispensations from the code. If the Inland Revenue list particular payments, benefits or facilities in an appropriate notice, then no additional tax is imposed under the code. This allows employers to deal with some of the benefits directly with the Revenue rather than each employee having to sort the matter out. It makes the job of a payroll department a lot easier. We now outline each part of the code.

Expense payments

8–16   Chapter 3 (ss.70–72) includes extremely wide rules that catch any sums paid to an employee in respect of expenses where the payment is "by reason of" the employment (s.70(1)). But every payment to an employee is assumed to be by way of the employment unless the employer is an individual and the payment is in the normal course of domestic, family or personal relationships (s.71(1)). Payments put at an employee's disposal are also caught. The nature of the expense payment is not relevant to the scope of the sections. The principle is that they should be included in the charge to tax, with the employee being left to claim a deduction if he or she can. In practice, this rule is much softened by the dispensations provisions. For example, the refund of approved travel or similar costs by an employer will usually be covered by a dispensation, so will not involve the employee being caught within s.70.

Vouchers and credit-tokens

The scope of Ch.4 (ss.73–96) requires a little more explanation—not to mention the translation into understandable English of "credit-token".   8–17

The chapter brings together three parallel sets of provisions designed to impose tax on what might be called indirect cash payments. Together they form a mini-code in their own right. The opportunity to rewrite the provisions into ITEPA has also allowed a number of minor problems to be ironed out. Nonetheless, to understand the scope of the provisions it is necessary to see just how wide are the definitions of the three key terms: cash voucher, non-cash voucher and credit-token.

A **cash voucher** means a voucher, stamp or similar document   8–18
capable of being exchanged for a sum of money that is at least not substantially less than the expense incurred by the person at whose cost the voucher is provided (s.75(1)). For example, an employer might provide employees with weekly "holiday stamps" that allow the employees to cash them in from time to time to receive sums from the employer towards the cost of a holiday. There are also special rules for "sickness benefits-related vouchers", which bring within these rules what would otherwise be cash vouchers save for the fact that a particular employee avoids sickness or personal injury, so is not claiming much in return for the vouchers.

A **non-cash voucher** means a voucher, stamp or similar   8–19
document, or token capable of being exchanged for money, goods or services. It includes "transport vouchers" and "cheque vouchers". But something that is a cash voucher cannot also be a non-cash voucher. A "transport voucher" is what most of us would call a ticket, and catches employer-provided season tickets. It also includes any form of pass or other document or token that can be used to obtain transport services. The wide wording has to cover the tokens used in some places to feed into machines, as well as for example Transport for London's Oyster cards. (s.84). A "cheque voucher" is a cheque given by an employer to an employee for the employee to buy particular kinds of goods and services. In practical terms, that means that

the cheque is made payable not to the employee but, for instance, to the local travel agents.

Section 89 is an interesting historical relic. It provides that when an employer provides employees with meal vouchers, the first 15p is exempt from tax. This enacts a previous extra-statutory concession first made in the 1940s. At the same time it shows both that such concessions can easily be enacted if the political will is there, but also the effect of fiscal drag and the limits of codification measures. Fifteen pence (then in old money a generous three shillings) could once buy you a lunch—and now? But there is no political authority to increase taxation in a rewrite bill, and any attempt at primary legislation to repeal it would run the risk that parliament increased it instead.

8–20   And what is a **credit-token**? You probably have some in your purse or wallet. They are credit cards, debit cards, or other cards, tokens, documents or other objects given by one person to another where the giver undertakes to provide money, goods or services on its production or to pay any third person for the supply of money goods or services on its production—unless the card or object is a cash voucher or non-cash voucher (s.92).

The mini-code provides that if any of these "documents" or "objects" are provided to an employee then income tax will be imposed on the "cash equivalent" of it or its use as if that were earnings. It defines the cash equivalent in each case and provides rules for the timing of such charges. The converse is that the goods, services or cash received are disregarded for tax purposes (s.95), in order to stop a potential double charge.

Living accommodation

8–21   Providing free or subsidised living accommodation to an employee is a long-standing method of attracting and keeping employees—and is a necessary aspect of some jobs. Chapter 5 (ss.97 to 113) lays down a series of rules to tax those who gain through employer-assisted accommodation. But it includes important exemptions for those who must live "on the job". There is no tax charge if it is necessary that the employee live in the accommodation for the proper performance of the employer's duties (s.99(1)). The classic example used to be a lighthouse keeper, but it still applies to many security and care posts. There is also no tax charge if the accommodation is provided for the better performance of the duties of the employment and it is customary to provide accommodation for employees in that kind of employment (s.99(2)). This would apply to many rural economy jobs. There is a further narrower exemption if the accommodation is provided as a result of a security threat (s.100).

The general rules catch accommodation provided not only for an employee but also for members of the employee's family. There are then two sets of rules to provide the cash equivalent of the use of the accommodation in any year. If the cost to the employer is over £75,000 then a stricter set of rules apply. That sum is calculated by reference to any purchase and improvement costs borne by the employer. Where the stricter rules apply the employee is charged tax not only on a notional rent but also on notional interest payable to fund the purchase or improvement costs.

Cars, vans and related benefits

Once upon a time (not that long ago) most cars on British roads belonged not to their drivers or families but to an employer. Of course, there are employees who are necessary car users, but not that many. The case of *Heaton v Bell* (1970) HL established that a well-designed car scheme (though not the one in the case!) would take the value of an employer-provided car outside the then tax rules. Given the popular status then attaching to big, new cars and the cost to an employee of buying them, the fact that your glossy new car was also indirectly subsidised by your neighbours through their taxes made "company cars" an almost irresistible perk to most. And, as governments were acutely aware, most fleet cars were then "built in Britain". Better still if it was full of extras that were also tax-free, and it was serviced and filled with petrol paid for by the employer but also free of income tax.

8–22

For those on the public payroll without access to these perks, it was necessary to pay employees for using their own cars and in some cases to help buy them. A generous "mileage allowance" could still be quite a help tax free.

The problem with all such schemes is that they are essentially unfair in tax terms. Company car users are subsidised by non-car users or those who have to buy their own cars without tax help. Those with big cars were more subsidised. Even given the political "clout" of car users—and car manufacturers—it was inevitable as car use grew that the tax shelter for company cars would be eliminated. But the ITEPA code rules for cars do more than that. As a result of recent changes, the code positively discourages some aspects of company car use. For example, having a second company car can now prove expensive in post-tax terms, while even the first car may not now be worth it to an employee. It is often now cheaper for an employee to buy a car and claim mileage allowances. Further, the rules have been designed to encourage the use of non-polluting vehicles. Gas guzzlers are definitely out—unless someone is prepared to pay for the privilege of polluting the neighbourhood. The only lobby that did prove successful in limiting the new rules was the classic cars lobby. Rules limit the tax charge on cars over 15 years old, but not old "bangers"—the car must be worth £15,000 to qualify (s.147).

Chapter 6 sets out rules to catch and tax the value of cars and vans provided by employers for the private use of employees or their families. It does not need to deal with the case where the employer gives the employee the car, because the ordinary rules tax the cost of doing so.

How cars are taxed

8–23   The starting point in taxing a car is to establish the cash equivalent of the benefit of the car. This is based on the price of the car together with any accessories. There are detailed rules to ensure that the price of the car is the list price or equivalent (to stop large employers securing large discounts on the price also securing tax discounts), and accessories (again to block avoidance). See ss.120–131. The tax charge is based on the "appropriate percentage" of this cost.

Turning first to new cars (post 1997), the appropriate percentage is based on the CO_2 emissions figure (in grams emitted per kilometre driven) with which the car was certified when first registered. Where emission figures are below the lower threshold for the year (itself being reduced year on year) then the appropriate percentage is 15 per cent. As the emission figure rises, so does the tax charge up to a yearly 35 per cent. In other words the income tax charge on new cars reflects both their full list price and their gas guzzling potential—regardless of how far they are actually driven. Until recently, the tax charge on a car that was (at least in theory) heavily used for business purposes was lower than one in light use. The result was that lots of people drove round almost literally in circles at the end of a tax year to get their business mileage up. That has now gone.

For older cars, the levy depends on their cylinder capacity, with a charge of 15 per cent on the cash equivalent for cars of 1,400 cc or less, and 32 per cent if over 2 litres.

There are inevitably a range of other rules dealing with vans, electric or diesel cars and vans and those run on liquid petroleum gas; for cars with shared use or which cannot be driven for a period; to take account of payments made by employees for their cars; for pooled cars and vans; but motor cycles are excepted.

Sections 149 to 153 catch the cash equivalent of car fuel provided to employees, unless they pay in full for it.

Mileage allowances and transport exemptions

So that we get the full picture about income tax and transport,   8–24 we should now note the provisions in Part 4 (and not in the code itself) dealing with exemptions from income tax for mileage allowances, passenger payments, transport and travel costs and subsistence away from home.

Sections 229–232 provide tax relief on approved mileage allowances paid to employees. These, again, have been trimmed back from past allowances. They are now 40p a mile for the first 10,000 miles and 25p a mile after that, regardless of the size of car, with 24p a mile for motor cycles and 20p a mile for cyclists—clearly aimed to get us all pedalling! If an employer allows less than this, then the employee can still claim tax relief on the differences between these figures and the actual allowances given.

Section 233 is another environment-friendly measure. It exempts from income tax any sums paid to a driver for using her or his car for carrying others for work reasons. Sections 237–249 list a series of further exemptions including, for example, workplace parking, works transport services, the provision of a cycle or cyclist's safety equipment, and transport and cars provided for disabled employees. The combined message of these tax provisions is clear (particularly when read alongside the message of our excise duties and other compulsory charges on cars and car use)—get on your bike.

Loans

Chapter 7 of the code (ss.173–191) is targeted on cheap loans   8–25 that are employment-related—that is, loans provided by reason of employment either interest-free or at a low rate of interest as compared with a commercial rate. The rules do not apply to loans totalling under £5,000, to bridging loans connected with employment moves (ss.288–9), to loans where tax relief can be claimed on the interest (for example, as a business expense), or to loans for necessary expenses. All other loans are assessed against "the official rate of interest". This is set from time to time by the Treasury (with different rates for sterling and foreign currency loans). If the interest rate is less than the official rate, and the loan is not an ordinary commercial loan by the employer available generally, then there is a tax charge on the interest that would be payable at the official rate less the actual interest paid.

A separate charge catches and taxes the amount of any loan written off (s.188).

There were linked provisions in Ch.8 of Part 3 of ITEPA as enacted dealing with notional loans in respect of acquisitions of shares. But these were repealed prospectively by the Finance Act 2003 for shares acquired after April 16, 2003, 10 days after ITEPA came into effect. Chapter 9 of that Part (on disposals of shares at more than market value) went the same way.

Residual liability to charge

8–26   Sections 201–210, forming Ch.10, provide a "sweeper-up" provision aimed generally at any other "employment-related benefit". It catches "a benefit or facility of any kind" provided for an employee (including past and future employees) or a member of the employee's family or household if "provided by reason of the employment". But everything provided by an employer is so regarded unless the employer and employee are members of the same family or household, or it is a normal personal benefit (such as a birthday present) (s.201). In other words, if it wasn't caught by the other parts of the code, it probably will be here. But if it is caught by other parts of the code, then those chapters apply and not this one.

The Chapter concludes by contrast with special rules for scholarships. They are designed to tax (the employee, rather than the student) the value of employer-provided scholarships to members of an employee's family or household. However, if the scholarship is part of a scheme funding full-time students in higher or further education then it can be exempted from the charge.

What's left

8–27   What's left that is not taxed, other than specifically exempted benefits? We must deal with the extremely important topic of pensions in the next chapter. Apart from what might be termed deferred earnings, the answer is not very much. Perhaps the other main two ways in which an employer can give a benefit to an employee without either incurring tax charges or having to establish some indirect (perhaps foreign) yet legal form of transferring value are the provision of free services (such as additional occupational health services or investment advice) and additional holidays.

The code and lower-paid employments

Sections 216–220 read with s.63(2) prevent the full rigours of   8–28
the benefit code applying to the low paid. The cash ceiling for
"lower-paid employment" is currently £8,500 (including any
benefits, payments treated as earnings, and sums deemed to be
earnings from personal service companies). To put that in perspective, someone earning the minimum wage of £4.85 an hour
in 2004 earns for a 40 hour week with four weeks paid holiday
about £10,000 for the year. In other words, the threshold
effectively now applies only to those working part time. [It is the
Inland Revenue's job to monitor minimum wage legislation.]
However, it should also be noted that in 2003 over one quarter
of all employees worked part time. And someone working only
part-time in each of two or more unconnected employments has
each employment considered separately. Even then, additional
safeguarding rules catch employees who are directors of
the employer company or who work in a series of related
employments.

For those who are within the lower-paid category, only the
following parts of the benefits code apply: Ch.4 (vouchers and
credit-tokens) and Ch.5 (living accommodation). The lower-
paid are therefore not subject to the code provisions on expenses
payments, cars and vans, loans, and the residual charge.
Remember, however, that the code provisions do apply to see if
the £8,500 limit is exceeded.

Where the code provisions do not apply, the pre-code general
income tax rules continue to apply. Those rules do not expressly
appear in ITEPA because most of them still rely on the judge-
made rules to work the old charge on "emoluments". The primary rule applying to benefits given to lower-paid employees is
that in *Tennant v Smith* (1892), HL, noted above. Employees
are taxed on the resale value—if there is one—of the benefit. The
rule in *Nicoll v Austin* (1935) should also be noted. If an
employer pays sums to a third party to meet an employee's bills,
then the employee is taxed on the amount the employer pays. If
the employer pays the employee's expenses, then they will only
be taxable if the expenses are not genuinely work expenses.

Amounts treated as earnings

We noted at the start of this discussion that what s.7 of ITEPA   8–29
calls "general earnings" are comprised of "earnings" and "any
amount treated as earnings". We have now examined fully the

meaning of earnings, and must turn to those other amounts. Section 7(5) lists them as being:

— the provisions for agency workers and arrangements made by intermediaries in Part 2;
— the benefits code provisions;
— payments treated as earnings under Ch.12 of Part 3; and
— certain balancing charges under the Capital Allowances Act 2001.

The provisions dealing with the benefits code and payments through intermediaries have already been discussed.

The agency provisions in ss.44–47 deal briefly with the treatment of workers who are supplied to employers by agencies. The legal problem is that the "employer" who pays the wages is the agency, not the person from whom the "employee" takes instructions. The result may be much like an ordinary employment contract, but it is not one, and so the income is not employment income. The solution adopted many years ago, and now universally applied, is to treat the agency as the employer and the sums paid as earnings for employment income purposes.

8–30 Chapter 12 brings together a small group of specific provisions catching sums and treating them as earnings. They are: payments to employees absent from wok because of sickness or disability (s.221); cases where the employer pays the employee's income tax (and so increases the employee's income by the amount of the tax paid (ss.222–223); certain payments to pension funds (s.224); and payments or consideration for restrictive undertakings (ss.225–226). Section 225 deals with a form of payment that cannot possibly be a payment for employment. If you offer to pay me a sum for not working at all, or for not working—say—within 10 miles of my office, that cannot be employment income. But it is income and parliament decided some time ago that it should be taxed and that it is best treated as income from employment.

Exempt income

8–31 Part 4 of ITEPA lists kinds of payments and benefits that are exempt from being taxed as earnings or as employment income. The list is a very long one, and it would be tedious indeed to plough through it. Nor is there any particular set of principles to emerge from it. The provisions are the accumulated wisdom (and lack of it) of many, many Finance Acts. So we will look only at the main structure, and leave the rest until any of you become tax practitioners (when you will need to know the lot). We have already seen the provisions on mileage allowances and transport payments that form Chs 2 and 3 of the Part. Chapter 4 brings together exemptions for education and training, including the failed individual learning accounts schemes. There are then exemptions for recreational benefits including the exemption (in s.264) for an annual "blow out" or staff party—provided the total cost does not exceed a generous £150 a head. (But is that kind of party really recreational?). This is followed by exemptions from the non-cash vouchers and credit-tokens legislation. For example, provisions protect transport company staff from being taxed on their free journeys to work. Removal benefits and expenses for employees moving for work reasons are also exempted, subject to some detailed revenue protection measures.

There are then measures for "special kinds of employees". However, when you look through the list (ss.290–306) you may wonder what is special about some of them. We have already dealt with redundancy payments in Ch.10, so we finish with the miscellaneous exemptions at the end of the Part. Three of these are of wide importance. First, there is exemption for subsidised meals at the workplace (s.317). Then provision is made to exempt employer-provided childcare facilities from tax (s.318). Finally, there is no income tax to pay on the advantage of an employer-provided computer or mobile telephone. (Does anyone other than a parliamentary drafter still call these omnipresent devices telephones?). See ss.319–320. These provisions show how fast technology dates tax laws, as you cannot use your computer as a mobile phone within the terms of exemptions under s.320, but may be able to use your mobile phone as a computer within the terms of exemption under s.319.

8–32

Deductions allowed from earnings

The rules allowing deduction of expenses from earnings were, until reorganisation took place under ITEPA, both over-compacted and dotted about in various parts of the Tax Acts. They are now found together in a properly codified form in Part 5 of ITEPA. This codification has also allowed the principles limiting deductions to emerge and in some cases to be made clear in the legislation for the first time.

8–33

The rules for deductions
The main rules for deductions are:

8–34

151

1 No deduction is allowed unless it is subject to express provision in the legislation. This is a general rule of income tax law to be found in s.817 of the Taxes Act 1988.

2 A deduction may only be made from the earnings of the employment in question (s.328).

3 The amount of a deduction must not exceed the earnings from which it is deductible (s.329).

4 A deduction from earnings is only allowed once in respect of the same cost (s.330).

5 A deduction is only allowed if the amount is paid by the employee (or by someone else but included in the earnings) (s.333). Where the employee is reimbursed for expenditure, the employee may only deduct the amount reimbursed if the reimbursement is taxed as earnings (s.334).

6 Subject to special provisions, a deduction is allowed only if—

(a) the employee is obliged to incur and pay it as holder of the employment, and

(b) the amount is incurred wholly, exclusively and necessarily in the performance of the duties of the employment (s.336).

"Wholly, exclusively and necessarily in the performance of"

8–35 Despite all the rewriting, the general rule for deduction is still to be found in one short phrase. It may be called the "general rule", but it is in fact several interactive rules. The words have not been changed because the meanings of these important few words have been exhaustively examined by the judges and because even the smallest change could prove very expensive.

The words "wholly" and "exclusively" are the same as those in the equivalent rule for trading income, and bear the same meaning. But there are two additional tests not required for claims for trading expenses, and which have proved to be exacting tests: the expenses must be necessary to the job, and must be incurred in the performance of the job.

The word "necessarily" has caused many a claim to founder. Stemming from *Ricketts v Colquhoun* (1926), HL, the test is, as Donovan L.J. put it in *Brown v Bullock* (1961), CA: ". . . not whether the employer imposes the expense . . . but whether the duties do." A bank manager was required by his employers (it was "virtually a condition of his employment") to be a member of a London club. It was held that the subscription fee was not a deductible expense. This is a harsh doctrine, and it may in time come to be softened if some of the ideas in *Taylor v Provan* begin to percolate through. But it will still be the case that the expense must not be necessitated merely by the personal circumstances of the taxpayer as distinct from the necessities of the job. Thus in *Roskams v Bennett* (1950) Mr Bennett was the district manager of an insurance company. Because of bad eyesight he could not drive a car, and so he found it necessary to maintain an office at home. It was held that the expense occasioned thereby was not deductible. In *Baird v Williams* (1999) the attempt of a Clerk to General Commissioners to deduct the interest on a loan to buy an office for hearing tax appeals similarly failed.

The phrase "in the performance of the duties" has had similar effects on non-travel expenses as on travel expenses. In *Simpson v Tate* (1925) a county medical officer of health joined certain medical and scientific societies so as to keep himself up-to-date on matters affecting public health. His claim to deduct these subscriptions was rejected, the court holding that the expense was incurred, not in the performance of the duties, but so that the taxpayer might keep himself fit to perform them. This seems a very restrictive doctrine, and indeed this particular point has been altered by statute. ITEPA now permits deduction of (we quote the title to the section) "fees and subscriptions to professional bodies, learned societies, etc." But the doctrine still stands where it has not been changed by statute. In *Fitzpatrick v IRC (No.2)*; *Smith v Abbott* (1994) HL, journalists incurred expenditure in purchasing newspapers and journals. They claimed to deduct this expenditure. The House of Lords by a majority (4–1) rejected this claim. Lord Templeman said "a journalist does not purchase and read newspapers in the performance of his duties but for the purpose of ensuring that he will carry out his duties efficiently". The rule surely tends to discourage employees from making themselves better employees. **8–36**

Travel expenses

Most employees' travel expenses are either travel to work or travel in employer-provided cars or other transport. We have already dealt with the rules that tax the provision of cars for private use, with some exemptions, and provide mileage allowances tax-free up to set limits. The final aspect of the taxation treatment of work travel is to note the rule for deducting employee-incurred travel costs. The practical importance of these rules is that they apply to long-distance travel for work reasons by air or train. But the political decision was taken **8–37** some time ago (after it had first been taken by the judges interpreting the then law) that the cost of travelling *at* work should be deductible, but the cost of travelling *to* work was not to be deductible. At the same time, it is unreasonable to exclude deduction of the costs of travelling to take up overseas jobs, and for similar major journeys, so the rules need exceptions.

The results are in ss.337 to 342. The main rule is that to claim a deduction for travel (besides meeting rules 1 to 5 of the main rules) the travel must be necessary for the employment and must be for travelling in the performance of the duties. As with the general rule about expenses, these words have been subject to close judicial attention, and we must note the main cases.

8–38   The expense of travel from one's home to one's work is not deductible. This basic rule is established by *Ricketts v Colquhoun* (1926), HL. Mr Ricketts was a barrister residing and practising in London. He was also the Recorder of Portsmouth (a part-time office). He claimed to deduct from the emoluments of his Recordership the expenses of travelling between London and Portsmouth and also his hotel expenses in Portsmouth. It was held by the House of Lords that neither the travelling expenses nor the hotel expenses were incurred in the performance of his duties, but rather before and after, and moreover, the expenses were attributable to the Recorder's own choice of residence and were not necessary to the office as such. This latter, very objective, point was rather softened by a later decision of the House of Lords, *Taylor v Provan* (1975), but on narrow facts.

The cost of travel from one place of work in an employment to another place of work in the same employment is deductible. In *Owen v Pook* (1970), HL, Dr Owen was a G.P. at his residence in Fishguard, and he also held a part-time appointment at a hospital in Haverfordwest, 15 miles away. Under his appointment Dr Owen was on stand-by duty to deal with emergency cases and he was required to be available by telephone. His responsibility for a patient began the moment he received a telephone call at home. It was held by a majority of the House of Lords that the duties of Dr Owen's employment were performed in two places (where he received the telephone calls and the hospital) and that he could deduct the expenses of travel between those places. This is akin to the Sch.D cases where a taxpayer is held to have his base at his home. But it is not identical, it is wider; sometimes Dr Owen received telephone calls when he was not at home. It seems to have been regarded as more important when he received the calls than where. But undoubtedly the case does establish that if his home is one of the places at which a taxpayer works (and rightly works) under his contract of employment, then the cost of travel from home to another place of work under the contract is deductible.

Other expenses

ITEPA also contains many other special rules for deduction, particularly for groups of employees with an international element to their jobs, such as seafarers and non-domiciled employees. Two specific rules are of internal importance.

8–39

Sections 343–345 allow employees to deduct various compulsory fees for being members of professions, and the annual fees for joining professional organisations. The scope of both sections is defined by a list: one in the statute and one prepared by the Inland Revenue. An example of the former is the fee and compensation fund payment payable by a solicitor for a practicing certificate. An example of the latter is the annual subscription to the Chartered Institute of Taxation. The test for claiming deduction of an annual subscription is that the activities of the body concerned are of direct benefit to, or concern the profession practised in, the performance of the duties of the employment.

By contrast s.358 put a bar on deducting most kinds of business entertainment or gift expenditure. These reflect rules mainly aimed at preventing employers from deducting business entertainment costs as business expenses. It is necessary therefore to control a deduction routed through an employee. The limit on business gifts is put at £50. The bar on deductions for any other form of hospitality expenditure is subject to a strictly limited exception.

Terminal payments

No, this is not something paid for using an airport, though it is about leaving. You may call them "golden handshakes", "golden parachutes", "golden handcuffs", "garden leave payments" or "payments and benefits on termination of employment, etc". They sound much more interesting if the officialese is avoided. But even ITEPA would look gimmicky if it dropped the formal language to adopt the headline texts. So we must use the "termination" language. Behind it are some important rules about payments made when people leave or change their work.

8–40

The problem is how to tax a payment made to get someone to leave his or her job. It is not employment income, because the payment is essentially to get someone to end the employment

155

contract. Further, the employee may have enforceable rights to keep that contract. At the same time, many payments to leave are PILONs (payments in lieu of notice) or are earnings by another name. When the employer wants someone to leave, it does not usually want to have the person around during a notice period. Indeed, it may be a security risk to the business for this to happen. So a payment is made and the work is ended. But if there is no continuing contract of employment, and no right to the payment because it is made (at least in form) as an ex gratia payment, is it not a gift?

8–41   Whether or not the payment is one within the general scope of the charge on earnings may depend on the precise terms of the employment. In *EMI Group Electronics v Coldicott* (1999), CA, the Court were faced with PILON payments made to employees entitled to six months' notice. The payments equalled six months pay. The Inland Revenue argued that this was earnings, while the employees argued that these were terminal payments. The reason, as we learn below, is that if the employees were right then the first £30,000 of their PILONs were free of tax, while if they were earnings they would be taxed in the normal way. The Court emphasised that payments in lieu of notice were separate from, and in addition to, any payments because the employment ended. Here there was contractual entitlement as an employee to the sum. It was therefore part of the earnings from that employment.

Had the Court found the sum not to arise from the employment, it would have had to apply the statutory provisions catching terminal payments, or the sums would have escaped tax entirely. In the past that approach was also used for tax planning by extending it to changes in an employment. I pay you a large sum to change the terms of your employment. I could probably, in practical terms, make you do that anyway but I have no legal right to do so. The sum you get is again not earnings—but in substance why not? The judicial answer was because it was not within the then charging provisions. The legislative answer to that was enacted in a series of provisions spread over time.

8–42   As elsewhere, ITEPA now presents us with a code. It is in ss.401 to 416. Section 403 imposes a single general charge on all forms of payment for ending or changing an employment which would have been taxable as earnings if paid for an employment, unless the payment is taxable under some other provision. It applies whether the change is a change in the duties of the employment or the earnings from it. It excludes any pension provision or payments for the death or disability of an employee. There are also limited exceptions that allow an ex-employee to keep only the car, the mobile phone and any computer equipment. Where the employee continues to work for the employer any removal expenses are ignored. Otherwise it applies if and to the extent that the payment exceeds a threshold of £30,000.

The rules are drawn widely to link a series of payments, and to catch payments made indirectly to an employee's family or (if deceased) survivors. There are also rules to ensure that the payment falls into tax and does not get missed because it is paid in a tax year after the employment ended or the employee died. The payment is brought into tax in the year in which it is received. If the payment is spread over a number of years, then it will be taxed in those years, but only the first £30,000 received will be exempt, not that sum each year.

Income relating to securities

The simple fact that companies are owned by their share-holders has been seen as one solution to the friction that can occur between employers and their corporate employees. It has also been seen as a way to offer incentives to employees, particularly senior employees, by linking them to the success of the employer. For 30 years various governments have pursued variants of the idea of making all employees, those employees that chose, or selected senior executives into owners of their employers.

8–43

At the same time, a straightforward gift of shares in the employer to the employee presented the employee with either an immediate windfall (if the shares were sold immediately) or the possibility of a much larger windfall if they were kept. If this was allowed to happen without a tax charge, then considerable sums could be lost to the exchequer. So it was necessary to impose conditions on employee shareholding schemes to prevent abuse.

The drafters of ITEPA were therefore faced with the formidable problem of converting a range of provisions into a single, sensible set of charging provisions. They worked hard on those provisions. The result was the 11 chapters and 140 sections of Part 7 of ITEPA. Actually, it wasn't. Or, rather, it was but only for 10 days. The real practical result, unknown until the last minute by those consulted by the rewrite team, was Sch.22 to the Finance Act 2003, and what are now 15 chapters to Part 7, with 28 of the sections entirely removed and 38 entirely new sections added. What is more, considerable amounts of detail relating to four kinds of scheme never went beyond being put in Schedules to ITEPA (Schs 2 to 5). To those we must add the provisions enacted in Sch.22 to the Finance Act and not read into ITEPA.

An understanding of these provisions demands a sound knowledge of corporate structure and finance laws, as well as of several new terms. For example, a SIP is not how you take your gin and tonic but a share incentive plan (ITEPA Sch.2). It tells you that in the Act. But it does not tell you what a CSOP is in Sch.5. You find it hidden in s.521(4) (company share option plan). And as far as we can see they do not bother to tell you what SAYE means anywhere in the Act (it stands for Save As You Earn).

The Part 7 rules

8–44   Let us then confine ourselves to the key aspects of the new Part 7 (after the Finance Act 2003 amendments). The "new" Part 7 is largely drafted in something approaching the full rewrite style—though without the advantage of the detailed professional scrutiny that ITEPA itself received. The signpost section, s.417, tells us that Part 7 contains rules "about cases where securities, interests in securities or securities options are acquired in connection with an employment."

The key word is "securities" and it is given a wide meaning by s.420. All the following are "securities":

(a) shares in any body corporate (wherever incorporated) or any non-UK unincorporated body;

(b) debentures, debenture stock, loan stock, bonds, certificates of deposit or indebtedness;

(c) warrants or instruments entitling holders to subscribe to present or future securities;

(d) certificates or documents conferring rights in securities held by third parties;

(e) units in collective investment schemes investing in any kind of property and allowing people to participate directly or indirectly from profits or income from the investments;

(f) futures, that is, rights under contracts for future delivery of any property;

(g) rights under contracts for differences or similar to them (that is, designed to secure a profit or prevent a loss against fluctuating prices).

But bills of exchange, money, bank balances, leases or dispositions of property or rights under insurance contracts are not.

And if the drafters got that list wrong, then the Treasury can amend it by order.

This section is then followed by similar sections creating potentially sweeping provisions to catch profits or gains from dealing with any security, interest in a security or option to purchase one. The aim is to identify any profit or gain (whether as a single sum or an ongoing benefit of holding a security on advantageous terms) and capture the tax value. But it is difficult to summarise usefully the complex provisions used to do this.

SIPs

Alongside these provisions are others to maintain approved   **8–45**
schemes for employees to hold securities. These include SIPs, under which employees can be given share incentives, including for example free shares. Under a SIP, any advantage on acquiring a share will be exempt from tax. If a dividend is paid on the share, but reinvested in the plan, then again it will be tax free. And if the employee holds the shares long enough (five years for a free share) then there will be no tax charge on disposal.

SAYE

Save As You Earn Option schemes allow employees to use   **8–46**
savings built up through a contractual savings scheme to hold and then use share options on advantageous terms again without a tax charge. Company Share Option Plans provide a parallel scheme without the external savings contract. Then there is an EMI (Enterprise Management Incentive) scheme and code (allowing a full tax advantage if the incentives are held in the company for 10 years), and provisions dealing with priority share allocations to employees on a public offer of shares.

The only safe conclusion in an introduction is to note that this   **8–47**
is now the territory of specialists of the same kind as those that can guide you safely across The Wash. They need to know exactly how the tide is flowing that day and where the shifting sands are safe to walk on. Easy when you know how. But those who venture in on their own are not likely to survive if the mists come down. You might like to reflect on how that fits in with the central aims of taxation we discussed in the first chapters.

National insurance contributions

Let us move on hastily to the other income tax levied   **8–48**
on employees and their employers. National Insurance (NI)

contributions started life as National Health Insurance stamps to be attached each week to contribution cards held by every employee. Part was paid by the employer and part by the employee, with the government topping the funds up. There was a fixed sum to be paid each week depending on the age and sex of the employee. Interestingly, my grandmother's contribution book from 1912 shows that contributions for women over 21 were at three different rates depending on the level of pay. But it was not until 1973 that the contributions stopped being mainly flat rate and became, in effect, a second income tax.

The income-based contributions were imposed by Social Security Acts 1973 and 1975. The provisions were consolidated into the Social Security Contributions and Benefits Act 1992, Part 1, itself now considerably amended. Further, under the Social Security Contributions (Transfer of Functions) Act 1999, responsibility for administering and collecting contributions was relocated from the Department of Social Security to the Inland Revenue; this is now run by HMRC from the NI Contributions Office. At that stage, however, the myth still continued that these were contributions to be set against the benefit entitlements of the contributors. And in form that endured up to the Social Security Contributions (Share Options) Act 2001.

In 2002 a subtle but fundamental change quietly took place. That year's contributions law, the National Insurance Contributions Act 2002, took the form of a money bill. Unlike all previous contributions legislation it started with the standard wording at the start of each finance bill: "We, your Majesty's most dutiful and loyal subject ... have freely and voluntarily resolved to give and grant unto Your Majesty the increases in national insurance contributions hereinafter mentioned ...". In constitutional form, as well as in substance, NI contributions are now a tax of exactly the same kind as income tax. Linked with this, the power to make regulations imposing contribution liability has moved from the Department to the Treasury. That is why, even though the primary legislation is still largely to be found in social security legislation, the government has quietly dropped all reference to "social security contributions" and so must we.

The form of tax imposed by the 1992 Act and regulations was relatively primitive. The liability was imposed by reference to weekly amounts of earnings, and by reference to a relatively simple tax base. The weekly nature of contributions continues, at least in form, and reflects the origin of the system in weekly stamps—although stamps are no longer issued. But over the last few years a steady series of changes have been conducted to align the tax base of NI contributions with the tax base for income tax. ITEPA provided the opportunity for some tidying up of the income tax rules. The equivalent tidying of the NI rules is largely to be found in regulations.

Contribution classes

Contributions are currently levied by reference to a series of Classes, of which there are currently six. These are: 8–49

Class 1	income-related contributions by employees (primary) and their employers (secondary) based on earnings;
Class 1A	similar to Class 1 but based on employee benefits under the benefits code;
Class 1B	contributions by employers on sums agreed with the Revenue as PAYE settlements (where no individual income tax is levied);
Class 2	flat-rate weekly contribution paid by those ordinarily self-employed;
Class 3	flat-rate weekly contribution payable voluntarily by those not otherwise liable to contributions;
Class 4	income-related contribution to be paid by the self-employed on their trading or professional income in addition to Class 2 contributions.

Class 2 and 4 contributions are discussed with trading income. Class 3 contributions are genuinely voluntary contributions that individuals can (and are invited to) pay to make up gaps in their contribution records for benefit purposes. They are not further discussed in this book.

Class 1 contributions

The rules for these contributions are found in the Social Security Contributions and Benefits Act 1992 (ss.1 to 9) and the Social Security Contributions Regulations 2001 (SI 2001/1004). The latter are very detailed provisions and have been amended several times since they were made. Almost every amendment serves to make the contribution rules closer to the income tax equivalent rules. 8–50

Nonetheless, the appearance of Class 1 contributions remains much in contrast to income tax. In particular, the burden is shared between the employer and the employee. And on higher earners, the main burden falls on the employer.

Contributions are still collected by reference not to tax years but to "earnings periods". The basic earnings period is a week, but this is adjusted for individual employees. So if you are paid weekly and I am paid monthly, then we have those different earnings periods. That means that contribution liability can lurch up and down for those who are paid weekly in a way that does not happen with income tax.

As a broad rule, if the sum is liable to income tax under the employment income provisions of ITEPA, it will now also be "earnings" liable to Class 1 primary and secondary contributions or, failing that, the Class 1A or Class 1B contributions. The "patching" by Class 1A and Class 1B deal between them with the largest difference until recently between Class 1 liability and income tax liability. They used to have completely different rules for non-cash benefits, including a rule excluding contribution liability on payments in kind. Nearly all those differences, even the detailed ones, have now gone.

In addition, Class 1 contributions are levied separately on each employment (though there are rules to link associated employments). So if I have two part-time jobs, then—again unlike income tax—they will be assessed separately to see what contributions I and my employers must pay. This separation serves to prevent one employer paying another's contributions.

The rates of contribution are discussed in Ch.12.

The fuller picture

8–51   A full flavour of the provisions of ITEPA can only be gained by assuming liability both to income tax and Class 1 (or 1A) contributions. As we have already noted, that extra £1 earnings will—depending on how much has already been earned that year (income tax) or earnings period (contributions)—impose a liability on the employee of 20 per cent or 40 per cent income tax once the personal allowance has been used up and (for those paying 20 per cent) another 11 per cent up to a weekly total of £770 with 1 per cent additional to other basic rate payers and all higher rate payers. Meanwhile the employer will also pay 12.8 per cent. Nor can this be sidestepped by the use of benefits in kind because of the combined effect of Class 1 and Class 1A. This is partly why it is now so much more expensive to have a company car. Not so long ago the rate of income tax was well below the rate on an equivalent amount of cash, and there was no NI contribution. Now the income tax levy may be higher in real terms than on equivalent cash, and there are contributions to pay.

But the fullest picture for most earners with families (and

most other low-paid earners) can only be obtained by looking also at the tax credits position. We will see in the next chapter that most—though not all—of the ITEPA rules also apply for assessing income for tax credits purposes. Where there is a claim for a tax credit at the margin (in other words, variable with the precise income of the claimant), then an extra £1 income or taxable benefit means 39p less credit. And in case you think that this can be safely left to those concerned with low pay, think again. The effective top limit at which precise levels of income affect tax credit entitlement is somewhere in the region of £65,000 a year in the extreme case—well into the category of people paying 40 per cent income tax.

PAYE

One of the real strengths of the income tax systems applied to employees in the UK is the Pay As You Earn system. This collects income tax and NI contributions from employees as they receive their earnings. This has the obvious advantage to the government that it not only knows that it is receiving the tax but that it receives it in a steady flow throughout the year and without delay. It has the second advantage—to the government—that it shifts the burden of collecting tax from most personal taxpayers from its own officials to employers.

8-52

The PAYE system is empowered by Part 11 of ITEPA, and the details are in the Income Tax (Pay As You Earn) Regulations 2003, (SI 2003/2682), rewritten at the same time as ITEPA.

Tax codes

Under the PAYE system each employee is issued with a tax code for a tax year by the local tax office. The employer is issued with the same code. Typically it will appear something like 496L. That means that the taxpayer is entitled to the personal allowance but that adjustments have been made to reduce it to leave the individual entitled to £4,960 income free of tax in the year. The employer is then provided by the Revenue with tables so that the employer spreads this amount over the year and collects tax and NI contributions at the correct level each pay day. By the end of the year, the employee should have paid income tax and NI contributions that are, within a few pounds, the correct amount for the year.

8-53

The tax code takes account of personal allowances, other deductions and reliefs, and in some cases also smaller amounts of tax due on other incomes (for example smaller untaxed earnings from another source). It therefore does far more in reality than merely collecting the tax on the earnings paid by the employer.

The power of the PAYE system has not only been built on to collect NI contributions at the same time as income tax. It is also now used to collect refundable student grants from graduates and to ensure payment of the four forms of statutory pay for sickness, maternity, paternity and adoption.

As a result of all these adjustments, what someone receives in his or her pay packet may be significantly different from the earnings that first go into it.

CHAPTER 9

PENSIONS, SOCIAL SECURITY AND CREDITS

Introduction

Huge changes have taken place in our social security systems   9–01
and their interactions with personal taxation since the first
edition of this book. These changes reflect major demographic
shifts in the British population. Put at its simplest, many more of
us are living much longer, so there are many more pensioners. At
the same time, the number of children joining us is dropping
(from an average of 2.4 children a family to approaching half
that). Each year there are fewer new members of our society and
more old ones. That means that each year there are fewer people
of working age to pay for the growing number of pensioners.
That also means that it is increasingly important to get as many
people of working age as reasonably possible to work. And we
need more children to pay our pensions in the future. So it is
regarded as responsible government for measures to be taken
both to cut the public cost of pensions and to encourage us all to
work and also to have children. Those social imperatives lie
behind the tax and credit measures in this chapter.

We start with the most important—pensions.

Pension income

"Pension income" is defined in ITEPA s.566 as pensions,   9–02
annuities and income of other types listed in the section. There
are 13 in the list, including voluntary annual payments. But the
Act carefully avoids defining "pension" beyond saying that it
includes pensions paid voluntarily or capable of being discontinued (s.570). The key for income tax purposes is that a
pension is normally payable to those who have stopped work
either permanently or on a long-term basis because of age, ill-
ness, disability or following the death of the husband or wife. In
such cases it is a form of deferred earnings from work, or work-
linked insurance against loss of earnings.

In this definition there is an obvious overlap between pensions, social security and other payments to those who are out of work but normally work. The approach of ITEPA is to treat as pension income those payments made to the retired (or widows and other survivors of deceased earners) and to treat as social security income those payments made to those whom it is assumed will return to work. So the state retirement pension—which is a social security pension—is treated as pension income and not as social security income. The main practical application of that divide is to treat as pensions those payments to claimants of 60 or over, and as social security income payments to those under 60. This reflects the state pension age of women, which is 60. From 2010 this divide will shift upwards to 65 by one year for each two calendar years.

The three pillars

9–03   There are three main forms of pension provision in the United Kingdom—often referred to as the three pillars of the retirement benefit system. The first pillar is the universal pension provided in the form of state basic flat-rate retirement pension, supplemented by the income-related state pension credit payable under the State Pension Credit Act 2002. The second pillar is the employment-based pension that most earners build up. In Britain there are three forms of this pension: the earnings-related occupational pension schemes run by employers and payable to employees when they finish work, the state second pension (previously known as the state earnings-related pension scheme or SERPS) which is available to those who do not have an occupational or personal pension, and personal pensions taken out by individual employees and the self-employed (to which employers may contribute). The third pillar is that of personal savings and investments, which need not be linked to retirement at all. This therefore does not give rise to "pension income", although it cannot be ignored in considering the overall tax treatment of retirement income.

The assumption of most pension provision is that the first pillar, the state benefit, is a "pay as you go" system. Current pensions are paid from current contributions and taxes. This is the basis of the basic state retirement pension and pension credit system.

The second pillar is assumed to be funded, that is, the occupational scheme collects contributions from individual earners to fund the future pensions payable to those earners. Currently there are two kinds of funded pension. The more popular form used to be the "final salary scheme" under which the pension paid on retirement is related not to the total contributions paid but to the salary payable to the employee in the last year or years of work. In other words, the scheme provides a defined benefit. If the available funds do not meet it, then the employer (usually) has to make up the difference. Because a final salary scheme can impose huge burdens on funds if people live longer than was originally anticipated, these funds are being replaced by "money purchase" or defined contribution schemes. In these schemes the pension an individual draws is related entirely to the contributions paid into the fund by that employee and the employer and the current value of those funds when the pension is claimed.

Both forms of funded pension raise important tax questions. How is the income of the fund to be treated, and how are gains and losses on investment to be dealt with? A complete account of the tax treatment of pension funds demands that we look at each stage of the funding: the payment in of the contributions, holding those contributions in the fund, and then paying the pension. ITEPA only deals with the last stage, so we need also to go to the Income and Corporation Taxes Act 1988 to get the fuller picture.

State retirement pensions

UK social security pensions, including pensions payable to widows and widowers, are taxable in full on the full amount accruing to the pensioner in the year irrespective of when the pension is actually paid (ss.577–578). War pensions are also taxable, but not pensions paid to survivors of those whose death was due to service. Similar treatment is given to foreign state and service pensions.

9–04

In practice, however, someone receiving these pensions (and the state pension credit) will not normally pay income tax if he or she has no other income. This is because the higher personal allowances granted to those over 65 are set at the appropriate level to stop income tax being paid by these taxpayers. But if the pensioner also has other pensions or income, then the state pension must be added to that other income to establish total tax liability.

To complete the picture, we must note that a contributor is not permitted to make a deduction against income tax for his or her NI contributions, nor is the reverse possible. NI contribution liability is calculated without regard to income tax liability in that year. But NI contribution liability, unlike income tax liability, stops when the contributor reaches 65 even if he or she continues to work. This is therefore a further cut in the tax liability of those over 65 in addition to the increased personal allowance. But an employer can treat NI contributions made for employees as deductible expenditure against profits. Against that, employers remain liable to pay secondary Class 1 contributions on earnings of employees over 65.

Occupational pension schemes

9–05   The tax treatment of funded pension schemes is important because a failure to make proper provision for pension funds may result in excessive taxation. That in turn may result in people failing to build up pension entitlement. And the reverse can be true. If the tax treatment is too generous, then people may save more than they need to do.

Tax theorists approach this by looking for the "triple E" scheme. There are three separate stages to any funded occupational pension scheme. First, earners and employers must make contributions from their earnings and profits. Second, the fund itself must ensure it produces adequate returns on the funds to maintain and enhance the value of the fund. Finally, the funds are paid out as pensions and/or lump sums.

If there is no fund, how will the individual be taxed? He or she will have to save from taxed income. The savings will themselves be subject to tax on income and gains. But when the individual cashes the savings and accumulated income, there will be no further tax. This is what the theorists call a "TTE" system. The first two stages are taxed and the third is exempt. That is normally regarded as fair taxation.

If we apply the pension income rules to the pension paid out of a fund without either helping the contributor or the fund, we will have a "TTT" system. It will be taxed at each stage. That is over-taxation and unfair as compared with non-pension savings.

So if we intend to tax the pension, then we must provide tax exemption or relief (an "E") to the contributors and/or the funds.

9–06   On this analysis, the standard British approach to funds is to give them an "EET" treatment, that is, to exempt both the contributions and the fund income, and collect the tax only on the pension. In substance this is to treat the pension as deferred earnings, and not to collect tax until the deferment ends. That is, of course, to give pension funds a tax preferred status compared with ordinary savings. But there is inevitably a condition attached. Or, to be more accurate, there are a very considerable number of conditions attached.

This is another area where income tax law has been rewritten —though on this occasion not by the Tax Law Rewrite Project.

Indeed, to the annoyance of some, the rewritten provisions about pension income in ITEPA Part 9 were replaced by new law from the Finance Act 2004 within days of enactment. The new rules took effect in 2006. The good news is that the new rules bring a much-needed common approach to the many different approaches to pension income taxation that previously applied. The bad news, as with all forms of pension law, is that the experts cannot forget the law applying in any year from the start of an individual's pension contributions. That requires keeping in existence the relevant rules and records for anything from 40 to 50 years for each individual who makes contributions. Therefore, typically, a properly-run fund has to look 60 years ahead from the entry of a new contributor to the point where most contributors have died. So even phasing a pension scheme out may take a long time. As a result, the tax and pension scheme rules have to deal not only with new schemes but also with older and closed schemes (ones that can receive no new members).

And inevitably as the rules about schemes became more complicated so did the scope for unauthorised schemes, or unauthorised payments under authorised schemes. The tax rules—as that list shows—must deal with each of these.

The Part 9 rules

The codified approach now in ITEPA Part 9 sets out general 9–07
rules about pension income and then follows this with specific rules about the kinds of pension included under the charge to tax on pension income. A glance at the contents of the Part shows how the reforms from 2006 have changed things. Section 579A now applies the provisions of the Act to a registered pension scheme. That replaces the former provisions for approved retirement benefit schemes (the previous form of occupational pension for most), approved superannuation funds, approved personal pension schemes, and retirement annuity contracts. Then follow the provisions dealing with foreign pensions and with pensions or pension schemes that are not registered or have broken the registration conditions.

But ITEPA only deals with the tax position of the contributor and pensioner. For the treatment of the funds themselves and of employers contributing to them, we must look elsewhere. Part 4 of the Finance Act 2004 defines a "pension scheme" and provides for the conditions that apply before a scheme can become a registered pension scheme.

The new rules permit both employers and financial businesses to set up pension schemes. The rules about this are liberal and do not require any particular form for a scheme. In every case the scheme must have an administrator who has satisfied HMRC of certain requirements.

The main conditions imposed on registered pension schemes set limits for the amounts of money that can be paid into schemes, or from schemes, from or to any one individual and how the funds are handled.

There are broadly three kinds of condition. The first kind is aimed at the amounts that can be paid into, and out of, a scheme with tax benefits. These rules have been relaxed considerably since 2006. There are now no limits on the sums that can be paid in, and the limits only apply to the amounts that gain tax privileges. But that is now potentially more generous. An employee can pay up to 100 per cent of her or his income into the fund and still receive tax relief. There is, however, an annual cap. It seems a high figure. In 2008–09 it was £235,000. For defined contribution schemes that is the total not only of any employee's contribution but also the employer's contribution. For defined benefit schemes, it is the benefit that is measured, not the contributions. The cap is based on the input amount to the fund for the individual in the year. That is measured as ten per cent of the added value of any additional benefits accruing to the employee in the year. Any excess over the maximum is charged to the higher rate of income tax.

There is also a new lifetime allowance limit. This places a single total allowance on all forms of pension fund held by an individual that may attract the favourable tax treatment. And anything exceeding the limit tends to attract instead a tax charge—sometimes two tax charges—at the higher rate level. So there is a strong disincentive against funds exceeding the limit. That limit currently stands at £1.6 million. That is the total level of funding that can be held for the benefit of any one individual in all funds added together. But there are important transitional provisions protecting those with large pension funds in place before the limit first applied in 2006.

Then there are limits on the payments out, including a general limit preventing more than one quarter of the entitlement being paid out as capital.

The second set of limits applies alongside the first. This imposes a minimum and maximum age band for drawing out entitlements. The current minimum age is 50, but that increases to 55 in 2010 as pension age is shifted upwards. The maximum age is 75. Gender equality already applied to all aspects of these pension funds, unlike state pensions. So the age limits of a fund must be the same for women and men and so must the benefits.

This is imposed by European equality laws as well as British law.

The third set of conditions is aimed at safeguarding the interests of the pensioners and prospective pensioners. There are therefore controls on how the fund is run.

Tax benefits

If a scheme meets all the conditions, then there are significant tax benefits. These generally follow the pattern of "EET". That is, the contributions receive tax preferred status as allowances, and the funds are tax exempt. Tax only applies when the payments out are made—or the rules are broken.

9–08

Contributions by an employee to a registered scheme can be set off in full against the earned income from which it is paid. Where the contributions are collected by the employer along with PAYE tax, the tax allowance will be set off directly against the tax payable that month by the employee. And employers can claim all their ordinary contributions to pension schemes as deductible expenses in calculating profits. That means they must meet the usual "wholly and exclusively" rule but no other. Compare this with NI contributions and the state pension. Employers can deduct the cost of their NI contributions. But employees get no deduction against income tax for the NI contributions paid.

There is a third tax exemption hidden behind those two. The employee is not regarded as earning the employer contribution. That is true of both NI contributions and contributions to registered schemes. This can be a valuable addition to total earnings. Say that an employee makes a 5 per cent contribution on gross pay to the fund, and the employer pays a further 10 per cent (plus of course the employer's NI contribution). In such a case the employee pays income tax on 95 per cent of gross earnings, while another 20 per cent or more of gross earnings goes out untaxed as employer's contributions and the employee's contribution to the registered scheme. And that means that considerably more gets paid to the fund than would be the case if these were taxed.

The second "E" is exemption from both income and corporation tax and any capital gains tax of all profits and gains of the pension fund.

Instead, income tax applies to the receipt of the pension by the pensioner. And, within limits, the "triple E" may still apply to lump sums payable to pensioners upon their retirement. But the general effect is to defer the taxation of pensions until the pensions themselves are payable. As compared with some other forms of tax-privileged savings, this has the advantage that the pension savings are therefore made from untaxed income rather than taxed income.

Social security income

9–09   Part 10 of ITEPA imposes tax, in principle, on all UK social security income. This principle is, however, subject to a list of exemptions that is considerably longer than the list of social security benefits that are taxable. Aside from retirement and survivor pensions (taxable as pension income) and statutory payments such as statutory sick pay (taxable as employment income), the only benefits subject to tax are some parts of employment and support allowance (payable to those of working age who have limited capacity for work), some forms of jobseeker's allowance (payable to those of working age who are unemployed but actively seeking employment), and some forms of income support (the state benefit for those with no other income and who do not need to look for work). Housing benefit and council tax benefit are not taxable.

Two forms of benefit are never taxable: first, the benefits to the disabled such as disabled living allowance; second, benefits payable for children, of which child benefit is the most important. As it is also now administered by HMRC and is in effect a precondition for receiving child tax credit, the following briefly outlines the benefit.

Child benefit

9–10   Child benefit is a weekly non-contributory flat-rate benefit payable on a claim by any person in the UK who is responsible for a child in the UK. It is payable by and under ss.141–147 of the Social Security Contributions and Benefits Act 1992. A "child" is anyone under 16 and also those under 19 receiving full-time education other than higher education. A person is "responsible for" a child or children if either the children are living with the person in that week or he or she is contributing to the cost of providing for that child at a minimum of at least the same amount as the child benefit. In addition both the child and the person responsible must be in the UK, save for limited absences Child benefit is not taxable. It is normally paid monthly into a bank account.

Because the rules are straightforward and obviously aimed at bringing immediate cash income into the home of every child in the country, they rarely cause difficulties. But child benefit is only payable once for any week for any child, and disputes can occur about who should get the benefit. There are also clear rules for this. The benefit cannot be shared—it is payable to one person only. As between two or more rival claimants, the mother will almost always have the better claim if the child is living with her at least part of the time, even in preference to the child's father when he is also her husband. In other cases preference is given to the claimant with whom the children live most of the time.

Tax credits

Two forms of tax credit were introduced under the Tax Credits Act 2002. "Tax credit" is one of those labels that sound so attractive that there is a temptation to overuse it. Some care therefore must be taken to sort out what it means. When paid with a dividend from a UK company, it means a notional amount of tax with which the shareholder is credited when being taxed on the dividend. A foreign tax credit means, in connection with double taxation, an amount of foreign income tax paid by a taxpayer that can be set directly off against income tax owed by that taxpayer in the UK on the same income. But the credit can never exceed the UK tax payable, so it is in reality not a credit but a deduction. An R&D tax credit means a deduction from the tax payable by someone in respect of expenditure on approved research and development costs. But again it is not really a credit, but rather a deduction.

9–11

The key difference is that a deduction may reduce or entirely remove tax liability, but it cannot result in a repayment. If a credit exceeds the income tax payable, then the taxpayer is entitled to receive the difference. Tax credits under the Tax Credits Act 2002 are, in that sense, truly credits—you can receive more credit than you pay in tax. The problem is whether they are actually anything to do with tax at all, or are social security payments better just referred to as "credits" like the state pension credit.

There is a further confusion in names because of the growing practice of referring to additional income tax deductions by reference to the underlying benefit in kind. Many taxpayers now find "benefits" on their tax coding notices such as "car benefit", "car fuel benefit", and "employer's loan benefit". This is a new label for an adjustment to the tax coding to reflect the tax payable on these forms of benefits in kind under the benefits code. That can be confusing when considered alongside housing benefit and industrial injuries benefit, both of which are weekly social security payments.

For the current forms of tax credit, we are unlikely to get a better name. This is not merely "spinning" the name of the payment to make it sound better. It represents a genuine problem in classification. Child tax credit is in reality an earnings-related addition to child benefit whether or not the recipients are working and is very probably a social security payment. Nonetheless, besides replacing previous social security benefits it also replaces an income tax allowance (children's tax credit). So it has a tax element too. Working tax credit is altogether more confusing. This is because part at least of the entitlement to working tax credit may not have much to do with income tax, but it also has little to do with social security either. It is (to borrow from a name of a former special tax) a negative selective employment tax for the lower-paid, designed to boost the pay packet of those with low earnings by using the extended form of the PAYE system on which we commented in the last chapter.

Child tax credit

9–12   Child tax credit (CTC) could be described as "child benefit plus" in the light of the above discussion about fashionable words. In nearly every case it is an additional payment to go with the child benefit payable for a child and payable to the same person that claims the child benefit for that child. The difference is that child benefit is a universal flat-rate weekly benefit, while CTC is income-based, adjusted to specific circumstances of the child and claimant, and payable for a tax year.

The "tax" significance of CTC becomes clear immediately when attention is paid to how the income of the claimant is worked out. It is, with a few tweaks, based on the income of the claimant for income tax purposes for that year or the previous year. Further, unlike most of our income-related social security benefits, any capital held by the claimant is ignored. So is any income or capital of the child. The most important difference in practice from both child benefit and income tax is that if the child is living with both parents (or with a couple both or either of whom are responsible for the child) then the couple must make a joint claim for CTC. Where a joint claim is made, the income of both claimants is taken into account. In the straightforward case where the child is living with both his or her parents, then both must claim. The only preference given to the mother is that the payment is in practice made not to the main earner but to the main carer and HMRC usually finds or assumes that this is the mother. The details are in the Child Tax Credits Regulations 2002 (SI 2002/2007).

CTC is made up of a number of "elements". All claimants are entitled to a family element, worth £545 a year (and double that if the child is less than a year old). There is then an element for each child in the family, worth a further £2,085. If the child is disabled, then the element is worth £4,265 or for severely disabled children £5,645. So a couple claiming for their three children, one of whom is born in the year, receives elements worth £7,345 plus any disablement additions. **9–13**

If the claiming couple have minimal or no income (other than jobseeker's allowance or income support), then the main carer of them will receive the £7,345 in regular cash payments. The dividing line for the benefits is that if either of the couple works for 16 or more hours a week, then neither income support nor jobseeker's allowance can be claimed. This is the same borderline as that for working tax credit, as we shall see. But it does not matter for CTC whether the claimants are working or not, save that income is taken into account.

If the couple are earning, then their joint incomes will be worked out in accordance with the rules in the Tax Credits (Definition and Calculation of Income) Regulations 2002 (SI 2002/2006).

The couple will receive the full amount of CTC if their total income does not exceed a lower threshold. They will receive the family element in full unless their income exceeds a higher threshold. The lower threshold is £15,575 and the higher threshold is £50,000. Where the income exceeds the thresholds, then the amount of CTC reduces by 39 per cent of the excess. For example, if the couple both work and have an income of £20,000, then their full entitlement of £7,345 is reduced by 39 per cent of (20,000–15,575), or £1,725, so they receive £5,620 cash credit. This is in addition to the tax free child benefit worth £18.80 a week for the first child and £12.55 each for the other two. That is a total credit and benefit entitlement of £7,902, though there will of course be income tax and NI contributions to pay.

Because the higher threshold is at £50,000, most families receive the £545 family element in addition to their child benefit.

Working tax credit

There are four different ways in which claimants can claim WTC. In each case the claimant (or joint claimants) must be working at least 16 hours a week. They are: **9–14**

- the claimant is responsible for a child;
- the claimant is disadvantaged in the employment market by disablement;
- the claimant is aged over 25 and works at least 30 hours a week;
- the claimant is aged over 50 and has come back into work after a period on benefit.

The most important of these categories of claimant is the couple or lone parent with children. A claim for WTC is of particular advantage to a lone parent, or to a couple both of whom are working, because the claim can include a child care element. In all other cases a claimant is entitled to a basic element of £1,800. A couple or lone parent also receive a further £1,770 second adult or lone parent element. If the claimant (or a couple between them) works more than 30 hours weekly, then a 30 hour element of £735 is added. The disability element is £2,405 with an additional severe disability element of £1,020. The 50 plus element is £1,840 if the claimant works over 30 hours a week, and £1,235 in other cases.

Parents can then claim a child care element of up to 80 per cent of approved child care costs of up to £300 a week for more than one child or £175 for a single child.

There is only one income threshold for WTFC, and it is much lower than the CTC lower threshold. For 2008–09 it is £6,420.

9–15   Will WTC help our couple from the CTC example? Assuming they both work, and that together they work over 30 hours a week, then they receive the basic element (£1,800), the second adult element (£1,770), the 30 hour element (£735) and potentially a child care element. Just for the sake of the example, we will award them the maximum possible child care element of 80 per cent of £15,600, or £12,480. (In practice, they may not be able to afford that). Total WTC entitlement is therefore £16,785. But, of course, their earnings are £20,000 and the threshold is £6,420. But they only lose 39 per cent of the excess, so they are entitled to WTC of £8,283 to help pay the child care costs. But, in addition, because they get *some* WTC, they get *all* the CTC—an additional £5,620. Add to that the child benefit, and HMRC will pay them a total of £16,185 tax free in credits and benefit. Perhaps they could afford some child care.

CHAPTER 10

SAVINGS AND INVESTMENT INCOME

Introduction

This chapter deals with what is for most individuals an untidy **10–01** and complex area of their tax affairs—the taxation of non-earned, non-business income. This is both untidy and complex for a series of reasons. Traditionally, different kinds of savings and investments have different tax treatments. Interest from certain kinds of savings were treated one way while other kinds of savings were treated in others. Then there was a different treatment again for dividends from shares in British companies and another for dividends from shares in foreign companies. Yet other rules applied to income in the form of annuities from capital invested in other ways.

Things are complicated further because of conflicting political and economic aims behind the tax laws. We are encouraged to save. So the income from some forms of savings are tax exempt. But we are only encouraged to save in certain ways, so other kinds of savings income have been subjected to higher taxes rather than lower taxes. At one time, for example, there was a rate of income tax called an investment income surcharge. By contrast, in 2008 the lowest rate of income tax applies only to some kinds of savings and cannot apply to earned income.

There is also the complication that people can gain from their savings by receiving capital gains instead of income. That is a considerable additional complication and we look at it in some detail later in the book.

We can quickly remove another complication. Pensions are not regarded as income from savings or investments even if that is what they actually are. The tax treatment of all forms of pension, including those purchased with capital sums, is now regulated by ITEPA and the Finance Act 2004. We discussed this in Ch.9.

To get the full picture, it is therefore necessary to look at the way in which savings income is taxed, then at the rates at which it is taxed, then at the rules of capital gains tax. In this chapter we look at the way the income is taxed, and at some of the main exemptions from tax. We set out the special rates in Ch.12.

10–02   None of these rules apply to UK resident companies. They do not pay tax (income tax or corporation tax) on dividends and distributions from other UK companies. Most of the other forms of income from their investments are taxed to corporation tax under special rules for receipts from loan relationships. These capture both income receipts and capital receipts from both UK investments and foreign investments and treat them in the same way. We deal with this in Ch.13.

10–03   The tax laws setting out the income tax treatment of income from savings and investments were rewritten completely for all individuals by the Income Tax (Trading and Other Income) Act 2005 (ITTOIA), Part 4 (Savings and Investment Income) and Part 6 (Exempt Income). The Act dealt with each kind of income and exemption in order of practical importance. It is useful to look at each chapter of Part 4 and then Part 6 to see what is covered. We must then look at some of the most important parts in more detail.

Part 4 covers:

- Interest
- Dividends and other kinds of distribution from UK companies
- Dividends and similar payments from non-UK resident companies
- Stock dividends from UK companies—that is, the issue of new shares instead of dividends or as an addition to a shareholding
- Sums released from loans made to individuals participating in a close company—this is to stop avoidance by schemes where money is loaned by small closely controlled companies to one of the owners and then the debt owed to the company is released or reduced
- Purchased life annuity payments—part of these payments are a return of the capital sum used to purchase the annuity while other part is income, so special rules are needed to separate the parts
- Income or capital sums generated from other specialised forms of savings instrument also require special rules, including in particular gains from life insurance

10–04   Part 6 sets out the main general exemptions from income tax applying to this kind of income. This is one of the areas of law where people try to impress others by giving things long complicated sounding names and then shortening them to a series of initials that only the initiate understand.

Part 6 contains special rules about:

- NS&I (National Savings and Investments) income exemptions
- Income from individual investment plans (better known as ISAs or individual savings accounts, and previously TESSAs)
- SAYE interest (interest from Save As You Earn savings plans)
- Dividends from VCTs, or venture capital trusts—a relief for shareholders who invest in smaller companies that are set up to undertake a new business
- FOTRAs—should be FOTTTNRITUKs, but that doesn't look as good—these cover income from securities that are Free Of Tax to Residents Abroad (or, rather, To Those Not Resident In The UK)
- Purchased life annuities (again—these add to the rules in Part 4)
- Other annual payments, and
- Other income—and, yes, there is a difference between these last two

Interest

Section 369(1) of ITTOIA has almost a beauty in its simplicity: **10–05**

"Income tax is charged on interest".

Sections 370 and 371 have a similar starkness. The tax is charged on the full amount of interest arising in the tax year. And the person liable is the person receiving or entitled to the interest.

The beauty starts to disappear swiftly when we turn to s.372. This tells us that "any dividend paid by a building society is treated as interest for the purposes of this Act." And it adds, spoiling the magic totally, that "dividend includes any distribution whether or not described as a dividend".

There follow a series of similar provisions ending with s.381. That informs us that "all discounts, other than discounts in deeply discounted securities, are treated as interest for the purposes of this Act."

Then we notice something missing. There is no definition of "interest". And don't go looking in the impressive Sch.4 list of defined expressions. The only definition of "interest" there is one that applies only to SAYE schemes—for which interest includes any bonus—and, anyway, does not define the term. Interest can be defined as the payment made by a borrower or debtor of money to the lender or creditor for the use of the money by reference to time. For most forms of saving that approach causes no problems. Both short-term loans such as those for the use of funds on a credit card or long term loans such as mortgages are expressly charged at a rate of interest.

In the straightforward case, I borrow £1,000 and pay, say, 10 per cent interest per annum on it. In commercial situations there may be fees, discounts and other variants. So, for example, I pay a facility fee of £100 to the lender for the loan or I receive the loan under a discount, so that I only get £900 of the £1,000 but have to pay the full £1,000 back. There are often good tax reasons (but VAT and corporation tax, not income tax reasons) for these arrangements. In practice they need not trouble us because the rules governing financial services largely prevent individuals lending money in such a way as to run into these problems. With that realisation, we can return to admire the simplicity of provisions that cause few practical problems.

10–06   We must add one important rider to this discussion. The Finance Act 2008 now recognises the problems involved in Islamic finance. Under some forms of religious belief it is wrong to earn interest on money. But it is not wrong to make arrangements so that the benefit of credit is recognised in other ways. This causes another problem. It is a major aim of taxation that it applies neutrally to all forms of income. So income tax must apply to any kind of income reward in a similar way.

Exempt interest
10–07   Another major reason why taxation of interest causes few practical problems is that most people hold savings in forms of security or investment that are exempt from tax. These exemptions are available to all of us. You will find all the details you need about individual forms of tax-exempt savings advertised by those who want to encourage you to save with them. But here is a quick guide to the main forms.

10–08   NATIONAL SAVINGS AND INVESTMENTS   The Treasury has power to exempt income or similar payments received from investments in government savings. A popular version of these schemes is the Premium Bond. Some bright person spotted that if you paid all the interest on a government bond issue into a prize fund rather than to the investors, and then gave some of the savers prizes instead of interest, you were giving them gambling winnings and not interest. That is not subject to income tax. Further, if you gave one or two of them large prizes, then you will attract wide interest (in another sense of the word). Then invent ERNIE (the electronic random number indicator equipment) to decide who gets the prizes and you have a winner—for the Treasury, that is. It is also in practice regarded as a winner by the many investors who put up to the maximum £30,000 into the fund. They pay no income tax on their winnings. (They don't count for tax credits either, making families with savings even bigger winners). The first £70 of income from National Savings Bank accounts are also free of income tax. And special tax exempt terms also apply to investments in National Savings Certificates. Together these schemes attract substantial levels of savings lent direct by individuals to the government (and therefore even safer than houses, as the saying goes). £50 billion savings bonds and £36 billion premium bonds were held in 2008.

ISAs Any individual can also put savings of up to £7,200   **10–09**
into an Individual Savings Accounts with a bank, buildings society or similar body each year and receive the interest from it free of income tax. ISAs are designed to encourage people to save generally, and not just with the Treasury. They are heavily advertised, as are the limits and conditions that apply to an ISA, so we need not set out more details here. In the past there were other forms of this scheme. Lovers of initials may like to note the immediate predecessor was TESSA (Tax Exempt Special Savings Account). But she has now morphed into ISA. Total ISA savings topped £180 billion in 2008.

SAYE Save As You Earn schemes are arrangements allowing   **10–10**
employees to buy shares in the employer company. The individual agrees to buy shares in the company under a share option scheme. This will usually allow the individual to buy the shares at some date in the future at a set or reduced price as compared with the market price. For example, the individual agrees to buy the shares in five years time at the current market price. The individual then enters a savings scheme to make regular contributions to save up the sum needed to exercise the option and buy the shares. This can give the individual a double advantage. The shares can be purchased at a discount if the shares gain in value during the period while the individual is saving, and the interest paid while he or she is saving is tax exempt.

Collecting income tax on interest

10–11   Another reason why these rules cause few practical problems is that where interest is subject to income tax the withholding tax rules usually apply. The bank, building society or similar organisation paying the interest is required to deduct income tax from it at the basic rate and account to HMRC directly for it. So the individual will receive the interest net of income tax. That has the practical advantage for the Treasury that there is limited scope for avoidance. It also receives the tax as the interest is paid and not, under the general rules, only at the end of the tax year. It also has the more general advantage that government departments generally can be kept informed of people's savings. For example, an individual claiming housing benefit without disclosing his or her savings may get a nasty surprise when the local authority asks for an explanation of why the council was not told about money held in such and such an account. The council will have found this out by cross-checking the individual's details with the HMRC records and found that tax has been deducted at source. So there has been no income tax avoidance, but another form of avoidance can also be stopped.

There is, however, another kind of tax advantage that can be offered here to taxpayers. Some forms of savings account are subject to income tax, but not to deduction at source. This means that the tax is paid only when it becomes due some time after the end of the tax year (for details see Ch.12). But the lender still has to tell the Treasury about the payment even when not collecting the tax.

10–12   One way round all these rules is to put money into an overseas investment, so that the interest is paid by a foreign bank not subject to the disclosure rules. That starts to get complicated, but it is worth noting even in an introduction to the subject that the common currency of the Euro assists such schemes, as does the complete removal of exchange controls over the last 30 years. This was a problem that could not have occurred even in the 1970s. But we are now in the European Union, and we are all entitled to the freedom of movement of our capital. The resultant problems are now being met by Europe-wide laws requiring either deduction of interest at source in all cases or as an alternative a report to all EU governments about interest paid to their citizens.

Dividends and distributions

10–13   Section 383(1) of ITTOIA charges income tax on dividends and other distributions received by an individual from a UK resident company. Subsection (2) provides that dividends and distributions are to be treated as income for these purposes. Subsection 383(3) adds an important rider. The fact that a distribution is capital" apart from subsection(s) "does not matter". In other words, requirements of company law that certain payments may only be made as capital do not apply for income tax purposes.

This section alerts us to the need to keep the law about the taxation of dividends separate from the company law provisions about dividends. In practice, to be a dividend or distribution, the payment must be made in accordance with company law provisions. So, for example, a payment out of a one-share company to the company's single shareholder/director/employee is technically only a dividend if the relevant formalities have been met. If they are not met, it may be open for argument that the payment that is said to be a dividend is in fact a payment of earnings (and so subject both to taxation under ITEPA and PAYE, and also NI contributions), or a loan.

10–14

Double taxation of dividends

There is also a theoretical problem of fairness involved in the taxation of dividends. Company law requires that the company paying the dividend must pay it from its profits. But corporation tax must be paid on those profits. So the dividend will normally be paid by the company from taxed income. And the company cannot deduct corporation tax as an expense when paying the dividend. Nor, the other way round, can it deduct the dividend when paying corporation tax on its profits. So to tax the dividend in the hands of the shareholder is to tax it a second time.

10–15

Is that fair? As always, that depends on what is meant by fairness. If that means equal treatment of the payments by the company to the recipient, then it can be argued to be unfair. Compare what happens when the same company pays interest to a stockholder and a dividend to a shareholder. The company can deduct the cost of the interest from its profits, and therefore pays the interest as a deductible expense. So when it pays the stockholder it is paying out of income that has not been subject to tax. If the stockholder is the same individual as the shareholder, then he or she will receive one form of income from the company subject to tax only once and the other subject to double tax.

In past times, this double taxation was ignored by the income tax system. Then it was taken into account by a system known as advance corporation tax or ACT. Thankfully for the student (but not the taxpayer) the complications of ACT have now been repealed and we need not waste time on them. What came into replace ACT was a special reduced rate of tax on dividends. It is a partial recognition of the double taxation that comes about when an individual receives a taxable dividend. The details are in Ch.12.

Tax exempt dividends

10–16   Individuals can avoid all taxation on dividends in the same way as with savings if they hold them through tax savings schemes. The main general provision is by using an ISA in the same way as for investing money in tax-free interest bearing accounts. Again, details are widely available from those who run the schemes and we need not repeat details here. As those details show, they allow investors to invest up to a set amount each year in stocks and shares without having to pay income tax on the dividends. But in practice the reduced income tax rates on dividends have meant that there is no real advantage for many taxpayers in doing this.

There are other schemes to exempt taxation where the shares are held by an employee in an employer share scheme. If the shares are held in an approved share incentive plan (or SIP for short) then dividends can, subject to limits, avoid tax both as earnings (under ITEPA) and under these provisions. However, there will be a charge to income tax under these provisions if any dividend is paid over as a cash dividend rather than held in the scheme.

Dividends and other payments from foreign companies

10–17   These are also subject to income tax, but they present different practical and theoretical problems to dividends paid from UK companies. This is because any tax payable by the company on its profits will be paid to a foreign tax authority. In addition, the foreign tax authority many have imposed a withholding tax on the payment of the dividend. So the UK resident shareholder will not be able to argue that tax has already been paid on the profits to the Treasury. And the individual may have suffered foreign tax on the dividend itself.

You will not find the solution to these problems in ITTOIA. They are to be found in the individual provisions of the bilateral double tax agreements that the UK government has concluded with over 100 other countries. The details vary from agreement to agreement and are beyond the scope of this introduction. You need note only that the terms of those agreements, when concluded in proper form, override the terms of ITTOIA, and so may stop the double taxation in the sense of tax by two different national tax authorities.

The same point—the application of double tax agreements overriding ITTOIA—also applies to interest and all other forms of savings income.

Annuities

Many annuities arise under a will or similar instrument of gift. These are taxed as "pure profit income". But it is perfectly possible to buy an annuity "in the market". These purchased life annuities, or some of them, have a special rule applying to them. The capital content of each periodic payment to the annuitant is exempt from income tax. The capital is found (putting it broadly) by dividing the purchase price of the annuity by the normal expectation of life of the annuitant, calculated at the date when the annuity begins. Once the calculation has been made the figure remains constant for every year. Income tax is charged each year on the amount by which the annuity payment exceeds this capital content, whether or not the annuitant survives for the period of normal expectation.

10–18

Other forms of non-earned income

This is a big heading, but it is a short reminder of a few short sections dealt with in Ch.7, and what they do not include. That is where we discussed the sections that tax annual payments and also any other kind of income that is not charged anywhere else in the tax legislation. But we see there that they also have limits.

10–19

There is no general definition of income tax. We have said it before, and we do not apologise for repeating it. So there may be forms of income that are not caught by those sections and are therefore not subject to income tax.

The provisions about employment income are broad enough to catch anything received by an individual because of his or her employment (whether or not he or she receives it as capital in finance terms). The provisions about trading income catch anything arising from a trade if it is income, not capital. And the same rules apply to any property business if again it is earned income. So no residual provision is needed for any form of earned income.

As this and other chapters show, the approach to non-earned income is not covered by similar broad provisions linking the receipt to a source in such a way as to make anything from that source subject to income tax. So we need to remind ourselves that there may be forms of unearned income that are not subject to income tax. Further, as the history of anti-avoidance provisions in our tax laws show (because, again, we have no general anti-avoidance provision), if there are gaps, people will find them and use them. Then, if the gaps are too big, Parliament will block them. But the hunt still goes on, and it can still be successful. It just gets harder each year now that you are required to share your clever ideas with HMRC under the disclosure regime so that they can (and will) bring forward blocking measures under a convenient Finance Act.

Tax credits

10–20   The rule for inclusion of income in the calculation of the total income of individuals for tax credits follows in general terms the same rules as for income tax. The most important aspect of this is that individuals can also use ISAs, Premium Bonds and other tax advantages to reduce their income for tax credits purposes as well as income tax purposes. So someone who is liable to income tax at the basis rate and also has income such that he or she is getting only part of the tax credit entitlement will gain substantially by saving (if they can afford to save) through, say, an ISA. For example, £10 earned in interest through an ISA account will be free of income tax (saving £2) and will not count for tax credit purposes (avoiding a reduction in tax credit payable of £3.70), so earning £10 from the investment rather than just £4.30.

CHAPTER 11

THE TAXATION OF TRUSTS AND ESTATES

Introduction

We need to look now at the way in which the income tax system works in relation to trusts and to the estates of deceased individuals.

11–01

In the general law—quite apart from tax law—there is a fundamental difference between the position of a person entitled to income of a residuary estate and a person entitled to income arising under a trust. The former is not entitled to anything until it is paid to him or at least appropriated to him: see *Corbett v IRC* (1938), CA. The latter is entitled to his share of the income of the trust from its inception, or, more strictly, to his share of the income of the investments which constitute the trust fund: see *Baker v Archer-Shee* (1927), HL.

We will look at the two situations in turn and then at charities.

Trust income

The existence of trusts causes great difficulties for tax legislators and for everyone else connected with tax, including students of tax law. Tax law would be very much simpler if there were no trusts. Lest that statement sound naive it may be pointed out that trusts fulfil a prominent role in tax planning. Nevertheless, many civil law countries do not recognise the concept of trusts. The subject is additionally complicated in Britain because Scottish trusts law is as developed as, but is markedly different from, English trusts law. Scottish lawyers rightly resent the fact that the (English-drafted) provisions in tax statutes are often passed in ignorance of Scottish law, although the provisions are supposed to work evenly on both sides of the border. But even confining ourselves to English law, the difficulties in squaring our trusts laws and our tax laws are considerable: for inheritance tax they have proved fiendish.

For income tax there is a kind of two-tier system: to some

11–02

extent income tax is charged on the trustees; to some extent it is charged on the beneficiary.

Tax payable by trustees

11–03   Trustees are not companies, so not liable to corporation tax. But they are also not "individuals" for the purposes of income tax. Consequently, they are in principle liable only to the basic rate of income tax on, for example, trading profits they receive, or income from investments. On the other hand, they are not entitled to personal allowances and reliefs. Generally, they are not liable to the higher rate of income tax, or the starting rate. But recently, with one eye on simplicity and the other on avoidance, trusts have been made subject to their own set of tax rates.

Exemption of first slice of income

11–04   Section 491 of ITA exempts from income tax the first £1,000 of trust income in any year. This is a simplification measure. Calculating income tax on trusts is not easy for the trustees, and chasing small trusts is a waste of time for HMRC officials. The apparent generosity of this exemption removes all small trusts from income tax altogether, so reducing the caseload for HMRC by about one third. Little local charities benefitting from what is left of the savings of a long dead benefactor no longer need to fill in endless forms to avoid tax.

The trust rate and dividend trust rate

11–05   Section 9 of ITA sets two special rates of tax for trusts. The trust rate is currently 40 per cent (the same rate as the higher rate) and the dividend trust rate is 32.5 per cent (the same as the dividend upper rate). Section 15 directs us to ss.479 and following for the details of when these apply. Section 479 applies the trust and dividend trust rates to non-charitable accumulation or discretionary trusts. Sections 481 and 482 set out a list of other situations when income received by trustees of non-charitable trusts is taxable at these higher rates.

The application of these rates is intended to prevent income being accumulated in a trust, or distributed by a trust, so as to avoid the individual's higher rate (or dividend upper rate) by deflecting the income elsewhere. It also prevents trusts postponing payment of tax by investing sums tax-free. It means that income can only be accumulated after the appropriate higher rate of income tax has been paid.

Note that these rates apply to the whole of the trust income after expenses and the first slice. So trustees of these trusts may end up paying more income tax on the trust income than a beneficiary would have done if the trust had not been interposed.

Trust expenses

The imposition of higher rates of tax directly on trusts highlighted the potential unfairness of the previous rule that trustees could not deduct trust expenses when paying income tax. There was an implicit trade-off between the lower rate of tax and the absence of allowable expenses for larger trusts. Removing one side of that trade-off meant that it was appropriate also to allow some expenses. Section 484 now allows trustees to deduct their expenses provided that they are not otherwise allowable (for example because they are trading expenses of a trade carried on by the trustees) and that they are properly chargeable to income. These expenses can be deducted both in calculating the taxable income of small trusts for the purposes of the exemption of the first slice, and also when calculating how much tax is payable at the trust rate or trust dividend rate.

Tax on beneficiaries

A beneficiary's income from a trust forms part of total income for determining reliefs and the rate of tax. It would be nice and neat if one could say that one works out the beneficiary's tax bill and then gives a straight credit for the tax already paid by the trustees. Unfortunately this is not precisely so. There is a case called *Macfarlane v IRC* (1929) (Ct. Sess.) which held that although trust expenses are not deductible in computing the trustees' income, they are deductible in computing the beneficiary's income. That position now, with the advent of the trust rate, is more complicated, because although trust expenses are not deductible in computing the trust's liability to basic rate tax, they are deductible in computing the trust's liability to tax which arises from the difference between the rate applicable to trusts and the lower or basic rate. Indeed, to further compound this complication, such expenses must normally be set off, in the first instance, against savings income. However, one can say this: the tax charge on the beneficiary *takes into account* (to some extent) the tax already charged on the trustees!

Income to which a beneficiary is *entitled* forms part of total income whether or not it is received. This follows from the general principle stated above, namely that a beneficiary who is entitled at all is entitled from the very inception of the trust. Of course this principle does not apply to a discretionary trust; if there is a discretion whether to pay any particular beneficiary, there is no entitlement until the discretion is exercised. When a sum is actually paid to such a beneficiary that sum forms part of his total income and is taxed, unless it is an annuity, in the same way as savings income. Whether one is talking of a fixed trust or a discretionary trust, payments in kind may, just as much as money payments, constitute income. This would be so, for example of a right to occupy a house rent free.

A payment may perfectly well be income in the hands of a beneficiary, even although it is made out of the capital (and not the income) of the trust. However, a payment out of capital does not become income in the hands of a beneficiary simply because it is to be used for an income purpose by that beneficiary (see *Stevenson v Wishart* (1987), CA).

11–09   An important tax point arises in connection with income which is accumulated by a trust. One has to make a distinction here between a vested interest and a contingent interest. This is a matter of general law rather than tax law and it involves some fairly complicated points. But broadly the distinction is that a vested interest is one which (generally) cannot be upset, whereas a contingent interest is one which is dependent on some contingency happening. The clearest example is where a trust provides that X is to have a certain interest under the trust when he attains a certain age. As X may never attain that age the interest is until then contingent. When X has attained that age the interest becomes vested. (A person may attain a vested interest in income before attaining, or without ever attaining, a vested interest in the capital of the fund.) For a person who has a vested interest in the income of a trust, that income (as has been said above) forms part of total income, and that is so even if it is not in fact received. But for a person who has only a contingent interest, until that contingency occurs, the income of the trust is not income. It follows that if the trust's income is accumulated it is not his income and it does not become so even if the contingency occurs (e.g. attaining the age of 18) and the accumulations are paid. The payments reach the beneficiary as capital. The leading authority on this point is *Stanley v IRC* (1944), CA.

11–10   With effect from 2004, there is specific legislation to protect trusts for the disadvantaged from paying more tax than the disadvantaged individual would pay personally.

Tax on settlors

We must now consider the detailed rules relating to settle- **11–11**
ments which are intended to curb the use of settlements for tax
avoidance. Section 620 of ITTOIA provides that for the purposes of Ch.5 of Part 20 a settlement includes "any disposition,
trust, covenant, agreement, arrangement or transfer of assets".
Broadly speaking, this encompasses two types of settlement,
namely, income settlements and capital settlements. An income
settlement is a settlement which involves the transfer of income
only, e.g. a covenant. A capital settlement is a settlement which
involves the transfer of income-producing property, e.g. a trust.
An income settlement is the handing-over of fruits; a capital
settlement is the handing-over of a fruit tree. An income settlement may provide for payment to trustees or for payment direct
to the beneficiary; a capital settlement necessarily involves
trustees. In neither instance, however, can a transaction constitute a settlement unless there is an element of bounty; a bona
fide commercial transaction is not a settlement for the purposes
of Part XV (see *IRC v Plummer* (1979), HL and *Chinn v Collins*
(1981), HL). Special rules are applied to both forms of settlement by Ch.5 of Part 5 of ITTOIA.

The background to that chapter is that settlements, histori- **11–12**
cally, have been a favourite means of tax avoidance, particularly
when individuals faced high marginal rates of tax. Indeed, in the
absence of statutory intervention, the potential for tax-saving
through settlements is self-evident—any settlement would
enable an individual with a high rate of tax to unload income on
to a comparatively poor member of the family to the advantage
of the family viewed as a whole, because the poor member has a
lower rate of tax or may not be liable to tax at all. Not surprisingly, therefore, governments have over the years sought to
counteract the fiscal efficacy of settlements.

The rules in Ch.5 are the most recent attempt. Where
applicable, the rules deem income arising under a settlement
during the life of the settlor to be the income of the settlor for *all*
income tax purposes. In such instances, the income is treated as
arising first in the settlement and then as being transferred to or
reverting to the settlor.

The important phrase, however, is "where applicable" for
many income settlements (annual payments) made by individuals are denied any effect for income tax purposes. Therefore,
in respect of such settlements, the rules in Ch.5 are redundant.

The rules in Ch.5 fall into three categories: **11–13**

(1) rules which apply where the settlor (or spouse or civil partner) retains an interest in the settled property (ss.624–28);

(2) rules which apply where a benefit is received by unmarried minor children from a parental settlement (ss.629–32);

(3) rules which apply where the settlor (or his spouse or civil partner) has received a capital sum from the settlement (ss.633–37).

We deal first with the strict provisions dealing with settlements of income (which normally take the form of a covenant or will trust), and then the more usual settlements of capital.

Income settlements

11–14   The ITTOIA provisions about annual payments stop most forms of income settlements (chiefly covenants) being effective to avoid income tax. The income of the payer is computed for income tax purposes without any deduction for the payments. Where they do not apply to an annual payment, the income will be treated as the income of the settlor (payer) under s.625, unless he can show that the income arises from property in which he has no interest or that the income is expressly excluded from the operation of s.625. In the latter respect, s.625 does not apply to income paid under a settlement by one party to a marriage to provide for the other after divorce, annulment or separation to the extent that the income is payable for the benefit of that other (s.626). This applies in a similar way to civil partners. In addition, s.627 provides that income which consists of annual payments made by an individual for bona fide commercial reasons in connection with his trade, profession or vocation or qualifying charitable donations falls outside s.625.

Capital settlements

Settlements where the settlor retains an interest

11–15   Broadly, s.625 of the Taxes Act deems all income arising under a settlement during the life of the settlor to be the *income of the settlor* for all income tax purposes unless the income arises from property in which the settlor has no interest.

The settlor is treated as having an interest where that property or any derived property (see s.626) is, or will or may become, payable to or for the benefit of the settlor or spouse or partner in any circumstances whatsoever. Section 625(4) provides that a spouse or partner of the settlor does *not* include a prospective or separated spouse or a widow or widower. Thus, it is the existence of the interest which attracts the charge to tax under s.625 and, perhaps, the most compelling example of where such an interest exists is where a settlement can be revoked and, on revocation, property reverts to the settlor or spouse (but note *IRC v Wolfson* (1949), HL).

The full scope of the section was tested before the House of Lords in *Jones v Garnett* (2007), known as the Arctic Systems case. Mr Jones set up a small company called Arctic Systems Ltd. He used it as a legal basis for his business as an IT consultant. There were two ordinary shares in the company. He held one and his wife held the other. In 1999–2000 the company earned nearly £80,000. It paid Mr Jones a salary of £6,000, and Mrs Jones a salary of £4,000, and made a profit of £26,000. After paying corporation tax of about £5,000, it paid a dividend that was said to be £25,000 to each shareholder for the year. It was accepted that this was to avoid National Insurance contributions and higher rate tax on Mr Jones.

11–16

The Revenue assessed Mr Jones on Mrs Jones' dividend under s.660A of the 1988 Act (now s.625). In the Revenue's view, on the grounds that this was a settlement of the one share by Mr Jones on Mrs Jones under that section. The House of Lords unanimously agreed that this was a settlement within the scope of the section. Mr Jones had given his wife the share in a situation that only made sense as a non-commercial transaction. But the Jones' plans were rescued by what was s.660A(6) (and is now s.626). This provides an exception to the charge under the section for outright gifts between husband and wife unless what is given is wholly or substantially a right to income. The House of Lords held this applied, as an ordinary share is not just a right to income. And it noted that this exception came in at the same time as separate taxation of husband and wife was introduced. That may explain why some call this the "husband and wife tax".

This is another case where judicial views varied as the appeal went up through the courts. Their lordships recognised this by conducting a survey of the case law of these sections. It is the best place to start studying these provisions in detail. The case also brings home just how wide these sections are. However, the government has announced it will reverse *Jones v Garrett* by legislation in 2009.

The operation of this is limited by subs.(2) and (3) by virtue of which the settlor is not to be regarded as having an interest if his or her interest can only take effect on the occurrence of certain

11–17

specified events, e.g. the bankruptcy of a person who is or may become entitled to the property or any derived property or on the death at any age of a child of the settlor who had become beneficially entitled to the property or any derived property at an age not exceeding 25. In addition, the section does not apply to the income arising under a settlement by one party to a marriage to provide for the other after divorce, annulment or separation to the extent that the income is payable for the benefit of that other (and likewise for civil partners).

If the section applies, the settlor is charged to tax, and the income is treated as the highest part of income. However, the settlor may recover any tax so paid from the trustees or any other person to whom the income is payable under the settlement (s.646).

Benefits received by unmarried minor children from parental settlements

11–18   Generally, any income arising under a settlement which is paid during the life of the settlor to or for the benefit of an unmarried minor (including a stepchild or illegitimate child) of the settlor is treated by s.629 of ITTOIA for all income tax purposes as the income of the settlor. However, this will not apply where the income is treated as the income of the settlor under s.624, nor will it apply where the income paid to a child under such a parental settlement does not exceed, in total, £100 in any tax year.

11–19   In addition, if income arising under a capital settlement in favour of the settlor's unmarried minor children is retained or accumulated by the trustees such income is not treated by reason of s.631 as income of the settlor. In certain circumstances, such a capital accumulation settlement can be used to secure tax savings for the family when it is viewed as a whole. For example, if the accumulated income belongs to the beneficiary because she has a vested interest, e.g. when capital is settled for a minor absolutely, there may be liability to basic rate tax, but this will, broadly speaking, have been borne by the trustees. Section 568 of ITTOIA (imposing the trust rates of tax) does not apply because the income belongs to the beneficiary. Moreover, depending on her other income and allowances, the beneficiary may be able to recover tax paid by the trustees so that the income as long as it remains within the settlement (or is distributed after the beneficiary has reached 18 or married under 18) will in some instances be free of income tax. However, if the beneficiary's interest is contingent, the accumulated income does *not* belong to him.

Income which is not accumulated but distributed is caught by **11–20** s.629. This will be so, for example, where income is applied for the child's maintenance, education or benefit under s.31 of the Trustee Act 1925. And it is no good the trustees thinking that they can avoid s.629 by accumulating income and using capital for maintenance, etc. of the unmarried minor beneficiary. This device is stopped by s.631 which provides that any sum whatsoever paid out for the benefit of an unmarried minor child of the settlor shall be deemed to be income (and not capital) to the extent that there is "available retained or accumulated income". "Available retained or accumulated income" is the aggregate amount of income which has arisen under the settlement since its inception *less* income already treated as income of the settlor or a beneficiary, income paid to or for the benefit of a beneficiary other than an unmarried minor child of the settlor and income properly spent on trust expenses.

If s.629 applies, the settlor is charged to tax, and the income is treated as the highest part of his income. However, as with s.625, the settlor may recover any tax so paid from the trustees or any other person to whom the income is payable under the settlement (s.646).

Capital sums paid to the settlor

Section 633 attacks capital sums paid *to* the settlor (or spouse **11–21** or civil partner) out of the settlement. "Capital sum" is defined to include "any sum paid by way of loan or repayment of a loan" (s.634). This is the key to the understanding of what the section is primarily aimed at. It is designed to stop a settlor (who is a higher-rate taxpayer) making a settlement, causing the trustees to accumulate rather than distribute the income, and causing them to let him (or his spouse) have the income in the form of a loan. For "other" capital sums which fall within this section, see s.634.

Where a capital sum is paid by the trustees to the settlor (or his spouse) such sum (grossed up at the rate applicable to trusts) is to be treated for all income tax purposes as the income of the settlor to the extent that such sum falls within the amount of "income available". "Income available" means, broadly speaking, the aggregate of all income arising to the settlement since its inception which has not been distributed and is not deemed to be income of the settlor under some other provision. The point of this is that what the section is attacking is the payment out as capital of money which came into the settlement as income.

If in the year in which the capital sum is paid such sum

exceeds the income available, the excess is carried forward and charged to the settlor in the following year (in so far as there is income available up to the end of that year) and thereafter, if necessary, subject to a maximum of 11 years. However, if the capital sum is paid by way of loan no charge can be raised in any year after that in which the loan is wholly repaid (s.638).

11–22   Section 641 of the Taxes Act stops the dodge of ensuring that the payment of a capital sum was made not by the trustees to the settlor but by an associated company which was in some way put in funds by the trustees. The section deems such sums to be paid by the trustees to the settlor and thus to be within the scope of s.638.

The settlor receives a tax credit for tax paid by the trustees, but cannot recover from the trustees any tax for which he may be responsible as a result of the operation of these provisions.

Estate income

11–23   What we are considering here is income arising during the period of administration of the estate of a deceased individual. When an individual dies the estate is administered by executors or administrators. The generic name for these is personal representatives; for tax purposes there is no need to distinguish between the two species.

Tax on administrators

11–24   As with trusts, so with estates, there is a kind of two-tier system of income tax. Personal representatives are like trustees in that they are chargeable to basic rate tax, are not chargeable to the higher rate of tax, and do not qualify for personal reliefs. In another respect, however, personal representatives differ from trustees; they are not chargeable to tax under the trust rates.

Tax on beneficiaries

11–25   How is the beneficiary taxed? That depends on the nature of the benefit. If the will gives an annuity, the annuity payments are part of total income from the date of death. So far as legatees are concerned it is perhaps worth stating the fairly elementary point that a legacy as such is not subject to income tax because it is not income; it is capital. But a legatee may be entitled to interest or (in the case of a specific legacy) to income from the date of death. In those cases the legatee is chargeable to income tax on the interest or income.

Residuary beneficiaries

What we have to look at in more detail is the position of a   **11–26**
residuary beneficiary. One has to distinguish between a beneficiary who has a limited interest in the residue of the estate and
a beneficiary who has an absolute interest in the residue. A
person has an absolute interest if he has an interest in the capital,
and a person has a limited interest if he does not have an
absolute interest.

An example of a person with a limited interest is a person who
gets a life tenancy. Everything that is paid to him by the personal
representatives must be income for the simple reason that he is
not entitled to any capital. Therefore very little complication
arises in his case. Each sum that is paid to him during the
administration counts (grossed-up) as part of his total income
for the year of assessment when it is paid. At the end of the
administration period any final payment is regarded as the
income of the beneficiary in the year of assessment in which the
administration ends.

Beneficiaries with entitlements

A beneficiary who has an absolute interest has, by definition,   **11–27**
an entitlement to capital. Therefore it is by no means certain
that everything paid to him during the administration of the
estate is income. To get at his tax liability the income element
must be sorted out from the capital element. The first step is to
calculate the "residuary income" of the estate for each year of
assessment during the administration period. To arrive at
residuary income the personal representatives are permitted to
deduct certain management expenses. The residuary income of
the estate is divided into a residuary income for each beneficiary
according to his share. For example, if there are three absolute
beneficiaries each with an equal share the residuary income of
each is one-third of the residuary income of the estate. Then any
sums which are paid to a beneficiary are treated as income for
the year of assessment in which they are actually paid in so far as
(grossed-up) they do not exceed his residuary income. In so far
as they do exceed it they are treated as capital. Finally, if at the
end of the administration the beneficiary has not received all the
residuary income which is his due, the outstanding amount is
regarded as having been paid immediately before the end of the
administration period.

Charitable Income

11–28   Charities (or, more formally, trusts and similar bodies such as companies limited by guarantee that are established solely for charitable purposes) are exempt from income tax and capital gains tax. That is an extremely valuable tax exemption. It has led to some interesting case law about what is a charity. That is not a question of tax law, and is beyond the scope of this book.

The most valuable tax exemption enjoyed by charities is that those giving money or assets to charities can also claim tax exemption. What is more, in many cases it is the charity that gets the advantage of the tax exemption, not the donor.

11–29   Traditionally, the only way that someone could get a tax advantage in giving money to a charity was by use of a covenant. Because of anti-avoidance rules no longer of importance, the covenant had to be for at least four years, or an uncertain period that could last at least that long. Because a covenant is a deed, it is legally enforceable without consideration being given by the recipient, and because the obligation was to pay so much a year for a number of years, the payments were annual payments. They were therefore charges on income and subject to the tax deduction regime explained in Ch.10.

Gift aid

11–30   The modern system of tax help to charities has at its centre a scheme known universally as gift aid. But before we deal with that we should mention that charitable covenants, that is annual payments payable to charities unconditionally for at least four years, or for an uncertain period that may exceed four years, still work as charges on income. So the payer deducts income tax at the basic rate when paying them, and can offset the sum paid against total taxable income. This can also be done by most forms of trust, if the objectives are charitable, without the settlor being caught by the anti-avoidance provisions set out earlier in this chapter. And it can sometimes be linked into the administration of estates, as gifts to charities on death do not suffer inheritance tax. Personal generosity was also encouraged in the past by giving additional sums when individuals permitted their employers to deduct sums from earnings to pay them directly to charities (payroll giving). And traders could justify some donations to charities as trading expenses.

11–31   HOW GIFT AID WORKS   Most people do not get involved in these complexities any longer. They can now make one-off payments and have them brought within the gift aid scheme.

The rules are in Part 8 of ITTOIA. If an individual makes a qualifying donation to a charity, then he or she is treated as making a donation after basic rate income tax has been deducted. At the same time, his or her basic rate limit is increased by the grossed up amount of the gift. See s.414.

How does that work? Mel decides to hand a £20 note to her favourite charity. Assuming that the £20 is a qualifying donation, she is treated as giving the charity the sum which, after deduction of basic rate tax, leaves £20. From 2008 the basic rate is 20 per cent. So she is treated as giving £25. And the amount of income tax on which she is charged at the basic rate goes up by £25, with the basic rate tax paid on it.

Mel's charity receives the £20 and makes a claim to HMRC to pay it the £5. (In 2008, the Treasury will give a little more than that to compensate charities for losing out when the basic rate was cut from 22 per cent to 20 per cent. That would add another 64p.) So it gets £25 (or more).

If Mel earns enough to be paying higher rate tax even after her basic rate limit is increased, then she can set the £25 against her income and reduce her total tax bill by the additional 20 per cent (higher rate less basic rate). So she can cut her tax bill by £5. The result is that it costs her £15 to hand over the £20 note and give the charity £25. Hence the "aid" bit of gift aid? Is it a reminder that the Treasury is providing the aid?

QUALIFYING DONATIONS The most important practical side **11–32** of making a qualifying donation is that the taxpayer must at some point fill in a gift aid declaration. This is the little form that any charity will give you to say that you are a taxpayer and are paying the amount from taxable income.

You must also give the money with no strings attached. Conditional gifts do not count. That presents some charities with a problem. If you pay the charity, for example, for copies of its magazine, then you are not making an unconditional gift. But if you decide to join the charity as an annual member, and annual membership allows you free copies of the magazine, the problem is solved. The annual membership is not a conditional gift, at least it is not if the benefits fall within the allowed benefits under ss.418 and 419. These impose limits on the amount of benefit that someone may be given in acknowledgement of a gift. The rules apply fully only if the benefit linked with the gift applies for a full year. If so, then a benefit worth 25 per cent of the amount of a gift of less than £100 can be ignored. If in addition to the magazine and the small piece of paper, you get a membership form telling you that you have joined the charity for a year, that's why.

11–33   Section 420 also allows charities to ignore rights of admission as benefits. These sections were brought in to help charities such as the National Trust and Royal Society for Protection of Birds. These charities are hugely influential not least because of their size. With several million members each they are the largest such organisations in the world. Both run huge estates and were giving free admission to those properties to members. But until this provision was introduced, there was a danger that the membership fees would be regarded as trading income and not charitable income. Again, there are conditions to the relief. Any benefit given for a gift must be for at least a year's admission. And the gift must be at least 10 per cent more than the individual entry fee to enter the property. And the property must also be open to the public.

So let's say Mel, instead of buying the magazine, wants to go into the museum run by her charity. It is open to the public at a fee of £15, but the public are invited to join the charity. Joining costs £20. On joining, Mel gets free admission for the year—and the bit of paper. She fills it in, hands over the £20, and—as before—her charity gets £25 and it costs her £15. And, as Mel pays higher rate tax, it costs her no more to join than she would have paid only for admission (provided she keeps the receipt). If Mel is a mum claiming child tax credit, she may get a similar benefit even if not paying higher rate tax. See the end of the chapter.

Tax Credits

11–34   The rules for calculating income for tax credits purposes also take into account both the rules for taxing trust income and most of the anti-avoidance rules. Section 629 is, in principle, of considerable importance here. A claim for tax credits must be based on the income of both the husband and wife (or unmarried or civil partners). This stops someone claiming more tax credits by shifting income sideways to the other spouse or partner, though this could work for income tax purposes to reduce the tax payable. So trusts to move income in this way will not work at all. But the income of children is not included in a tax credit claim for child tax credit for those children. That leaves open the obvious route of moving the income to the children so as to increase the tax credit claim. Here HMRC has a ready weapon with s.629. That, as we have seen, moves the income back to the settlor (the parent), and so will stop this being effective for tax credit purposes.

Tax credits and gift aid

Gifts to charities that are tax effective are also tax credit effective. So Mel, if she can claim tax credit, perhaps because of her children and childcare costs, will again find her gift of the £20 note costing her less than it seems. Let's say she joins the local wildlife park, which is a charity, for a year so she and her children can visit. Section 420 allows the individual who makes the gift to bring members of the family along as well. Her £20 became £25 under gift aid. But she can also deduct the £25 (not £20) from her income for tax credit purposes. If she is also working, she is probably losing 39p for every £1 increase in income (2008 rates). So if she reduces her income by the £25, by giving it to the wildlife park charity, then her entitlement to tax credit goes up by £9.75. On this basis, her £20 note costs her £10.25.

11–35

CHAPTER 12

TAXATION OF INDIVIDUALS

Introduction

12–01　　We have entitled this chapter "Taxation of Individuals" because "individual" excludes companies (which, in tax law as in law generally, are "persons" but are not "individuals") and also excludes trustees and personal representatives, to whom special tax rules apply, as we saw in the last chapter. Since 1990 husbands and wives are taxed separately as individuals.

Income tax

12–02　　So far we have set out the rules for identifying the taxable income of individuals from each separate source. We must now see how those individual items are added together to produce the amount of income tax the individual must pay in any year. This process used to be conducted entirely by the Revenue, and did not matter too much to many individuals. But now individuals must self-assess and should work out their own income tax liability each year (or have their accountants do it). The Tax Law Rewrite Project paid particular attention to making this aspect of the codified tax laws clear and systematic. The method used is to divide the process into individual steps in the legislation itself. The details are then fitted round the steps. The process is now set out as follows:

Step 1
"Income" is income under any charging provision. The first step is to aggregate all the separate amounts of income under these provisions from all sources on which the individual is liable to income tax for the tax year.

Step 2
Deduct from Step 1 income any deductions to which the individual is entitled for the tax year. This will include losses, charges on income, and any other deductions that are not limited to being offset against a single source. This is known as "total income".

Step 3
Deduct from the Step 2 income the total of any personal allowances to which the individual is entitled for the tax year. This produces the "taxable income" for the year.

Step 4
Calculate the total income tax payable on the Step 3 (taxable) income.

Step 5
Deduct from the Step 4 tax calculation any tax reductions to which the individual is entitled for the tax year. This produces the individual's income tax liability for the year.

The individual is then liable to pay to HMRC the difference between the amount of tax for which he or she is liable and the amount of tax already paid by deduction at source, through the PAYE system, or in any other way.

Before we move on to the details of these steps, we should remember that for most people there is also a liability to NI contributions to be paid, and that for nearly all families and nearly all lower-paid employees or the self-employed there is an entitlement to tax credits.

Tax credits

A similar, but not identical, set of steps is laid down in the Tax Credits (Definition and Calculation of Income) Regulations 2002 for the calculation of the income of a claimant for any tax year. As noted above, the definitions of the relevant income are now based closely on those of income tax. Further, tax credits are now claimed and awarded separately for each tax year. The main difference between the calculation of income tax liability of an individual for a tax year, and the calculation of the tax credit entitlement for that year is that one is a positive calculation and the other is a negative calculation. What that means is that the calculation starts for income tax assuming no income tax is payable. But the tax credit calculation starts assuming the individual gets the maximum tax credit. As income rises, so the tax bill also rises by the set rates. But the tax credit entitlement falls by a tax credit withdrawal rate, as set out below.

12–03

NI contributions

The process of establishing liability to NI contributions is simpler and also fundamentally different in several ways.

12–04

The most important difference is that NI contribution liability is source-specific. There is no single overarching assessment of NI contribution liability similar to what we have just seen for income tax and tax credits. The liability of an employee and the employer to pay contributions on employment income under Class 1 is specific to that employment. So an individual may have to pay two sets of contribution if he or she has two jobs with different employers. And the employers are separately liable on the separate employment.

Similarly, an individual who is both employed in employment with a contribution liability and also self-employed is liable separately to the Class 1 contributions on the employment and the Class 2 and Class 4 contributions on the self-employment.

Another difference is that Class 1 contributions are imposed by reference not to a tax year but to individual earnings periods with an underlying liability for individual weeks. So a weekly-paid employee might be liable to contributions in one week but, because earnings are lower in the following week, none in that week. There is no equivalent to the annual assessment or self-assessment of income for income tax purposes.

But there are annual limits to prevent an individual paying more than a maximum amount where he or she has two or more employments and/or is both employed and self-employed. These in effect prevent the individual paying more than would be paid if the income came from a single employment. An employee who is going to pay maximum Class 1 contributions in a year can be excused from Class 2 and Class 4 contributions, or have them deferred. Any excess payment can be claimed back.

Step 1: Income from all sources

12–05   The first step is to identify and add together the separate calculations of income from each of the charging provisions in the Tax Acts. We must check for each source that we include only the income from that source that is taxable in the tax year with which we are concerned. We have seen that most of these provisions have their own rules for identifying in which year income is to be regarded as taxable, allowing in some cases averaging and instalments. The separate provisions also provide for the expenses that are allowed against the gross income received in computing the amount of income for income tax purposes.

What also requires to be emphasised here is that this is not the total of all income. It is the total of income that is taxable. Some forms of income are not taxable. This applies, for example, to social security benefits such as child benefit, to most student grants and scholarships, to most betting winnings, and to cash gifts (unless they are annual payments). Income tax only applies to those forms of income that are taxable under specific tax provisions.

Kinds of income

An individual's income may include items of the following kinds: 12–06

(a) Income not taxed by deduction before receipt
An important example of this kind of income is income from a trade. Another example is income from rents from land. 12–07

(b) Income taxed by deduction before receipt
This is where we take account, as we must, of all receipts which were subject to withholding taxes. The point we want to make here is that income taxed by deduction of tax before receipt has to be grossed-up, that is, converted into a gross sum, for the purpose of computing total income. We will explain grossing-up in a moment. The most important example of income taxed by deduction before receipt is salary or wage income. Tax is charged as employment income and is deducted by the employer under the PAYE system. The gross amount, which includes the tax calculated according to the various tax bands, is included in total income, but of course the employee is credited with the tax deducted by his employer. The same is true of pensions taxed at source. 12–08

Interest received from a building society or a bank is also subject to deduction of tax before receipt.

GROSSING-UP An employee usually knows what his or her gross pay is (because the pay slip must state what it is) and so grossing-up does not present any problem. Moreover, it is, perhaps, simpler (and we are very much in favour of simplicity when it is a matter of arithmetic) to consider the mechanics of grossing-up in the case of taxable interest. The payer will deduct tax at the basic rate. If the lender receives £80 (net), the gross amount is £100. The gross amount is made up of the net payment (£80) plus tax deducted at the basic rate (at present 20 per cent), £20. With less obvious figures, you gross-up by multiplying the net amount by 100 over 80. The explanation (for simple lawyers, not accountants) is that if basic rate is 20 per cent, net income is gross (which is 100 per cent) less 20 per cent of gross, so net income is 80 per cent of gross.

Trust income

12–09   A beneficiary under a trust has to include in the total income an amount equal to his or her share of the trust income, grossed-up. He or she will have received the share after deduction of tax, and will be credited (depending on the circumstances) with all or some of the tax paid by the trustees. The taxation of trust income is dealt with in Ch.11.

Partnership income

12–10   A partnership is defined in the Partnership Act 1890 as the relation which subsists between persons carrying on business in common with a view of profit. There is no definition of partnership in the tax legislation, but the existence of partnerships is, as might be expected, acknowledged.

Three non-tax points we wish to make are extremely elementary, but we have found that they come as a surprise to some students. First, a partnership is quite different from a company registered under the Companies Acts, of which the main species is a limited company, e.g. BP. Thus a partnership, unlike a registered company, is not, in English law, a legal entity separate from its members (although, as we shall see, under the old regime it is for purposes of assessment and collection treated as though it were a separate legal entity). Nevertheless, the name of a partnership may contain the word "Company", or "Co.", e.g. Price & Co. This does not make it a company in law; it is a partnership. The word "firm" is equivalent to the word "partnership", and should not be used in reference to a company. Secondly, there is no requirement of law or practice that the shares of each partner in the profits (or losses) of the partnership should be equal. Thirdly, a company can be a partner in a partnership.

Broadly speaking, the responsibility for the tax payable on the profits of a trade or profession carried on in partnership lies not with the partnership but with the individual partners. Assessments are made on the individual partners, not on the partnership. Each partner is treated as if his share of the partnership profits is derived from a separate trade or profession carried on by him alone, i.e. as a sole trader or professional. This notional sole trade or profession is deemed to begin when he becomes a partner. It comes to an end when he ceases to be a partner or where the actual trade or profession is subsequently carried on by him alone or when it is actually discontinued. The partners are individually liable for tax in accordance with their respective shares in the partnership profits during the period in which the profits accrued.

Classifications of income

For nearly 90 years the law of income tax made a distinction between two kinds of income, earned income and unearned income, and until 1984 taxed the latter more heavily than the former. At one time the system was to have a "standard rate" of tax applicable to all income, but to have also a relief on earned income. In this respect, the system between 1973 and 1984 was to have a "basic rate" of tax applicable to all income, and also to have a further rate imposed (as well) on unearned income. This further rate was called in the legislation "additional rate", but it has now been repealed. Since 1992, the situation has become more complicated, with different rates applying to different kinds of income.

12–11

The legislation does not use the phrase "unearned income", but rather "investment income". And it does not define investment income except to say that investment income is any income other than earned income. Earned income includes employment and other income taxable under ITEPA and any trading income immediately derived by an individual from the carrying on of a trade, profession or vocation either as an individual or partner. This definition is consonant with commonsense, but there are some difficult borderline cases.

Income which is charged on property businesses, notwithstanding its computation according to the principles of trading income, is investment income.

Step 2: Total income

It is necessary to find a taxpayer's total income for two purposes: first, to determine whether it is enough to entitle him to personal reliefs; secondly, to determine liability (if any) to the higher rate of tax.

12–12

To arrive at total income one deducts what are called "charges on income", certain payments (outward) of interest and any other non-source-specific deductions.

Charges on Income

Most payments that used to be deductible at this stage are now dealt with in other ways. But a deduction may still apply at

12–13

this stage for a covenant of income by partners to a retired partner. The new rules applying to most payments to charities are at the end of Ch.11. Those paying higher rate tax will also be entitled to a deduction for that purpose.

Deductible Interest Payments

12–14 We are not speaking here of interest paid out as one of the expenses of a business; that is deductible *in computing* the income of that business. We are speaking of payments of interest in respect of which an individual can secure relief from income tax by deducting them *from* income. Relief of this sort was at one time widely available. It has been progressively restricted over recent years. In particular, what used to be called "mortgage interest relief", a deduction for interest paid when buying a home, was abolished in 2000.

Perhaps not surprisingly, these exceptional cases do not include many of the payments of interest most people make, e.g. on a bank overdraft or under a credit card arrangement or hire purchase contract. This is so regardless of the purpose of that kind of loan. Rather they relate to instances where the loan for which the interest is being paid is for one of a number of specified purposes. However, even if the loan is for one of these purposes there are two general restrictions which come into play: first, relief is only given up to the amount of reasonable commercial rate of interest, see s.384 of ITA 2007, and secondly, no relief at all is given if the sole or main benefit that might be expected to accrue to the claimant from the transaction under which the interest is paid was the obtaining of a reduction in tax liability by means of such relief: s.787 of the Taxes Act.

12–15 There is a full list of the purposes for which loans may be taken out so that individuals can claim tax relief on the interest paid in s.383 of ITA 2007. The details of each kind of purpose, and the conditions attached to loans for that purpose, follow in code form from s.388 to s.412. Section 386 provides a general rule that where a loan is partly for one of the purposes in the list and partly for some other purpose, then the qualifying part of the mixed loan must be identified for any claim to be made.

12–16 LOANS TO INVEST IN A BUSINESS STRUCTURE A series of provisions allow a deduction to be claimed on interest paid on loans taken out to invest in close companies, employee-controlled companies, trading partnerships or co-operative enterprises. Together they reflect part of the policy of encouraging individuals to become entrepreneurs by allowing the cost of borrowing stake money to invest in any of these forms of enterprise.

LOANS TO BUY PLANT AND MACHINERY This fills a gap   12–17
between the provisions under which a company can borrow to buy plant and machinery on which it can claim a capital allowance and the provisions allowing an individual trader to do that. The rule here allows a partnership to borrow for the same purpose and to offset the interest cost of the loan against the partnership profits. The rule is focussed by requiring that the expenditure be on plant and machinery subject to a capital allowance claim.

LOANS TO PAY INHERITANCE TAX This is a narrow but   12–18
pragmatic relief. It is available only to the personal representatives responsible for settling an estate. With any larger estate the personal representatives will need to settle the inheritance tax bill with HMRC when they submit their account of the estate to HMRC. So they may have to borrow to pay the tax. But even then, they can only claim relief on a loan for one year.

Step 3: Taxable income

Step 2 gave us the total amount of income for any tax year   12–19
after taking account of all taxable sources of income and all the allowances and deductions to which an individual is entitled by reason of the nature of her or his income and expenditure. We must now take account of other provisions, known as personal reliefs, which depend on personal characteristics of the taxpayer. This step used to be far more important than it is now. The former child allowances and child tax reliefs are now all dealt with separately by the child tax credit. With one exception (blind people), help for disabilities is now given only by social security benefits. And the rules dealing with married couples have largely gone with the introduction of separate taxation. There are two sorts of personal relief left:

- personal allowances. These are sums deducted from total income to produce taxable income; and
- tax reductions. These sums are set off against the income tax liability to produce the amount of tax payable.

Personal allowances are taken into account at this step. Tax reductions are taken into account at step 5.

Personal allowances

12–20 Every individual taxpayer is entitled to a personal allowance, provided that she or he claims and meets, or is exempt from, the residence requirement. The allowance is paid at three levels:

- Those aged 75 or over at some time in the tax year are entitled to an annual allowance of £9,180.
- Those aged 65, but not 75, at some time during the year are entitled to an annual allowance of £9,030.
- All other individuals (including children with taxable income) are entitled to an annual allowance of £5,435.

These reflect sharp increases in 2008, removing many pensioners from the income tax system. Both the higher personal allowances are subject to a clawback if the individual's total income is greater than a set annual sum, which is currently £21,800. But the deduction cannot take the personal allowance below that given to those under 65. The allowance is given in full (subject to any clawback) in the tax year in which the individual dies.

Another way of looking at these allowances is that they are age-related zero-rate bands. In other words, no taxpayer pays income tax on the first band of his or her income. The amount of the band depends only on his or her age. The allowances work in this way because their value cannot be transferred from year to year or from one taxpayer to another. If my income is, say, £3,000 this year, then I pay no income tax. But I cannot transfer the unused part of the allowance to last year or next year or to my wife.

Do not forget that I may get tax credits as a result of my low income. But there are no personal allowances for these credits. Nor are there any personal allowances to set against NI contribution liability. Instead there is a lower earnings limit and a primary threshold set each week. Where earnings for a week are below the primary threshold then the contributor is either exempt from contributions or is liable to a zero-rate contribution (which amounts to the same thing for current purposes).

Blind person's allowance

12–21 This is the one remaining personal relief that takes into account an individual's disabilities. Other forms of disablement affecting the ability to work or earn are covered by social security benefits or the disabled worker's entitlement to working tax credit. It is also the only remaining allowance that can be transferred from one spouse to the other. To claim it, the individual must be registered as blind (or unable to do work for which eyesight is essential) and not merely partially sighted. The annual amount of the allowance is £1,800.

Blind people who are working and are also low earners may claim working tax credit with the disability element. This applies equally to all other working people who suffer disadvantage in their earning capacity because of their disablements. This is separate from, but linked to, their entitlement to social security disability benefits.

Step 4: The rates of income tax

Having deducted from total income certain of a taxpayer's personal reliefs, we have arrived at taxable income. We must now proceed to establish what amount of tax is payable. This is primarily determined by the rate or rates of tax applicable to an individual's taxable income.

12–22

The Rates of Tax

If one searches for any consistency of application or purpose in the rates of tax which are applied to taxable income one searches in vain as the following brief excursus through recent history shows.

12–23

Income tax is all one tax, though levied at various rates. Until 1977–78 there were the basic rate, higher rates and additional rates. For 1978–79 there was a lower rate. The introduction of a lower rate complicated the system, mainly because of the many cases in which at that time income tax was "deducted at source" at the basic rate. It also greatly complicated the PAYE codes. On the other hand it was thought that the introduction of a lower rate had achieved one social good by reducing the number of people caught in the "poverty trap". The poverty trap is the situation in which a family can actually be worse off if the bread-winner gets a rise than they were before. This absurdity arises from the interaction (at a certain low level of income) of income tax, national insurance contributions and means-tested social benefits. It was found, however, when detailed research was undertaken that the main beneficiaries were married women. So it was abolished. From 1984–85 there was another change in the rate structure. The additional rate, levied on investment income over a certain threshold at the rate of 15 per cent, was abolished. Again, research suggested that in practice it operated in a different way to that which theory suggested. It was mainly paid by retired people. This left a basic rate and a series of progressive higher rates of tax. From 1988–89 a single higher rate of tax of 40 per cent was introduced.

Since then there has been the resurrection from 1992–93 of a lower rate (levied at 20 per cent) as a first step towards the government's proclaimed goal of achieving a basic rate of 20 per cent; a goal further enhanced from 1996–97, by the taxation of savings income of many taxpayers at the lower rate. A special 10 per cent rate was applied to dividends (with a special higher rate) in 1999 to offset the effect of other reforms of corporation tax. And in 1999 a new "starting rate" of income tax of 10 per cent was imposed on the first slice of taxable income. This was aimed specifically at poverty trap victims. Further steps to avoid the poverty trap were taken in 2003 by basing the working tax credit and child tax credit on the same rules for determining income as income tax. The rate of that negative tax is, as we have seen, 39 per cent. The 20 per cent main rate finally arrived in 2008 and other rates were then simplified. As part of this, the Finance Act 2007 abolished the starting rate from 2008. But an unprecedented "rebellion" of backbench MPs led to a last minute compensation for this to low-paid taxpayers. It cost over £2 billion.

The current rates of income tax

12–24   The following rates of income tax apply for the tax year 2008–09.

Zero-rate
There is no formal zero-rate but do not forget that this is the effect of the personal allowance to which each individual is entitled each tax year.

Starting rate for savings
The first £2,320 of savings income only is taxable at 10 per cent. However, if the individual has other taxable income of more than that amount, then the starting rate is not payable and the savings income is subject to the basic rate. Remember that this applies after the personal allowance has been taken into account. In practice it will cut the income tax payable to pensioners whose savings income and pensions together add up to a little more than the annual personal allowance for a pensioner.

Basic rate

Income above the personal allowance level is taxed at the basic rate of 20 per cent up to a ceiling of £36,000. This applies to all earned income, but note however the following rates.

Dividend ordinary rate

The rate of income tax on dividends paid to individuals by UK companies is 10 per cent. This rate reflects the fact that, in effect, both the company and the individual are paying tax on profits that are distributed as dividends. This rate applies instead of the basic rate up to the same ceiling as the basic rate.

Higher rate

The rate payable on all income over £36,000 in the tax year is 40 per cent. This applies to all forms of taxable income other than dividends from UK companies.

Dividend higher rate

This is 32.5 per cent, not 40 per cent.

The existence of several different positive rates of income tax inevitably leads to complications. As a result, there are rules that we need not look at here defining precisely the order in which the rates are applied to the different forms of income. But that is, of course, not where the complexity stops for most taxpayers. Most of the income subject to the basic rate, rather than the savings rate, will also be subject to NI contribution liability rates. Then there are the tax credit withdrawal rates to apply. We note these below. We have not finished with income tax yet.

Step 5: Income tax liability

The result of Step 4 is a total of income tax at the various rates on the income for the year. We must make one final adjustment to find out the income tax liability of the individual for the year. This is the deduction from that total of tax payable of the amount of any tax reductions. We saw in Step 3 that tax reductions are the other form of personal reliefs along with personal allowances.

12–25

There is now only one tax reduction of general importance: that for married couples one or both of whom was born before April 6, 1935 (that is, is over 73 at the start of the 2008–09 tax year). This is the last residue of the married couple's allowance formerly available to every married taxpayer. But it also has complicated rules applying to it. For present purposes, we say

213

only that those who qualify can deduct about £560 from the tax payable at Step 4 to reach their individual tax liability for a year.

In all other cases, the total of tax at Step 4 is the total tax liability for the year.

The current rates of NI contribution

12–26   We must now return, in effect, to Step 4 for NI contributions. As we see, there are only two steps in calculating NI contribution liability. These are the equivalent of Step 4 for income tax plus a second step when the maximum annual liability for contributions of individuals is determined.

Class 1

This applies to earnings from employment and some forms of social security income. Because individuals are not liable to pay NI contributions when over the age of 60 (women) or 65 (men), neither the earnings nor the pensions of most retired people fall within the scope of contribution liability. However, their employers remain liable to the secondary rate on their earnings regardless of age.

The current Class 1 primary threshold is £105 a week. If the weekly earnings are below this figure no contribution is payable by either the employee or the employer. That figure is the weekly equivalent of the main (under 65) level of individual personal allowance for income tax. The current Class 1 upper earnings limit is £770 a week. For many years there was a gap between the upper earnings limit of NI contributions and the starting point of the higher rate. Earnings between those levels were subject, in effect, to a lower rate of tax than either the higher rate or the basic rate plus contributions. But in 2008 the upper earnings limit for NI contributions was increased sharply. It stands in that year at an annual level of £40,040. The starting point for higher rate income tax is £36,000 taxable income, or £41,435 with the personal allowance. So the gap has largely disappeared. Employees do not pay contributions on earnings above that level (but may pay the higher rate of income tax instead). Employers pay 1 per cent on those earning without upper limit.

Employees pay a primary rate on earnings between the primary threshold and the upper earnings limit. The current rate is 11 per cent, but most employees also have contract-out pensions (denying them certain state pension rights). Those employees pay a contracted out rate of 9.4 per cent but they will usually also be paying a contribution to the contracted-out pension scheme.

Employers pay a secondary rate on earnings over the primary threshold of 12.8 per cent, and 1 per cent above the upper earnings limit. If the employee's pension is contracted-out, the employer's rate is 9.1 per cent or 11.4 per cent (depending on the type of scheme) but the employer will usually be paying a much higher rate of contribution to the employee's pension fund. These also apply to Class 1A and Class 1B contributions.

Class 2

This is a weekly flat rate of £2.30 for all those who are ordinarily self-employed, regardless of the earnings in that week. The small earnings exception (in effect an annual lower earnings limit) is £4,825.

Class 4

This is 8 per cent of total earnings from self-employment for the tax year so far as they exceed a threshold of £5,435 a year (the amount of the personal allowance). It is payable on earnings up to £40,040 (the same as the upper earnings level for Class 1). There is a liability of 1 per cent on all earnings above that limit. There is, of course, no employer's contribution.

The current rates of tax credits

Tax credits are not allowances or reductions, but genuine   12–27
payments *to* claimants/taxpayers that increase their incomes rather than reduce the taxes deducted from their incomes. But the credits are designed in part to replace tax allowances and deductions. At the same time they also replace certain forms of social security allowances and benefits.

The child tax credit has now replaced the former income tax children's tax credit and all forms of social security allowance for children apart from the universal child benefit. The working tax credit is directly set off against the income tax and NI deductions under PAYE from low-paid employees, and is also available to the low-paid self-employed. It partly replaces former social security allowances, but is in part a genuine negative income tax in the sense that it is designed to add money to, rather than take it from, some individuals simply because of their low pay levels (and without reference to any social security criterion). Both forms of tax credit are income-related, and the relevant rules are noted at the end of each main chapter in this part. The details of the tax credits themselves are set out in Ch.9.

There are three parts to the calculation of the amount of tax credit to which an individual or family is entitled. First, the maximum entitlement to tax credits must be calculated. Then the income of the claimants must be calculated. This is done by much the same approach as applies for income tax, and we will not repeat it in full here. Finally the one is set off against the other at the tax credit withdrawal rate.

Maximum child tax credit

This consists of a family element of £545 for the year (double if a child is under a year old), and £2,085 for each child. There are substantially higher amounts if any child is disabled. It is separate from entitlement to child benefit.

Maximum working tax credit

This includes a basic element of £1,800 in all cases. Where the claim is joint, or by a lone parent, there is an additional element of £1,770. If the claimant works 30 hours or more there is an additional £735. There are higher sums for disabled workers and those over 50 returning to work.

In addition, anyone who is working and is responsible for children may be able to claim the childcare element. This is 80 per cent of actual and approved childcare costs up to £175 a week for one child and £300 a week in total for more than one child.

Tax credit withdrawal rates

There are three annual income thresholds for tax credit purposes. The first, currently £6,420 is the figure at which working tax credits (including the childcare credit) start to be withdrawn. The second, currently £15,575, is the figure at which child tax credits start to be withdrawn, apart from the family element. The third, currently £50,000, is the figure at which the family element starts to be withdrawn.

The tax credits withdrawal rate is 39 per cent at both the first and second income thresholds and 6.67 per cent at the third of the thresholds.

In other words, someone who is entitled to child tax credit will lose entitlement of the maximum tax credit at 39p for every £1 by which income exceeds the second threshold, save for the family element of £545. This is removed at the rate of 6.6p per £1 only when income exceeds £50,000.

"The rate of tax"

There is much talk about "the rate of tax" (usually with the comment that it is "too high"). We hope that this chapter has shown that there isn't one. If we look at personal allowances as being in reality a zero-rate of income tax, then we have seen that there are seven rates of income tax, two rates of tax credit withdrawal, and all sorts of rates of NI contribution.

12–28

What is more, there is no neat interaction between the three sets of rates. For example, someone receiving employment income pays at the basic rate and also pays the appropriate Class 1 NI contribution rate. The self-employed also pay at the basic rate but pay the Class 4 contribution rate. Those receiving interest income pay at the lower rate but do not pay NI contributions. Those receiving property income pay at the basic rate but do not pay NI contributions. Those receiving dividends pay at the Schedule F lower rate, and do not pay NI contributions. Those with higher incomes pay at the higher rate, and pay contributions on some of their income at 1 per cent.

Now add in the complication that currently some six million families or individuals get tax credits. In some cases this will reduce the income tax payable. In others, the tax credit exceeds the income tax and NI contributions payable.

What then is "the rate of tax". There is no such thing. There are in policy terms two rates that matter. The first is the *marginal rate of tax*. This is the answer to the question: if I earn or receive another £1 of income, how much will I have to pay in tax? For example, I earn £1 extra this week, but have to pay 20p income tax at the basic rate and 11p NI contribution, and also lose 39p tax credits. So my marginal rate of tax is 70 per cent. I also receive an extra £1 interest income this week. But my savings are in an ISA and are tax exempt. I pay no extra income tax, and lose no tax credits. There are no NI contributions on interest income. So my marginal rate of tax is 0 per cent. That is one basis on which to argue whether rates are "too high". It is important in considering, for example, whether the rates of tax stop people working harder or saving more or encourage them to do so.

12–29

The other rate is the *effective rate of tax*. This means the total tax I pay on my total income for the year. For example, if all my income is £20,000 and my total tax and NI contributions liability, after personal allowances and reductions and tax credits, comes to £5,000, then my effective rate of tax is 25 per cent. You will have realised by now that working this out is fiendishly complicated. It is the effective rate—the total amount of tax that the individual actually pays in the year divided by the total amount of income (including any forms of income that are not taxable at all) for the year—which is, many argue, the only way of judging the overall fairness between individuals and the tax system in any year.

12–30 EXAMPLE Now one for you. You are the sole shareholder/director/employee of a small company. It earns £50,000 profits this year from your efforts. Your partner does not work, but is at home looking after the two young children you both have. What is the effective rate of tax if (a) the company employs you and pays you all the profits as earnings; (b) the company pays your partner £5,000 earnings and the rest to you as a dividend. (No, we don't expect an answer but it shows how difficult it is to talk about effective rates of tax. But you do need to go to the next chapter to get the full context.)

12–31 National Statistics publish generalised answers. For 2008-09 those figures show that the average rate of tax on earnings was 21 per cent for the top 10 per cent of earners (but not including NI contributions). For the bottom 10 per cent (of taxpayers) childless single taxpayers *pay* 11 per cent of earnings. Couples with two children *receive* 32 per cent of average earnings of the decile. It is interesting to note that the average rate for the top 10 per cent has been much the same for 20 years. But the lowest 10 per cent pay noticeably less, and those with children have been net gainers since 2000.

CHAPTER 13

TAXATION OF COMPANIES

Introduction

Income tax was invented before joint stock companies. While that was a long time ago, its significance has yet to leave our direct tax laws. United Kingdom companies do not pay income tax. Nor do they pay capital gains tax. Instead, they pay a tax on both income and capital gains tax called corporation tax. However, until recently the laws of income tax and corporation tax were completely intertwined together in the Income and Corporation Taxes Act 1988.

13–01

The Tax Law Rewrite Project

One of the major achievements of the Tax Law Rewrite Project is the separation of most provisions of corporation tax from those of income tax. However, as at the time of writing this edition, the income tax laws have been rewritten, but the process of rewriting the corporation tax laws is still underway. When it is completed, there will be two separate Corporation Tax Acts alongside the Capital Allowance Act 2001, the three Income Tax Acts, and a final Act that is likely to mop up a few special provisions from both income tax and corporation tax (chiefly with international content).

13–02

The first of the draft Corporation Tax Bills was published in 2008. It is a parallel law to ITTOIA and relevant parts of ITA. Remember that companies cannot be employees or pensioners so ITEPA is not relevant. But there are also major parts of ITTOIA that do not apply to companies. And there are rules that treat the distinction between income and capital in different ways for companies than the ways in which they are treated for individuals.

The unfortunate result—for a short period—is that all the relevant Schedules and Cases harking back to 1803 are still lurking in the Taxes Act 1988 with effect for companies even though they have now been swept away from the income tax laws. That is why you will find the major standard books setting out the tax legislation record most parts of the Taxes Act as both in force (for companies) and repealed (for income tax purposes).

Taxing companies

13–03   The charge to corporation tax is still to be found in s.6 of the Taxes Act 1988. It is a charge on "profits" of the company. This is defined by s.6(4) as meaning income and chargeable gains. Section 6 also misapplies income tax and capital gains tax from those profits. Instead, s.9 provides that the amount of any income shall be computed in accordance with income tax principles and shall be determined in accordance with income tax law and practice.

That provision sits uncomfortably with the current transitional regime under which income tax law has been rewritten. Once the new Bills have been enacted, that will change. The new approach is set out in cl.1 of the draft Corporation Tax Bill. Clause 2 of that Bill repeats the provisions now in s.6, but there is no equivalent of s.9. Instead, the Bill and its successor will set out charging provisions entirely separately from those in income tax.

The charging provisions as drafted in the current draft Bill are:

- Trading income (Part 3)
- Property income (Part 4)
- Investment income (Part 5)
- Profits from loan relationships (Parts 6 and 7)
- Profits from derivative contracts (Part 8)
- Gains from intangible fixed assets (Part 9)
- Miscellaneous income (Part 10).

But until they are enacted, we must go to the Taxes Act and the various schedules and cases.

What is a "company"?

13–04   What is a "company"? It is defined in the Taxes Act, s.831 as meaning (except in certain contexts) "any body corporate or unincorporated association, but does not include a partnership, a local authority or a local authority association."[1] (An authorised unit trust is deemed to be a company, but some special rules apply to it; see Taxes Act, s.48).

13–05   A non-resident company, i.e. one not incorporated in the

---

[1] Nor does it include the Conservative Party's Central Office—that is not an unincorporated association. But members' clubs are included: *Conservative and Unionist Central Office v Burrell* (1982); *Blackpool Marton Rotary Club v Martin* (1990) (CA). In a member's club there is no liability on the members to share profits or losses as there is in a partnership

United Kingdom and whose central management and control are located elsewhere, is not within the charge to corporation tax unless it carries on a trade in the United Kingdom through a branch or agency. If so it is chargeable to corporation tax on trading income from the branch on income from property held by the branch and on chargeable gains accruing from the disposal of assets within the United Kingdom in the same circumstances as would make an individual chargeable. In so far as it is not liable to corporation tax, a non-resident company is liable to income tax on the same footing as a non-resident individual.

Why tax companies?

It may be asked, why have a tax on company profits at all? Why not simply tax, in the hands of the shareholders, what emerges from the company in the form of distributions? The answer originally was because of the different rates of tax between income tax and capital gains tax. Taxing only distributions would have meant that that would enable a company to be used as a kind of receptacle in which profits could be stored up tax-free; distribution (and hence income taxation) could be avoided by storing up the profits for years on end and then eventually selling the shares (causing only liability to capital gains tax at a flat rate). This "receptacle problem" (a problem for HMRC) is particularly acute in the case of narrowly-owned companies, such as one-member companies and family companies. Special rules were devised to deal with such companies, called "close" companies and, although the harmonisation of income tax and capital gains tax rates has solved *most* of the "receptacle" problems, other possible tax advantages remain. These include the use of investment companies to avoid higher rate tax on "hidden" distributions.

13–06

To incorporate or not?

The question whether a particular individual or partnership would gain (tax-wise) by forming a company is not easy to answer except in very general terms, or alternatively in minutely particular terms with a full knowledge of all the circumstances of a particular case. In general, a major pointer is the comparison between the individual's marginal rate of income tax and the relevant rate of corporation tax. This has changed very sharply recently. For example, back in 1979 when the first edition of this book was written the top rate of income tax had just fallen from 98 per cent to 75 per cent. The main rate of corporation tax was then 52 per cent. But by 2003 the starter

13–07

rate for companies had dropped to zero. That was almost too good to be true. Many self-employed individuals turned their businesses into "pocket-book" companies, and turned themselves into directors and shareholders. They paid themselves next to nothing, but took dividends or loans instead. The result? A corporation tax rate of 0 per cent, lower income tax bills, and no NI contributions to pay. Rules were quickly introduced to stop this in 2004 because of the loss of corporation tax. Those rules are in addition to the provisions that we saw in the chapter on employment income that treat some earnings of the self-employed as being employment income.

If a trader or professional does form a company, he or she ceases to be self-employed and is taxable on any earnings from the company (including director's fees) as employment income. If the money is taken out as dividends, then the dividend rates apply.

13–08   The change from income tax to corporation tax is done by a discontinuance of the trade (see Taxes Act, s.63); loss relief (income tax) can be carried forward (Taxes Act, s.35); and hold-over relief (capital gains tax) is available.

13–09   The decision whether to trade individually or by means of a company is not wholly, perhaps not even primarily, a tax decision. There is one great advantage of incorporation, namely limited liability even for a single member company, although for small companies that may be largely illusory in practice. Also, it is easier for a company to arrange finance (either from inside or outside the business) for expansion, particularly by the use of a floating charge. The disadvantage from more (and expensive) paperwork arising from the requirements of the Companies Acts has to some extent been reduced for small companies in recent years. And, of course, it must be borne in mind that some *professions* do not permit their practitioners to become incorporated. A final point is that, until 2000, individuals could impose a "pocket book" company between themselves and their clients or customers to save some income tax and NI contributions. There are now anti-avoidance provisions to curb this.

The tax laws that apply

13–10   The corporation tax, along with income tax and capital gains tax, is under the care and management of HMRC, and the detailed provisions for administration set out in the Taxes Management Act 1970 apply to corporation tax. It is important to appreciate, at the outset, that corporation tax *is* the income tax and capital gains tax on companies. Its administration is closely tied in with that of income tax and CGT.

The substantive law of corporation tax is to be found (at least for the time being), for the most part, in ss.6–13A, Part VIII (ss.337–344), Part X (ss.392A–413), and a few sections of the Taxation of Chargeable Gains Act 1992, and Chapter II of Part IV of the Finance Act 1996 and s.117 and Sch.18 to the Finance Act 1998. The special rules for companies are not currently being looked at by the Tax Law Rewrite Project.

Taxable Periods

Corporation tax is levied by reference, not to "years of assessment", but to "financial years". A financial year begins on April 1 and ends on March 31. And each financial year is named by reference to only one calendar year and that is the year in which it begins, not the year in which it ends. So the financial year 2010 is the year from April 1, 2010, to March 31, 2011. Assessment is on a current year basis; the tax assessment for 2010 being based on the profits of 2010. But where a company's accounting period does not correspond to the financial year, the profits of the accounting period are apportioned into the appropriate financial years. This is important in that the rate of tax may differ in the two financial years.

    13–11

Companies are subject to self-assessment. Large companies pay the tax due in quarterly instalments during the year, with rather more generous treatment for smaller companies—but then the many small companies pay hardly any serious amounts of tax.

Rates of corporation tax

The rates of corporation tax are, unlike income tax, usually set a year ahead. This is in part because corporation tax does not suffer from the technical problem that it is an annual tax. So we can assume it will be there next year even if we have to pretend that income tax might not be. But that has not stopped the corporation tax rates going up and down somewhat over the years. There is, however, a general trend downwards in the main rate of corporation tax, as paid by the larger businesses. At the time of the first edition of this book it was 52 per cent of profits. By 2009 that has almost halved to 28 per cent for most large companies. Many companies are not big enough to pay the main rate. For them the rates went down to zero, but have now come back up to 21 per cent for most small companies. But those are the headline rates, and the actual position is somewhat more complicated.

    13–12

Small companies' rate

13–13 The lower rate of tax (21 per cent for 2009) applies to "small companies". Except that it doesn't. The size or total value of a company is irrelevant for this rate. What counts is the amount of profits it earns in a year. If the company—regardless of size—has total taxable profits of under £300,000 then it can claim what is called small companies' relief by s.13 of the Taxes Act 1988. For 2009 that means, as we have noted, that the tax rate is 21 per cent (up from 19 per cent in 2008). There are special rules to prevent companies making themselves "small" in this sense by sharing profits out among associated companies. The rate is payable on all the profits of the company. There are no corporate "personal allowances" or exempt slices of the kinds available to small trusts.

And remember in considering the effect of this rate that dividends are not deductible from profits (although most kinds of interest payment are). So from 2009 the effect is that a pocket book company will bear 21 per cent tax on its profits, with the shareholder/director/employee then paying tax again at the dividend rate on any money paid as dividends. If the main dividend rate is paid, then this is 10 per cent, while it will be 32.5 per cent if total income is over the higher rate limit.

EXAMPLE A pocket book company has profits of £40,000. Corporation tax is payable at 21 per cent, so leaving 79p of each £1 of profits left. If that is dividended in full to the single shareholder/director, then the company's owner will receive £31,600. If the owner has no other income, then this will be subject, after personal allowances, to the 10 per cent rate. In back-of-envelope terms that means a further £3,000 or so tax. So the total tax on the £40,000 is about £11,400 or an effective rate of 28 per cent or so. What would it be if there were no company and the individual were self-employed? (Don't forget the NI contributions).

The corporation tax rate

13–14 This is the main rate of tax. For 2009 it is 28 per cent, down from 30 per cent in previous years. This applies to all the profits of a company if those profits are in total over £1,500,000 in the year.

13–15 Many companies fall in the large in-between area with profits over £300,000 and below £1,500,000. They are subject to a sliding scale. It can claim a reduction from the full rate of 7/400ths overall. But this must be done on a sliding basis so that it ends up paying at the main rate when its profits reach the upper figure. Translated into a percentage, this means that the company pays 21 per cent on its profits up to the £300,000 level and then 33.25 per cent on profits above that level up to £1,500,000. And in case you are puzzled, this obscurely worded provision does, as shown, produce a marginal rate for the mid-range companies that is higher than either the lower rate or the main rate.

The pre-2009 rates continue to apply to "ring fence profits" but those only apply to profits from oil extraction, so need not delay us.

Computation of Profits

A company is charged to corporation tax on its total profits; that is, its income plus its chargeable gains. (Profits = income + chargeable gains). It is declared in the Taxes Act, s.9 that in general a company's income is to be computed on income tax principles, excluding income tax enactments which make special provision for individuals. This, however, does not mean that there are no differences at all. One difference is that the rules for computing a company's income and gains from either borrowing or lending are different from those for individuals (see below). But the differences are minor compared with the broad principle which (we say again) is that a company's income is computed on income tax principles. If the law of income tax changes during the accounting period of a company, the law which applies for the computation is the law applying to the year of assessment in which the accounting period *ends*.

Similarly, s.8 of the Taxation of Chargeable Gains Act 1992 declares that the chargeable gains of a company are to be computed on the principles of capital gains tax. That is subject to what we say about "loan relationships" below.

The income of a company is allotted to Schedules. So, for example, a company's trading income is assessed under Case I of Sch.D and its income from rents under Sch.A. Under Case I, directors' emoluments are on the same footing as salaries and wages of the company's employees; they are deductible to the extent that they are reasonable.

It is worth stressing that the way in which the schedules apply to companies is inevitably different to the application to individuals. Companies cannot be employees, so ITEPA is not usually relevant. Nor can companies hold a profession or vocation, ruling out Case II of Sch.D. The loan relationship rules below replace Case IV of Sch.D. Schedule F is not relevant as that does not apply to distributions from UK companies paid to

13–16

13–17

other UK companies. That leaves only Sch.A, Cases I, III and V of Sch.D, and parts of the TCGA applying.

13–18   More fundamentally, the government is currently considering if any part of this approach should continue to apply to companies, and is consulting on a number of options. These range from levying corporation tax as a single undifferentiated charge on all profits, income and capital, regardless of source, and based on the company's accounts, through to a simplified version of the current rules treating trading profits and investment profits separately. Most options would develop the approach to corporate earnings successfully started with the loan relationships provisions.

The several classes of income of a company together with the total of its chargeable gains constitute the total profits of the company.

Loan relationships

13–19   Chapter II of Part IV of the Finance Act 1996 introduced a new regime for companies in respect of all profits and losses made by companies on loans. In general the idea is to treat all such profits and losses as income, whether or not for individuals they would be treated as capital gains or losses. (The original idea was to apply these rules to individuals as well but that did not find favour during the consultation process.) The new rules apply whether the company is the borrower or lender. The most obvious category is the treatment of interest paid by a company on its debentures, from the company's point of view.

The 1996 rules apply to what are termed "loan relationships". These are defined as any relationship in which a company is either a creditor or debtor for a money debt, whether in sterling or another currency, which under the general law is a loan. Thus all forms of bond and corporate debt are covered. In calculating the profits and losses from such relationships companies may use one of two accounting methods: an accruals basis, under which payments and receipts are allocated when they accrue to the accounting periods to which they relate; or a mark-to-market basis, which means that a loan relationship must be accounted for in each accounting period at a fair value. In general companies may use whichever method they use in their statutory accounts prepared for Companies Act purposes.

13–20   The central concepts of the new regime (in ss.82 and 83 of the 1996 Act) are: (i) that where companies enter into loan relationships for the purposes of a trade, the profits, losses and expenses relating to those relationships (known in the legislation as debits and credits) will be treated as receipts of expenses of that trade; i.e. they will form part of the Sch.D, Case I computation; and (ii) in the case of profits and losses arising from other, i.e. non-trading, loan relationships any net profit (taking into account the company's other income subject to those rules) will be taxable under the rules of Case III of Sch.D.

Any net loss on a non-trading loan relationship, calculated in **13–21** the same way, may be used to give relief in one of four ways. First, it may be used against any profits for corporation tax of the year in which the loss occurred; secondly by way of group relief (see below); thirdly by way of carry back against similar non-trading profits of the preceding three years; and fourthly by carry forward against non-trading profits generally of the company for succeeding accounting periods.

These new rules apply to all interest payments made by companies but do not apply to payments which are distributions for corporation tax purposes so that the basic distinction remains between dividends payable on shares and interest payable on debentures. The former cannot be deducted from taxable profits. The latter are now part of the tax computation as outlined above. Perhaps the most significant feature of the new rules is the general shift from capital gains tax rules to income tax rules for the many forms of corporate and government debt.

Intellectual property and other intangibles

There is a second major exception to the application of the **13–22** Schedules and Cases of the income tax to companies applied to all forms of intangible assets. This follows the lead of the loan relationship provisions in moving towards accounts-based tax assessments and away from the traditional split between income and capital.

The Finance Act 2002, s.84 and Sch.29, introduces a new regime for taxing gains from a company's intangible fixed assets. The purpose of the regime is to reflect accounting practice in the way that income and gains from such assets are taxed. For this purpose, the key definition "intangible asset" is defined as having "the meaning it has for accounting purposes" (Sch.29, para.2). This includes intellectual property, and the Schedule goes on to define intellectual property widely as including not only patents, trade marks, copyrights, and similar forms of property copyrights, but also techniques and information of value not protected by rights. The rules are also expressly applied to goodwill.

The Schedule sets out rules for inclusion in the tax accounts of debits and credits in express accounting language. Further, where the company decides for accounting purposes to write off expenditure over a period, then the basic rule is that the same period applies for the inclusion of the debit (deduction) for tax purposes. Similarly, the general rule is that where a receipt in respect of intangibles is recognised (included) in the accounts, then a corresponding credit (addition) is to be brought into account for tax purposes. There are also rules for the realisation (in capital gains terms, disposal or part-disposal) of intangible assets.

These rules are applied not only to the tax accounts of a trading company, but also to assets held for the purposes of a (Sch.A) property business and also for non-trading gains and losses (taxable under Case VI of Sch.D). The result is the removal of any tax based on chargeable gains.

Deductions from total profits

13–23   Having arrived at the total profits of the company the next thing to do is to consider what items are permitted to be deducted in order to determine the amount on which corporation tax is to be charged. There are four kinds of permitted deductions: (1) charges on income; (2) management expenses; (3) minor capital allowances; (4) losses. We will deal with these in turn.

Charges on income

13–24   It will be remembered from Ch.12 ("Taxation of Individuals") that, for income tax, certain payments out are called "charges on income" and are deductible in computing "total income". Those deductions are separate from the deductions which are expenses in earning the income under any particular Schedule or Case. The position is similar for corporation tax. Payments out which are expenses in earning the income under a particular Schedule or Case are deductible in computing the income of a company under that Schedule or Case. That still leaves some payments out which, although not deductible *in computing* income, are deductible *from* (or "against") the total profits of the company. Many payments are not deductible in either way. Those which are deductible against total profits are called "charges on income": see s.338 of the Taxes Act. Of course deductibility is only completely effective if the charges on income are less than the total profits. If the charges exceed the total profits in a particular accounting period, and the charges include payments made wholly and exclusively for the purposes of a trade carried on by the company, then up to the amount of that excess (or of those payments, if less) the charges are deductible as if they were trading expenses of the trade for the purpose of computing a trading loss: Taxes Act, s.393(9). Or, where a company is a member of a group of companies, it may in certain circumstances "surrender" its excess of charges on income to another company in the group: Taxes Act, s.403(7).

There are various conditions with which a payment must comply if it is to count as a charge on income. The conditions are set out in s.338. In summary, a payment is not to be treated as a charge on income in any of the following circumstances: if the payment is charged to capital; if the payment is not ultimately borne by the company; if the payment is not made under a liability incurred for a valuable and sufficient consideration (subject to the rules for charitable donation, below); if (in the case of a non-resident company) the payment is incurred for the purposes of its overseas operations, if it would be deductible in computing the company's taxable profits. It must be made in *return for* consideration and not just in the hope of receiving consideration. Thus in *Ball v National & Grindlay's Bank* (1973), money paid under a covenant for the education of overseas employees' children in order to retain their services was held not to be a charge on income. It was a hope of a business advantage only. It is an open question whether payment by the company for the benefit of A with consideration supplied by B will be a charge on income.

Certain further stringent rules apply to payments made by companies to non-residents: see Taxes Act, ss.338(4) and 340.

A company that makes a gift of a sum of money to a charity is treated as if it made an annual payment of the sum: Finance Act 2000, s.40, amending s.339 of the Taxes Act.

Investment management expenses

Section 75 of the Taxes Act 1988 allows deduction of management expenses to any company, whether or not resident in the United Kingdom, with investment business here. The rules are broadly compatible with accounting practice. The point of this provision is to make up for the fact that a company, unless trading, has no opportunity of deducting expenses of management in the actual computation of profits. "Management expenses" are given a wide meaning by the courts, but they must relate to some act of management and not be part of the cost of acquiring an asset; e.g. a commission paid by one investment company to another company in return for that company's

13–25

13–26

guarantee of a loan raised by the first, was held by the Court of Appeal to be an acquisition and not a management expense. It was part of the price of raising the loan. See *Hoechst Finance Ltd v Gumbrell* (1983), CA. Individuals cannot claim these expenses.

Minor capital allowances

13–27   Another possible deduction relates to what one might call the "minor" capital allowances. An example is the agricultural buildings allowance for non-traders. The rules are complicated, but in certain circumstances such an allowance can be implemented by way of a deduction from total profits.

Losses

13–28   Losses of companies under corporation tax are dealt with in ways similar to losses of individuals under income tax. Let us first make the general point that a loss in a trade is computed in the same way as trading income is computed. In other words, the computation process may lead to a plus answer or a minus answer.

There are two main ways in which a trading loss of a company may be relieved: see the Taxes Act, ss.393, 393A.

Carry-forward

13–29   The company may claim, to set off a trading loss of one accounting period against trading income from the same trade in succeeding accounting periods. Relief is given against the first available year and then each successive year as appropriate. For the purposes of this carry-forward relief, if a company in a Deductions from Total Profitsparticular accounting period has an excess of "charges on income" over profits and the charges on income include payments made wholly and exclusively for the purposes of a trade carried on by the company, then, up to the amount of that excess or of those payments, whichever is the less, the charges on income so paid shall in computing a loss be deductible as if they were trading expenses of the trade: Taxes Act, s.393(9).

Set-off against current and previous profits

13–30   The company may claim to set off a trading loss in any particular accounting period against profits of whatever description (including chargeable gains) of that accounting period. If the loss is not in this way completely absorbed, it can be set against the profits of preceding accounting periods, subject to the limitation that the loss can only be carried back for accounting periods falling within the previous three years. Such a claim must be made within two years and relief is given against a later accounting period before an earlier period. The company must have been carrying on the same trade in the carry-back period. Set-off against general profits, but not carry forward relief, is not allowed unless either (a) the trade is being carried on in the exercise of functions conferred by an Act of Parliament or (b) the trade is being carried on on a commercial basis. It will be noticed that (b) above is parallel to a requirement for income tax (s.384) designed to exclude hobby-trading from the relief. And the special rules for hobby-farming (s.397) apply to corporation tax as well as to income tax.

Case VI
Apart from the above modes of loss relief there is also a 13–31 limited relief for Case VI losses. The company may claim to set off the loss against any other Case VI income for the same or any subsequent accounting period.

Company reconstructions
Where a company ceases to carry on a trade and another 13–32 company begins to carry it on, the change of company is ignored if the fundamental ownership (e.g. by shareholding) is (to the extent of three-quarters or more) the same before and after the change of companies. So if Company A has accumulated losses, and its trade is transferred to Company B (and the common ownership test is satisfied) Company B can use the carry-for-ward provisions and set off the accumulated losses against profits of the transferred trade (but not against other profits): Taxes Act ss.343, 344. There are restrictions if Company A is insolvent at the time of transfer.

Change of ownership
Sometimes the converse case arises; that is, the company 13–33 carrying on the trade remains the same but the underlying ownership changes. There used to be a brisk business in the sale of companies which were bulging with unrelieved tax losses. This commerce was largely struck down by a section which is now the Taxes Act, s.768. If in any period of three years there is both a substantial change in the ownership of a company and a "major change in the nature or conduct of a trade carried on by the company" past trading losses will not be available for carry-forward relief. A substantial change in ownership is basically a change in the ownership of more than 50 per cent of the voting

share capital. Nor is the relief available if "at any time after the scale of the activities in a trade carried on by a company has become small or negligible, and before any considerable revival of the trade, there is a change in the ownership of the company." The point of this latter provision is to strike at what was once a common practice keeping a company in existence simply because it was big with losses. Similar rules apply to prevent losses incurred *after* the change of ownership from being carried back against profits incurred *before* the change under the three year carry-back reliefs: Taxes Act, s.768A.

Group relief

13–34   A company which is a member of a group or of companies may "surrender" a loss to another company which is a member of the same group. This enables the transferee company to claim loss relief: Taxes Act, ss.402 and 403(1). The claimant company must use the relief in the year it was surrendered. A group for this purpose is where 75 per cent of the ordinary shares of one company is owned by the other. The availability of this relief has, however, led to the creation of strange "groups" of companies the object of which is to allow a profitable company to take the benefit of a loss of a company with insufficient profits. This has led in turn to complex anti-avoidance legislation and many complex cases as to what constitutes a group for this purpose.

A similar relief is available within a consortium of companies which together own trading companies.

Distributions

13–35   Some payments out made by a company are "distributions" and some are not. A dividend is a distribution; interest on loan stock is not. A distribution which is made by a company resident in the United Kingdom is chargeable to income tax on an individual recipient under Sch.F. A payment which is not a distribution is not subject to Sch.F, though it may be chargeable to tax under some other Schedule. For example, interest on loan stock is chargeable on an individual under Case III of Sch.D.

What is a distribution?

13–36   The concept of "distribution" is defined in the Taxes Act, ss.212 and 218, as amended. The definition is widened where the paying company is a "close company". A distribution is never deductible from the total profits of the paying company, be it close or non-close.

The definition of "distribution" is involved, but putting the matter broadly it covers (amongst other things) dividends (including capital dividends) and anything else (other than a repayment of share capital) distributed in respect of shares in cash or otherwise out of the assets of the company (meaning that the cost falls on the company) and where the company does not receive any new consideration for that which it distributes. It follows that a bonus issue is not a distribution, because there is no cost falling on the company; and a rights issue is not a distribution, because there is new consideration.

What is not a distribution?
The Companies Act gives companies power to repurchase   13–37
their own shares and to issue redeemable ordinary shares without requiring a court order. The avowed intention of these provisions was to provide small companies with shares which would be attractive to an outside investor in that he could resell to the company and not be "locked-in" with no opportunity to sell the shares. (Private companies in general have no open market for their shares.) But such a repurchase or redemption will be a distribution for tax purposes in so far as it amounts to more than the original investment. The Government therefore introduced an exemption from the distribution rules for certain repurchases and redemptions. We may say, however, that the exemption is extremely limited and in some cases will frustrate the intentions of the companies legislation.

There is one other exemption from the distribution rules   13–38
allowed for by ss.213 to 218 of the Taxes Act. This will be on a "demerger"—i.e. splitting up one company into two or more. In certain circumstances an issue of shares by the original company to the members of the new companies will not invoke the distribution rules. As with purchases and redemptions this relief only applies to trading companies when the de-merger is wholly or mainly for the benefit of the trade. Advance clearance is possible and desirable.

Close companies

Lurking in ss.414 to 422 of the 1988 Act are the remaining   13–39
legislative "ruins" of a once-great Revenue weapon for use in tax collection: the provisions aimed at breaking open close companies. What are left are complicated definitions which have limited practical effect. So instead of the full treatment in previous editions of this book, we will attempt only a brief summary.

The aim of the provisions was to break down the fiscal "walls" of companies to ensure that they were not used to hide money from the national coffers. (The more polite euphemism of "lifting the corporate veil" suggests making love, but these were wartime measures). The sections contain complicated language but the key issue was to define the targets so that they could not move out of range, and then provide high-calibre ammunition to hit the target. Close companies were at their most important when the top rate of income tax was 98 per cent and anything was, in most people's view, better than incurring that rate. Further, there could be double tax when dividends were paid out, as both the company and the shareholder were taxed. The obvious answer was to keep the money in the company and not to pay it out as a dividend—or to pay it out in disguised ways such as loans. The "ammunition" consisted of provisions that deemed dividends to occur, deemed loans to be dividends, and so on.

The targets were all companies that were, in effect, closely controlled. There were elaborate definitions that caught any combination of arrangements where private companies were controlled by five or fewer groups of people or by their directors.

In practice, the sections are of limited importance for two very different reasons. The first is that in the modern "global" economy, companies move out of range by the simple process of decamping to an offshore jurisdiction. The second is that the tax burden is now much lower.

PART THREE

TAXATION OF CAPITAL GAINS

CHAPTER 14

CAPITAL GAINS TAX

Introduction

Capital gains tax is, not surprisingly, a tax on capital gains. It **14–01** is not a tax on income and is generally free from any overlap with income tax. Nor is it a tax on capital as such (as a wealth tax would be) but only on gains. It is in this latter point (gains) that it differs from inheritance tax. Both inheritance tax and capital gains tax are concerned, broadly speaking, with the movement of capital from one person to another, but whereas on such a movement inheritance tax charges tax on the whole amount of capital which moves, capital gains tax charges tax only on the gain as between the value it has at the time of this movement (e.g. sale by A) compared with the value it had on the occasion of its last previous movement (e.g. purchase by A). There are a few occasions when there will be a charge to both taxes where some limited relief is available, but on the whole they are complementary. In general, inheritance tax was designed to tax voluntary transfers whereas capital gains tax was designed to tax commercial transfers. But changes made to both taxes have led to the paradoxical position that lifetime gifts are now subject to capital gains tax and only occasionally to inheritance tax.

Effect of inflation

The social idea behind capital gains tax is that it is too arbi- **14–02** trary, and therefore unfair, to tax a person on his income (e.g. dividends) and not to tax a person on his capital gains (e.g. buying shares on the stock exchange and selling them at a higher price). The latter is thought of as being as much a taxable resource as the former.[1]

But the theory was initially spoiled by high rates of inflation. If you bought something in 1978 for £400 and sold it in 1982 the probability is that you would have got around £600 for it. On paper you would have made a gain of £200; in real terms, taking into account the fall in the value of £1 due to inflation,

---

[1] But see "The Meade Report and the Taxation of Capital" [1979] B.T.R. 25.

237

you would not have made any gain at all. Until 1982, however, the legislation made no allowance for such a paper gain. In fact the point was tested in court, and in *Secretan v Hart* (1969) it was held that no adjustment for inflation was allowable.

Development of the tax

14–03   The tax was originally introduced in 1965 and taxed all gains accruing after March 1965. Conservative governments between 1979 and 1997 sought to reduce the impact of the tax (by introducing extensive reliefs) and to remedy the perceived injustice of taxing inflated gains. In 1982 a form of index-linking was introduced, which was refined in 1985 so that some relief was available for the effects of inflation from March 1982. Thus if a person bought an asset in 1972 for £1,000 and sold it in 1992 for £11,000 he would have been able to discount from the total gain of £10,000 a sum for inflation from 1982 to 1992. But he or she was still liable in full for all gains incurred before 1982. In 1988, therefore, it was decided to take out of the charge all gains, paper or real, incurred before 1982. Thus in our example the gain would be calculated by treating the market value of the asset at March 1982, say £7,000, as the cost of acquiring the asset and deducting that from the sale price of £11,000. That gain of £4,000 would then also have attracted relief for inflation between 1982 and 1992.

In 1998 the Labour Government decided that, for individuals, there should be no more relief for the effects of inflation but that instead relief should be given according to the length of time that the asset has been held by the taxpayer. The avowed intention was to discourage short-term gains. This taper relief, as it was known, reduced the chargeable gain by a percentage which increased the longer the asset was held, to a maximum achieved after two years for a business asset and 10 years for other assets. This favourable treatment of business assets was balanced by the phased withdrawal of a relief on the transfer of such assets, known as retirement relief. Indexation relief was still available, however, for inflation between 1982 and 1998 and there was still no charge for any gains accruing before 1982. This complex structure whereby the chargeable gain depended upon whether the asset was acquired before 1982, before 1998 or after that date, was abolished as from the 2008/9 tax year. There is no longer any relief either for the effects of inflation or length of ownership. Rebasing to the market value of a pre 1982 asset as at March 1982, however, still remains. At the same time, by way of compensation, the rate of tax was changed from the taxpayer's marginal rate of income tax (e.g. 40 per cent for a higher rate taxpayer) to a flat rate of 18 per cent.

The immediate combined effect of losing the reliefs and changing the rate was that those owning unquoted shares or interests in a business (supposedly tax favoured as wealth-creating) had their effective rate raised from 10 per cent to 18 per cent, whereas the owners of a second home (regarded as luxury assets) had their rate cut from a minimum of 24 per cent to 18 per cent. Further, for all, relief for inflation up to 1998 was lost. As a result of sustained pressure from industrialists after these changes were announced a new form of relief, entrepreneurs' relief, was introduced for 2008/9. In effect that relief reduces the effective rate on certain business disposals to 10 per cent but only on the first £1 million of such disposals during a taxpayer's lifetime. These matters are considered more fully at paras 15-14 and 16.22 below.

Companies and individuals

For administrative and assessment purposes capital gains tax, which applies only to individuals and not companies, is similar to income tax and is thus subsumed into the system of self-assessment and payment already explained. It is assessed and charged annually and payment is due by January 31 of the year following the year of assessment. For companies, chargeable gains, although computed in general in the same way as for individuals, are then liable to corporation tax and not capital gains tax.

14-04

The law relating to capital gains tax was consolidated in the Taxation of Chargeable Gains Act 1992. **Unless otherwise stated all references in this part of the book are to that Act**. Most amendments made since then have been incorporated into that Act. It is, as we shall see, quite a technical tax and there have been many cases for the courts to decide. Those which relate to the principles of the tax are included below.

Rate of tax

Until 1988 the tax was charged at a flat rate of 30 per cent. From 1988 the rates of capital gains tax and income tax were harmonised. A taxpayer's chargeable gains were treated as if they were the top slice of that person's taxable income and thus the appropriate income tax band—lower or higher—applied. As from 2008 the rate is once again a flat rate of 18 per cent: s.4.

14-05

CAPITAL GAINS TAX

Exempt amount
14–06   An individual subject to capital gains tax can take advantage of the "exempt amount" for each year. This is specified by a statutory instrument issued in advance by the Treasury for each tax year and is index-linked unless Parliament decides otherwise: s.3. The amount for 2008–09 is £9,600. Tax is therefore only payable in so far as an individual has taxable gains (chargeable gains less allowable losses) in excess of that amount in the year. The exempt amount is in effect the tax threshold for the year in question and so fulfils the same role for capital gains tax as the personal allowances do for income tax. Because capital gains tax is charged by reference to a transaction it is therefore possible to allocate such transactions between years so as to maximise the use of this exemption.

Spouses and civil partners
14–07   Spouses and civil partners are taxable as separate individuals for capital gains tax as they are for income tax. Thus, for example, they both have an exempt amount. However, there are two consequences for capital gains tax if the spouses or civil partners are living together. For this purpose an individual is deemed to be living with his or her spouse or civil partner unless they are legally separated or the circumstances are such that the separation is likely to be permanent: s.288(3). The first consequence is that a transfer of assets between the parties is treated as if neither a gain nor a loss has occurred (so that the transferee is deemed to have acquired the asset at the price paid by the transferor) (see below) and the second is that they can only have one main residence to qualify for exemption from the tax (see para.16–16). Thus a cohabiting couple can each have a house which they can sell free of the tax, but not so married couples or civil partners.

Trustees
14–08   Trustees, who may be liable to pay the tax in relation to changes in the beneficial ownership of the trust property, are only entitled to half the annual exempt amount (Sch.1, para.2). Personal representatives, however, are entitled to the full amount for the year of the death and the two following years. After that they cease to have any exempt amount (s.3(7)). Both trustees and personal representatives are taxed at 40 per cent.

240

The charge to tax

Section 1(1) declares: "Tax shall be charged in accordance **14–09** with this Act in respect of capital gains, that is to say chargeable gains computed in accordance with this Act and accruing to a person on the disposal of assets."

This subsection contains in summary form the whole of the law relating to capital gains tax. We shall know that law when we know what a chargeable gain is, how the Act requires computation to be made, what a person is, what an asset is, and, above all, what a disposal is. This chapter tells us what a chargeable gain is and what amounts to a person, an asset and a disposal; i.e. the basic charge, including the complications caused by settled property. The next chapter concerns itself with the computation of the gain and the final chapter with the various exemptions and reliefs from the tax.

Chargeable gains

All gains, other than exempted gains, are chargeable gains **14–10** (s.15(2)). The chargeable gain is, broadly speaking, the difference between the cost of the asset and the consideration received on its disposal. The cost is usually referred to as the "base cost". It is important to realise that the consideration received by A on a disposal to B will be B's base cost on a subsequent disposal to C. Capital gains tax operates thus by charging the gains on an asset by reference to specific events, known as disposals. In general, as we have seen, where an asset was acquired before March 31, 1982, the base cost will be its market value at that date.

Although each asset disposed of in a year of assessment has to be considered separately, the tax is charged on the total amount of chargeable gains in the year after deducting allowable losses (s.2(2)).

The key requirements for a charge are the disposal of an asset by a chargeable person. Let us now examine each of these in turn (in reverse order).

Persons

"Person" has the same meaning as in income tax law. So not **14–11** only individuals are persons but so also are companies and trustees and personal representatives. As we have seen, however, companies are liable to corporation tax and not capital gains tax on their gains. For capital gains tax purposes in all parts of the United Kingdom partners in a general or limited partnership are treated separately as individuals for their share of the gains or losses arising from the disposal of partnership assets or other partnership dealings: s.59. The same principle also applies to members of a limited liability partnership by virtue of s.59A, even though it is a body corporate. That tax transparency (as it is called) will cease, however, if the LLP goes into liquidation, when the LLP is deemed to have always owned the relevant assets and the members will instead be assessed on the disposal of their interests in the LLP.

Residence, etc.

14–12 A person is chargeable to capital gains tax in respect of chargeable gains accruing to him in a year of assessment during any part of which he is resident in the United Kingdom, or during which he is ordinarily resident in the United Kingdom (s.2(1)). The meaning of "resident" and "ordinarily resident" are the same as for income tax (s.9).

On the other hand, the disposal of an asset which is situated in the United Kingdom only imposes tax on a person who is not resident and not ordinarily resident here if he is carrying on a trade through a branch or agency in the United Kingdom and the asset is connected with the trade (s.10(1)). To prevent an individual from acquiring a temporary residence outside the United Kingdom and then disposing of a UK asset free of tax, s.10A provides a charge on such gains realised during the period of non-residence which is triggered by the individual's return to the United Kingdom. The section applies if the individual was resident or ordinarily resident in the United Kingdom for some part of four of the seven tax years prior to departure from the United Kingdom, and the period of non-residence is less than five full tax years. In general, the gains will be computed as if the individual had been resident in the year in question but will be charged at the rate applicable in the year of return.

An individual who is resident or ordinarily resident but not domiciled in the United Kingdom is taxed only if the proceeds are remitted to the United Kingdom on gains from the disposal of assets outside the United Kingdom (s.12(1)), and losses on the disposal of such assets are not allowable losses (s.10(4)). In *Young v Phillips* (1984), the disposal of letters of allotment to shares in a United Kingdom company, although taking place in Sark, was held not to fall within s.12(1). The letters carried rights enforceable in the United Kingdom and so were not assets situated outside the United Kingdom.

Assets

Section 21(1) provides that all forms of property are assets, **14–13** and this is so whether they are situated in the United Kingdom or not. Thus a United Kingdom resident is liable for disposal of non-UK assets. (Section 275 contains rules for determining where certain kinds of assets are situated.) That subsection then declares that assets include: (a) options, debts and incorporeal property generally; (b) any currency other than sterling; and (c) any form of property created by the person disposing of it, or otherwise coming to be owned without being acquired. Notice that head (b) excludes sterling, so that, e.g. a gift of cash is not subject to capital gains tax, and is only rarely subject to inheritance tax. On the other hand, head (c) brings into charge things which were never acquired but were on the contrary created by the taxpayer, such as a building, the copyright of a book, and (very importantly) the goodwill of a business[2] which of course may have been built up from nothing. Some items, as we shall see later, are expressly stated not to be chargeable assets.

Personal and other rights

Since assets are defined by reference to all forms of property it **14–14** is important to note that this will include all interests in property; for example a lease of land is itself an asset as well as the reversion. There was originally some doubt as to whether purely personal rights could be assets for this purpose; these would include assets such as the right of a protected tenant or a right to damages for an action in tort. The problem is that such rights cannot be assigned or sold, but they can, for example, be surrendered. The point was resolved in *O'Brien v Benson's Hosiery Ltd* (1980) where B was appointed a director of the company in 1968 on a seven-year contract. In 1970 the company released him from this contract in return for a payment of £50,000. The Revenue sought to assess the company on this receipt on the basis that it had disposed of an asset, viz its rights against B under the contract. The House of Lords, reversing the Court of Appeal, held that these rights were assets. The fact that the company could not assign their rights did not matter. The

---

[2] See, e.g. *Butler v Evans* (1980). In *Kirby v Thorn EMI Plc* (1987), the Court of Appeal held that where a company, having sold three subsidiaries, agreed not to compete with their businesses it had disposed of its goodwill in those businesses. That was an asset. They overruled the judge's opinion that the company was merely fettering its freedom of commercial activity.

important point was that they could be turned to account, as in fact they had been in this case. As we shall see even the fact that an asset has no obvious market value does not prevent it being an asset—one can always calculate a hypothetical market value.

Non-assignable rights under a contract are therefore assets. Can the same be said of a disputed or moral claim? Some assistance may be derived from the decision in *Zim Properties Ltd v Procter* (1985) that a right to sue for damages in the tort of negligence was an asset on the basis that it could be turned to account (e.g. by a compromise settlement). The judge, applying the *O'Brien* test, thought that all such actions would be assets unless clearly frivolous or vexatious. "Assets" is a wider concept than "property". Since in practice the question will only arise if the "assets" are turned into account (e.g. there is a disposal), the *O'Brien* test suggests that all such rights and claims will be assets if the point arises. Put another way, we can almost say that if you can dispose of something in any of the ways possible under the Act, it is an asset.

Disposals

14–15   The basic event on which capital gains tax depends, therefore, is the disposal of an asset. It has been judicially pointed out that, subject to certain exceptions such as options, there can be no disposal of an asset unless the asset existed and was owned by the taxpayer prior to the disposal. Thus creating a contractual right to a payment of money is not a disposal: *Burca v Parkinson* (2001). Whenever a disposal does take place, however, a calculation must be made to see whether there has been a gain or a loss or neither.

The word "disposal" has first of all to be given its ordinary meaning before going on to consider the extended meaning given to it by the Act. In its ordinary meaning a disposal occurs whenever the owner of an asset (which, remember, may be an abstract entity such as a right) divests himself of his entitlement to the asset. Thus the ordinary meaning includes sale, exchange and gift.

Gifts and disposals not at arm's length
14–16   It is very important to grasp that the making of a gift is a chargeable event. At first sight this may seem very odd. Clearly the giver of a gift has made a disposal, but how on earth can he be said to have made a gain? The point was challenged in court in *Turner v Follett* (1973), CA. It was held that a gift is a chargeable event. In s.17(1)(a) it is now enacted that where a

person acquires an asset by way of gift, the disposal of it to him (as well as the acquisition of it by him) shall be deemed to be for a consideration equal to its market value. So if a father gives to his son an asset which he bought for £10,000 and at the time of the gift its market value is £14,000, father has made a chargeable (albeit notional or unrealised) gain of £4,000. But remember that if the gift is a gift of British money there is no charge to *this* tax (though there may possibly be to inheritance tax) because sterling is not an asset; s.21(1)(b). Otherwise, there would be no yardstick to measure gains.

When capital gains tax was introduced there was no other charge on gifts (except those made within seven years of a death). Capital transfer tax, introduced in 1975 originally applied to all gifts and there was therefore a potential double charge to tax on a gift. When capital transfer tax mutated to inheritance tax most gifts (except those made within seven years of a death) were again excluded from the charge. Thus the relief from capital gains tax introduced in 1980 to avoid the double charge was substantially repealed.

ARM'S LENGTH The market value rule for gifts stated in s.17 **14–17** applies not only to a disposal by way of gift but also to a disposal "otherwise than by way of a bargain made at arm's length". The idea is that if two people are closer than arm's length away from each other their dealings may be not wholly governed by commercial considerations, with the result that a deal may be done at less than market value. This might be so, for example, where a person sells a sailing dinghy to a friend. In such a case, if the section applies, the disposal is deemed for the purpose of capital gains tax to be at market value. So if Fred bought a boat for £50,000 and later sold it to Greg for £60,000 when its value was really £100,000, Fred has a chargeable gain of £50,000 and Greg gets a base cost of £100,000. In *Zim Properties Ltd v Procter* (1985) a potential negligence action was held not to have been acquired at arms length or by way of bargain and was thus acquired at market value at the date the right of action accrued.

Where the parties to a transaction are "connected persons" the transaction is automatically treated as a transaction otherwise than by way of a bargain at arm's length; s.18(2). "Connected person" is defined in s.286(2) as follows: "A person is connected with an individual if that person is the individual's spouse or civil partner, or is a relative, or spouse or civil partner of a relative, of the individual or of the individual's husband or wife." And by s.286(8) "relative" means "brother, sister, ancestor or lineal descendant". There are also definitions in s.286 of "connected person" in relation to trusts, partnerships and companies.

Where the parties are not connected persons, as with Fred and Greg above, the question as to whether they are at arm's length or not is a question of fact, which amounts in effect to deciding whether there was an element of gift involved. In *Bullivant Holdings Ltd v IRC* (1998), it was held that where X purchased a 25 per cent shareholding in a company from Y for £12,500, they were at arm's length and so that was X's base cost, even though X had acquired a 50 per cent holding in the same company on the same day from Z, which had had its market value of £350,000 attributed to it as X's base cost since X and Z were connected persons. In *Mansworth v Jelley* (2002), Lightman J. said that a bargain at arm's length meant a transaction between two parties with separate and distinct interests who have each agreed terms (actually or by inference) with a mind solely to his or her own interests.

Where there is a gift or a sale at an undervalue by persons not at arm's length, the donor or vendor is primarily liable for the tax, subject to the relief mentioned above, but if he does not pay it the donee or purchaser can in certain circumstances be required to pay it.

Other market value cases

14–18   Section 17(1)(b) also applies the market value rule to cases where the consideration cannot be valued, or is connected with the loss of employment, reduction of emoluments or is in respect of the provision or services. In *Whitehouse v Ellam* (1995) it was said that there must be a direct link at the time of the disposal between the disposal and the loss of emoluments.

Part disposals

14–19   A "disposal" includes a part disposal (s.21(2)). Thus where a person disposes of less than the whole of an asset (or disposes of less than his whole interest in an asset) that counts as a part disposal of the whole asset and not a disposal of part of the asset (see *Watton v Tippett* (1996)). Generally speaking, the gain accruing on the disposal is calculated by reference to a proportion of the cost of the entire asset. A part disposal also includes the disposal of an interest in an asset, which interest is created by the disposal and did not exist before the disposal. If the owner of freehold land grants a lease (for a premium) over the land the granting of the lease is a part disposal, notwithstanding that the lease only comes into existence at the moment when the part disposal takes place. The freeholder has disposed of part of his interest in the land.

While we are talking of leases let us point out that a premium for a lease is only chargeable to capital gains tax in so far as it is not chargeable to income tax as income from land (Sch.8, para.5(1)). This is part of a wider principle, namely that any sum charged to income tax is not to count as part of the consideration for a disposal for the purposes of capital gains tax (see s.37(1)).

Deriving capital sums from assets

There is an extended meaning of "disposal" in s.22(1) where a **14–20** capital sum is derived from assets by their owner, notwithstanding that no asset is acquired by the person paying the capital sum. The clearest example of this is where a shareholder receives a capital distribution in respect of his shares. This section also applies to fix the charge on those personal, non-assignable rights and claims, discussed above, which are assets if they can be turned into account. The "turning to account" is the derivation of a capital sum from the asset, hence the disposal and the charge: *O'Brien v Benson Hosiery (Holdings) Ltd* (1979), HL; *Zim Properties Ltd v Procter* (1985). In the latter case it was stated to be a matter for the exercise of common sense as to the asset from which the sum is derived. It might be the right to payment itself or the property giving rise to that demand (e.g. by a vendor of a house). The section was also applied in *Kirby v Thorn EMI Plc* (1987) to a company entering into a restrictive covenant not to compete with the business it had just sold. It had derived a capital sum from an asset (its goodwill). In *British Telecommunications Plc v HMRC* (2006), Sp Comm, however, it was held that if the payment is not for giving up rights under an agreement but rather to give effect to the agreement, it has not been derived from an asset.

SPECIFIC CASES   Section 22(1) then goes on to say that the **14–21** principle applies in particular to four defined circumstances: (a) capital sums received by way of compensation for any kind of damage or injury to assets or for the loss, destruction or dissipation of assets or for any depreciation or risk of depreciation of an asset. An example would be compensation for infringement of copyright; another example would be damages paid by a tortfeasor for physical damage done to an asset; (b) capital sums received under a policy of insurance covering the risk of any kind of damage, etc. to assets. This hardly needs examples;

(c) capital sums received in return for forfeiture or surrender of rights, or for refraining from exercising rights. An example would be a payment received by A for releasing B from his obligation under a contract;[3] (d) capital sums received as consideration for use or exploitation of assets. This seems to point towards such transactions as the grant of a right to use a copyright. In *Chaloner v Pellipar Investments Ltd* (1996) it was said that this head could not apply where the owner granted a lease over his property. That would be a part disposal under s.21(2). The head might apply where the owner retained full title to the property, e.g. on the grant of a licence.

The question might be asked as to why a taxpayer should argue for a disposal under head (d) rather than for a part disposal. The answer is that a disposal under heads (a)–(d) takes place when the capital sum is received (s.22(2)), whereas a part disposal takes place on the disposal and, as in the case itself, that can affect the computation of the gain. Curiously, s.22(2) does not apply to other disposals caught by the general wording of s.21(1); it only applies to the specific examples in heads (a)–(d).

14–22   WIDE APPLICATION   Section 22 has produced other problems of interpretation for the courts. In *Marren v Ingles* (1980) the House of Lords held that the meaning of "notwithstanding that no asset is acquired by the person paying the capital sum" was "whether or not" he acquired such an asset, e.g. absolute title to an asset on payment of a contingent sum. The effect of that means that the general wording of s.22(1) can apply to all commercial disposals, including basic sales. In the *Chaloner* case, above, it was therefore held that the general wording in s.22(1) could apply, but since s.22(2) could not apply, it availed the taxpayers little. Conversely, in *Davenport v Chilver* (1983) the judge decided that if a capital sum was received within one of the specific headings (a–d) the section could apply even if the capital sum did not strictly derive from an asset as required by the general wording of the section (e.g. access to an independent compensation fund).

In *Davis v Powell* (1977), on the other hand, money paid to a tenant farmer as compensation for disturbance on the ending of his lease as required by the Agricultural Holdings Act 1948 was held not to be *derived* from the lease but from the statutory right to compensation. Nor was it money received under (c) as money received for the surrender of rights under the lease—there was

---

[3]   e.g. the disposal of the company's rights in *O'Brien v Bensons' Hosiery (Holdings) Ltd* (1979), see para.14–14, above.

no element of bargain but simply a statutory computation. A similar result has been applied to business tenancies: *Drummond v Austin-Brown* (1983), but not where the right to compensation is an independent property right, e.g. to a compensation fund for loss of foreign appropriated property, see *Davenport v Chilver* (1983).

Loss, destruction and negligible value

Another extended meaning of "disposal" is set out in s.24(1):   **14–23**

> "...the occasion of the entire loss, destruction, dissipation or extinction of an asset shall ... constitute a disposal of the asset whether or not any capital sum by way of compensation or otherwise is received in respect of the destruction, dissipation or extinction of the asset."

The *entire* loss, destruction, etc. of an asset would normally mean that it had become valueless, so the deemed disposal is a disposal for a nil consideration. The next subsection—s.24(2)—deals with a situation where there has not been entire loss, destruction, etc., but where the value of an asset has become "negligible". The effect here is that the owner is deemed to have sold and immediately re-acquired the asset at its then market value. The deemed disposal, being at a negligible value, may well give the owner a loss (compared with the price for which he had acquired the asset); the point of the deemed re-acquisition is that if the value of the asset picks up so that there is a gain on its subsequent disposal, that gain is calculated by reference to this new, low, acquisition value. This subsection only applies if the taxpayer makes a claim to the commissioners to that effect.[4]

BUILDINGS   In deciding whether an asset becomes entirely   **14–24**
lost, destroyed, etc. or whether it merely becomes of negligible value, if the asset in question is a building it is treated as an asset separate from the land on which it stands. But the owner is deemed to have disposed of the land (as well as of the building) and also to have immediately re-acquired the land at its then market value. The effect of this is that any loss relief that the owner gets in respect of the building will be reduced by the amount of any appreciation in the value of the land itself since he acquired it.

---

[4] The disposal (loss) is deemed either to have taken place at the date of the claim or at any earlier time within two years prior to the tax year at the claim, if specified in the claim. It cannot be deemed to take effect any earlier: *Williams v Bullivant* (1983).

14–25   EFFECT OF INSURANCE PAYMENTS   Let us look now at the inter-relation between the destruction, etc., of an asset and the subsequent receipt of a capital sum. If an asset is totally destroyed that will produce a loss, because the deemed disposal is for a nil consideration. If the destroyer pays a sum in damages or an insurer pays insurance money that may reduce or wipe out the loss. Suppose A bought an asset for £6,000. Subsequently it was totally destroyed. A is deemed to have disposed of the asset for nothing. That produces a loss of £6,000. A few weeks later an insurance company pays A £6,000. That produces a gain of £6,000. The one balances the other, so all in all there is no loss or gain. Of course, the insurance company may pay A less than £6,000, say £5,500, in which case there is an overall loss of £500. Or the insurance company may pay A more than £6,000, say £7,000, in which case there is an overall gain of £1,000.

There are provisions in s.23 whereby in some situations tax on such a gain may be deferred until there is a disposal in the future. This is a kind of "hold-over" relief. ("Hold-over" relief is another splendid piece of tax jargon, to be found nowhere in the dictionary, but everywhere in the Acts. There are several kinds of hold-over relief in CGT, all amounting only to post-ponements of tax, rather than complete exemptions.) For example, if our friend A spends the insurance money within one year of receipt on buying a replacement asset for £7,000 the £1,000 gain is dealt with by deducting £1,000 from the acquisition cost of the replacement asset. This will have the effect of increasing by £1,000 the gain to A when he comes to dispose of the replacement asset in the future. So A will be in exactly the same position as he would have been in if the asset had never been destroyed. Suppose A sells the asset (the replacement asset) eventually for £9,000. When he sells the asset, he deducts £1,000 from the replacement cost (which was £7,000) so his gain is £9,000 minus £6,000 = £3,000. If the original asset (which cost £6,000) had never been destroyed his gain would equally have been £3,000.

14–26   DAMAGES   These provisions apply not only to insurance money received but also to damages received. A somewhat similar system operates where an asset is not destroyed but only damaged.

Timing of a disposal by contract

14–27   Section 28 provides that where an asset is disposed of and acquired under a contract, then, unless the contract is conditional, the time at which the disposal and acquisition takes place is the time when the contract was made and not the time when the asset is subsequently transferred or conveyed. This is of course particularly relevant to a disposal of land by the traditional method of an exchange of contracts (which transfers the equitable title) followed by the conveyance or transfer of the legal title. But there must be a disposal by the contract, even one of land, for s.28 to operate. In *Underwood v HMRC* (2008), the taxpayer agreed to sell some land on a set date but at the same time exercised an option to repurchase. There were no conveyances and the only result was that he paid £20,000 (the difference between the sale and repurchase prices) to the other party. It was held that, since there had been no actual transfer of the beneficial title to the purchaser at any time, s.28 did not apply (the taxpayer was seeking to create a loss in that year). There had been no performance of the contract and so no disposal under a contract.

It is clear that s.28 fixes the date of the disposal, for timing purposes, as being the date of the exchange of contracts but it does not have the additional effect of fixing the parties to the disposal and acquisition (and their interests) as being the parties to that contract as distinct from those at the date of completion where they are different.

This was the decision of the House of Lords in *Jerome v Kelley* (2004), reversing the Court of Appeal. In 1987, A, B and C agreed to sell some land to X. In 1989, A and B each assigned half their interest in the land to D. The transfer of the land to X was completed in 1992. The disposal was held not to have been made by A, B and C only, as to their shares in the land in 1987 but by A, B, C and D as to their shares in 1992. (D was a nonresident trust). The 1989 assignments were part disposals, by A and B to D. That was the straightforward analysis. Section 28 only found the date of the disposal as 1987. Their Lordships were, however, concerned with the potential difficulty with this solution if D had not been in existence in 1987. Although a person could dispose of an asset which he did not own at the time, could he dispose of an asset at a time when it, e.g. a trust, did not exist? The point was left open.

Conditional contracts

Where there is a conditional contract, however, the date of the disposal/acquisition is the date when the condition is fulfilled. In *Lyon v Pettigrew* (1985), it was held that this only applied where all the liabilities under a contract of sale were

14–28

conditional and not, as in that case, where title in only part of the property was to pass on payment of all instalments. The condition must be a condition precedent to the incurring of a binding contractual obligation. In *Hatt v Newman* (2000), contracts for the sale of a property were exchanged in February 1995, with a completion date of March 20, 1995. This was conditional, however, on planning permission for conversion of the building being granted. Planning permission was granted on March 29, 1995 and legal completion took place on April 6, 1995. The taxpayer's argument (made in person) that the disposal had taken place on April 6, (and so in the next tax year) failed. If this was a conditional contract within s.28(2), the date when the condition was satisfied was March 29. Alternatively, if the condition was merely a condition subsequent to the incurring of binding contractual obligations, then s.28(1) would fix the date of disposal as being in February 1995. (The Revenue actually calculated that the taxpayer's liability would have been greater if he had succeeded in his argument.)

Section 28 does not apply to disposals by derivation of a capital sum from an asset under s.22(1)(a)–(d) where, as we have seen (para.14–22), s.22(2) defers the disposal to the time when the capital sum is actually received.

Disposals for a deferred or contingent consideration

14–29   Suppose that A sells an asset to B for £5000 payable immediately and £1000 per month payable for the next 10 months. The consideration received by A for that asset for capital gains tax purposes is £15,000 (£5,000 + 10 × £1,000) and he is deemed to have received this amount at the date of sale, i.e. in accordance with s.28, just discussed. Section 48 makes it clear that no allowance is to be made for the fact that A will not receive the full amount at that time. This is an example of a disposal for a deferred consideration (i.e. a future payment which will become payable).

The position is more complex in relation to disposals for a contingent consideration (i.e. a future payment, which may or may not become payable, usually of an uncertain amount). This has caused problems which had to be resolved by the House of Lords in *Marren v Ingles* (1980). In that case the taxpayer agreed to sell 60 shares in an unquoted company for £700 each, payable immediately, and a stated percentage of the sale price quoted for those shares if the company was floated on the stock exchange. When the company was floated the purchaser became liable to pay the taxpayer £2,825 for each share. Clearly there was a disposal of assets for at least £700 each but how to deal with the additional amount?

The Revenue did not seek to charge the tax by reference to a single disposal on the original agreement but by reference to two disposals—one of the shares on the agreement and one of the right to the contingent payments under s.22(1) as the receipt of a capital sum derived from that right on payment of the extra amount. After much technical argument by the judge and the Court of Appeal on the merits of applying s.22(1), the House of Lords held that the section could apply whether the purchaser was thereby acquiring full title to the shares or simply extinguishing a liability to pay an additional sum. The judge, Slade J., also discussed whether s.17 could have applied (i.e. a disposal where the consideration cannot be valued is to be charged at market value) or whether it could be regarded as two part-disposals, but expressed no opinion on the matter.

Section 48, which provides that deferred or contingent consideration be added back onto the proceeds of the disposal as if paid at the time, relates only to the first disposal, and in a *Marren v Ingles* situation any such contingent consideration can only be valued then on an actuarial (i.e. reduced) basis. The second, deemed, disposal catches the full amount actually paid. Thus the argument of the taypayer in *Marson v Marriage* (1980) that since the original disposal was prior to 1965 (at that time the starting date for the tax) and the contingent payments (in that case for land subsequently developed) after 1965, s.48 required all the considerations to be regarded as pre-1965 and so out of the charge, failed, and the principle of *Marren v Ingles* was applied.

Appropriations to and from stock in trade

It will be remembered that in income tax where a trader **14–30** disposes of part of his stock in trade not by sale either but for his own use or for some other non-commercial purpose, he must, for the purposes of income tax, bring into his accounts as a receipt the market value of the asset at that time. And of course the converse applies—where a trader transfers an item from his own recreational enjoyment into his trade he can show in his accounts the market value of that item as an expense of the trade.

Transfer to stock

14–31   Now, how does capital gains tax bear on these events? Where a person who is a trader transfers a personal asset to his trade that appropriation is treated as a disposal, thus involving a gain or a loss compared with its earlier acquisition cost: s.161(1). But he can, if he wishes, avoid payment of capital gains tax by electing to bring the asset into trading stock not at its then market value simply, but at its then market value reduced by the amount of the chargeable gain or increased by the amount of the allowable loss (s.161(3)). (A partner can only make this election if the other partners concur.) Take the case of a gain: the effect is that the item appears in his trading account amongst "purchases" at a figure below its true value by the amount of the gain, thus swelling his trading profits for that year by that amount.

Transfer from stock

14–32   In the converse case, where a trader transfers an item of trading stock to his personal enjoyment he is treated as having acquired it for a consideration equal to the amount then brought into the accounts of the trade in respect of that item for income tax purposes. Thus the closing figure for the item for income tax purposes is taken as the base cost for capital gains tax purposes: s.161(2). For income tax purposes no doubt the trader would like to put a low figure on the item, thus reducing his trade receipts and so his profits. But a low figure for income tax means a low base cost, which will in the end involve him in more capital gains tax.

     To some extent, the practical importance of s.161 is reduced by the presence of an exemption from capital gains tax in the case of a disposal of an asset which is tangible movable property and which is a wasting asset: see below at para.15–12. But of course not all stock in trade is tangible movable property. It may be tangible without being movable (e.g. land) or movable without being tangible (e.g. stocks and shares).

Groups

14–33   The benefits of s.161(3) are available to a group of companies if they can ensure that one company transfers a non trading stock asset to another member of the group in such a way that the asset is acquired by the second company as trading stock (s.171). In this way, e.g., an allowable capital loss may be converted into a trading loss by electing to use s.161(3). The only requirement is that the acquisition must be by a trading company as trading stock. In *New Angel Court Ltd v Adam* (2003), the judge, after considering a number of cases, said that to qualify the transfer must have some commercial justification or conceivable reason, be normal and the asset must not only be of a kind which is sold in the ordinary course of the second company's trade but must also be acquired for the purpose of that trade with a view to a resale at a genuine profit.

Capital distributions by companies

Where a person receives a capital distribution (other than a new holding, on which see the next heading) in respect of shares in a company, he is treated as if in consideration of that distribution he had disposed of an interest in the shares (s.122). This applies for example when a company makes a "rights" issue of shares[5] and a shareholder sells his rights to a third party. Another example of its application is when a liquidator makes a repayment of capital to shareholders in the course of a winding-up. If, however, the amount of any capital distribution is "small"[6] as compared with the value of the shares the occurrence is not treated as a disposal, but instead the amount of the distribution is deducted from the expenditure allowable as a deduction in computing a gain when the shareholder comes to dispose of the shares in the future. This of course has the effect of increasing the gain and hence the tax. It is a kind of hold-over relief.

14–34

Company adjustments

There are detailed provisions (in ss.126–140) as to the bearing of capital gains tax on the re-organisation of a company's share capital, the conversion of securities and the amalgamation of companies.

14–35

These provisions are very detailed but the general principle with regard to reorganisations is that where a shareholder's former interest in the company (the original holding) now involves different shares which represent the original shares (the new holding), the reorganisation is not to be regarded either as a disposal of the original holding or as an acquisition of the new holding. Instead the two holdings are to be regarded as a single

---

[5] This is an issue of shares which are offered first to existing shareholders.
[6] Revenue and Customs take the general view that "small" means less than £3,000 or 5 per cent of the value of the shares, if greater. But it is a question of fact and degree: see *O'Rourke v Binks* [1992] S.T.C. 703.

asset acquired by the shareholder at the cost of the original holding. In *Unliver (UK) Holdings Ltd v Smith* (2003), the Court of Appeal held that this principle did not apply where the shareholder held all the shares of one class in the company and the other class was cancelled on a scheme of arrangement. A new holding must result from the reorganisation, which required there to be either a disposal or acquisition which would then be negatived by the sections. There was no such disposal or acquisition in that case because (a) cancelling shares is not a disposal; and (b) the rights attaching to the retained shares had not been altered. Thus the shares could not be regarded as a new holding.

An example where this continuity principle will operate is where a company makes a "bonus" issue or a "rights" issue of shares and a shareholder takes up the shares (a "new holding"). The new shares are treated as acquired when the original shares were acquired, and the acquisition cost of the total holding is the cost of the original shares plus the sum (if any) which the shareholder pays for the new holding. In the case of a company amalgamation (or take-over) then, subject to certain conditions, the exchange of shares in one company for shares in another company does not count as a disposal.

Avoidance conditions

14–36   This rule led to a great deal of tax avoidance and the relief has been subjected to two conditions, namely that the change must be effected for bona fide commercial reasons and it must not form part of a scheme or arrangements of which the main purpose or one of the main purposes is avoidance of tax liability: (s.137).

In *Snell v HMRC* (2007), these two conditions were discussed. It was held that provided there was evidence of bona fide commercial reasons for the deal, the fact that the transaction might have been structured differently did not matter. But that in assessing the avoidance test, the tax liability being avoided could be one which was prospective, contingent or simply deferred.

Debts

14–37   The "satisfaction" of a debt is a disposal by the creditor. "Satisfaction" of a debt includes payment of the debt, and it also includes assignment of the debt. It may be worth discussing what the creditor whose debtor pays him a debt is disposing of.

The answer is that he is disposing of the debt itself i.e. the right to the money, which is intangible property. There are many circumstances in the law of capital gains tax where it is more obvious that a person is acquiring something (e.g. money in satisfaction of a debt) than that he is disposing of something. If one looks closely one sees that he is disposing of the right to obtain that which he acquires. Where does the capital gain come in in connection with a debt? The answer to that is that the capital gain is the difference between what the creditor lent and what he gets back as a capital sum.

Claiming an allowable loss—loans to traders

Although, in general, satisfaction of a debt is a disposal **14–38** (s.251), so far as concerns the original creditor no chargeable gain accrues on the disposal. And the same is true of the original creditor's personal representative or legatee. At first sight this seems very good of the Revenue, but the point is really directed against losses. It is a general principle of capital gains tax law that a loss cannot be claimed from a transaction upon which, if there had been a gain, it would not have been a chargeable gain. This principle is modified for debts which prove to be bad debts by s.253, first introduced in 1978. That section was enacted because huge losses had been incurred during the slump of the mid-1970s. The section applies where a loan or part of a loan *to a trader* which has been used wholly for the purposes of the trade becomes irrecoverable. In that case, the original creditor or a guarantor can claim the loss as an allowable loss. In *Robson v Mitchell* (2005) CA, it was held that where a trader borrowed money to refinance an existing debt, the purpose of the original debt was the relevant purpose for s.253. Whether it was actually wholly for the purposes of the trade was a question of fact. The Court did not express an opinion on whether, since the section did not include the word "exclusively" as in the trading income expenses provisions, if *part* of the borrowed money was *wholly* expended for the purposes of the trade that would suffice.

Debt on security

The rule that no chargeable gain (and hence—subject to **14–39** s.253—no allowable loss) can arise to the original creditor (or his personal representative or legatee) does not apply to a "debt on a security." The courts have struggled to decide what exactly amounts to a debt on a security. The most recent decision is that of the Court of Appeal in *Taylor Clark International Ltd v*

Lewis (1998). It does not mean the same as a secured debt, e.g. a debt secured by a mortgage or charge. Instead it is said to encompass debts which are really held as investments, and so can lead to a gain or loss, whether protected by a security or not. One important factor seems to be whether the debt is held in a marketable form. The obvious example is loan stock of a company or local authority (see s.132(3)(b)). However, gains on what are known as "qualifying corporate bonds" (company debentures) are exempt from the charge to capital gains tax for individuals and so cannot give rise to any allowable losses (s.117).[7]

Assignees

14–40   The assignee of a debt (as distinct from the original creditor) does make a chargeable gain (or an allowable loss) when the debt is satisfied, whether it be a debt on a security or not. This rule (if it stood alone) would open the way to a great deal of tax avoidance, because it is very easy to contrive a loss on a debt. So there are provisions to stop up these possibilities. A loss made by a person on the disposal of a debt is disallowed if he acquired the debt from a "connected person": s.251(4). So if A sells a debt to B for £1,200 and later X (the debtor) pays up £1,000 to B, B cannot claim a loss of £200 if A and B are connected persons. If this were not so, and B *could* claim a loss, it would be a way of B making a gift of £200 to A, to which gift the Revenue would be contributing.

Property in satisfaction of a debt

14–41   Sometimes a creditor takes property instead of money in satisfaction of a debt. In that case the base cost of the property is its then market value and no more. This looks as though it is going to prejudice the creditor when he comes to sell the property. And so it does in the case of a creditor who is not the original creditor, but is a person who has acquired the debt by assignment. So if A assigns to B a debt of £5,000 for £5,000 and then X (the debtor) hands over to B in satisfaction of the debt property worth £4,500, the base cost of the property is £4,500. So if, later, B sells the property for £5,200 he has made a gain of £700. But if the *original* creditor (A) (not having assigned the debt) accepts from the debtor in satisfaction of the debt property worth £4,500 the chargeable gain to A, when he comes to sell

---

[7]   Companies may still get relief on such losses under corporation tax rules. As to the need for the bonds to be normal commercial loans see *Weston v Garnett* (2005).

the property, is not to exceed the chargeable gain which would have accrued to him if he had acquired the property for a consideration equal to the amount of the debt. So if the debt was £5,000, the property was worth £4,500 and A later sells it for £5,200, A's acquisition cost is £5,000 and his chargeable gain is £200 (not £700). These matters are dealt with in s.251(3).

Options

An option is an asset. The grant of an option is treated as a disposal. Where the option is exercised, the grant and the exercise are treated as all one transaction. So if A grants to B an option to buy certain property (a put option)[8] and B subsequently exercises the option and buys the property, the sum paid for the option and the sum paid for the property are added together to ascertain the disposal cost (for A) and the acquisition cost (for B). Supposing, on the other hand, that an option is granted and then abandoned (i.e. not exercised): A is left with the gain on the grant of the option; for B the abandonment of the option does not count as a disposal for the purposes of s.24 (total loss, asset becoming of negligible value, etc.)—with the result that, although he has lost money, he does not get any loss relief. On the other hand if the option is abandoned by agreement for a consideration, i.e. A pays B to release the option, that will be a disposal by B under s.22(1) (derivation of a capital sum from an asset). Thus if the option is released for a nominal amount, loss relief will be available. These and other rules are set out in ss.144–147, as interpreted by Vinelott J. in *Golding v Kaufman* (1985).

14–42

Options not at arm's length

Where both the grant and exercise of the option take place in circumstances where s.17 would apply (e.g. because they are not transactions at arm's length), the perceived position was that when the option was exercised, the disposal proceeds/ acquisition costs were to be calculated by reference to the sum of the market value of the option when it was granted and the amount actually paid under the terms of the option when it was exercised. In *Mansworth v Jelley* (2003), however, the Court of Appeal decided that this was wrong and that the true interpretation of the sections was that the disposal proceeds/ acquisition costs should be simply the market value of the asset

14–43

---

[8] A put option is where the seller must sell on request. A call option is one where the buyer must buy on request.

at the time of the exercise of the option, thus ignoring the cost or value of the option when granted. As a result, s.144ZA was introduced by the Finance Act 2003 to restore the position to that which had been applied prior to the decision—i.e. the market value of the option when granted plus the actual sum paid for the exercise of the option. Further amendments were made by the Finance (No.2) Act 2005. Principally these are where the exercise price of the option (now generally used in such cases) is such that it would not normally be exercised in a commercial situation (e.g. if in the case of a call option it is greater than the value of exercise price). In such cases the market value of the asset will be substituted.

Value shifting

14–44   This is the dramatic and cryptic heading given to ss.29 to 34. Section 29 begins with a general introduction, and it then proceeds to deal with four specific situations.

First, if a person having control of a company exercises his control so that value passes out of his shares (or other rights) or out of the shares (or rights) of a person with whom he is connected into other shares (or rights) that is a disposal of the shares (or rights). An example would be if A, who holds the only shares which carry voting rights in a company, were to pass a resolution to transfer the voting rights to the shares held by other shareholders. It is, after all, a kind of gift. For a more sophisticated example, see *Floor v Davis* (1980) (HL).

Secondly, if there has been a shift of value as above, and subsequently the transferor disposes at a loss of some other asset which has depreciated in value by reason of the shift, that loss is not an allowable loss.

Thirdly, if there is a sale and lease back of land or other property and then subsequently there is an adjustment of the rights and liabilities under the lease which is favourable to the lessor, that counts as a disposal by the lessee of an interest in the property. The idea behind this rule is that the seller has really sold the property for less than its true value. Suppose A, the owner of a factory, sells the freehold of it to B for £100,000 and B immediately leases it back to A at a rent of £5,000 a year. Later an adjustment is made in the terms of the lease in favour of B, so that in effect B is to get £6,000 a year from the property. On this footing the price that A received for the freehold turns out be less than what he could have got for it, with the result that A paid less capital gains tax on the disposal of the freehold than he "should" have done. This present provision, by treating the adjustment in the lease as a disposal by A, enables the Revenue to pick up the lost tax.

Fourthly, if an asset is subject to some right or restriction and then the person entitled to enforce the right or restriction abrogates it, that abrogation counts as a disposal by that person of the right or restriction. An example of this would be if A, who had chartered a ship from B, were to release B from his obligations under the charterparty. That would be a disposal by A of his rights under the charterparty.

Section 30 was enacted (originally in 1977) to strike at some tax avoidance schemes which were based on transferring some of the value of a chargeable asset into a non-chargeable asset. The section is in very wide terms and has the potential to become a general anti-avoidance weapon. It will not apply if the taxpayer can show that tax avoidance was not the main purpose of the scheme.

Sections 31 to 34 (enacted in 1989 and amended in both 1999 and 2002) are aimed at preventing a group of companies from selling a subsidiary company with a reduced value, having shifted that value into other companies within the group prior to the sale.

Spouses and civil partners

As we have seen, disposals *between* spouses or civil partners who are living together are treated (by s.58) "as if the asset was acquired from the one making the disposal for a consideration of such amount as would secure that on the disposal neither a gain nor a loss would accrue to the one making the disposal[9]." Broadly the effect of this is that the transferee takes the asset at the original or base cost which it had in the hands of the transferor. But it is a little better than that, because the words of the section seem to imply that if there are some incidental costs of such a transfer the base cost for the transferee is to include those costs. Thus if H bought an item for £100 and subsequently transferred it to W and the costs of the transfer were £5, the base cost for W (looking to a future disposal by her) would be £105.

14–45

---

[9] This rule does not apply if (a) the asset is trading stock of the transferor or is acquired as trading stock of the transferee, or (b) the disposal is by way of *donatio mortis causa*.

Death

14–46 Until 1971 death was in itself a chargeable event (i.e. as a disposal by the deceased) for capital gains tax thus providing a double charge with estate duty (the predecessor of inheritance tax). The Finance Act 1971 abolished the capital gains charge. But a person's death still has important consequences—for his or her survivors. The subject of death is now dealt with in s.62 of the 1992 Act. Section 62(1) provides:

> "...the assets of which a deceased person was competent to dispose—
> (a) shall be deemed to be acquired on his death by the personal representatives or other person on whom they devolve for a consideration equal to their market value at the date of death; but
> (b) shall not be deemed to be disposed of by him on his death..."

The main point of the phrase "assets of which a deceased person was competent to dispose" is to exclude settled property in which the deceased had an interest. Settled property is governed by different rules which are discussed in the next section. To take an example, if, when A dies, he is the life tenant under a settlement, he is not "competent to dispose" of the settled property. One can speak of property of which a deceased person was competent to dispose as being his "free estate".

Uplift effect

14–47 The effect of s.62(1) is that so far as concerns the deceased's free estate, the death does not give rise to a charge to capital gains tax, but it does give rise to an "uplift" in the base cost of his assets. This, of course, is advantageous for the future. If A bought an asset for £50,000 and later died when its market value was £60,000, the base cost becomes £60,000. On a future disposal of the asset for £65,000, the gain is £5,000 and not £15,000 so that £10,000 gains have been written off. It must be borne in mind, however, that inheritance tax will (or may) be payable on the death of A on the full value of £60,000. Indeed the idea behind the exemption from capital gains tax on death is that death should not be an occasion of charge to both taxes. But it goes a bit further than that, because there is no charge to capital gains tax on death even if there is no charge to inheritance tax either, as for instance where assets are left to a surviving spouse. (See para.19–02 below).

Disposal to legatee

14–48 The next question which arises is this: when the personal representatives come to dispose of the assets in the course of the administration of the deceased's estate, is that disposal a chargeable event? The answer is that if the disposal is to a legatee that is not a chargeable event, but if the disposal is to anyone else it is a chargeable event.

A legatee gets as his base cost the market value of the asset at the time of the deceased's death; s.62(4). "Legatee" is given an extended meaning by s.64(2) and (3). It includes any person taking under a testamentary disposition (a will) or under an intestacy or partial intestacy, whether he takes beneficially or as trustee. And where the personal representatives appropriate assets to satisfy a legacy, the person taking under the appropriation is deemed to be a legatee. Also, by s.62, subss.(6) to (9), if the deceased's dispositions are varied by an instrument in writing made expressly for the purpose of invoking the subsections by the persons entitled within two years of the death, the variations do not count as disposals, except such variations as are made for a consideration (other than a consideration consisting of some other variation).

Disposal other than to legatee

14–49 A disposal by personal representatives otherwise than to a legatee *does* involve a chargeable gain or allowable loss. This is so, for example, if they sell an asset in order to pay inheritance tax, or if they simply re-arrange the investment portfolio. There is no provision for personal representatives to offset their losses against gains of the deceased. If the deceased had, in the year of assessment in which he died, an excess of losses over gains these may be "rolled backwards" as deductions from gains by the deceased for the preceding three years before taper relief is applied: s.62(2), (2B).

Settled property

Definition

14–50 "Settled property" is defined in s.68 as "any property held in trust[10] other than property to which s.60 ... applies." So the first thing to do is to find out what s.60 is all about. It deals with the situation where one person is nominee for another person or is a

---

[10] A unit trust scheme does not count as a trust (nor does an investment trust company). Both count as companies, though with some special rules of their own.

bare trustee for another person. Neither a nominee nor a bare trustee counts as a trustee, and the property they hold is not settled property. The property is treated as though it were vested in the person for whom the nominee or bare trustee is holding it, i.e. the beneficiary. Unfortunately (from the point of view of clarity) s.60 itself does not use the phrase "bare trustee," but there is an illuminating translation of the phrase used in the section, namely "trustee for another person absolutely entitled as against the trustee, or for any person who would be so entitled but for being an infant or other person under disability (or for two or more persons who are or would be jointly so entitled) ...". The phrase "bare trustee" does occur in the marginal note to s.60. Section 60(2) says this:

> "It is hereby declared that references in this Act to any asset held by a person as trustee for another person absolutely entitled as against the trustee are references to a case where that other person has the exclusive right, subject only to satisfying any outstanding charge, lien or other right of the trustee[11] to resort to the asset for payment of duty, taxes, costs or other outgoings, to direct how that asset shall be dealt with."

Jointly so entitled

14–51　The words "jointly so entitled" in s.60 do not refer only to persons who are technically joint tenants; they cover also persons who are tenants in common. So *concurrent interests* can exist (whether in the form of a joint tenancy or a tenancy in common) without the property in which the interests subsist being settled property, provided the "tenants" can direct the trustee how the asset shall be dealt with: see *Kidson v MacDonald* (1974). This point is not confined to real property; the word "jointly" refers to "persons who are, as it were, in the same interest", whatever the subject matter of the trust (per Walton J. in *Stephenson v Barclays Bank Trust Co Ltd.* (1975)). On the other hand it was held in both those cases that where there are *interests in succession* (e.g. where there is a trust for A for life with remainder to B) the trustees can never be bare trustees and the property must be settled property. This is because, although A and B are *together* entitled absolutely as

---

[11] This does not include payment of an annuity under the trust. Thus the presence of an annuity prevents the beneficiaries being absolutely entitled: *Stephenson v Barclays Bank Trust Co Ltd* (1975).

against the trustee, they are not entitled "jointly" and so s.60 can never be satisfied.[12]

Absolutely entitled

If the beneficiaries' interests are contingent they are clearly not absolutely entitled as against the trustees, even if the only contingency is on their obtaining the age of majority. They are not absolutely entitled "but for their infancy" but because they only have contingent interests: see *Tomlinson v Glyns Executor Co* (1970).

14–52

The essential criteria for a bare trust is that the beneficiary (or beneficiaries) must be able to direct the trustees as to how to deal with the trust property and to give a valid receipt for it. Actual transfer is not required, just the right to do so: *Stephenson v Barclays Bank Trust Co Ltd* (1975). This has been applied to what are known as "putting arrangements." Thus where all the members of a private company transferred their shares to trustees and subjected themselves to restrictions on transfer they were held to be absolutely entitled since they could collectively end the trust and so destroy or override any discretions or powers vested in the trustees.[13] Similarly where a family entitled to farming property set up a trust in which each member's interest was equivalent to their previous entitlements there was held to be no settlement for capital gains tax purposes.[14] The importance of this is that there is no exit charge if one member takes his interest out of the trust (see para.14–58, below).

Class and individual gifts

On the other hand, in the case of class gifts, e.g. "to such of my grandchildren born within 21 years of my death", the beneficiaries cannot be absolutely entitled until the class has closed, i.e. there can be no more potential beneficiaries. Until then the size of each grandchild's share is unknown.[15] Different considerations apply where each potential beneficiary has a defined share, irrespective of how many satisfy the contingency, e.g. "one quarter to each of my grandchildren on attaining 21". In this case when each beneficiary attains a vested interest (i.e.

14–53

---

[12] In *Booth v Ellard* (1980) it was accepted that the interests of the beneficiaries must be concurrent and all must be the same. See also *Harthan v Mason* (1980).

[13] *Booth v Ellard* (1980).

[14] *Jenkins v Brown* (1989).

[15] For this purpose any individual is deemed to be capable of having children until he or she dies: *Figg v Clarke* (1997).

attains 21) the question of whether he becomes absolutely entitled to that part of the settled property depends upon whether he can require the trustee to appropriate that part of it to him. In the case of land held on trust, for example, under the law no single beneficiary can require the trustees to sell the land and allocate a share of the proceeds. Only where all the beneficiaries have satisfied the contingency could such a sale be enforced by them. Thus in *Crowe v Appleby* (1975) where only one beneficiary had satisfied the contingency, it followed that he was not absolutely entitled against the trustees. The position would usually be different if the trust property consisted of money or quoted securities which are easily divisible.

If the trustees are not bare trustees then "any property held in trust" is settled property.

Trustees of the settlement

14–54   Section 69 provides that the trustees of a settlement are to be treated as a single and continuing body of persons. This is irrespective of any changes in the actual trustees themselves. Liability for the tax falls on those trustees in that capacity and not as individuals (s.65). Thus the trust through the trustees has a separate identity for capital gains tax purposes. Thus, the residence etc. of the majority of the trustees fixes the residence of the trust for capital gains tax purposes.

In that context, it was held in *Jasmine Trustees v Wells & Hind* (2007), that persons operating as trustees de son tort (those acting as trustees but not appointed as such) were not trustees of the settlement within s.69. Thus their residence did not count. As to their liability, they would be personally liable under s.1, but their acts would also be the acts of the proper trustees since they would be absolutely entitled to any trust property as against the trustees de son tort and s.60 could apply.

Disposals and settled property

14–55   We must now consider the events connected with settled property (as defined above) which count as disposals.

Putting property into a settlement

14–56   A transfer of property into a settlement (but not a bare trust under s.60) is a disposal of the entire property which thus becomes settled property (s.70). This is so even if the donor takes some interest as a beneficiary under the settlement or is a trustee or the sole trustee of the settlement. This is a pretty harsh rule. Suppose Mr Smith wishes to give his house to his nephew, but to retain for himself the right to occupy the house for the rest of his life, so that the nephew will only come into occupation when S dies (S for Smith and also for "settlor"). S can only carry out this transaction by putting the house into settlement. It is a transfer of property into a settlement and so it is treated as a disposal of the entire property. That means that the deemed consideration for the disposal is the whole capital value of the house. This does not accord with the reality, because in reality all that S has given away is the remainder interest. The same point can occur the other way round: S may want to allow his aged aunt to live in the house for her life. He makes a settlement under which the aunt gets a life interest and he retains the remainder interest. There is a charge to tax based on the value of "the entire property" when this transfer is made. In reality all that S has given away is a tiny fraction of the value of the entire property.

Actual disposals by the trustees

Trustees, as we have seen, though they are not "individuals," are "persons", and they are chargeable to capital gains tax at the fixed rate of 40 per cent. They are chargeable, for example, on gains made in the course of switching investments in the trust's portfolio. But where the settlor or the settlor's spouse or civil partner has an interest in the settlement the gains are taxable as if they had been realised by the settlor and not the trustees.   14–57

Deemed disposal on a person becoming absolutely liable as against the trustees

Under s.71(1) the trustees are deemed to have disposed of the assets (or part of them) comprised in the settlement whenever a beneficiary becomes absolutely entitled to the property (or part). This is subject to a few exceptions where the reason for the absolute entitlement is the death of another beneficiary.   14–58

Suppose assets are held in trust for A contingently on his attaining the age of 25. When A becomes 25 that is an occasion of charge under s.71(1). The assets are deemed to have been disposed of by the trustees and immediately re-acquired by them, in their capacity as bare trustees within s.60(1), for a consideration equal to their market value. After that it makes no difference whether the trustees hand over the property to A at once or keep it as bare trustee for him. The actual handing over of the property to A is not a chargeable event because it is deemed to be A's already by virtue of s.60(1). The upshot is that the trustees pay tax on the gain represented by the increase in value of the assets between the time when they were put into trust and the time when A became 25, and A takes as his base cost the market value on the day when he attained 25.

14–59   LOSSES   If an asset has fallen in value so as to create a loss on the deemed disposal by the trustees, that loss is transferred to A only if the trustees cannot set it off against gains arising at the same time or earlier in the same tax year. For this purpose such a loss is deducted before any other losses. But A can only use that loss to offset a subsequent gain by him on the disposal of that asset, or if the asset is land, any asset which is derived from it, although, if the loss cannot be deducted in that year (insufficient gains) it can be carried forward by A as if it were a loss incurred in the next available year. Any such losses are a first deduction before other losses. In no circumstances can a loss incurred by the trustees on the actual disposal of an asset be transferred to A (ss.71(2)–(2D)).

Limited exceptions to the deemed disposal rule

14–60   In certain situations inheritance tax charges the whole settled property where the holder of a life interest in a settlement dies. To avoid a potential double charge therefore, capital gains tax does not apply where a beneficiary becomes absolutely entitled as the result of a death of a prior beneficiary where there would also be a potential charge to inheritance tax. This is achieved by providing that there is an acquisition by the trustees at the value at the date of the death, but no corresponding disposal by them. In effect therefore, not only is there no charge but there is also an uplift in the base cost of the trust property, such as there is, as we have seen, on the death of an individual.

Until 2006, there was a universal charge to inheritance tax on the death of the prior beneficiary in all such "fixed interest" trusts. But then the law was changed so that that type of inheritance tax charge was limited to a few categories of prior interests (the remainder being subsumed into the more draconian discretionary trusts regime—see Ch.21). At the same time therefore the no-disposal/uplift exceptions for capital gains tax were limited to those specific categories. As these categories are set out extensively in inheritance tax law we will only refer to them by name here.

The exceptions (in s.73) are therefore limited to where a person becomes absolutely entitled on the death of a person having one of the following interests:

(i) an immediate post-death interest (see para.21-10, below)
(ii) a transitional serial interest (see para.21-12, below)
(iii) a disabled person's interest (see para.21-11, below)
(iv) an interest in a trust for a bereaved minor (see para.21-43, below)
(v) the death under 18 of a person entitled under an age 18-to-25 trust (see para.21-47, below).

Revertor to settlor

Even those limited exceptions to the deemed disposal rule are qualified if the person becoming absolutely entitled on the death is the settlor. This is known as revertor to settlor.

The background to this point is that no inheritance tax is payable on the death of X in those limited situations where X has been given a life interest by S (settlor) in such terms that the property reverts, on X's death, to S. If in this situation S could also get, on the death of X, an uplift in the base cost for purposes of capital gains tax that would be too favourable to S. So he cannot: see s.73(1)(b). If, on the life tenant's death, property reverts to the disponer (settlor), the disposal and re-acquisition shall be deemed to be for such consideration as to secure that neither a gain nor a loss accrues to the trustee. Thus, suppose S grants a life interest to X in property which at the time of the grant is worth £10,000. X dies at a time when the market value of the property is £14,000. The property reverts to S. The trustee is treated as re-acquiring the asset for £10,000 (not £14,000) and that figure (£10,000) becomes S's base cost.

14-61

Termination of a prior life interest in possession—no-one becoming absolutely entitled

This situation is dealt with by s.72(1). Naturally, the termination of an interest in possession by the death of the person entitled to it and the absolute entitlement of some person often happen on the same event. If property is held in trust for A for life with remainder to B, the event of A's death brings about the termination of a life interest (A's) *and* the absolute entitlement of some person (B). In this situation it is s.71(1) and 73 which apply. Section 72(1) applies only where there is a termination of an interest in possession by the death of the person entitled to it but still no one becomes absolutely entitled. This would be so, for example, where property is settled on A for life, remainder to B for life, remainder to C absolutely, and A dies. On A's death there is the termination of his interest by his death but no one becomes absolutely entitled; B becomes entitled for life and so

14-62

s.72(1) applies. On B's subsequent death (or surrender) s.71(1) applies, because C does then become absolutely entitled. If B died before A, however, s.72(1) would not apply since B's interest is not in possession. Nor would s.71(1) apply because no one would become absolutely entitled.

14–63   Section 72(1) provides that there is a deemed acquisition (but no disposal) by the trustees at the then base price if there is a death of the person entitled to the interest in possession. As in s.73, there is no corresponding disposal by the trustees so that there will be an uplift in the base price. But also like s.73, after 2006 this only applies if that interest was one of the five types set out in para.14-60, above.

Person entitled to the interest

14–64   It is important to note that the limited exemption from charge and base uplift given by s.73(1)(a) and the limited base uplift given by s.72 (which we have just been speaking about) only apply where the event causing a person to become absolutely entitled or causing the termination of an interest in possession is the death of the person *entitled* to the interest. If A is life tenant with a relevant interest (with remainder to B) and A dies still holding the life tenancy, there is no charge to capital gains tax, only an uplift. But if A assigns his interest to X, there is a charge when A dies, even though X's interest comes to an end on A's death. B becomes absolutely entitled, and s.71(1) imposes a charge to tax. The charge is not relieved by s.73(1)(a) for the reason that B's becoming absolutely entitled is not caused by the death of the person *entitled* to the interest because A was not (at death) *entitled* to it.

Similarly, if A is life tenant with a relevant interest under a settlement for A for life, then for B for life, then for C absolutely. If A is still holding the life tenancy when he dies there is the termination of a life interest and an uplift of the base price, because the termination arises on the death of the person entitled. But if A had assigned his interest to X there is a charge on A's death; s.72(1) does not apply and there is no uplift of the base price.

The charge to tax under s.71(1) which arises on the death of a former life tenant who has assigned his interest will be in addition to a charge to inheritance tax.

Transfers between trusts

Creation of separate settlement

Trustees are liable for capital gains tax in respect of their own **14–65** settlement. As we have seen, by virtue of s.69 the trustees for the time being are regarded as one body for this purpose, so that there is no charge on a change of trustees. The position is more complex, however, where under a power in the settlement the trustees transfer assets to another trust, of which they may or may not be the trustees. The crucial question is whether that second settlement can be regarded as a separate settlement or as merely a subsidiary part of the first. If they are separate settlements then it appears that the trustees of the second trust will become absolutely entitled as against the trustees of the first, and an exit charge can be made under s.71(1), discussed above. In *Hoare Trustees v Gardner* (1978) the judge decided that the second trustees need not be beneficially entitled as against the original trustees, nor did the section require them to be absolutely entitled as against the whole world (clearly they were not so as against the second beneficiaries). This was so even though the trustees of both trusts were identical.

Subsiduary settlement

If the second settlement is, however, merely a subsidiary of **14–66** the first trust then the trustees of either trust will be liable for the gains of both but there will be no exit charge. This has been a particularly useful device for the Revenue where one set of trustees is non-resident and so not chargeable to the tax. In *Roome v Edwards* (1982) Lord Wilberforce laid down the test to determine whether there are one or two settlements as follows:

> "The question whether a particular set of facts amounts to a settlement should be approached by asking what a person, with knowledge of the legal content of the word under established doctrine and applying this knowledge in a practical and common-sense manner to the facts under examination would conclude."

In that case, since the original settlement was still in existence and the second settlement was treated as being held on the trusts of the first as added to and varied by the first, the two settlements could be treated as one.

Making the distinction

14–67   Each case depends upon its facts and there are no golden rules. Separate administration and separate trust accounts may be relevant.[16] In *Bond v Pickford* (1983) the Court of Appeal drew a distinction between trustees transferring property under a power which altered the operative trusts of a settlement, thus allowing removal of the assets from the original settlement altogether (referred to as powers in the wider form) where there would be a charge under s.71, and powers in a narrower form which do not confer such authority. In that case a power to allocate funds for discretionary beneficiaries which were subject to the rules of the trust was held to be a narrower form power. The trustees of the original settlement continued to be responsible in that capacity for the allocated funds.

The Revenue have indicated in a Statement of Practice (SP 7/84) that there will be no charge under s.71(1) (and so no separate settlement) if there is an exercise of a power in the wider form if either it is revocable or where the trusts declared are not exhaustive so that they may at some time come back into the trusts or reference still has to be made to the trustees' original powers of administration or disposition. There will equally be no deemed disposal if the duties of the trustees of the second settlement fall to the trustees as trustees of the first. Separate identity of the trustees is irrelevant, as is the location of the mechanical powers of the trustees. However, in *Swires v Renton* (1991), Hoffmann J. suggested that even if the funds were transferred under a wider form power the question remained as to whether there was a new settlement or whether it was being "grafted onto" the existing settlement. If any reference back to the original settlement was required then this would indicate that no new settlement had been created.

Tax position of the beneficiaries

The general rule

14–68   The legislation is not notably generous to trustees or beneficiaries, but beneficiaries do have one crumb of comfort. It is to be found in s.76(1). If a person, other than the settlor or settlor's spouse or civil partner, is holding an interest under a settlement and that interest was created for his benefit, then, unless the trustees are non-resident, no chargeable gain arises if he disposes

---

[16] Vinelott J. in *Ewart v Taylor* (1983) regarded this as an important factor together with the fact that the transfer to the second settlement was part of a scheme to wind up the first, in finding that the two settlements were separate.

of his interest. Thus, suppose property is held in trust for A for life with remainder to B absolutely. If A assigns (e.g. sells) his life interest that is not a chargeable event. The same is true if B sells his remainder interest. And if it happens that B dies while A is still alive, B's personal representatives can sell B's remainder interest without tax arising. But a person who acquired an interest for consideration in money or money's worth (other than consideration consisting of another interest under the settlement) and then sells the interest is liable to tax on any gain involved. So if X bought A's life interest (or B's remainder interest) and then sold it at a gain he would be liable to tax. And if X, having bought B's remainder interest and still holding it when A died, would be treated as disposing of the remainder interest in consideration of obtaining the settled property itself and so a charge to tax would arise: s.76(2).

Settlor, spouse or civil partner

There is an exception to the general rule that the disposal of a **14–69** non-purchased interest is not a chargeable event where the relevant interest is held in a settlement in which the settlor or his spouse or civil partner has an interest. Where such an interest, whether owned by the settlor or not, is disposed of for actual consideration (other than another interest in the settlement) the trustees will be deemed to have made a disposal of the assets to which that interest relates to themselves at market value: s.76A and Sch.4A. Unless the interest is in a specific fund or in a specific fraction of the income or capital, this means a deemed disposal of all the trust assets. This is intended to prevent, e.g. a settlor transferring an asset into a settlement (using one of the roll over reliefs) and then selling his interest in the settlement, thus effectively transferring the asset tax free. Liability for the tax falls on the trustees, but they have a right of recovery from the person disposing of the interest.

Adjustments

The legislation also permits adjustments of the interest of **14–70** several beneficiaries amongst themselves without a charge to tax arising. "Partition" of settled property is quite a common occurrence. A, a life tenant, may surrender his life interest in part of the trust property in return for an interest in the capital. A is not treated as acquiring his interest in capital for money or money's worth because he has acquired it in exchange for "another interest" (i.e. his life interest) "under the settlement" and that does not count as money or money's worth. Consequently, if A were to carry out the above transaction and then sell his interest in capital (a remainder interest) at a gain, he would not be liable to tax.

Payment of the tax

14–71   A beneficiary may become liable to pay tax which has been assessed on the trustees. This will be so where the tax is not paid within six months of its due date and the asset concerned or a part of it or the proceeds of it are transferred by the trustees to the beneficiary. He can be assessed at any time within two years from the due date on the chargeable gain or, in the case of a transfer of a part, on a proportionate part of the chargeable gain; s.69(4).

CHAPTER 15

GAINS AND LOSSES

Introduction

Essentially the amount of a chargeable gain or of an allowable   **15–01**
loss is arrived at by comparing the consideration received on the
disposal of an asset with the cost of its acquisition. What we
must now do is to look in more detail at the way in which the
computation is done. If the asset is a foreign asset the consideration received and the costs of acquisition must first be
converted into sterling at the rate of exchange applicable at each
event so that the gain or loss may be affected by fluctuations in
exchange rates.[1] Further, by s.16(1), a loss is to be computed in
the same way as a gain.

We will look first at the general rules of computation laid
down in Part II, Ch.I (ss.15 to 20) and Ch.III (ss.37 to 52) of the
Act. Following the abolition of the reliefs for inflation (indexation relief) and length of ownership (taper relief) as from 2008,
those rules alone will now produce the chargeable gain. That
will then be subject to a flat rate charge of 18 per cent once the
total exceeds an individual's exempt amount for the year.[2] Next
we shall look at the special rules where the asset disposed of was
owned by the taxpayer on March 31, 1982. These are necessary
because it should be remembered that no gains accruing before
then are taxable. Finally we look at the position where the
computation produces a loss rather than a gain.

General Rules—Computing the Chargeable Gain

Income receipts and expenditure

First, there is to be excluded from the consideration for a   **15–02**
disposal any sum which is taken into account for income tax
(s.37). An example would be the whole of the consideration for

---

[1]   *Bentley v Pike* (1981); *Capcount Trading v Evans* (1993), CA. This is not the
position with regard to income taxation.
[2]   Companies pay corporation tax on their chargeable gains and have no
exempt amount. The effective rate for certain business disposals is 10% under
entrepreneurs' relief. See para.16–28, below.

the sale of an asset by a dealer in such assets. Another example would be that part of a lease premium which was chargeable to income tax. Special rules apply to assets which have enjoyed capital allowances.

Similarly expenditure which would be allowable in an income tax computation is not allowable for capital gains tax (s.39). In making this decision the section requires that the asset is presumed to be a fixed asset of a trade and the question asked whether the expenditure would have been allowable in an income tax computation of that, hypothetical, trade (the statutory hypothesis).[3] Since under income tax law extensive repairs may be carried out to an asset and still be allowable for that tax, (*Odeon Cinemas Ltd v Jones* (1972)), this, in practice, restricts many claims.

Consideration

15–03   This is basically the gross money price paid. If the consideration is in money's worth it can be valued (exchange of assets is a disposal). Remember also that where the consideration cannot be valued it will be taken to be the market value of the asset. That rule, in s.17, also applies to gifts and sales at an undervalue.

Sometimes the relevant consideration may depend upon the terms and form of the transaction adopted by the parties. The courts will apply the agreed terms of the parties unless they are a sham or a fraud. It is not open to the taxpayer or the commission to argue that some other construction should be put upon the agreement simply because it would have achieved the same economic effect and be more advantageous or disadvantageous for tax purposes.[4] Further, as we have seen, s.48 provides that where the right to receive payment is postponed (e.g. on a payment by instalments) or contingent, the whole amount is treated as the consideration at the time of the disposal without any discount for delay in payment or the possibility that it might not be paid at all, although if either of the latter can be subsequently shown to have happened an adjustment can be made.[5]

---

[3]   See, e.g. *Emmerson v Computer Time International* (1977), CA.

[4]   Per Lightman J. in *Spectros International Plc v Madden* (1997). See also *Fielder v Vedlynn Ltd* (1992); *Collins v HMRC* (2007) SpC.

[5]   The actual consideration must be irrecoverable and not just its sterling equivalent (i.e. where because of the need to convert foreign currency transactions into sterling at the rate in force at the time when the contract was made, the amount ultimately received when the instalments are paid, calculated at the rates then in force, is less in sterling terms than that originally charged): *Goodbrand v Loffland Bros North Sea Inc* (1998).

Applying s.48

An example of these rules of interpretation by the courts and   **15–04**
the operation of s.48 is the case of *Garner v Pounds Shipowners
and Shipbrokers Ltd* (2000), HL. The taxpayers sold an option
to purchase land to M for £399,750. That money was paid to
independent stakeholders who were to pay over the money only
when the taxpayers obtained the release of some restrictive
covenants over the land or as directed by M. If the taxpayers
failed to obtain those releases then the money was to be repaid
to M unless M decided in any event to exercise the option. The
releases were achieved by the taxpayers at a price of £90,000.
The stakeholders then paid £309,750 to the taxpayers and
£90,000 to the holders of the restrictive covenants. In the event
the option was never exercised. The question therefore arose as
to what was the consideration for the grant of the option (and
not the land).

The House of Lords held that the consideration for the grant
of the option was the full £399,750. In doing so they distinguished the earlier case of *Randall v Plumb* (1975). In that
case consideration for an option to purchase land was paid
directly to the taxpayers on terms that they would have to repay
part of it if planning permission was not subsequently obtained.
Walton J. allowed a discount from the consideration paid for the
option by taking into account the contingent possibility of
repayment. This is allowed as an adjustment under s.48. The
House of Lords expressly approved that decision but said that it
had no application to the present case since the whole amount
was paid to the taxpayers and no part of it was ever repaid to M.
A payment to a third party did not alter the consideration
received by the taxpayers for the grant of the option since it was
clear that the parties had agreed that the payment of £399,750
was for the grant of the option only and not for both the option
and the taxpayer to obtain the release of the covenants. The
parties were bound by their clear agreement. If the contingency
was directly related to the value of the consideration (as in
Randall v Plumb) it could be taken into account in computing its
value but if it was related to matters which did not directly bear
upon that value it did not follow that it should be taken into
account. As we shall see in a moment they were also unable to
deduct that £90,000 as allowable expenditure.

The principle in *Garner* was applied by Park J., in *Burca v
Parkinson* (2001) where A sold his shares to B having agreed to
pay 60 per cent of the proceeds to C. The whole consideration
had been received by A for tax purposes. The judge also said
that the position would have been the same even if, which was

not the case, A had received that amount as trustee for C; A had still disposed of 100 per cent of the shares himself and the total amount paid by B was the consideration for that disposal.

Allowable expenditure

15–05   The gain (or loss) is computed by deducting the allowable expenditure from the consideration. As we shall see the expenditure may in some cases be increased by way of a relief to counter the effects of inflation up to 1998. Section 38(1) provides the following heads:

(a)   expenditure wholly and exclusively incurred in the acquisition of the asset (together with the incidental costs) or, if the asset was not acquired, the expenditure incurred wholly and exclusively in producing it (e.g. the expenditure incurred in writing a book and thereby creating a copyright). Where the taxpayer acquired the asset on a market value disposal to him, e.g. a gift, that will form his acquisition cost;

(b)   the expenditure incurred wholly and exclusively for the purpose of enhancing the value of the asset being expenditure reflected in the value of the asset at the date of disposal (e.g. extensions to a building) and expenditure incurred wholly and exclusively in establishing, preserving or defending one's title to, or right over, the asset (e.g., the costs involved in taking out probate);

(c)   the incidental costs of making the disposal.[6] In *Administrators of the Estate of Caton v Couch* (1997), it was held that whilst the cost of employing a valuer to value shares in a private company was allowable as an incidental cost of their disposal, subsequent costs in negotiating that value with the Revenue and in (successfully) appealing against an assessment were not so allowable.

15–06   WHOLLY AND EXCLUSIVELY   The expenditure under (a) and (b) must be "wholly and exclusively" for the acquisition of the asset or for establishing, preserving or defending title to the asset. This has enabled the court to disallow an acquisition cost where acquiring the asset was part of an avoidance scheme,[7] but in *IRC v Richard's Executors* (1971) the House of Lords, by a

---

[6]   Inheritance tax payable on a gift may also be allowable if a claim is made for roll-over relief on a gift of business assets; see para.16–33.
[7]   *Eilbeck v Rawling* (1982).

narrow majority, held that those words must be given a reasonable interpretation. They allowed the costs of obtaining a valuation for estate duty purposes as an expense establishing title since such a valuation was a necessary prerequisite for obtaining their title to the estate.

In *Garner v Pounds Shipowners and Shipbreakers Ltd* (2000)[8] the taxpayers also failed to have the £90,000 paid to the owners of the restrictive covenants deducted from the consideration for the grant of the option under either paras (a) or (b). Since the option could have been exercised by M whether or not the restrictive covenants were removed, payment to achieve that so could not be said to be wholly and exclusively incurred by the taxpayers in providing the option for the purposes of para.(a). Further, for para.(b) neither the obligation nor the payment of £90,000 was reflected in the value of the option (as opposed to the land itself) at the date of the agreement. The option was to purchase specified land at a specified price. In effect the expenditure was extraneous to the option and it was even arguable that the obligation to remove the covenants was part of the asset (option) being disposed of so that it could not also be expenditure relating to it. As the House of Lords pointed out, the position might have been different if M had exercised the option, since the £90,000 may then have been deductible from the purchase price for the land itself as distinct from the option.

APPORTIONMENT Expenditure or consideration received on two or more assets may be apportioned between those assets if it is just and reasonable, so that where a company sold the shares of a subsidiary company and agreed to waive a debt owed to it by that subsidiary, the consideration received for the sale of the shares was held to be divisible between the two disposals—the sale of the shares and the waiver of the debt: *Aberdeen Construction Group Ltd v IRC* (1978). If, however, the consideration for the shares and the waiver are expressed as separate sums no further adjustment can be made: *Booth (E.V.) (Holdings) Ltd v Buckwell* (1980). **15–07**

CONTRACT PRICE In the absence of fraud or collusion, the acquisition cost (base price) is the value placed on the amount provided by the parties in the contract at the date of the acquisition. Thus if an asset is acquired by a company issuing new shares, credited as fully paid up, to the vendor, it is the **15–08**

---

[8] See para.15–04, above.

value placed on those shares by the parties which forms the acquisition cost of the asset to the company for any subsequent disposal: *Stanton v Drayton Commercial Investment Co Ltd* (1982). The Revenue's argument that market value should apply was rejected. Expenditure, to be allowable, however, must be in money or money's worth. In *Oram v Johnson* (1980) personal work by the taxpayer on renovating an old cottage was not allowed as an expense as enhancing the value of the asset; nothing had passed out from the taxpayer. If he had used a builder the expenditure would have been allowable. Certain kinds of expenditure are not deductible, notably expenditure on insuring an asset in respect of damage, injury, loss or depreciation. Another notable non-allowable expenditure is the payment of interest (except as provided by s.40 in relation to loans for construction work taken out by companies where the resulting building, etc. is being disposed of).

15–09 DEEMED DISPOSALS It will be recalled that there are many instances where there is deemed to be a disposal (and re-acquisition). Can there be incidental costs of such a notional disposal? Section 38(4) says (rather laconically):

> "Any provision … introducing the assumption that assets are sold and immediately re-acquired shall not imply that any expenditure is incurred as incidental to the sale or re-acquisition."

It has been held in the courts that real expenditure on a notional disposal is allowable (e.g. legal costs), but that notional expenditure is not. Real lawyers' fees could arise, for example, in respect of a deemed disposal and re-acquisition by trustees on the death of a life tenant. Such real fees are deductible. But where the deemed disposal and re-acquisition arises because the asset in question was held by the taxpayer on March 31, 1982 (see para.15–25 below) the taxpayer cannot say: "If I had really sold and re-bought the shares on the stock exchange on that day I would have incurred brokers' fees and stamp duty, and I claim to deduct those notional expenses."

15–10 VAT A word must be said about Value Added Tax. If VAT has been suffered on the purchase of an asset but that VAT is available as input tax for set-off in the purchaser's VAT account, the cost of the asset for the purposes of capital gains tax will be the cost exclusive of VAT. Where no VAT set-off is available, the cost will be inclusive of the VAT which has been borne. Where an asset is disposed of any VAT chargeable as output tax will be disregarded in computing the capital gain (because the disponer will have to pay over the VAT to Revenue and Customs). If the disponer is not selling in the course of a business VAT is not chargeable.

Part disposals

Where there is a part disposal the amounts of acquisition or production expenditure (see (a) above) and subsequent expenditure (see (b) above) have to be apportioned between the part disposed of and the part retained (s.42). The apportionment is done by applying to the total of expenditure the fraction

$$\frac{A}{A+B}$$

where A is the consideration for the part disposal and B is the market value of the property retained. To take an example, suppose Mr Smith owns an asset which has a base cost of £10,000 and he sells part of that asset for £7,000 and the market value of the part he retains is £21,000. The "attributable" expenditure from the £10,000 is:

$$£10,000 \times \frac{£7,000}{£7,000 + £21,000} = £2,500$$

So the gain on this part disposal is £4,500 (i.e. the difference between the sale consideration (£7,000) and the attributable expenditure (£2,500)). The balance of expenditure (£7,500) which was not allowed on this part disposal is carried forward for use on any future disposal of the part of the asset which was retained.

Wasting assets

There is a restriction on the amount of expenditure that may be deducted in respect of what are called "wasting assets". A wasting asset means (per s.44(1)) an asset which has a predictable life not exceeding 50 years. Plant and machinery are expressly regarded as having a life not exceeding 50 years. The residual or scrap value of the asset is deducted from the acquisition cost and the resulting sum is written-off on a straight line basis over the life of the asset. Let us take an example. Suppose Mr Jones bought an asset which had a predictable life of 30 years. He paid £10,000 for it. Ten years later Mr Jones sold the asset for £8,000. It has a scrap value of £1,000. The

15–11

15–12

computation for calculating the gain on the occasion of the sale goes like this:

Proceeds of sale		£8,000
Less: cost	£10,000	
Deduct scrap value	£1,000	
	9,000	
Deduct written-off amount		
$\frac{10}{30} \times £9,000^9$	£3,000	
	£6,000	
Add on scrap value	£1,000	
	£7,000	£7,000
	Gross gain	£1,000

Notice that this procedure, on the above facts, converts what at first sight looked like a loss (cost price £10,000; sale price £8,000) into a gain. The idea behind this is that if you buy a wasting asset and use it for a number of years and then sell it you have had the enjoyment of part of its useful life and you have sold it when its prospective useful life is diminished. So the Act deals with this situation by providing that the buying price must be notionally reduced to take account of the enjoyment of the asset which you have used up.

15–13   LEASES   A lease is a wasting asset when its future duration is 50 years or less. But for leases the straight line basis of writing-off is not used. What is used is a fixed Table set out in Schedule 8. On this Table the line of wastage is curved and it accelerates as the lease approaches its end since leases depreciate more rapidly towards the end of their life.

Charging the gain to tax

The 2008 flat rate system

15–14   Having calculated the total gains (i.e. the consideration for each disposal less the relevant allowable expenditure), of an individual in a tax year, then, from 2008/9, insofar as they exceed the exempt amount for that year, they are charged to capital gains tax at a fixed rate of 18 per cent (s.4). There is, as

---

9   This is the writing-off. 10 is the length of ownership; 30 is the life of the asset.

we have seen, from that date no longer any relief for the effects of inflation (indexation relief) or for the length of ownership of the asset (taper relief). At the same time, that fixed rate also replaced the prior application of the taxpayer's marginal rate of income tax. (That assumed that the gains were added on to the taxpayer's total income and charged at either the higher (40 per cent) or lower (savings) rate (20 per cent) as appropriate.) It is no longer necessary therefore to spend much time on either indexation or taper relief or the complex computation structure which they provoked. But it is worth while considering the effect of these changes on taxpayers—as ever there are winners and losers. To do that does require a very brief outline of the two former reliefs.

The pre-2008 indexation and taper reliefs

Indexation relief applied to any asset acquired before March 15–15 1998. It worked by increasing the allowable expenditure by reference to the increase in the retail prices index from the date of acquisition to March 1998. Taper relief applied to all assets and reduced the chargeable gain to a percentage. The amount of the reduction depended on how many years from March 1998 onwards the taxpayer had owned the asset prior to the disposal and whether or not it was a business asset. For a business asset the chargeable gain was reduced to just 25 per cent of the computed gain after just two years ownership. For other assets it took ten years to reduce the gain to 60 per cent of the chargeable gain.

If the asset had been owned prior to March 1998 that tapered gain had first also been reduced by indexation relief up to that date, which was known as the indexed gain. So it was then the indexed gain which was tapered. But ignoring index relief, the interaction of taper relief and income tax rates for a higher rate tax payer meant that after two years the effective rate of the tax on a business asset was 10 per cent (40 per cent on the tapered 25 per cent of the gain). For a non-business asset it was a minimum of 24 per cent achieved only after ten years (40 per cent on the tapered 60 per cent of the gain). Now it is 18 per cent on the whole of the gain and that will not have been indexed whenever the asset was acquired. The major factor in this change was the political need to be seen to be taxing so-called private equity groups at more than 10 per cent, far less than the rate of income tax paid by the employees of the companies involved.

Effect of the changes

15–16   To take three examples of the effect of these changes: suppose A sells a business asset (e.g. private company shares in a company which he has set up and developed) which he has owned for two years and makes a gain of £2,000,000. Without any relief (see below), he will pay 18 per cent tax on that (£360,000). Before, as a higher rate taxpayer, he would have paid 40 per cent but only on the tapered gain of £500,000 (£200,000). Result a sharp increase in the tax bill.

Suppose B sells a non-business asset (e.g. a second home) which he has owned for ten years and makes a gain of £200,000. Now he will pay 18 per cent tax on that (£36,000). Before, as a higher rate taxpayer, he would have paid 40 per cent on the tapered gain of £120,000 (£48,000). If the house had been owned for less time, the tapered gain and so the previous tax bill would have been even higher. Result, a substantial tax saving.

Finally, suppose C sells her second home which she has owned for twenty years and makes a gain of £200,000. Her current bill will be £36,000 as above. Before, however, she would have only paid 40 per cent on 60 per cent of the *indexed gain* (i.e. the gain as reduced for inflation up to 1998—say £160,000) which would have been £38,400. Result, a small reduction. Thus the abolition of indexation relief penalised those who had owned their assets the longest.

15–17   The announcement of those changes in the Pre Budget Report in the autumn of 2007 produced an outcry from the business community. The capital gains tax regime had always favoured business assets, as being wealth creating, over private assets. There had, until 1988, been a specific relief for those disposing of an interest in a business or unquoted shares in a trading company (misleadingly known as retirement relief). When that was repealed, it was replaced by the favourable taper regime for such assets, which became more favourable as it went along.

15–18   INTRODUCTION OF ENTREPRENEURS RELIEF   Yet here was a change which favoured second home owners, especially short term second home owners, over entrepreneurs. As a result of substantial pressure, a new relief, entrepreneurs relief, was introduced in the year 2008/9. The effect of that is to reduce the effective rate on the disposal of certain business assets (largely the same as those formerly eligible for retirement relief) to 10 per cent on gains up to £1 million over a taxpayer's lifetime (see para.16–22, below).

Rebasing—assets owned before April 1 1982

Assets acquired before April 1 1982 but after April 5 1965

These assets are subject to rebasing in the calculation of the gross gain as if they had been acquired at market value at March 31, 1982.

15–19

REBASING It is s.35 which takes all gains accrued before March 31, 1982 out of the charge to tax. That date was chosen because indexation relief started at that point. Section 35(2) accordingly provides that where a taxpayer disposes of an asset which he held on March 31, 1982 then "in computing ... the gain or the loss accruing on the disposal it shall be assumed that the asset was on March 31, 1982 sold by the person making the disposal, and immediately reacquired by him, at its market value". Thus the base price of that asset is uplifted to its market value at that date. Thus it can be said to have been "rebased" to March 1982. Where the taxpayer has acquired the asset after March 31, 1982 on a no gain/no loss transfer, e.g. as between spouses, from a transferor who owned the asset on March 31, 1982, the transferee is also deemed to have owned it then and rebasing will apply.

15–20

From 2008, all pre-1982 assets will have that base price of their market value at that date. The former exceptions to that rule (where the original cost figure could be used) no longer apply.

Special rules for shares—pooling arrangements

Until indexation relief was introduced in 1982, shares of the same class in the same company held by a taxpayer were treated as a single asset, i.e. a pool of shares. Every time some were bought they were added to the pool (and the acquisition cost added to the acquisition costs of the pool) and when some were sold they were deducted from the pool and charged as a part disposal of the single pooled asset. Thus, if half the shares were sold, half the allowable expenditure of the pool was available. Between 1982 and 1985 such pooling was abolished but in 1985 new rules reinstated the pooling arrangements and accommodated indexation relief.

15–21

Those rules were in their turn replaced by another set of rules for individuals with the introduction of taper relief in 1998. The 1985 rules, however, still apply to companies. With the abolition of taper relief (and deferred indexation relief) in 2008, however, the 1998 rules for individuals were themselves largely repealed. There was no longer any general need to identify particular shares sold with shares acquired. The length of ownership since 1998 and the effects of inflation between 1982 and 1998 were no longer of any relevance in computing the gain. As anti-avoidance devices, however, two identification rules (the same day rules and the "bed and breakfasting" rules) were maintained.

15–22   THE CURRENT POSITION   As from April 6, 2008, subject to two exceptions, all shares of the same class in the same company are treated as forming a single asset (a share pool). It is irrelevant when they were acquired. This restores the pre-1982 position described above in para.15-21.

15–23   SAME DAY RULE   The first exception to the single pool concept is that any shares disposed of must first be identified with any such shares acquired on the same day.

15–24   BED AND BREAKFASTING RULES   The same day rule would not on its own prevent what was known as "bed and breakfasting". That was a simple tax planning device whereby the taxpayer sold a number of shares at the close of business on one day and bought them back again at the start of trading on the next day. The gain thus incurred would be equivalent to the exempt amount for the year. Thus there would be no actual charge to the tax, the annual exempt amount would have been utilised and the base price of the shares raised to the repurchase cost. Accordingly any shares sold must first be identified with any such shares acquired in the next thirty days after the disposal. Thus there will be no gain and so no uplift in the base price. This will not, however, prevent a spouse or civil partner selling shares, giving the proceeds to the other spouse or partner who then buys the shares back with those proceeds.

Losses

15–25   We want to collect together under this heading certain leading points about losses. Some of the points have been mentioned before; some are new.

Losses are, in general, computed in the same way as gains are computed; s.16(1).[10] If a transaction is such that a gain (if there had been one) would not be a chargeable gain, then if a loss occurs (instead of a gain) that loss is not an allowable loss; s.16(2). This provision has some very important consequences. A good example arises in connection with the disposal of gilt-edged securities or qualifying corporate bonds.

Loss relief

Capital gains tax is charged on the total amount of chargeable gains in a year of assessment after deducting any allowable losses.　　　　　　15–26

EXEMPT AMOUNT   If in any year a person has a taxable amount (chargeable gains minus allowable losses) not exceeding the exempt amount for that year the accumulated losses of earlier years are not required to be used in eliminating that taxable amount. For example if at the end of year 1 a person has accumulated losses of £5,000, and in year 2 his taxable amount is £4,000, no part of the £5,000 needs to be used in knocking down the £4,000 to nil. He goes forward into year 3 with his accumulation of losses (£5,000) intact: s.3(5)(a). Similarly, if his taxable amount in year 2 had been £20,000, he need only use so much of his accumulated losses as is needed to reduce that taxable amount to the exempt amount and the remaining losses could be carried forward into year 3: s.3(5)(b).　　　　　15–27

Losses incurred in a disposal to a "connected person" are only allowable against gains made on subsequent disposals to the same connected person: s.18(3).

CARRY BACK   Losses may only be carried *back* against gains of previous years on three occasions. First, under s.62(2), where the loss is incurred in the year of the taxpayer's death, the loss may be carried back for three years. Second, where the loss accrues in respect of a mineral lease it may be carried back for 15 years. The third is where the disposal of the asset was partly for contingent consideration, or what the Revenue calls unascertainable deferred consideration, i.e. in the *Marren v Ingles* type of case which we dealt with in para.14–22. Remember in such a case where, e.g., shares are sold say for £100,000 and a percentage of the price of those shares if the company is floated on the stock exchange, there is an immediate disposal both of　　　15–28

---

[10] In general, losses must be realised but remember the deemed disposal provisions where an asset has been destroyed, extinguished or become of negligible value, where an allowable loss may be claimed.

the shares and of the right to the as yet unknown additional payment. The consideration for that right is deemed to be an actuarial value which takes into account the possibilities of actually getting the money.

Sections 279A-D are concerned with the situation where the taxpayer subsequently sells that right to the contingent payment, say three years later, for less than that actuarial value, thus incurring a loss in that later year. The taxpayer may have no gains against which to set off that loss, so he is now entitled to elect so that that loss is deemed to have accrued in the original year of the contract. That will reduce the gain on the original disposal. Any other gains available in that year must be used first. If necessary the carried back loss can be used against gains of the intermediate years. As with other losses, no carried back loss need be used to cancel gains up to the exempt amount.

CHAPTER 16

EXEMPTIONS AND RELIEFS

Introduction

An exemption arises where either some asset is expressed not to be a chargeable asset or some gain is expressed not to be a chargeable gain A relief arises where although there is a chargeable asset and a chargeable gain the full amount of tax is not exacted or the chargeable gain is postponed. Remember that there is an annual exemption for all gains accruing to an individual up to the exempt amount for the year in question. This chapter deals with the other important exemptions and reliefs.

16–01

Hold-over Relief for Gifts Immediately Chargeable to Inheritance Tax

Between 1980 and 1989 all gifts between individuals were eligible for what is known as hold-over relief from capital gains tax. This was because gifts were also subject to inheritance tax and it was thought inequitable to apply both taxes. This general relief was, however, abolished in 1989 on the (slightly flawed) basis that inheritance tax now rarely applies to lifetime gifts. Hold-over relief still applies to gifts of business assets (see para.16–27 below) and under s.260 gifts which attract an immediate charge to inheritance tax. Section 260 also applies to some specific types of gift which are exempt from inheritance tax. Before we look at the relief under s.260, it is important to understand the concept of a hold-over relief since it applies in other areas we shall come to (gifts of business assets, replacement of business assets, transfer of business to a company).

16–02

How hold-over relief works

Hold-over relief works by allowing the amount of the chargeable gain which would otherwise be payable on a disposal from A to B to be deducted from the acquisition cost of B rather than chargeable on A. Suppose A buys an asset for £10,000. He disposes of it to B for £15,000. A therefore makes a gain of £5,000. If hold-over relief is available then instead of charging

16–03

that gain on the disposal it will be deducted from B's acquisition cost. Thus B will be deemed to have acquired the asset for £10,000 (i.e. £15,000–£5,000). If B subsequently disposes of the asset to C for £20,000 he will therefore be treated as having made a gain of £10,000 (£20,000–£10,000). Thus A's original gain of £5,000 and B's actual gain of £5,000 both become chargeable on B's disposal to C. In other words hold-over relief postpones or holds over the first gain, it does not exclude it.

If B's disposal to C had also been eligible for hold-over relief then B's gain of £10,000 would not be chargeable but C's acquisition cost would be reduced by that amount, and so on. Thus whilst the general relief for gifts applied it was possible by simply making a series of gifts of an asset to postpone all the gains. If the final donee died so that the asset passed under his will or intestacy, those held-over gains would disappear because of the provisions (already dealt with para.14–46) whereby his executors would be deemed to acquire the asset at its then market value but make no chargeable gain on transferring the asset to the beneficiary.

Current limited relief for any type of gift

16–04 Hold-over relief for any type of gift is now only available where the gift would attract an immediate charge to inheritance tax: s.260. This means that the gift must be an immediately chargeable transfer for inheritance tax purposes. It does not apply to gifts which are potentially exempt transfers, because they will only be chargeable to inheritance tax if the donor dies within seven years of making the gift, so that there is no immediate charge to the tax. Even if they do then become chargeable no hold-over relief is available. These concepts are discussed at para.18–05, below, but the effect broadly is that the relief only applies to the creation or termination of most trusts[1] or a transfer which is not made to an individual.

Provided there is a charge to inheritance tax, however, it does not matter that the amount of tax actually payable is negligible—see *Melville v IRC* (2000), para.18–05 below. The relief is not available to companies or on the transfer of shares or securities to companies, or where the donee is neither resident nor ordinarily resident in the United Kingdom. Where it applies, the relief for gifts of business assets (para.16–33 below) does not apply. A claim for hold-over relief must be made jointly by the

---

[1] Those trusts which are outside this relief are those set out in para.14–60 above.

donor and donee and if made entitles the parties to postpone the gain in the way set out above.

The relief also applies to bad bargains taxable on full market value under s.17. In that case the amount which can be held-over is the difference between the price paid and the market value, i.e. the gift element. Finally we should note that the relief is available to certain gifts which are exempt from inheritance tax altogether thus taking them outside the tax net. These include gifts to political parties and to maintenance funds for historic houses. The relief will also apply where a trust for a bereaved minor or an 18-25 trust[2] ends and no charge to inheritance tax arises.

Restriction of gifts general relief

To prevent a number of avoidance schemes, often combining gifts relief, either under s.165 (gifts of business assets—see para.16–33 below) or s.260, with the private residence exemption (para.16–09, below), ss.169B to 169G (introduced in 2004) provide that gifts relief is not available on a transfer to trustees of a settlement in which the donor either has an interest at the time of transfer or acquires an interest in it within six years of the transfer (referred to as settlor-interested settlements) Thus the initial gift will be chargeable under the usual rules rather than being held over. In the latter case the relief is "clawed back" when the donor acquires such an interest. The schemes worked by the trustees being able to dissipate the held-over gain before selling the property on.

For example, David owns a house which is not his principal main residence (and so not exempt from tax). It has, say, a market value of £250,000 with a potential gain of £150,000 if it is sold. David transfers the house to trustees of a settlement in which he has an interest, claiming gifts relief so that the gain is held over. Erica, his daughter, is entitled to occupy the house under the terms of the trust and does so as her sole main residence. Erica then moves out and the trustees sell the house for £250,000. The held-over gain of £150,000 which would normally be chargeable at that stage is lost because the disposal by the trustees is, as we shall see, exempt under the private residence exemption rules. David therefore has de facto access to the full proceeds of the house without paying any CGT. Under the new rules, David could not claim gifts relief so that the gain would be chargeable in full on the transfer to the trust. The

16–05

---

[2] These concepts are considered in Ch.21 below.

trustees, selling the house for what they are deemed to have acquired it for, would make no gain.

Some Miscellaneous Exemptions

16–06   Private motor cars are not chargeable assets (s.263). Nor are savings certificates or premium bonds chargeable, (s.121) or betting winnings.

There is no chargeable gain when a person disposes of foreign currency which he had acquired for personal expenditure abroad (s.269).

Sums obtained by way of compensation or damages for any wrong or injury suffered by an individual in his person or in his profession are not chargeable gains. Were it not for this provision, the law might otherwise produce the slightly macabre result that someone who received compensation, for example, for an injury at work, would be regarded as part-disposing of himself for CGT purposes.

There are also exemptions for gains arising from individual savings accounts and a relief for transfers of shares into an approved employee share-ownership plan.

Gilt-edged Securities and Qualifying Corporate Bonds

16–07   A gain is not a chargeable gain if it accrues on the disposal of certain specified gilt-edged securities and qualifying corporate bonds: see ss.115, 117 and Sch.9. The list of specified gilt-edged securities has been added to from time to time by statutory instrument and now comprises virtually all government stocks. At first sight this seems a generous gesture on the part of the Revenue, but losses occur in dealings on the gilt-edged market, and the rule that where no chargeable gain (if there had been a gain) would have arisen there can be no allowable loss has meant that this exemption has frequently operated to prohibit losses rather than to exempt gains. Qualifying corporate bonds, which similarly cannot give rise to a loss for an individual are defined to include normal[3] non-convertible corporate debentures; but for companies most qualifying corporate bonds have been subsumed into their trading profits for corporation tax purposes and taken out of the chargeable gain regime.

[3]   See e.g. *Weston v Garnett* (2005).

Life Assurance and Deferred Annuities

In principle the receipt of policy monies under a policy of life **16–08** assurance, or the receipt of the first instalment of a deferred annuity, is a disposal (a disposal of the right in return for the money). But no chargeable gain arises where the money is paid to the original holder of the policy or his personal representatives or trustees. Nor is there a chargeable gain if he surrenders (or they surrender) the policy. But if the policy is assigned for money or money's worth (e.g. sold) and then the policy money is paid to the assignee (or the policy is surrendered) that is a chargeable event.

These matters are dealt with by s.210, but that section was revised by the Finance Act 2003 principally to deal with one simple gap under the previous version. Suppose X buys a policy for £25,000 as a investment. He would be liable to capital gains tax when the policy monies become payable to him (as an assignee for value). But suppose just before the policy is due to mature he gives it to Y, his spouse or civil partner who receives the £45,000 from the insurance company. The gift from X to Y would be regarded as being neither a gain nor a loss (under the normal spouse rules); i.e. at £25,000—so no tax is payable by him. Y's gain of £20,000 would not have been taxable either since Y gave no consideration for the assignment to Y. The amended section now charges Y's gain on the basis that a previous assignee had given consideration.

Private Residences

This important exemption is dealt with in ss.222–226B. A **16–09** gain on the disposal by an individual of a dwelling-house or part of a dwelling house, together with a certain amount of land attached, is not a chargeable gain if the house was the individual's only or main residence. This exemption in practice takes most people's main asset out of the charge to capital gains tax and is extremely important in practice in a country where most families now own their own homes, which are generally of ever-increasing value. But that benevolence does not extend (as we shall see) to inheritance tax; for that tax a private residence is no different from other property. The capital gains tax exemption does not apply if the house was acquired wholly or partly for the purpose of realising a gain from its disposal: s.224(3).

Sole or main residence

16–10   To get the full capital gains tax exemption the house must have been the individual's only or main residence throughout his period of ownership, ignoring any period of ownership prior to March 31, 1982, except that it does not matter if it has not been such for all or any part of the last 36 months of his ownership. The point of this exception is (we take it) to meet the case where an individual has moved to a new house before he has been able to sell his old one. If the house has not been the taxpayer's only or main residence throughout his period of ownership a fraction of the gain is exempted corresponding to the period of occupation.[4] In certain circumstances a period of absence can be disregarded. These include periods where the taxpayer was employed abroad and any period not exceeding three years. Where the taxpayer has to live in job-related accommodation the exemption will apply to a house bought as a future main residence even if he never lives in it.

16–11   TEMPORARY OCCUPATION   The relief applies to a dwelling-house or part of a dwelling-house which is the taxpayer's sole or main residence. In *Goodwin v Curtis* (1998), the Court of Appeal upheld a decision of the General Commissioners that mere temporary occupation of premises by a taxpayer may not be sufficient to make it his residence for the purposes of the relief. Thus there is a distinction between temporary accommodation and a permanent residence. In that case the taxpayer had already advertised a farmhouse as being for sale before he moved into it. He lived in it for just over a month until the sale was completed. In the view of the Court of Appeal the facts indicated that there was an insufficient degree of permanence for it to be his residence. Each case will depend on its facts, but the important criterion will be the intention of the taxpayer when he occupies the house and not the length of occupation. A clear intention to occupy the house permanently will be sufficient, even if he has to move out after a short time, e.g. because he has changed jobs, whereas a longer period of occupation which is always temporary may not be so.

Dwelling-house or part of a dwelling house

16–12   What amounts to a dwelling-house or part of a dwelling-house for this relief has been the subject of several cases. It has

---

[4]   As in *Henke v HMRC* (2006) Sp Comm. The land was bought in 1982 but the house was not occupied until 1993.

been held to include a caravan (admittedly connected to mains services),[5] but that is always a question of fact.[6]

More difficulties have arisen as to what amounts to part of a dwelling-house. This has for example been held to include the disposal of a bungalow built in the grounds of a house for the gardener and housekeeper[7] so that a dwelling-house can clearly consist of more than one building. The criteria applied to decide whether the building being disposed of is part of the dwelling house or a separate entity have varied. Initially the question asked was whether the two buildings together formed an entity so that taken together they could form a dwelling-house. Thus in *Williams v Merrylees* (1987) Vinelott J. held that a lodge built some 200 yards from the main house could form part of a single dwelling-house with the main house, the dwelling-house being split up into different buildings fulfilling different functions. The scale and layout of the buildings was important. But in the same year, Walton J. applied a much more precise (and restrictive) test in *Markey v Sanders* (1987). To succeed in a claim for relief the taxpayer would have to show that the second building (1) increased the taxpayer's enjoyment of the first dwelling; and (2) was very closely adjacent to it. Since the employee's bungalow in that case was a long way from the main house and was screened from it, the judge was able to decide that it did not form part of the taxpayer's dwelling-house.

PROXIMITY TEST   The Court of Appeal in *Lewis v Lady Rook* (1992) seem to have adopted the narrower geographical (or proximity) approach as opposed to the entity approach. The test set out in that case was to ask whether the building being sold was within the curtilage of, and appurtenant to, the main building so as to constitute an entity which could be described as a dwelling-house. The Court of Appeal were cheerfully of the   16–13

---

[5] *Makins v Elson* (1977).
[6] *Moore v Thompson* (1986), where the caravan was not connected to main services and only occupied sporadically it was held not to come within the exemption.
[7] *Batey v Wakefield* (1981).

opinion that everyone would know what the curtilage of a house was, but it is nowhere defined in the tax legislation.[8]

In *Honour v Norris* (1992) the above test was said to be applicable to the "country house" situation but not to the facts of that case. The taxpayer had acquired four separate flats in a block of flats and the fourth, acquired to accommodate their grown up children and their guests, was sold separately. The judge refused to lay down any general test for such urban cases. On the facts the fourth flat had never formed part of a single entity—it had been acquired as a separate unit conveniently close to the others. It was like a country house owner acquiring a bungalow in the nearby village.

Land occupied and enjoyed with the residence

16–14   The exemption also applies to land occupied and enjoyed with the residence, up to half a hectare in area. If this land is disposed of separately from the house it must be disposed of first, otherwise it will no longer be occupied and enjoyed with the house at the time of its disposal.[9] A larger area may be allowed if it is required for the reasonable enjoyment of the house, given the size and character of the house: s.222. In *Longson v Baker* (2001) it was stressed that, to qualify, the additional area of land must be objectively assessed by relation to the house and not for a particular use of the land by the owners, in that case the land needed to keep horses. That had nothing to do with the house. There is no requirement that the land is actually physically attached to the house, e.g. if it is the natural garden of the house. On the other hand land owned apart from the house will not count just because it is used as a garden.[10] Where the land is greater than the permitted area, the gain will be apportioned

---

[8]   There are many cases in other areas as to what amounts to the curtilage of a building. One example, for the purposes of the Housing Act 1980, is the definition laid down in *Dyer v Dorset County Council* (1988) that the curtilage is a small area of land which is part and parcel of the building it contains or is attached to it. But in *Skerrits of Nottingham Ltd v Secretary of State* (2000), the Court of Appeal said that it was wrong to include smallness as a criterion. It was a question of fact and degree, so that a manor house might well include stables and other outbuildings. The Court also said that "curtilage" was an expression which not even lawyers could define precisely! Sometimes it depends on the facts and context—e.g. in relation to listed buildings for planning permission purposes: see e.g. *Sumption v Greenwich LBC* (2007).

[9]   *Varty v Lynes* (1976).

[10]   *Wakeling v Pearce* (1995).

according to the respective areas of the exempt and non-exempt land.[11]

Partial business use or private letting

16–15

If the gain accrues from a disposal of a dwelling-house part of which is used exclusively for the purposes of a trade, business, profession or vocation the exemption applies only to that part of the gain which falls to be apportioned to the "private" part of the house. (This is a point to be weighed against the income tax advantage of claiming that a part of one's house is being used exclusively for business, etc. purposes.) Similar provisions apply to any reconstruction, conversion or change of use of the property, but it seems that such events will only justify an apportionment if they amount to a change in the taxpayer's occupation[12]: s.224.

If the owner lets his house during his period of ownership the part of the gain attributable to that period is chargeable on a straight line basis (e.g. owned 10 years during which it was let for two, one-fifth of the total gain is chargeable). Further relief is available under s.223(4) where the house is let as residential accommodation.[13] The chargeable gain is then reduced by the lower of the exempt gain (i.e. four-fifths of the gain in the example above) or £40,000. In practice lodgers are not treated as affecting the relief.

Settlements, spouses and civil partners

16–16

The exemption also applies, on a claim by the trustees, to occupation of a dwelling-house held under a settlement by a person entitled to occupy it under the settlement: s.225. Usually this will be the life tenant but it can include a beneficiary under a discretionary trust where the trustees have a power to allow this.[14] Under s.225A, the relief may be claimed by personal representatives if the house has been occupied by persons entitled to at least 75 per cent of the proceeds of the house, or a 75 per cent interest in it, under a will or intestacy. This is calculated on the basis that the house is not needed to pay any IHT or other debt of the estate.

Spouses and civil partners can only have one residence or main residence. If they are not separated it is no good claiming that Mon Repos is one's main residence and Dunromin is the

---

[11] *Henke v HMRC* (2006) Sp Comm.
[12] *IRC v Green* (1982).
[13] This includes short-term holiday lets: *Owen v Elliott* (1990).
[14] *Sansom v Peay* (1976).

other's main residence: s.222(6). Where a taxpayer, spouses or civil partners, have two or more residences, they must choose which is to be the "main" residence. This choice must be made within two years of the acquisition of a second or subsequent residence in which case it will be backdated for that period. In *Griffin v Craig-Harvey* (1993) the court held that the taxpayer had no right to make an election after two years from the second acquisition, a decision which leaves many taxpayers out of time to make an election. If there is no election the inspector of taxes can decide which is the taxpayer's main residence.

Restriction if exemption is combined with gifts relief

16–17   A number of avoidance schemes were used to extend the private residence exemption to a second house where it was combined with gifts relief under s.260 (see para.16–04). For example, suppose Harriet has a second home (with in-built gains) which she wishes to sell and give the proceeds to her children Mike and Emma. She gives the house to trustees of a settlement of which the beneficiaries are Mike and Emma (if Harriet had been a beneficiary then no gifts relief would have been available as it would be a transfer to settlor-interested settlement—see para.16–05). Harriet claims hold-over gifts relief so that no tax is payable at that stage. The trustees allow Mike to occupy the house as his sole residence. When the trustees sell the house—that sale will be exempt since the private residence exemption will apply to it (relevant occupation by a beneficiary under the settlement). Thus the held-over gain will disappear and the full proceeds of sale will have effectively passed from Harriet to the children without any tax being paid. To prevent this, s.226A, introduced in 2004, provides that, in such circumstances, if Harriet claims the gifts relief the trustees cannot claim the private residence exemption. Thus the tax is payable either on the transfer of the house to the settlement or on the sale by the trustees.

Chattels Disposed of for £6,000 or Less

16–18   Section 262 provides that "a gain accruing on a disposal of an asset which is tangible moveable property [i.e. a chattel] shall not be a chargeable gain if the amount or value *of the consideration* for the disposal does not exceed £6,000." Section 262 does not apply to a disposal of currency of any description, nor to a disposal of commodities by a person dealing on a terminal market. A terminal market is not defined but it means a market in which you can buy or sell, e.g. cocoa, for a price fixed now but for delivery at some future date (e.g. three months hence). It is sometimes called a futures market. Notice that the figure of £6,000 refers to the amount of the consideration, not to the amount of the gain.

Marginal relief   Where the amount of the consideration   **16–19**
exceeds £6,000 there shall be excluded from any chargeable gain so much of it as exceeds five-thirds of the difference between the consideration and £6,000. Thus if X buys a chattel for £1,000 and sells it for £6,400, the chargeable gain is not £5,400 but $^5/_3 \times £400$ (£6,400–£6,000), i.e. £667.

But the section is far from generous as regards losses. If there is a disposal at a loss, and the consideration for the disposal is less than £6,000, the consideration is deemed to be £6,000. Thus if a chattel was bought for £6,200 and sold for £5,800 the actual loss (£400) is not allowable; the loss relief is limited to £200.

Sets   If two or more assets forming part of a set of articles   **16–20**
(say a set of Chippendale chairs) are disposed of by the same seller to the same buyer (or to different buyers who are acting in concert or who are connected persons) whether on the same or different occasions, the two or more transactions are treated as a single transaction.

The disposals of two (or more) quite separate articles qualify separately for the relief. It is no bar to getting the relief that you have (in the same year) sold a table for £6,000 and a stamp for £6,000, or even for that matter two unconnected stamps for £6,000 each.

Where there is a disposal of a right or interest in a chattel, the consideration is deemed (for the purposes of the exemption only) to be the aggregate of the sum received and the market value of the remainder—that avoids selling successive part-interests in a chattel to obtain the relief.

Tangible Moveables which are Wasting Assets

No chargeable gain (or, more likely, an allowable loss) shall   **16–21**
accrue on the disposal of an asset which is tangible moveable property (i.e. a chattel) and which is a wasting asset: s.45. It will be recalled that a wasting asset is an asset which has a predictable life not exceeding 50 years. This exemption applies (unlike the exemption mentioned above, since it is not really an exemption from any charge) irrespective of the amount of the disposal consideration.

Entrepreneurs' relief

Introduction and amount of the relief

16–22   As a result of the abolition of taper and indexation reliefs and the change to a flat rate charge as from 2008/9 (see para.15-14, above), a new relief, known as entrepreneurs' relief was introduced to assist owners of small businesses. The relevant provisions are to be found in ss.169H to 169S.

The relief, which must be claimed, applies to the first £1 million of lifetime gains (after deducting the annual exempt amount, if available) which arise from a qualifying or associated disposal. The various disposals which together constitute a qualifying disposal, e.g. on the sale of a business and its assets, are treated as a single composite disposal for this purpose. Thus any losses so incurred, e.g. on the sale of a particular business asset, must be deducted from the gains arising on, e.g., the sale of other business assets. It is the resulting composite net gain (if any) which qualifies for the relief. If there are more losses than gains, then the relief does not apply to that disposal.

The net gains on such a disposal are then reduced by four-ninths. This results in an effective rate of 10 per cent on such gains (five-ninths x 18 per cent). Thus a qualifying net gain of £450,000 would be reduced to one of £250,000. That would give a capital gains tax liability at 18 per cent of £45,000, which is of course 10 per cent of £450,000. Additional gains in excess of the £1 million limit do not qualify for the relief. Further, once the £1 million figure has been used by a taxpayer, the relief is exhausted for all future disposals. This is not a serial entrepreneur's relief.

Qualifying disposals

16–23   There are three principal categories of qualifying disposals by individuals. Ironically these are based on those for retirement relief which was abolished in favour of taper relief in 1988. In categories (a) and (b) the assets in question must have been owned by the taxpayer for at least the whole of the year prior to the disposal. The categories are:

(a)   gains on the disposal of the whole or part of a trading business (this includes sole traders and partners who may use this relief when they dispose of their interest in the partnership). A trading business, which is any business carried commercially with a view of profit, includes professions and vocations but does not include a property letting business other than furnished holiday lettings.

The relief only applies to relevant business assets, i.e. those used in the business. Further, there is no relief for excluded assets which are held by the business such as shares or other investments. Goodwill is not an excluded asset for this purpose;

(b) gains on the disposal of assets or an interest in assets within three years of the cessation of (the whole of) such a business. The assets must be relevant business assets and not excluded assets (see above); and

(c) gains on a disposal of shares in a trading company (or the holding company of a trading company) provided

    (i) the taxpayer has been an officer or employee (not necessarily full time) of the company (or its holding company or other member company of its trading group);

    (ii) it is his personal company, i.e. he owns at least 5 per cent of the ordinary share capital of the company which carry 5 per cent of the voting rights in the company; and

    (iii) conditions (i) and (ii) have applied either throughout the year prior to the disposal, or throughout the year prior to the company ceasing to be a trading company, if that cessation was itself within three years prior to the disposal. That does not apply, however, if the company ceases to be a trading company but becomes a member of a trading group.

A trading company and a trading group is one which is trading commercially and for profit and which does not carry on other activities to a substantial extent.

ASSOCIATED DISPOSALS If a partner or a shareholder/officer/ **16–24** employee of the company makes a qualifying disposal under either (a) or (c) above, the relief will also be available on an associated disposal of an asset (e.g. the premises on which the business is carried on) owned by the taxpayer.

Such disposals are associated if they take place at the same time as the qualifying disposal and are part of the individual's withdrawal from the business or company. Unlike a sole trader, there is no requirement that the business itself ceases. Further, the assets must have been used in the firm's or company's business for the year prior to the disposal or, if earlier, the year prior to the withdrawal from the business.

There are reductions where: (i) the asset was not wholly in business use throughout the period of ownership; (ii) only part of the asset was used in the business; (iii) the taxpayer was not involved in the business or company throughout the period of the business use of the asset; and (iv) rent was charged for the use of the asset (it is seen as an investment then). In each case only a "just and reasonable amount" of relief will be allowed.

16–25   TRUSTEES   The relief applies to gains by trustees on disposals of shares in a company or assets used in a business. There must be a beneficiary with an interest in possession relating to those assets who is a qualifying beneficiary. That person must satisfy the same criteria as would have applied if he had had been making the claim in his own name as an individual under (a), (b) or (c) above.

If there is another beneficiary, other than the qualifying beneficiary, with an interest in possession under the trust in the relevant assets, the amount of the relief is reduced to the proportion held by the qualifying beneficiary. That proportion is calculated by reference to the respective entitlements of the beneficiaries to the trust income.

The £1 million limit on the relief is calculated by reference to the qualifying beneficiary, so that a qualifying disposal by the trustees counts towards the beneficiary's lifetime allowance. For that purpose, where there is such a disposal by the trustees on the same day as one by the qualifying beneficiary in his own right, the disposal by the trustees is deemed to have occurred after that by the beneficiary. Thus the personal disposal will have first bite at the relief.

Potential difficulties

16–26   Since the categories of qualifying gains are derived from those for retirement relief, they will have inherited the problems of that relief relating to the interface between categories (a) and (b) where some but not all of the assets of a business are disposed of. Case law established the following propositions in relation to that relief:

(i) because roll-over relief for replacement of business assets is available (see para.16–27 below), category (b) is only available if the *whole of the business* has permanently ceased: *Marriot* v *Lane* (1996); if there is no such total cessation then category (a) requires a disposal of the whole *or part of* a business;

(ii) the disposal of some of the assets of the business does not amount to the disposal of a part of that business for that purpose if the business is in fact substantially still continuing: *McGregor v Adcock* (1977);

(iii) but if a disposal of business assets has the effect of creating a de facto disposal of part of a business that will suffice: *Pepper v Daffurn* (1993); *Wase v Bourke* (1996);

(iv) in deciding whether there has been such a disposal of part of a business, the courts will look at the position before and after the disposal of the assets and ask whether the changes caused by the disposal amount to a cessation of part of the business by the taxpayer. That is a question of fact: *Jarmin v Rawlings* (1994); *Barrett v Powell* (1998); *Purves v Harrison* (2001).

Replacement of Business Assets

Sections 152 to 159 are the operative sections here. They provide not a complete exemption from tax but a relief in the hold-over form. The relief arises when a trader disposes of business assets (of certain types) at a gain, and uses the disposal consideration to acquire replacement assets for use in the trade.

The relief is given by allowing the trader to defer payment of tax on the disposal gain and (instead) to deduct the gain which he makes on the disposal of the old assets from the acquisition cost of the new assets. This will have the effect of increasing the tax payable when he comes (if he does) to dispose of the new assets in the future.

This causes a particular problem with respect to LLPS which go into winding up before the new asset has been disposed of. A similar problem arises with respect to the relief on gifts of business assets and the two are dealt with in that section—see para.16–27 below.

CONDITIONS FOR THE RELIEF Despite some reservations expressed by the courts it is sufficient for the relief to apply if the consideration on the disposal of the old assets is at least matched by the cost of the new assets. There is no need to demonstrate any form of tracing of the proceeds into the new asset. This enabled the judge in *Wardhaugh v Penrith Rugby Union Football Club* (2002) to ignore the effect of a Sports Council grant which partly funded the building of a new clubhouse, where the

16–27

16–28

other part-funding came from the sale of land. The whole of the gain arising from that sale could be held-over.

To get the relief the trader must acquire the new assets within three years after the disposal[15] (or within 12 months before the disposal). Once the replacement asset is acquired it must be used in the taxpayer's trade "on the acquisition." A gap will prevent the relief applying.[16] Both the old and new assets must have been so used for the purposes of the taxpayers trade.

It is possible to acquire the "new" asset one year before the disposal of the old asset, provided of course that the old asset was part of the trader's assets when the new asset was acquired. But in *Watton v Tippett* (1997) no relief was allowed where a trader, having bought a single asset, disposed of part of it within a year and claimed to deduct the gain from the cost of the part retained. The original cost for the whole asset could not be severed since the part retained had never been acquired as such, it was never a "new asset."

16–29   The relief only applies to assets set out in classes in s.155 (which can be added to by a Treasury Order). These are currently: (i) land and buildings; (ii) fixed plant and machinery[17]; (iii) ships; (iv) aircraft; (v) hovercraft; (vi) goodwill; (vii) satellites, space stations and spacecraft (!); (viii) certain farming quotas; (ix) fish quotas; and (x) rights of members of a Lloyd's syndicate. The old and new assets need not be of the same type, however.

16–30   LIMITS   There is no relief for a non-resident where the replacement asset is outside the charge to tax because it is outside the United Kingdom: s.159. In addition there is no relief if the new assets were acquired wholly or partly for the purpose of realising a gain from their disposal.[18] There are further restrictions if the replacement asset is a wasting asset.

Where the whole of the proceeds of sale are not reinvested in acquiring a new asset, i.e. where the cost of the new asset is less

---

[15] This period can be extended by the Revenue, but there is no appeal against their refusal to do so: *Steibelt v Paling* (1999).

[16] See *Campbell Connelly & Co Ltd v Barnett* (1993). There are special rules for groups of companies in this respect. In practice, if an asset requires capital expenditure on it before it can be used in the taxpayer's trade, the relief will apply if the work is completed within a reasonable time and it is then used in the trade. See *Steibelt v Paling* (1999).

[17] Thus excluding moveable machinery: *Williams v Evans* (1982).

[18] See e.g. *Re Loquitur Ltd* (2003).

than the proceeds of the sale of the old asset[19], the amount not reinvested will be treated as a chargeable gain and only the balance will be held over. Similarly where the new asset is only partially used for the purposes of the business the relief will be restricted to the proportion used in the business.[20]

Transfer of Business to a Company

Hold over relief is also available, unless the transferor elects to the contrary, where an unincorporated business (and not just its assets) are transferred to a company in return for shares in the company; ie where the business is incorporated: ss.162, 162A. The company is deemed to acquire the assets at market value (s.17 will apply).[21]

16–31

Concessions applicable to hold-over business reliefs

The operation of the two reliefs discussed above are amplified by a number of published extra-statutory concessions which in effect allow a gain to be deferred in the same way as hold-over relief even though the statutory provisions might not strictly be applicable. As we have seen, the basic principle of hold-over relief is that there is no charge on the first gain but that that amount is then deducted from the acquisition cost of the replacement asset thus increasing the gain on any disposal of that asset. It appears that under the wording of these concessions there is no undertaking required from the taxpayer at the time when the first gain is deferred that it will be so deducted from the acquisition cost on the second disposal. Further it appears that the Revenue conceded that they have no powers to compel any such deduction. Consequently for events occurring only after March 9, 1999, ss.248A and 248B give them the power to assess the held-over gain under a concession as it would have been under the sections. This was not made retrospective, however, so some taxpayers appear to have been able to both have their cake and eat it.

16–32

---

[19] In *Wardhaugh v Penrith Rugby Union FC* (2002), above, the Revenue's argument was that the grant should be deducted from the cost of the new asset so as to apply this restriction.

[20] For an unfortunate example of this restriction see *Todd v Mudd* (1987).

[21] See, e.g. *Gordon v IRC* (1991).

Gifts of Business Assets

16–33   There is a relief for gifts of business assets which is now enacted in s.165. The relief arises where an individual makes a disposal otherwise than under a bargain at arm's length to a person resident or ordinarily resident in the United Kingdom of any asset[22] used for the purposes of a trade, profession or vocation carried on by the transferor or by his personal company or by a trading company which is a subsidiary of his personal company[23]. The relief also applies to a similar transfer of shares of an unquoted company or of the transferor's personal company but not if the gift of those shares is to a company.

Since this relief is a hold-over relief, the amount of the gain can be deducted from the deemed acquisition cost of the donee (market value under s.17). Because the donee will therefore become liable to a potentially higher capital gains tax bill on a subsequent disposal any claim for this relief must be made by both the donor and donee. The Revenue's view is that the gain so "held-over" is that before any available entrepreneurs' relief has been applied. That relief will therefore be lost if the gain is so held-over. As with the relief for gifts subject to inheritance tax (para.16–04), this relief is not available on transfers to a settlement in which the donor has an interest or in which he acquires an interest within six years of the transfer.

Where the relief is available on sales at an undervalue only the amount of that undervalue is available for the relief. If the gift was the subject of a charge to inheritance tax the donor can add that tax paid to his acquisition cost.

Hold-over relief and LLPs

16–34   The reliefs for gifts of business assets and replacement of business assets (see paras 16–27 and 16–33, above) both operate by postponing the held-over gain until the asset, or new asset, is disposed of on a chargeable transaction. Because members of an LLP are taxed as if they and not the LLP own the assets they may well have postponed a gain by using one of those two reliefs. But when an LLP is wound up that tax transparency ceases, so that the LLP is deemed always to have owned the

---

[22] There are no restrictions similar to those applicable on business asset replacement relief—para.16–23.

[23] This is a company in which the taxpayer can exercise at least 5% of the votes.

business assets as a body corporate.[24] Accordingly, when it makes a disposal of those assets it will be able to claim the full acquisition cost as an expense and no account will be taken of the reduction resulting from the hold-over relief already claimed by the individual members. Accordingly, ss.156A and 169A provide a charge on the members who claimed the hold-over relief, for replacement or gifts of business assets respectively, equivalent to the amount of the postponed gain.

Charities

A gain which accrues to a charity and is applicable and applied for charitable purposes is not a chargeable gain: s.256(1). But if property is held on charitable trusts and then ceases to be so held there is a deemed disposal at market value and any gain so accruing is chargeable: s.256(2). Where a charity has an interest under a trust, money paid to it by the trustees on the disposal of surplus assets are not gains accruing to the charity but to the trustees, unless it is a bare trust.[25]

16–35

Turning now to a disposal *to* a charity, such a disposal if by way of gift is exempt from capital gains tax under s.257 in the sense that neither a gain nor a loss is treated as accruing on the disposal. If the charity subsequently disposes of the property which was given to it, and disposes of it at a gain, the gain will not be a chargeable gain if the gain is applicable and applied for charitable purposes.[26]

---

[24] s.59A(5).
[25] *Prest v Bettinson* (1980).
[26] An outright transfer by a charitable company to another charity is deemed to be applied for charitable purposes: *IRC v Helen Slater Charitable Trust* (1980).

CHAPTER 17

EVOLUTION OF INHERITANCE TAX

Inheritance Tax

Ever since 1894 there has been a tax aimed at non-commercial 17–01
transfers of capital, charging tax on the whole of the value so
transferred. The current version of this tax is known as inheritance tax, although as we shall see it is neither calculated by
reference to what a person inherits nor limited to inheritance on
a death. It is different from capital gains tax since that taxes only
the gain on a transfer, does not apply on a death and applies in
the main to commercial transfers of capital. The relationship
between the two taxes is usually complementary, although there
are overlaps in the area of lifetime gifts, where paradoxically
capital gains tax is more likely to apply than inheritance tax.

Estate duty

The evolution of inheritance tax can be traced back to estate 17–02
duty introduced in 1894. That tax charged all the property of an
individual which passed on his death, unless specifically
exempted. In its final form this included not only property which
the deceased owned at his death and which passed under his will
or intestacy but also property which was deemed to pass on his
death. Such property included the full value of any settled
property in which the deceased had an interest (including certain
discretionary trusts) and the value of any gift made by the
deceased either within seven years prior to his death or at any
time if the deceased had retained any interest in the property
given. The whole amount of the property so passing on the
death was then aggregated and tax charged on that amount.
Thus estate duty was a mutation duty (i.e. one charged on the
property passing from the deceased) and not an acquisition duty
(i.e. one charged according to the amount each person acquired
on the death). But only a death triggered a charge.

Capital transfer tax

In 1974 the incoming Labour Government announced its 17–03
intention to repeal estate duty, which it finally did in 1975. The
replacement was known as capital transfer tax. The central idea

311

of this tax (introduced as the precursor of a wealth tax which never materialised) was to charge all non-commercial transfers of capital (known as chargeable transfers) made by an individual throughout his lifetime, with death being regarded as the final transfer. The important concept was that all such transfers were taxed on a cumulative basis. Thus the rate of tax for each successive transfer was calculated on the basis of the transferor's cumulative total at that time. Thus if X, having already made transfers of £100,000, made another transfer of £50,000, the rate of tax for that transfer would be calculated at that applicable for transfers between £100,000 and £150,000, and so on, until on X's death the rates payable would depend upon his whole cumulative total of lifetime transfers. The value of each transfer was calculated not on the value of the transfer as such but on the loss to the transferor. There were special rules for settlements. The law on capital transfer tax was consolidated in 1984 into the Capital Transfer Tax Act.

Inheritance tax

17–04   But by then this principle of taxing all transfers made by an individual throughout his lifetime had been reduced by the rule that the cumulative principle should only apply to gifts made within the previous 10 years. Thus in our example above, if X had made the £100,000 transfers more than 10 years before the transfer of £50,000, the latter would be taxed only on the rates between £0 and £50,000. If only £60,000 of the earlier transfers had been made within the past 10 years, the rate of tax on the £50,000 transfer would be calculated according to the rates between £60,000 and £110,000. More importantly, on a death the deceased's cumulative total would only be those transfers made within 10 years of the death and not those throughout his lifetime. In 1986 even more fundamental changes were made to the structure of capital transfer tax and the resulting product was renamed as the inheritance tax we have today. **Even the 1984 consolidation, as amended, was renamed the Inheritance Tax Act 1984[1] and references to sections in the following chapters are to that Act unless otherwise stated.**

---

[1]   Technically the law provides that the 1984 Act *may* be referred to as the Inheritance Tax Act 1984 rather than the Capital Transfer Tax Act, but, in practice, everybody does so.

1986 CHANGES What then were the 1986 changes? Apart **17–05**
from a simplification of the rates of the tax, the major change
was to take some lifetime transfers out of the charge to the tax
altogether.[2] With one or two fairly significant exceptions[3] lifetime transfers will only be chargeable if either they were made
within seven years prior to the death of the transferor or the
transferor has retained a benefit in the property transferred.
Most non-settlement lifetime transfers are now regarded as
potentially exempt transfers which will only become retrospectively chargeable in their own right if the transferor dies
within seven years of making them. Since the cumulative principle for those transfers which are chargeable was reduced from
ten to seven years, on a death the deceased's cumulative total
relates to those transfers charged (at the time or retrospectively)
within the past seven years.

HYBRID TAX Inheritance tax has therefore resurrected the **17–06**
old estate duty concepts that a death rather than a lifetime
transfer is the major trigger for a charge to the tax and that gifts
made within seven years and those with a reservation of benefit
(gifts with reservation) become chargeable on that death. But
many aspects of capital transfer tax also remain. Charges on a
death and on discretionary trusts[4] remain much as before, the
way in which the value of the transfer is calculated is still the
loss to the transferor, there is still a limited form of cumulation
and in certain cases there is a charge even though no death has
occurred. Thus inheritance tax is a hybrid between estate duty
and capital transfer tax, which charges more than just an
inheritance on a death and which does so by reference to the
total of the transfers made by the transferor and not by reference
to the amount inherited; i.e. it is still a mutation and not an
acquisitions tax. One curious consequence of the changes to this
tax is that non-settlement lifetime gifts will rarely be chargeable
to inheritance tax (the non-commercial tax) on the full value
transferred but to capital gains tax (the commercial tax) on the
notional gain made by the donor. Where both taxes are
chargeable there is, as we have seen in para.16–04, a relief from
capital gains tax.

---

[2] Thus triggering the reintroduction of the charge on lifetime gifts under capital
gains tax.
[3] Notably those relating to the creation and continued existence of most trusts,
which are immediately chargeable.
[4] Other trusts are now also taxed in the same way as discretionary trusts since
2006.

17–07   STRUCTURAL CHANGES POST 1986   After almost twenty years of the status quo, another change to the structure of the tax came in 2006 when the regime for fixed interest trusts was radically altered with almost immediate effect. There was no prior consultation or warning and a limited time given for damage limitation.

The next change came in 2008, in response to political pressure resulting from the rapid advance in domestic house prices, which, unlike capital gains tax, are not exempt from inheritance tax. The percentage of the nil band (effectively the IHT threshold) unused by a spouse or civil partner on their death could be carried forward and added to that of the survivor. This could occur e.g. because all the property was left to their surviving spouse/partner and so, as we shall see, is exempt from the tax. In that case 100 per cent can be carried forward. Alternatively, if part of the estate was chargeable, e.g. as being left to the children, but that part is say only 60 per cent of the nil-band limit, then 40 per cent can be carried forward. This change effectively doubled the tax threshold for most couples (but not co-habitees).

Scope of this part

17–08   In the following chapters we shall examine the scope and effects of this hybrid known as inheritance tax. The first question which needs an answer is what amounts to a chargeable lifetime transfer so as to give rise either to an immediate lifetime charge or to a retrospective charge if the transferor dies within seven years, explaining as we go the way in which gifts with reservation fit into this. Then we need to examine the charge which arises on the death of the transferor. Having established what is chargeable or potentially chargeable we need to look at the various exemptions and reliefs which are available against this charge. Having thus established the net charge so to speak we then examine how the charge is actually calculated and who ultimately has to account for and pay the tax. Because settlements are the subject of many special rules these are dealt with in a separate chapter.

CHAPTER 18

CHARGEABLE TRANSFERS

Introduction

Inheritance tax is only chargeable if there is a *chargeable*   **18–01**
transfer. These may be made either during the transferor's lifetime or on his death, although, as we have seen, many of the
former do not attract an immediate charge to the tax. Instead
they may become retrospectively chargeable if the transferor
dies within seven years of making them. Until then they are
known as *potentially exempt transfers*. There are special rules
for lifetime transfers in which the transferor retains some
interest in the property transferred, known as *gifts with reservation*. This chapter deals with what is meant by a chargeable
lifetime transfer, what is a potentially exempt transfer, the rules
for gifts with reservation, transfers on death, and one or two
special charges, e.g. involving close companies as defined for
corporation tax purposes). Settled property, being inevitably the
most complex area, is dealt with separately in Ch.21. Remember
that there are many exemptions and reliefs which apply to these
various charges—these are set out in the following chapter.

Lifetime Transfers

Section 1 declares: "Inheritance tax shall be charged on the   **18–02**
value transferred by a chargeable transfer." What, then, is a
"chargeable transfer"? The answer is in s.2(1): "A chargeable
transfer is a transfer of value which is made by an individual but
is not an exempt transfer."

So we need to know what is a transfer of value, what is the
value transferred, what is an individual and what is an exempt
transfer.

A "*transfer of value*" is defined by s.3(1) as: "... a disposition
made by a person (the transferor) as a result of which the value
of his estate immediately after the disposition is less than it
would be but for the disposition: and the amount by which it is
less is the *value transferred* by the transfer." The two essential
criteria for a charge are therefore a disposition and a loss to the
transferor's estate.

The word *"individual"* is not defined by the Act, but of course it is a word well-known in tax law; it does not include companies, nor trustees nor personal representatives. However, as we shall see later, certain dispositions made by trustees of settled property give rise to charges to tax as if they were chargeable transfers, and transfers of value made by companies which are close companies may also give rise to tax liability.

Transfers which are *"exempt transfers"*, and therefore not changeable transfers, are dealt with in Ch.19.

It is also as well to say here that some kinds of property are designated as *"excluded property"*, though these are mainly overseas assets and certain assets, such as unit trusts, held by non-UK domiciled investors (s.6). Reversionary interests under settlements are also excluded property—we shall deal with those in Ch.21. Transfers of such property are not taken into account; s.3(2).

Loss to the transferor's estate

18–03   It is very important to appreciate that the *value transferred* by a transfer is measured under s.3(1) by the diminution in value of the transferor's estate, and not by the increase in value of the transferee's estate, which in this legislation is not limited to the property of a dead person. Of course, in many circumstances the result would be the same whichever measure one took. If Albert gives a motor car to his son Ben, Albert's estate is diminished and Ben's estate is increased by the same amount, namely the value of the car. But there are circumstances in which this is not so, and some of them are very important. For example, if Albert owns 51 per cent of the shares in a company and Ben owns none, and then Albert transfers 2 per cent of the shares to Ben, the diminution in Albert's estate is much greater than is the increase in Ben's estate, because Albert has given up control of the company and Ben has not obtained control.

18–04   ESTATE   The word *"estate"* is defined in s.5(1) as the aggregate[1] of all the property to which [a person] is beneficially entitled, except excluded property and most interests in settled property.[2] The only interests in settled property which now (since 2006) form part of a person's estate are *an immediate post-death interest, a disabled person's interest, a transitional serial interest* or an interest in a *bereaved minor's trust* or in an *18-25 trust.* Those various terms are explained in Ch.21, below.

[1]   See *St Barbe Green v IRC* (2005).
[2]   Because the settlement itself is regarded as the taxable entity.

POWERS OF APPOINTMENT   The word "*property*" is stated in **18–05**
s.272 to include "rights and interests of any description." In
particular, s.5(2) includes any general power of appointment as
being part of a person's estate. The definition of a general power
for this purpose seems to continue the estate duty concept[3] of
any power which a person can appoint in his own favour, e.g.
"to such person as X shall appoint", or "to such of X, Y, and Z
as X shall appoint". It follows that the exercise of such a power
will be a transfer of value (disposition plus loss to the estate) and
also in some cases the omission to exercise it (loss to estate and
gain to the estate of the person entitled in default of appointment—s.3(3)). If not exercised it will also form part of the
deceased's estate on death. In *Sillars v IRC* (2004), the Special
Commissioner held that the wording of s.5(2) was wide enough
to include all of a building society account to which the deceased
had added the names of her two daughters some years before her
death. The deceased could dispose of the entire balance at any
time—the amount was never divided up.

PROPERTY   The meaning of property in the context of a loss   **18–06**
to the transferor's estate was considered by Lightman J. and the
Court of Appeal in *Melville v IRC* (2001). The taxpayer had
settled property on discretionary trusts (an immediately
chargeable transfer) but had included a provision in the trust
deed whereby he had the right to require the trustees to transfer
the whole of the trust fund back to him at his request at any time
90 days after the date of the settlement and also had a veto on
any exercise by the trustees of their powers of appointment
under the trust. The judge and the Court of Appeal held that
those rights were property under s.272 and therefore formed
part of the taxpayer's estate for the purposes of s.3(1). There
was nothing in the legislation to prevent the full meaning of the
word property being applied. It followed that the loss to his
estate consequent on the transfer into the settlement was negligible. It did, however, remain a chargeable transfer for the
purposes of relief from capital gains tax, since there was some
loss to the estate (see para.16–04) which was the object of the
exercise. That object was, however, negatived by a change in
the law in 2002 (see para.21–55), but the general principle in the
case remains valid.

GROSSING UP   One very important aspect of this diminution   **18–07**
principle is that if the transferor pays the inheritance tax the tax

---

[3]   See e.g. *Re Parsons* (1943).

is itself taxable, because his estate is diminished not only by what he transfers to the transferee but also by what he has to pay to the Revenue. The payment of the tax forms part of the loss to the transferor's estate. So there is a grossing-up process. We will deal with this concept more fully later on.

Disposition

18–08   It will be noticed that the definition of transfer of value includes the word "disposition". There is no general definition of this but it probably includes not only obvious transfers such as sales and gifts but also disclaimers[4] and waivers of possible future rights.[5] There have been two attempts since 1975 to charge interest-free loans but both have been repealed and the position remains obscure. It is, however, provided by s.3(3) that a disposition can be merely the omission to exercise a right. This provision prevents many possible avoidance devices. For example, but for this provision Albert could make a tax-free transfer to Ben (his son) by engaging him, for a lump sum paid in advance, to work for a specified time in his (Albert's) business and then standing by and omitting to sue for damages when Ben does not turn up. Section 3(3) only applies, however, if, as the result of an omission by you, your estate is diminished and another's[6] is increased, and it can be avoided if you can show that the omission was not deliberate.[7]

Associated operations

18–09   It is stated in s.272 (the definitions section) that a "disposition" includes "a disposition effected by *associated operations*" and "associated operations" are defined by s.268. They are

> "(a)   operations which affect the same property ... or
> (b)   any two operations of which one is effected with reference to the other, or with a view to enabling the other to be effected or facilitating its being effected, and any further operation having a like relation to any of those two, and so on: whether those operations are effected by the same person or different persons, and whether or not they are simultaneous; and 'operation' includes an omission."

---

[4]   Some disclaimers are expressly excluded from the charge, (e.g. of a legacy within two years of death: s.142). So it presumably follows that other disclaimers are included.

[5]   Again some waivers, (e.g. of future dividends not declared for at least one year afterwards: s.15) are expressly excluded from the charge.

[6]   Including most settlements.

[7]   Does this include for example failure to exercise a beneficial option owing to lack of funds?

A simple example of how this provision might work arises from an attempt to manipulate the exempt transfer provisions. As we shall see transfers between spouses are, in general, exempt and each individual may make exempt transfers up to £3,000 in each tax year. Suppose Albert is a wealthy taxpayer who has already given £3,000 to his son, Ben in the current year. Albert could give £3,000 to his wife Zoë, who could then give that money to Ben, using her exempt amount. None of the transfers is a chargeable transfer. Under the associated operations provisions the transfer of the second £3,000 to Ben could be treated as if it had been made by Albert and so chargeable if Albert were to die within seven years, even if Zoë is still alive.

LIMITATIONS The definition of associated operations is on **18–10** the face of it very wide. The section has been before the courts on a number of occasions involving settlements. In *Macpherson v IRC* (1988) the trustees entered into two transactions which together had the effect of lowering the charge to tax on the second. The House of Lords had no difficulty in deciding that these were associated operations but the case is worth noting because their Lordships imposed a restriction on the width of the section by insisting that each operation must be relevant to the scheme which created the benefit for the transferee.

That restrictive theme was taken up and developed by Park J. and the Court of Appeal in *Rysaffe Trustee Co (CI) Ltd v IRC* (2003). The taxpayer had made five separate but basically identical discretionary settlements. The Revenue sought to treat them as being one settlement, i.e. that together they amounted to a single disposition, the creation of a settlement. The judge held that each settlement was a separate settlement, each of which had been effected by a single disposition and not by a series of dispositions. Whilst the definition of "associated operations" was quite wide, its practical operation was very limited. It was simply a definition and not a catch-all anti-avoidance provision which could be invoked to nullify the effectiveness of any scheme or structure which could be said to have involved more than one operation and which was intended to avoid or reduce tax (i.e. it was not a *Ramsay* type of provision). Where two or more transactions take place, they may be associated operations in the sense that they were effected by reference to each other, etc. but they will only be *relevant* associated operations if they contribute to the actual transfer of value.

The judge approved and followed a decision of the Special Commissioners in *Reynaud v IRC* (1999). In that case the tax-payers transferred shares in a private company to trustees. The company then purchased those shares from the trustees for cash. The Revenue sought to add these two events together to say that the gifts were therefore of cash and not shares and so not eligible for business relief. The Commissioners refused, saying that the transfer of value (the shares) was effected by a single disposition and not by a series of dispositions. The same was true of each of the settlements in the present case, the value transferred had been completed by each transfer—no other transaction was needed to effect that, unlike the example given earlier of two transactions being used to effect a transfer from Albert to Ben. The judge's reasoning was subsequently upheld by the Court of Appeal. The inclusion of associated operations in the description of a disposition was not intended for cases where there was clearly a disposition of property falling within the Act, but where there was a dispute as to whether there was such a disposition at all.

18–11   CONSEQUENCES If the associated operations provision applies then the consequence is that the chargeable transfer is deemed to take place at the time of the last of them: s.268(3). There is one statutory exception in s.268(2). The grant of a lease for full consideration is not to be associated with any operation effected more than three years earlier, e.g. a gift of the landlord's reversion.

Non-commercial transfers

18–12   It has been said above that inheritance tax is (in part) a tax on non-commercial transfers, i.e. "gifts tax". That phrase is not used in the legislation, but it is made clear by the use of other words "*gratuitous benefit*" in s.10(1) that the tax only bites on transfers which contain an element of gift. Sales at market value are not taxable because they do not involve any diminution in the value of the seller's estate. If Albert owns a car which is worth £800 and he sells it to Charles for £800 Albert's estate has the same value after the sale as it had before the sale; he has merely exchanged one asset (the car) for an equivalent asset (cash). But suppose Albert sells the car, not for £800, but for £500. That may occur either (1) because Albert wished to confer a benefit on Charles or (2) because he made a bad bargain. A gift (as in (1)), is taxable: a bad bargain (as in (2)), is not taxable. This point is dealt with in s.10(1) which declares:

"A disposition is not a transfer of value if it is shown that it was not intended, and was not made in a transaction intended, to confer any gratuitous benefit on any person and either—

320

(a) that it was made in a transaction at arm's length between persons not connected with each other, or

(b) that it was such as might be expected to be made in a transaction at arm's length between persons not connected with each other..."

The subsection requires two conditions to be met; a subjective non-donative intent *and* the objective fact stated in (a) or the apparently objective fact stated in (b). Where the parties are connected (i.e. they are relatives, linked in a trust, partners or involved with a close company) the criterion imposed by (b) of what would be expected to amount to an arm's length sale was discussed in *IRC v Spencer-Nairn* (1991).

CONNECTED PERSONS This was an unusual case in that the   **18–13**
vendor was unaware that he was selling to a connected person (a company) and had negotiated on the basis that they were unconnected. He sold the property for £94,000 below the market value because he mistakenly thought that he was liable for repairs to the property. The Revenue agreed that he had no gratuitous intention but argued that the discrepancy between the market value and the actual value of the land meant that it was not one which could have been expected on an arm's length sale. The Court of Session in Scotland dismissed the argument that any such discrepancy would automatically invoke the section, stating that it was merely one factor which had to be taken into account. They decided that a hypothetical arm's length vendor should be taken to have had the actual vendor's (reasonable) belief that he was liable for repairs and so, since the price was not unreasonable given that belief, they found for the taxpayer. They were impressed by the fact that the price had been negotiated between persons who thought they were acting at arms length. One consequence of this decision is therefore that in assessing what can be expected on an arm's length sale certain subjective factors, such as the reasonable belief in this case, are to be taken into account.

INTENT TO CONFER A GRATUITOUS BENEFIT Where the par-   **18–14**
ties are not connected, the central issue is whether the transferor can show the negative intent of not conferring any gratuitous benefit on the transferee. This was considered by the Special Commissioners in *Executors of Postlethwaite v HMRC* (2006). They pointed out that the fact that there was a gratuitous benefit actually conferred was not determinative but simply a factor as to intent, which was the key issue. They considered that a

payment made under a binding legal obligation would not be so intended. They also thought that past consideration might well negative the intention. On the facts they found no such intention since the money paid was a sum to which the recipient already had an economic entitlement.

Potentially exempt transfers

Definition

18–15   Lifetime transfers do not necessarily attract an immediate charge to tax. Only those which are not potentially exempt transfers as defined in s.3A become immediately liable to a charge. A potentially exempt transfer (PET) is now defined as (i) one made by an individual, (ii) which would otherwise be a chargeable transfer, (iii) which is made to another individual or into a *disabled trust* or on the coming to an end, during the lifetime of the beneficial holder, of an *immediate post-death interest* in the settlement, which then continues as a *bereaved minor's trust*.[8] Thus transfers to companies, and most of the various charges involving trusts are not potentially exempt transfers. They are therefore immediately chargeable transfers.

In the case of a transfer to an individual the transfer will only be a PET if the property becomes part of that individual's estate or his estate is increased. Thus if David decides to pay his grandson's school fees and does so by paying the school direct he has not made a PET—the grandson's estate has not been increased. It would be a PET if David gave the money to his son who then used the money to pay the school fees as the son's estate will have been increased. Gifts with a reservation, i.e. where the donor retains some interest in the property, are the subject of special rules, set out in the following part of this chapter.

Effect of being a PET

18–16   We will explain the somewhat tortuous rules for calculating the charges to inheritance tax in Ch.20. For the moment it is sufficient to note that a lifetime transfer which is not a PET attracts an immediate charge based on the cumulative total of such transfers within the previous seven years. The current (2008/09) rate for immediately chargeable lifetime transfers is 20 per cent on cumulative transfers above £312,000. Thus if Edward, having made no previous transfers, creates two discretionary trusts in 2007 and 2008, each with a value of

---

[8]   All these terms are explained in Ch.21.

£312,000—the first will be tax free but the second will be chargeable at 20 per cent.

If the transfer is a PET then there is no immediate charge to tax and if the transferor lives for more than seven years there will be no charge at all. If, however, the transferor dies within that period the PET becomes chargeable at the appropriate rate for deaths (which is currently double the rate for lifetime transfers, subject to some relief if he has survived at least three years). This is the rate at the date of death rather than the rate in force when the transfer was made, unless the former is higher. Another effect of a PET ceasing to be exempt is that it retrospectively becomes a chargeable transfer. Thus it will have to be taken into account in working out the transferor's cumulative total for subsequent lifetime transfers. This can retrospectively affect the liability for those other transfers. Thus if in our example above, Edward had made a PET of £312,000 in 2006, which subsequently becomes chargeable on Edward's death in 2008, not only is that transfer itself charged to tax but the relevant cumulative total of previous transfers for, say, a discretionary trust transfer in 2007 will change from zero to £312,000 and the latter will become chargeable at 20 per cent.[9]

In *Re Griffiths* (2008), PETS made by the deceased, who then died within two years, were set aside by the court. At the time of the gifts he was, unknowingly, suffering from cancer. Had he known that, he would not have made the PETS as part of a tax planning device.

Gifts with reservation of benefit

Purpose of the legislation

18–17
With the introduction of the potentially exempt transfer regime in 1986 it was inevitable that measures would be taken to prevent a transferor making a gift, e.g. of his house to his son or daughter, whilst retaining a benefit in that property, e.g. by continuing to live in the house. If the transferor lived for more than seven years after making the gift he would avoid any inheritance tax and would have passed on his house to his son or daughter tax free, whilst in practice having made no material change in his circumstances. To prevent taxpayers having their cake and eating it in this way the concept of a gift with reservation was introduced by s.102 of and Sch.20 to the Finance Act

---

[9] In fact, as we shall see, because Edward has died within seven years of setting up the discretionary trusts, additional tax above the 20% becomes payable, up to the full death-rate, depending on the length of time Edward survived.

1986. In fact this concept was really reintroduced because it had been necessary under estate duty law to prevent exactly the same abuse. The basic legislation is similar to that for estate duty and some of the cases decided under those rules are relevant here. One issue which also arose under the 1986 rules was decided in such a way by the House of Lords under the new rules that additional legislation, ss.102A, 102B and 102C was introduced in 1999. Further changes, also as the result of a court decision, were made in 2003.

One problem with using the former estate duty concept of a gift is that it does not always square with the inheritance tax concept of a transfer of value. Thus, whilst a bad bargain may be a transfer of value if it is between connected persons because there will be a loss to the transferor's estate and it will not fall within the gratuitous benefit exemption, it is hard to see that there is any element of bounty so as to classify it as a gift.[10]

18–18   Section 102 of the Finance Act 1986 applies when an individual disposes of any property by way of gift and either:

  (a) possession and enjoyment is not bona fide assumed by the donee at, or before the beginning of the relevant period; or
  (b) at any time in the relevant period the property is not enjoyed to the entire exclusion, or virtually the entire exclusion,[11] of the donor and of any benefit to him by contract or otherwise.

The *relevant period* in which both possession and enjoyment must be assumed and the entire exclusion of the donor is assessed, is seven years prior to the death of the donor. Thus if at any time in the seven years prior to his death the donor was not so excluded or possession was not taken up by the donee, the gift will be regarded as one subject to a reservation. It follows that if any such benefit is given up and possession has been assumed more than seven years before the death then there is no gift with a reservation and in fact no charge to inheritance tax.

---

[10] It is also arguable that a disposition which is deemed by the 1984 Act not to be a transfer of value, e.g. one for the maintenance of the family (see para.19–29), will still be a gift for this purpose.
[11] This was not present in the original estate duty provisions and is intended to allow e.g. the donor of a house to return to it on visits or a short holiday.

Effect of a reservation

There are two possible consequences of a gift being regarded   **18–19**
as one subject to a reservation. First, whenever it was made, if
the gift is still subject to a reservation at the date of the donor's
death, the property given is deemed to be part of the donor's
estate at death and so chargeable as if he had never given it
away.

Thus in *Sillars v IRC* (2004), where the deceased and her two
daughters were joint tenants of a building society account, the
deceased was deemed to own the whole amount at death. When
the daughters' names were added to the account, the deceased
was still entitled to a share of the whole and the property had
not been enjoyed to the entire exclusion of the deceased.

Secondly, if the gift ceases to be subject to a reservation within
seven years before the donor's death, the donor is treated as if he
had made a PET at that date. Thus the property will be retrospectively charged under the PET rules as if the donor had made
a chargeable transfer of the property at the date when the
reservation ceased.

Interpreting the legislation

Using, in part, the old estate duty cases it is possible to shed   **18–20**
some light on how the courts will interpret the various parts of
s.102 of the Finance Act 1986. With regard to the concept of the
donee assuming bona fide possession in para.(a) it is clear that to
do so the gift must be a perfect transfer in equity.[12] This was the
decision in *Letts v IRC* (1957). Looking at para.(b), it has been
held that the donor will not be entirely excluded from possession
of the property unless that is the position in fact as well as in
law. Thus in *Oakes v Commissioner of Stamp Duties* (1954), a
settlor who settled property in which he had no interest was
caught when he was appointed as a trustee with a right to
remuneration, and in *Stamp Duties Commissioner of New
South Wales v Permanent Trustee Co* (1956), where the settlor
borrowed the interest arising from the settlement on his
daughter, with no legal entitlement to do so, a similar result
applied.

The inclusion of a benefit "by contract or otherwise" is
intended to catch collateral benefits to the donor. In *Att-Gen v
Seccombe* (1911) it was held that such benefits had to be the
subject of a legal entitlement. It is doubted whether that would

---

[12] Remember that in general, equity will not perfect an imperfect gift so that if
any formalities required to effect a gift have not been undertaken by the
donor, there is no perfect gift.

now be the law. Thus it has been held that a gift into a discretionary trust of which the donor is a potential beneficiary is a gift with reservation under ground (b), (donor not entirely excluded etc). Further, if the donor may exercise a significant control over the trust, it will also be a gift with reservation under ground (a), (possession by the trustees not assumed etc).[13] Under s.102ZA, in the few situations where the holder of a beneficial interest in settled property is treated for tax purposes as owning the whole settled property,[14] for the purpose of s.102 that holder is treated as enjoying the whole property prior to the gift or termination of the interest.

Schedule 20 expressly excludes two factual situations from being a reservation of a benefit. Paragraph 6 provides that actual occupation of land by the donor in return for full consideration in money or where the donor comes back into actual occupation of land owing to his incapacity and it is for reasonable provision for his care and maintenance by the donee who is a relative of the donor, are not to be regarded as a reservation of a benefit by the donor.

Benefits reserved or retained

18–21   The most complex of the cases are those which draw a distinction between a benefit reserved out of the property given away and a benefit retained by the donor which was never given away in the first place. The importance of this is that in the second case the property actually given away has never been the subject of a reservation. This is easier to state than to apply in practice, however. The trick is to separate the part retained by the donor from the part given away. This is sometimes explained by reference to *vertical and horizontal separation*.

For example if Fred owns two adjoining houses and gives one to Gillian whilst retaining the other this is said to be vertical separation. The fact that Fred has retained one house does not mean that he has retained any benefit in the other which thus becomes a PET.

Suppose, instead, Fred creates an interest, such as a lease, in his property and then gives away the rest, he has horizontally separated the two and so has no benefit in the part given away. It would be different if he gave away the whole property and

---

[13]   *Lyon's Personal Representatives v HMRC* Sp Comm (2007), following Lightman J. in *IRC v Eversden* (2002). The latter case was decided by the CA on a different point (2003), but the CA accepted the position of the judge on this point.

[14]   See Ch.21 below.

was then given back the interest in it—he would have reserved a benefit in the property.

TIMING With regard to such horizontal separation the timing of the separation is crucial. The original authority for its effectiveness is *Munro v Commissioner of Stamp Duties* (1934), where the donor gave away land subject to his interest as a partner in its use which had been created prior to the gift. He was held to have given away only the land subject to the partnership interest. He had not reserved his interest as a partner, he had simply never given it away at all. This decision was distinguished in *Nichols v IRC* (1975) where the donor gave his land away subject to a condition that it was leased back to him by the donee. He was held to have given away the whole property and reserved the benefit of the lease. The lease had not been created by a prior transaction unlike the partnership interest in *Munro*.

18–22

In *Ingram v IRC* (1999), decided under the new law, the donor transferred property to trustees and, in an attempt to avoid the decision in *Nicholls, at the same time* created the right to a lease of the property to herself. The Court of Appeal agreed with the general principle as to the timing of the separation in *Nichols* but it was rejected by the House of Lords. In their opinion a gift of the freehold of land with a condition that a lease back to the donor be granted was not a gift with reservation. All that the donor had given away was the reversion in which she had no benefit. The ban was against a reservation on the *interest* disposed of and not the *property*. *Nichols* was distinguished on the basis that in that case there was an additional reservation under a different head because the donee had covenanted to repair the land and so the donor, in occupation of it under the lease, was not entirely excluded from benefit by contract. This allowed the House of Lords to decide that the general reservation point in *Nichols* was *obiter*.

Special rules for land

The success of what was known as the "lease carve out scheme" in *Ingram* "disappointed" the Revenue, who then, in time-honoured fashion, took the first opportunity to introduce legislation to reverse the decision. The main section is s.102A inserted into the Finance Act 1986. It applies only where the gift is of an interest in land and where it would not otherwise be a

18–23

gift with reservation under the general rules.[15] In practice it is of course in relation to land that such schemes will mainly apply because of the possibilities of creating horizontal interests in land. The section provides that where X makes a gift of an interest in land there will be a gift with a reservation if within the relevant period[16] either: (1) X (the donor) or his spouse has a *significant right or interest* in relation to the land; or (2) X or his spouse is a party to a *significant arrangement* in relation to the land (s.102A(2)).

18–24   SIGNIFICANT INTEREST   An interest, right or arrangement is significant for this purpose if it *entitles* or *enables* X to occupy all or part of the land or to enjoy some right in relation to all or part of the land[17] otherwise than for full consideration in money or money's worth (s.102A(3)). This means that for the section to apply it must be X who occupies the land or enjoys the right, even if it is his spouse who has the interest. Thus if X gives some land to Y on condition that it is leased back to X's spouse, but X occupies the land with his spouse's consent, it will be caught because X's spouse has an interest which is a significant one since it has enabled X to occupy the land. The use of the word *enables* may cause problems since it is far less precise than *entitles*. For example, suppose that X gives land to Y on condition that it is leased back to Z who is not X's spouse. Z then allows X to occupy the land. Is X a party to a significant arrangement, i.e. one which enables him to occupy the land?

18–25   SEVEN YEAR LIMIT   An important limit on the scope of s.102A is that subsection (5) exempts interests or rights which X or his spouse were granted more than seven years before the gift of land.[18] Thus, at first sight, if X grants his spouse a lease in year one and gives the reversion to Y in year nine, there will be no reservation even if X continues to occupy the land. But this seven-year period does not apply to arrangements, so that any arrangement made at any time before the gift will count if it is significant. Therefore, if the above example can be regarded as an arrangement, it will still be a gift with reservation since X's occupation will make it significant. Thus it can be seen that

---

[15]   Such as a reservation of benefit by a contract (the covenant to repair) as in *Nicholls.*

[16]   Remember that this is the seven years before X's subsequent death.

[17]   This will include rights such as shooting rights, etc.

[18]   Be careful not to confuse this with the period of seven years before X's death in which the significant right, interest or arrangement must still exist before there can be a charge, whenever the gift was made.

these provisions apply to interests, etc., created well before the gift and not just to lease carve out schemes of the *Ingram* type. Under the old rules the Revenue used to ignore events prior to the gift if they were "prior independent transactions".[19]

EXCEPTIONS Section 102A does not apply in certain cir-   **18–26**
cumstances where the general rule in s.102 would also not apply, e.g. occupation by X due to unforeseen circumstances. Nor does it apply where X gives Y a lease and retains the reversion (s.102A(4)(b)) which is the converse to a lease carve out.

UNDIVIDED SHARES More fundamentally s.102A does not   **18–27**
apply to gifts of an undivided share (i.e. in England the creation of a tenancy in common) in land. In fact in such a case even the general provisions in s.102 are not to apply (s.102C(6)). Instead s.102B applies. Under that section, where X gives Y an undivided share in his land so that X and Y become tenants in common, he will have made a gift with reservation unless: (1) X does not occupy the land;[20] (2) X occupies the land to the entire exclusion of Y for full consideration in money or money's worth[21]; or (3) X and Y occupy the land and X does not receive any benefit, other than a negligible one, provided by Y or at his expense for some reason connected with the gift. This last situation will therefore protect X if Y pays only his fair share of the outgoings of the land. There will also be no charge where X occupies the land due to unforeseen circumstances.

Effect of exempt transfers

The second case decided after 1986 also caused the Revenue   **18–28**
much concern. Section 102(5) provides that where the gift is one of a selected number of exempt transfer categories, including transfers to a spouse, then the gift with reservation principle will not apply. In *IRC v Eversden* (2003), D created a settlement for her husband for life, then to a number of discretionary beneficiaries including herself. She then transferred 95 per cent of her house to the trustees. When her husband died she was allowed to live in that house and was so doing when she died. It was agreed that her interest under the trust and her occupation of the house meant that she had prima facie made a gift with reser-

---

[19] Which of course they seldom were in practice.
[20] Since s.102 does not apply X can receive rent, etc. from the land provided he is not in occupation of it.
[21] This is similar to the position under ss.102 and 102A.

vation of the house and that the value of the house should therefore be added to her estate on death. But since the gift was initially of a life interest to her husband and that was a relevant exempt transfer, s.102(5) applied and took the whole property out of the charge under s.102.

As a result, a number of schemes were marketed, typically setting up a trust giving the settlor's spouse a short interest, say for three months, with discretionary remainders, including the settlor; the effect being to exempt both the creation of the settlement and the passing of the house on the settlor's death. The Revenue took action and the Finance Act 2003 inserted subss.(5A), (5B), and (5C) into s.102. The effect is that where a trust is set up and the settlor's spouse has an interest in possession which comes to an end (whether by death or otherwise under the settlement) s.102 will apply to the settlor on the facts as they exist from the time that interest so ends. Thus, both in the case and the example above, whilst the creation of the settlement will be exempt, after the spouse's interest ends the settlor's living in the house or her interest as a discretionary beneficiary will make the transfer of the house into a gift with reservation from that date and so it will be added onto her estate at death.

Income tax alternative

18–29   Despite these changes, a further number of successful avoidance schemes were marketed which enabled taxpayers to obtain a benefit from assets which they had given away without being caught by the gift with reservation rules. The Revenue therefore changed their point of attack and Sch.15 to the Finance Act 2004 imposed a charge to **income tax** (from 2005/6) where a person enjoys a benefit (either free or at low cost) from an asset he formerly owned or provided the funds to purchase (known as a pre-owned asset) at any time since March 1986. There are detailed provisions as to how the benefit is to be quantified for land, chattels and intangible assets.

It is clear that this new charge is intended as a residual charge where the IHT rules have been avoided. Thus it does not apply: (i) where the asset was disposed of at arms' length or on arms' length terms; (ii) where the disposal was into a trust in which the taxpayer or spouse has an interest in possession (potential IHT charge then anyway); (iii) where the disposal was to a spouse; (iv) where the IHT gifts with reservation rules apply or would apply but for existing IHT exemptions such as gifts to charity; (v) where the IHT rules do not apply because the taxpayer has given part of their interest to someone with whom the share occupation; and (vi) where the IHT rules would apply but for the exception for cases where the former owner needs to move back into the gifted property following a change in his circumstances (e.g. for reasons of age). As an alternative to this charge, a former owner may elect to have the asset(s) treated as part of their estate for IHT purposes.

Property subject to the charge

The final question involving gifts subject to a reservation is that if they do become chargeable to IHT what property is actually subject to the charge? The answers to this are to be found in Sch.20 to the Finance Act 1986. If the property originally given is still held by the donee unchanged in form then of course it will be that property, valued now, which is chargeable. But if the donee has parted with the original gift an alternative is required. In outline, if the donee sells or exchanges the asset for full consideration then that sum or replacement asset becomes the subject of any charge. In other cases the property with which he parted (including any replacement asset taken in full exchange) becomes the subject of the charge. The same rules apply broadly to gifts into a settlement. 18–30

Transfers on Death

Transfer of value

Section 4(1) declares that: "On the death of any person tax shall be charged as if, immediately before his death he had made a transfer of value and the value transferred by it had been equal to the value of his estate immediately before his death." It is this enactment which brought in inheritance tax as a replacement of estate duty. 18–31

The effect of s.4 is that the deceased is deemed to have made a disposition of all his assets the moment before death. The total of those assets must then be added to the cumulative total of his chargeable lifetime transfers made in the past seven years and charged at the appropriate rate. The rate of tax on a death is twice that on a lifetime transfer, although the former may also be liable to capital gains tax.

Retrospective effect

We have already seen that the death of the transferor will also make all PETS made within the past seven years retrospectively chargeable (and part of the cumulative total for subsequent previous transfers) and that a gift still subject to a reservation at the death will also become chargeable at the rates for a death. 18–32

The death will also increase the rate of tax already paid on an immediately chargeable lifetime transfer made by the deceased within seven years prior to the death. One minor blessing is that since the deceased has transferred all his assets on his death there can be no question of grossing up the transfer to include the tax payable—that must come out of the assets transferred. Questions as to who pays the tax and who ultimately bears the cost (e.g. as between the beneficiaries) are the subject of Ch.22.

Timing of transfer

18–33   What is the point of deeming the transfer of value to have been made "immediately before" the death, not "on" the death? Presumably it is to knock out any argument that at the moment of death certain interests of the person dying cease to exist and therefore do not form part of his estate. This argument could have been put forward, for example, in relation to the interest of a joint tenant which is extinguished "on" the death: s.171(2).

Similarly exercising a power of appointment by will does not affect the fact that such a power formed part of the estate immediately before the death. Estate has the same meaning as for lifetime transfers. Moving the deemed transfer from the moment of death to "immediately before" the death also makes it easier for the legislation to lay down its own code of rules, untrammelled by the general law, as to which assets are to be treated as forming part of the estate and which are not. Such a code is laid down in ss.171 to 177. For example, there is an allowance for reasonable funeral expenses under s.172.

Comorientes

18–34   It is important to know what is the tax position if two (or more) persons die (for example in a car accident) virtually at the same instant. The law of succession to property in such a case is stated in s.184 of the Law of Property Act 1925, namely that the younger person is deemed to have survived the elder person. For tax purposes s.4(2) provides that "where it cannot be known which of two or more persons who have died survived the other or others they shall be assumed to have died at the same instant." Suppose that the two persons are Albert and his son Ben. The effect is that the estate left by Albert to Ben is charged to tax on Albert's death but not also on Ben's death. Similarly, if Ben has left anything to Albert, that estate is charged on Ben's death but not also on Albert's death. Where the order of death *is* known (e.g. Albert dies five minutes before Ben) s.4(2) does not apply, but there may be "Quick Succession Relief": see para.19–15. An alternative is to provide in a will that property will only pass to a beneficiary if he survives the testator by a specified period. Such survivorship clauses if limited to six months will avoid a double charge in such cases: s.92.

Other Charges

This rather curious chapter title is taken from the Finance Act 1975 where "Other Charges" was used as a cross-heading to describe four sections, 39–42, grouped together in that Act as being, broadly speaking, anti-avoidance measures. It is a fair comment on the haste with which the 1975 Bill was prepared that these problems had not been thought through very thoroughly. Indeed, when the Bill was first published the problem of close companies (obvious with hindsight) had not been dealt with at all. When the 1984 consolidation took place some attempts at rationalisation over the 10 years was evident. Section 39 (beefed up in 1976) become ss.94 to 98 *and* s.102 *and* s.202. Section 41 was repealed before it came into effect. But ss.40 and 42 (now ss.262 and 263) still defy classification and were assigned to the "Miscellaneous and Supplementary" part of the 1984 Act.

18–35

Close companies

In general, inheritance tax is not charged on companies because they are not "individuals". But, by s.94, where a company which is a close company makes a transfer of value a tax charge may arise. Such transfers cannot be PETs and so attract an immediate charge to the tax. The intention is to prevent such companies from being used to avoid the tax. Tax is charged as if each participator, domiciled here, had made a transfer of value proportionate to his interest in the company.[22] But against this can be set the amount (if any) by which the value of his estate is increased. So (for example) a return of capital would be a gratuitous transfer by the company, but no tax would be payable because each member's estate would be increased by the amount received. His estate (for this purpose) does not include any rights or interests in the company.

18–36

Section 98 provides that where there is an alteration of such a company's shares or debentures or rights attaching to them so that there is a loss to a transferor's estate there will be a chargeable transfer by the participators. This is to prevent value being passed in ways that it might be impossible to establish that

---

[22] We have come across these terms for corporation tax purposes. But see s.96 which excludes the ownership of preference shares for this purpose.

the transferor shareholder has made a disposition, e.g. on a reduction of capital or a purchase by a company of its own shares. The sections are aimed at various avoidance devices, and consequently s.102 provides that a "close company" includes not only a company which is a close company for purposes of corporation tax but also a company which would be such a close company if it were resident in the United Kingdom.

Future payments

18–37   This matter is dealt with (in rather obscure language) by s.262. Where a transfer of value takes the form of a disposition for which payments are made (or assets are transferred) more than a year after the disposition, each payment is taxed separately when it is made, the tax being based on a proportionate part of the value transferred. For example, if A buys a property for more than its market value, that is, on the general principles of the tax, a transfer of value by A of the amount by which the price exceeds the market value—the gratuitous element. The effect of this present section is that if A agrees to pay by instalments, each instalment counts as a separate transfer of value. (The rule does not apply to a disposition for no consideration at all, such as an ordinary seven-year covenant.) The point of the section is (presumably) to spread the amount of value transferred. Thus some of the instalments may fall within seven years before A's death, thus attracting a charge, whereas the earlier ones may escape such a charge under the PET rules.

Interest-free loans

18–38   This matter was originally intended to be dealt with by s.41 (of Finance Act 1975) but that was replaced by Finance Act 1976, s.115 before it came into effect. That section was itself repealed and there are no specific provisions now to deal with interest-free loans. The position is therefore covered only by the general provisions of the Act. It follows that a fixed-term loan of money or assets may be a transfer of value. For example, if A lends B £1,000 interest-free for five years, gratuitously, A is making a transfer to B of the then value of using the money for that period. But if the loan was repayable on demand, there would be no value transferred, and no inheritance tax charge.

Annuity purchased in conjunction with life policy

18–39   Section 263 imposes a charge to tax where the purchase of an annuity is an associated operation with the issue of a life policy on the life of the annuitant and the policy is vested in someone other than the purchaser of the annuity. The purchaser is treated as making a transfer of value at the time the life policy becomes vested in that other person. The amount of the transfer of value is whichever is the less of the following: (a) the sum paid for the annuity plus premiums paid under the policy up to the time of the transfer; (b) the greatest benefit capable of being conferred at any time by the policy. Such transfers are PETs.

It seems that this special charge to tax is additional to the charge which may arise (if no exemption applies) from the transferor's keeping the policy on foot by paying the premiums, each premium payment being a transfer of value.

The reason why the Revenue are so concerned about back-to-back policies is that a linked contract for life assurance and an annuity with the same company can be obtained on very favourable terms, because if the company loses on the assurance policy it will gain on the annuity contract. Because of this background, the Revenue will be prepared to treat the arrangements as not being associated operations (and hence not taxable) if the life policy has been issued on full medical evidence[23] and on no different terms from those which would have been obtainable without the annuity link.

Settled property

The application of inheritance tax to settled property is the subject of Ch.21, below.   **18–40**

---

[23] See *Smith v HMRC* [2008] S.T.C. 1649 on that point.

CHAPTER 19

EXEMPTIONS AND RELIEFS

Introduction

19–01 The legislation gives relief from tax in various ways. Some kinds of property are declared to be excluded property. Some transactions are declared not to be transfers of value. Some transfers of value are declared to be exempt transfers, thus attracting no tax. Some transfers of value, though they are taxable, attract a reduced amount of tax. Some apply to lifetime transfers only, some to transfers on a death and others to all types of transfer.

No great benefit would accrue from expounding the exemptions and reliefs under separate heads corresponding to the various modes of relief mentioned above. Until the 1984 Act they were somewhat randomly placed through the legislation, and even the 1984 consolidation has to resort to calling two of its nine parts "Miscellaneous". In order to continue to show how the history of this tax lacks coherence the order in which the exemptions and reliefs are expounded in what follows is based largely (but not wholly) on the order in which they stood in the Finance Act 1975 and then on the order in which further reliefs have been added since. References in this chapter are, however, to the 1984 Act.

Transfers between spouses and civil partners: s.18

19–02 Transfers between spouses and civil partners are exempt transfers. This is true both of lifetime transfers and of transfers on death. This exemption is obviously of immense importance in tax planning. As we shall see in the next chapter, spouses and civil partners also have transferable nil-rate bands on death. The fact that no such largesse applies, e.g. to siblings sharing a house, was held not to be a breach of the human rights legislation by the European Court of Human Rights in *Burden v United Kingdom* (2008).

The exemption is stated in s.18:

"A transfer of value is an exempt transfer to the extent that the value transferred is attributable to property which becomes comprised in the estate of the transferor's spouse or civil partner, or, so far as the value transferred is not so attributable, to the extent that that estate is increased."

The first part of the section gives exemption to the straightforward case where one spouse or civil partner transfers some item of cash or property to the other. The second part of the section deals with less clear-cut cases. An example would be a case where one spouse or civil partner forgives a debt owed to him (or her) by the other. The forgiveness is a transfer of value, but it is an exempt transfer because, although no property becomes comprised in the estate of the forgiven spouse or civil partner, that estate is increased by the amount of the debt.

Exceptions and limitations

The exemption does not apply if the disposition takes effect   **19–03** on the termination *after the transfer of value* of any interest or period. So if H (husband) leaves or settles property to X (any third party) for life and then to W (H's wife) the exemption does not apply.[1] Similarly if H leaves property to X for 10 years and then to W. Also, the exemption does not apply if the disposition depends on a condition which is not satisfied within 12 months. An example would be if H left property to W provided she survived him by 18 months. But the exemption is not excluded by reason only that the gift is conditional on one spouse or civil partner surviving the other for a specified period. So a survivorship clause in a will does not knock out the exemption provided the survivorship period is not more than 12 months. In practice wills are commonly drawn with a survivorship period of 30 or 60 days.

As an anti-avoidance measure, the exemption does not apply if the spouse or civil partner has purchased the reversionary interest in the property: see s.56(2).

There is no requirement that the spouses or civil partners must be living together. But if the transferor is domiciled in the United Kingdom and the transferee is domiciled abroad, the exemption has a limit of £55,000 (calculated as a value on which no tax is payable. i.e. without grossing-up).

---

[1] But if H is either still alive when X dies, or he died no more then two years before, there will be an exemption on X's, death: s.53(4).

Values not exceeding £3,000: s.19

19–04   Lifetime transfers of value made by a transferor in any one year are exempt to the extent that the values transferred do not exceed the now small amount of £3,000. That figure has not been increased for many years, probably because of the PET regime. The values are to be calculated for this purpose as values on which no tax is payable; in other words, without grossing up. The year ends on April 5. Unused relief may be carried forward into the next year to be used after the amount for that year. The shortfall cannot be carried forward any further. Thus if in year 1 X gives away £2,500 he can carry forward £500 to year 2. If in that year he gives away £3,200 he uses the £3,000 for that year and £200 from year 1. The remaining £300 is lost.

As husband and wife and civil partner are separate chargeable individuals for the purposes of inheritance tax, each can make gifts up to £3,000 per year without either of them incurring any inheritance tax.

Where the transferor makes more than one transfer of value in a tax year the relief is given against earlier rather than later transfers. Where, as in most cases, a transfer is a PET then the relief is first given against any transfers which are not PETs in that year. If the PET subsequently becomes chargeable it will be treated as having been made at the end of the year in which it was made and in so far as the exemption for that year is still available it can be claimed retrospectively against the retrospective charge.

Small gifts to same person: s.20

19–05   Lifetime transfers of value made by a transferor in any one tax year to any one person are exempt to the extent that the values transferred by them (calculated as values on which no tax is chargeable) do not exceed £250. This exemption does not apply to transfers on death, and it only applies to lifetime transfers which are "outright gifts", as distinct from gifts in settlement. It does not apply to part of gifts in excess of £250. Again the figure has not been increased for many years.

Learned articles have been published arguing that the wording of the legislation is such that this "small gifts exemption" and the £3,000 exemption" (and some other exemptions) are not wholly independent and that in some circumstances they are not cumulative.[2] The position is unclear, however, and there is a

---

[2]   See particularly David Feldman in [1977] B.T.R. 164.

good argument that the two exemptions are cumulative. So we think one can say that a taxpayer (Albert perhaps) can give up to £250 to any number of different persons in a year and can also make £3,000 worth of gifts, all exempt from tax: e.g. £3,250 to B plus £250 to C plus £250 to D and so on through the alphabet (if his generosity runs so far). The small amounts involved, however, mean that a resolution of this problem is unlikely.

Normal expenditure out of income: s.21

A lifetime transfer of value is an exempt transfer if, or to the extent that, it is shown (a) that it was made as part of normal expenditure of the transferor: and (b) that (taking one year with another) it was made out of his income; and (c) that, after allowing for all transfers of value forming part of his normal expenditure, the transferor was left with sufficient income to maintain his usual standard of living.

19–06

Some guidance as to what is meant by "normal expenditure" for this purpose was provided by Lightman J. in *Bennett v IRC* (1995). Mrs Bennett had been given a life interest under her husband's will with her sons taking the whole amount after her death. Initially the income produced by the trust fund was sufficient to meet her needs, which were described by the judge as "modest". Subsequently the income produced by the fund increased substantially and she instructed the trustees that since she did not require any additional income, the surplus income should be paid out to the sons. Her needs did indeed continue to be modest. The trustees did as instructed, although on a conservative basis. Mrs Bennett died unexpectedly two years after giving this instruction and the Revenue sought to charge the payments to the sons as PETs by her, which were activated by her death. The sons argued that the normal expenditure out of income exception applied.

Lightman J. put forward three propositions. First, that for expenditure to be normal, each payment had to be shown to conform to an established pattern of expenditure by the payer. Such a pattern could be established by proof of the existence of a prior commitment or resolve (e.g. a regular payment) or by reference to a sequence of payments, e.g. by paying the instalments on a life assurance policy.[3] Thus a death bed commitment would not satisfy either requirement. There was no need, however, either for a legal obligation or a minimum period.

---

[3] For an example of a case where there was no pattern of expenditure, see *Nadin v IRC* (1997).

Second, the amount need not be fixed and the recipient need not be the same, so that, e.g. paying the costs of elderly relatives' nursing home expenses would suffice. Third, the fact that the income was unreasonable or idiosyncratic did not mean that it was not normal for the particular individual. Applying all this to the facts, the judge held that the exception applied in this case. There was a pattern in respect of the surplus income, which she genuinely did not need, and the payments to the sons had been made in accordance with that pattern.

Gifts in consideration of marriage or civil partnership: s.22

19–07   A gift in consideration of marriage or a civil partnership is not defined in the legislation. It has been established by previous case law that a gift is a gift in consideration of marriage if it fulfils three requisites: it is made on the occasion of a marriage; it is conditional on the marriage taking place; and it is made for the purpose of, or with a view to encouraging or facilitating, the particular marriage: see the estate duty case of *IRC v Lord Rennell* (1964), HL.[4] We can assume that the same criteria will apply to a civil partnership.

Transfers of value made by gifts in consideration of marriage or civil partnership are exempt under s.22 (if they are lifetime transfers or certain transfers under a settlement, as distinct from transfers on death) to the extent that the values transferred by such transfers made by any one transferor in respect of any one marriage (calculated net) do not exceed:

(a)   in the case of gifts satisfying the conditions set out below by a parent of a party to the marriage or civil partnership, £5,000;

(b)   in the case of other gifts satisfying those conditions, £2,500; and

(c)   in any other case, £1,000.[5]

The conditions which have to be met to obtain the £5,000 or £2,500 exemption are:

(i)   it is an outright gift to a child or remoter descendant of

---

[4]   Provided these conditions are fulfilled the motive of the donor is irrelevant. See *Re Park Dec'd.* (No.2) (1972).

[5]   Again these amounts have not been raised to cover the effects of inflation.

the transferor (thus each parent can give £5,000, and each grandparent £2,500, to the couple); or

(ii) the transferor is a parent or remoter ancestor of either party to the marriage or civil partnership, and either the gift is an outright gift to the other party to the marriage or civil partnership or the property comprised in the gift is settled by the gift; or

(iii) the transferor is a party to the marriage or civil partnership, and either the gift is an outright gift to the other party to the marriage or civil partnership or the property comprised in the gift is settled by the gift.

There are limits on who can benefit. To qualify for exemption an outright gift must be to a party to the marriage or civil partnership; and a settled gift can only include certain persons (notably the parties to the marriage and their issue) as beneficiaries or potential beneficiaries.

Gifts to charities: s.23

Transfers of value to charities are exempt transfers. There is no limit as to the amount and the exemption applies to both lifetime and death transfers. There are provisions which prevent the relief applying if the transfer is not an immediate and outright transfer, or if it could be used for other purposes.

19–08

Gifts to political parties: s.24

There is a similar unlimited exemption for gifts to political parties defined as one with either two members of Parliament or one member and at least 150,000 votes at the last general election.

19–09

Gifts to housing associations: s.24A

There is also a similar unlimited exemption for gifts to housing associations.[6]

19–10

Gifts for national purposes, etc.: s.25

A transfer of value is an exempt transfer if it is made to certain bodies (sometimes referred to as "heritage bodies") being cer-

19–11

---

[6] These are defined by reference to the Housing Associations Act 1985 and Part 1 of the Housing Act 1996.

tain galleries, museums, libraries, national collections and preservation bodies, universities, university colleges, local
authorities, or any government department. The bodies given
this benefit are listed in Sch.3. They include the British Museum,
the National Gallery, local authority museums, the National
Trust, and "any government department," which would therefore include other national museums such as the Victoria and
Albert Museum. The exemption applies to lifetime and death
transfers, and there is no limit in amount. The exemption also
applies where a PET is followed by a transfer to a Sch.3 body or
the property is accepted by the Revenue in satisfaction of tax
under s.230: (s.26A).

Cash options under approved annuity schemes: s.152

19–12   *All the provisions listed above are exempt transfers. The
reliefs that follow take several different forms for no particular
reasons, so each should be looked at as self-contained.*

Where, under an approved annuity scheme, an annuity
becomes payable on a person's death to the deceased's widow,
widower, surviving civil partner or dependant and the scheme
gave an option for the deceased to require that, instead, a sum of
money should be paid to his personal representatives, that
option will not involve that the deceased be treated as being
beneficially entitled (under s.5) to that sum. In other words, that
sum does not form part of his estate.

Death on active service, etc.: s.154

19–13   This exemption applies to death on active service against an
enemy (or on other service of a warlike nature) and to death
arising out of such service.[7] The exemption operates by means of
excluding s.4, the section which charges to tax a transfer on
death.

Visiting forces and staff of allied headquarters: s.155

19–14   This paragraph gives certain exemptions to pay and tangible
movables of members of visiting forces of designated countries
(not being citizens of the United Kingdom and colonies) and
personnel attached to a designated allied headquarters.

---

[7]   This includes service in Northern Ireland.

Relief for successive charges: s.141

This is generally called "quick succession" relief. Prior to 1981 two somewhat confusingly different forms were in operation, one relating to deaths and the other to settlements. Under the new "unified" relief the tax charge on a death or a settlement where the life tenant is treated as owning the whole settled property[8] is reduced if the death or settlement charge occurs within five years after some previous chargeable event relating to the same property. For a death the previous charge may be of any type, but for a settlement it must have been a previous charge on that settlement, or the creation of the settlement itself.

The relief operates by way of a "tax credit" against tax payable on the second charge by reference to a percentage of the tax paid on the first. This will be 100 per cent if the gap between the two transfers is one year or less, reduced by 20 per cent for each subsequent year between the transfers, so that if the gap is between 4 and 5 years it will only be 20 per cent.

19–15

Conditional relief for works of art, historic buildings, etc.: sections 30–35A (as amended)

The things to which this conditional relief relates are chattels of pre-eminent interest, works of art, scientific collections, land and buildings which are of outstanding scenic, architectural, historic or scientific interest and chattels historically associated with them. The sections apply to all transfers including discretionary trusts, but the relief can only be sought in relation to a PET if it subsequently becomes chargeable. It is provided (no doubt as an anti-avoidance measure) that for relief to apply to a lifetime transfer the property must have either been owned for six years or the transferor must have acquired the property on a death which was itself a "conditionally exempt transfer" (see below). The relief must be claimed within two years.

19–16

To gain the relief the property has to be "designated" by the Revenue, and "undertakings" have to be given concerning preservation, access, etc. The rules relating to these undertakings were tightened in 1998, so that, for example, it is no longer sufficient to allow public access only by prior appointment.

A transfer is then called a "conditionally exempt transfer" so that any tax payable will be postponed. It is conditional because

---

[8] See Ch.21, below.

if an undertaking is not observed tax becomes payable on the current value of the asset by reference to the transferor's cumulative total, but at the lifetime rate if the conditionally exempt transfer was not made on a death. Also, tax becomes payable on a subsequent sale or disposal of the property (including disposal on death).

There are two cases where a subsequent disposal is not a chargeable event: (a) if the subsequent death or gift is itself a conditionally exempt transfer or the undertaking previously given is replaced by an undertaking given by such person as the Revenue think appropriate; (b) if within three years of the death the deceased's personal representatives (or, in the case of settled property, the trustees or the person next entitled) give the property or sell it by private treaty to one of the "heritage bodies" listed in Sch.3 (see para.19–11, above) or transfer the property to the Revenue in satisfaction of tax.

Where the conditionally exempt transfer loses its exemption on a subsequent gift which is a PET, any inheritance tax triggered will be available as a tax credit against the tax payable if the PET becomes chargeable.

The point of the exemption which has been discussed under this head,[9] as distinct from the heritage bodies exemption discussed above is that an ancestral home (for example), or a Rembrandt in an ancestral home, can be kept in the family.

A maintenance fund for historic houses etc can be set up under s.27. It is possible for property to be settled on trusts to finance the maintenance, repair or preservation of, or public access to, historic buildings or adjoining land without liability to inheritance tax. This relief, again, takes the form of a conditional exemption which becomes chargeable on the fund failing to meet the criteria.

Voidable transfers: s.150

19–17   This relief refers to transfers set aside by law. An example would be a gift made within five years before bankruptcy, because such a gift could be set aside (under the Insolvency Act 1986, s.339) by the transferor's trustee in bankruptcy. Similarly equity will set aside a transfer made under a relevant mistake, e.g. as to the life expectancy of the transferors *Re Giffiths* (2008). If a transfer is so set aside, tax is repaid (with tax-free

---

[9]   It is sometimes called the "national heritage exemption". So we have the "national heritage exemption" as well as "heritage bodies" and "heritage property".

interest) and also the transfer is wiped out from the transferor's cumulative total of values transferred.

Relief for business property: ss.103–114

Nature and extent of the relief

This relief was brought in in 1976 in response to claims that   **19–18** without some such relief many small businesses would face closure because of the tax on transfers, e.g. from parent to child. The relief has been liberalised by subsequent amendments and, in many cases, stands at 100 per cent. Transfers of value in this context include not only lifetime transfers but also transfers on death and chargeable events in relation to settled property.

Where the whole or part of the value transferred by a transfer of value is attributable to the value of any relevant business property, the whole of that part of the value transferred shall be treated as reduced by either 100 or 50 per cent. The value transferred is to be calculated as a value on which no tax is chargeable, i.e. without grossing up. Relevant business property means:

  (i) a business or an interest in a business. This includes sole traders and partners disposing of all or part of their interests in a business[10];

  (ii) a holding of shares in or securities of a listed company which, together with others held by the transfer or, gave him control of the company on all questions affecting the company[11];

 (iii) a holding of securities in an unquoted company which together with other such securities and unquoted shares held by the transferor, gave him control of the company (as defined above);

  (iv) a holding, of any size, of shares in an unquoted company;

  (v) any land or building, machinery or plant which was used wholly or mainly for the purpose of a business carried on

---

[10] In *Fetherstonaugh v IRC* (1984) a sole trader who used land owned by a settlement of which he was the life tenant in his business was allowed the relief on that land under this head. In *Russell v IRC* (1988) the relief was allowed where a legatee was entitled to a cash sum payable only out of the proceeds of sale of a business.

[11] Control is to be assessed at the time of the transfer. In assessing whether the transferor has voting control of a company no account is to be taken of the fact that other shares are held by an individual who cannot in practice exercise his votes, e.g. a five-year-old child: *Walding v IRC* (1996).

by a company of which the transferor had control (as defined above) or of which he was a partner.

Exceptions—land and investments

19-19 No business, interest in a business or shares or securities in a company are eligible for business property relief if the business (or the company's business) consists wholly or mainly either in dealing in securities, shares, land or buildings or in making or holding investments. Letting out land is regarded as holding an investment for this purpose, so the question can then arise as to whether that is wholly or mainly what the business is about. In *Martin v IRC* (1995) the Special Commissioner held that letting industrial units on three-year lets remained an investment business even though the taxpayer managed and maintained the units; all that was simply referable to the obligations under the leases—there were no additional charges for other services.[12]

This issue has also arisen in connection with the owners of caravan sites. In several cases, culminating in *Weston v IRC* (2000), it was held that receiving rent in respect of caravan lets was investment business. The judge then stated that in deciding whether such a business was therefore excluded from the relief, it was first necessary to identify and separate the investment and non-investment activities and then to determine whether the business did consist wholly or mainly of the investment activities. In *Farmer v IRC* (1999), however, another Special Commissioner held that a farm which let properties, the income from which exceeded that of the farming business, was still predominantly a farming business. The matter had to be looked at in the round.[13]

The matter finally came before the Court of Appeal in *IRC v George* (2004) where the question as to whether a caravan site business was wholly or mainly one of making investments was held to be largely a question of fact for the commissioner whose decision had been reversed by the judge. Rejecting the approach of the judge below and, by implication the *Weston* approach, Carnwath L.J. said there was no requirement to open an investment bag into which were placed all the activities of the caravan park, including even the supply of water, gas and electricity. Nor was it necessary to determine what was the

---

[12] This approach, that actively managing land leased to tenants is still an investment business, was approved in *IRC v George* (2004) and in *Clark v HMRC* Sp C (2005). As to a company making loans see *Phillips v HMRC* Sp C (2006).

[13] As to balancing investment activity (rents) with others (building, sales etc.) see *Clark v HMRC* Sp C (2005).

"very" business of the company. The holding of property was only one component of the business and the commissioner had found that it was not the main component. An active family business of this kind should not be excluded from the relief merely because a part of it involved the use of land.

Excluded items

Certain items are excluded from the definition of relevant **19–20** business property, e.g. shares or securities of a company which is in the process of liquidation, or surplus cash not required for the future use of the business.[14]

And, putting it broadly, property is not relevant business property unless it has been owned by the transferor throughout the two years immediately preceding the transfer. But there are provisions adjusting this rule where there have been replacements of property, the incorporation of a business, and acquisitions of property on the death of a spouse.

Reduction in value of transfer

The relief is given by reducing the value of the net business **19–21** assets that have been transferred. This means the value of the assets used in the business less any liabilities incurred for the purposes of the business. In *Mallender v IRC* (2001), the taxpayer negotiated a bank guarantee for the purposes of his business as a member of a Lloyd's insurance syndicate. In order to do that he had to give the bank a charge over the freehold reversion of some land held by him. The court refused to allow the value of that reversion as a business asset for the purposes of the relief. The only asset used in the business was the guarantee. There was no sufficient nexus between the business and the charge. An asset used to secure a loan for the purpose of a business was not itself an asset used in that business.

The relief is given automatically. For transfers within categories (i), (iii) and (iv) this relief is 100 per cent, so that most family businesses will be outside the tax. For categories (ii) and (v) the relief is 50 per cent. It is generally better therefore for a taxpayer's company to own the plant and machinery, etc. used in its business, rather than the taxpayer.

Interface with PETs and gifts with reservation

Where the transferor makes a PET of relevant business **19–22** property and then dies within seven years so that it becomes a chargeable transfer, the relief will only be available if the

---

[14] *Barclays Bank Trust Co Ltd v IRC* (1998).

transferee still owns the property (or what is known as replacement property) and it would have qualified for the relief immediately before the transferor's death. Similar rules apply where additional tax is payable on a lifetime transfer on the death of the transferor within seven years (see Ch.20). There is no such clawback, however, where a beneficiary sells the business after inheriting it on a death.

In deciding whether the relief applies to a gift subject to a reservation (either one which is still in existence at the transferor's death or which ceased only within the last seven years and so is a deemed PET), the criteria in the various categories are applied to the donee and not the donor, although the ownership of the donor can be added to that of the donee to establish the two year minimum ownership requirement. Paradoxically, however, in assessing whether the shares give control of the company, the shares will be regarded as being owned by the donor.

Interface with agricultural relief

19–23   Business property relief may be available where agricultural relief is also available. In such cases agricultural relief takes priority, through business property relief is also important to farmers and farm owners.

Relief for agricultural property: ss.115–124C (as amended)

19–24   This relief applies to lifetime transfers and transfers on death, and it applies to transfers involving certain settlements as well as to "outright" transfers. It was included in the 1975 Act, but drastically remodelled and extended in 1981.

Conditions for the relief

19–25   Short-term purchasers of farms are excluded from the relief; for the relief to apply, both the transferor and the land must fulfil certain conditions. The transferor must have either occupied the land for agricultural purposes throughout the last two years or have owned the land for the last seven years, it having been occupied by someone for agricultural purposes during that time. A person who inherits a farm from his or her spouse or civil partner, provided the spouse or civil partner fulfilled the above condition, can transfer the farm with benefit of the relief.[15] For the land to qualify it must be agricultural property

---

[15] See e.g. *Rosser v IRC* (2003).

in the United Kingdom. If one farm has been replaced by another, it is sufficient if occupation of the farms viewed together lasted for at least two out of five years immediately preceding the transfer.

Applying the relief

The relief, where it is available, takes the form of reducing the "agricultural value of the agricultural property". "Agricultural property"[16] means:

19–26

> "agricultural land or pasture and includes woodland and any building used in connection with the intensive rearing of livestock and fish if occupied with agricultural land or pasture and the occupation is ancillary to that of the agricultural land or pasture; and also includes such cottages, farm buildings and farm-houses[17], together with the land occupied with them, as are of a character appropriate to the property".[18]

"The agricultural value" is "the value which would be the value of the property if the property were subject to a perpetual covenant prohibiting its use otherwise than as agricultural property": s.115(3). Thus there is no relief for any development value, although business relief may be available for that.

REDUCTIONS   The reduction is either of 100 or 50 per cent. In broad terms owner occupiers are entitled to a 100 per cent reduction, whilst agricultural landlords are entitled to a 50 per cent reduction unless the tenancy began or a tenant succeeded to the tenancy after August 1995 when 100 per cent relief is available, although of course on the value of the reversion and not the whole farm. The reduction in value because of the agricultural tenancy will, of course, reduce the inheritance tax payable on the land. There are no limits as to size of the farm or as to amount of the relief. As with business relief, this relief is

19–27

---

[16] This includes land used for "short rotation coppicing" by virtue of s.154 of the Finance Act 1995. In essence this is the planting and harvesting of permanent trees within 10 years. It also includes "habitat land" and genuine farm cottages.

[17] A farm-house is a house for the farmer from which the farm is managed: *Rosser v IRC* (2003).

[18] s.115(2). The criteria for establishing whether the various buildings are included were set out in *Lloyds TSB v IRC* (2002). If the buildings do not fall within that test, e.g. because they are very valuable compared to the farmland involved, they cannot be included in the other category as agricultural land: *Starke v IRC* (1995). In deciding whether the building is appropriate, the relevant property must be owned by the owners of the building a common occupation is not enough: *Rosser v IRC* (2003).

given automatically. It is given in priority to business relief but both may be available. The availability of the relief for PETs and gifts with reservation is governed by the same rules as those for business relief.

Transfers of shares or debentures in a farming company controlled by the transferor can qualify for agricultural property relief.

Relief for woodlands: ss.125–130

Nature and extent of the relief

19–28   Relief is available where any part of the value of a person's estate immediately before his death is attributable to the value of land in the United Kingdom on which trees or underwood are growing but which is not agricultural property. Deathbed purchases of woodland as a tax avoidance ploy will not work. For the relief to apply the deceased must either have been beneficially entitled to the land throughout the five years immediately before his death or have become beneficially entitled to it otherwise than for a consideration in money or money's worth, i.e. by a gift or inheritance.

Retrospective charge

19–29   The relief takes the form of leaving out of account, in determining the value transferred on death, the value of the trees or underwood. Notice that the relief does not apply to a lifetime transfer and also that it is only the value of the timber which is relieved, not the value of the land on which it is growing.

The relief is not absolute; a subsequent lifetime transfer of the timber can give rise to a retrospective charge to tax at the full rate at the date of the transfer. Tax will be charged on the sale proceeds of the timber if the transfer is for full consideration; otherwise on the then net value of the timber. If the transfer following the death is itself a chargeable transfer, e.g. a gift, there may be a tax charge on that disposal as well as the retrospective tax charge relating to the death, but the value transferred by the subsequent disposal will be calculated as if the value of the trees or underwood had been reduced by the amount of tax charged in respect of the death. Business relief (at 50 per cent) will be available if the growing timber formed a business asset of the deceased at the date of death.

If another death occurs, and there has been no disposal between the first death and the second death, the second death wipes out any possibility of a tax charge arising in respect of the first death.

Dispositions for maintenance of family: s.11

The official Revenue view is that s.11 only applies to lifetime transfers, and not to transfers on death. The point has never been tested in the courts, but the Revenue view is probably correct, for one or other (or both) of two reasons: (1) The section uses the word "disposition". It is noticeable that the section relating to death (s.4) nowhere uses the word "disposition". It would seem to be a fair inference that wherever in the inheritance tax legislation the word "disposition" occurs the enactment is referring only to lifetime transfers; (2) the section uses the phrase "not a transfer of value", and it may well be (as some commentators assume) that wherever the legislation gives an exemption by saying that such-and-such shall "not be a transfer of value" that exemption is confined to lifetime transfers and does not cover transfers on death.

19–30

Section 11(1) declares that a disposition is not a transfer of value if it is made by one party to a marriage in favour of the other party or of a child of either party and is:

(a) for the maintenance of the other party; or
(b) for the maintenance, education or training of the child for a period ending not later than the year in which he attains the age of 18 or, after attaining that age, ceases to undergo full-time education or training.[19]

CHILDREN "Child" includes a step-child and an adopted child. A similar disposition in favour of an illegitimate child is exempt, but in this case only if the child is the child of the disponer (not of the other party to the marriage). A similar disposition in favour of a child who is someone else's child is exempt if the child is not in the care of a parent of his. But in this case, if the disposition is made after the child attains 18 years of age, it is only exempt if the child has for substantial periods before attaining that age been in the care of the disponer.

19–31

DEPENDENT RELATIVES Also, a disposition is not a transfer of value if it is made in favour of a dependent relative of the disponer or his spouse or civil partner and is a reasonable provision for his or her care or maintenance. Here there is an explicit reference to reasonableness (of amount), whereas in the

19–32

---

[19] Quaere the position where the "child" leaves school, takes a gap year and starts university aged 19? Technically he/she ceased full-time education on leaving school, but not permanently.

case of a disposition to a spouse, civil partner or child there is no explicit mention of reasonableness. However, such a limit seems to be implicit, because it is stated that, where a disposition satisfies the conditions to a limited extent only, so much of it as satisfies them and so much of it as does not satisfy them shall be treated as separate dispositions.

Uses of the relief

19–33   Since all transfers between spouses or civil partners are exempt,[20] this exemption has very little effect whilst either the marriage or civil partnership is on-going. In *Phizackerley v HMRC* Sp C (2007), it was argued, as part of a tax planning scheme, that s.11 applied where a husband put his house into the joint names of himself and his wife during their marriage. The special commissioner rejected that argument on the basis that such an act was not for the maintenance of the wife. It was to give her security. But so far as a child is concerned s.11 is very useful as it exempts a payment made by a parent to assist (for example) a child who is a student if the payment is outside the "normal expenditure out of income" exemption (see para.19–06 above).[21]

The section applies also, however, to a disposition on the occasion of the dissolution or annulment of a marriage or civil partnership (and to a disposition varying a disposition so made) by subs.(6) which provides that in relation to those events "marriage" and "civil partnership" (see subs.(1)) includes a former marriage or civil partnership. In *G v G* (1975) a High Court judge held that the court has power to defer a decree absolute in order to prevent inheritance tax arising.[22]

Alteration of dispositions taking effect on death, etc.: ss.17, 29A, 93, 142–145

19–34   The scheme of the sections is this: certain re-arrangements of the deceased's estate shall not be treated as transfers of value and tax shall be charged on the death as if the deceased had left his property in accordance with the re-arrangements. The main provisions can be stated in six numbered points.

---

[20] Under s.18, see para.19–02, above.
[21] The section may not apply if the child leaves school, goes out to work and re-enters full-time education after the age of 18. Has he already ceased to undertake full-time education?
[22] Such orders will usually be exempt under s.10 (no gratuitous benefit).

Variation of deceased's dispositions on death

(1) By s.142(1), where within two years after a person's death **19–35**
any beneficiary makes an instrument in writing which effects a
variation or disclaimer of any of the dispositions (whether
effected by will or under the law relating to intestacy or otherwise) of the property comprised in the deceased's estate
immediately before his death, the variation or disclaimer shall
not be a transfer of value and tax shall be charged as if the
variation had been effected by the deceased or (as the case may
be) the disclaimed benefit had never been conferred. In the case
of a variation, all those making the variation must state in the
document that they intend s.142(1) to apply to the variation.
Where the variation results in additional tax being payable, the
deceased's personal representatives must also make that statement, but they can only decline to join in an election if
insufficient assets are held by them for discharging the additional tax. Additional tax could become payable, for example, if
some item of property which had been left by the deceased to his
widow is now, by family agreement, to go to his daughter.

EFFECTIVENESS OF DEED To be an effective deed of variation **19–36**
for the purposes of s.142, it must operate so as to affect the
destination of the property of the deceased comprised in the
deemed transfer on death under s.4. The deed cannot operate to
remove property from that estate so that is no longer part of the
deceased's estate at death and so subject to that deemed transfer.
If it purports to do so, it has no effect for tax purposes and the
estate will be taxed on the dispositions as made under the will or
intestacy.[23]

CONSIDERATION The section does not apply to a variation **19–37**
or disclaimer which is made for any consideration in money or
money's worth other than consideration consisting of the
making of another variation or disclaimer relating to the same
estate. For the purpose of this section the deceased's estate
includes excluded property but not settled property in which he
had an interest in possession. It does not matter whether or not
the administration of the estate is complete, and it does not
matter that a benefit has been received under the original dispositions, and there is no objection to the variations extending
beyond the deceased's family or beyond the original beneficiaries. Where a variation results in property being held in trust
for a person for a period which ends not more than two years

---

[23] *Glowacki v HMRC* Sp Comm (2006).

after the death the disposition at the end of the period is treated as though it had had effect from the beginning of the period.

19–38   SECOND DEED RECTIFICATION   In *Russell v IRC* (1988), Knox J. upheld the Revenue's argument that s.142 could not apply where the beneficiaries, having already executed one deed of variation, executed a variation of that deed. The section only allows the first one to count as being read back into the will. On the other hand in *Lake v Lake* (1989), Mervyn Davies J. held that a deed of disclaimer could be rectified by the court if the wording had failed to give effect to the joint intention of the parties, even though the amended wording would substantially improve the parties' tax position. The deed was also rectified in *Wills v Gibbs* (2008) on the basis that it gave effect to the maker's intentions and resolved a dispute between the parties.

Variation of settlement in a will

19–39   (2) Section 144 (as amended) applies where a settlor creates a settlement by his will, other than one in which there is an immediate post-death or disabled person's interest (as defined in ss.49A and 89B[24]). If within two years of the death and before any immediate post death or disabled person's interest has actually arisen under the settlement, an event causes the property to be held as if the deceased had created an immediate post-death interest, a bereaved minor's trust (see s.71A[25]) or an 18-25 trust (see s.71D[26]), there will be no charge to inheritance tax and tax will be charged as though the event in question had been provided for in the will.

In *Frankland v IRC* (1997) the section was held by the Court of Appeal not to apply to a variation within the first quarter after the death of the settlor because within that time no capital distribution charge is levied and the section requires that, without its application, a capital distribution charge would otherwise apply. The section was not ambiguous and the absurdity not too great!

Request to legatee

19–40   (3) Section 143 deals with the case where assets are left to a legatee with a request (which is not legally binding) that the legatee should distribute them in accordance with the testator's wishes. If within two years after the death the legatee does so

---

[24] See Ch.21, below.
[25] See Ch.21, below.
[26] See Ch.21, below.

distribute the assets, the transfers by the legatee are not transfers of value and tax shall be charged in relation to the death as if the property had been bequeathed by the will to the transferees. (Such a provision in a will is called a precatory trust; it is quite common, particularly in respect of household effects, etc.)

Surviving spouse or civil partner election

(4) Section 145 deals with the case where a surviving spouse   **19–41**
elects, under s.47A of the Administration of Estates Act 1925, to redeem for a capital sum his or her life interest which arises under the intestacy rules. Where such an election is made, the election does not count as a transfer of value and tax is charged in relation to the death on the footing that the surviving spouse had from the outset been entitled to the capital sum.

Disclaimers

(5) By s.93, where a person becomes entitled (on death or   **19–42**
otherwise) to an interest in settled property but disclaims the interest, then, if the disclaimer is not made for a consideration in money or money's worth, the inheritance tax provisions shall apply as if he had not become entitled to the interest.

Linked exempt transfer

(6) Section 29A is rather different in that it is in reality an   **19–43**
anti-avoidance provision. It applies whenever there is an exempt transfer on a death, e.g. to a charity,[27] and the exempt beneficiary subsequently makes a disposition of property, which does not derive from that transferred on the death, in settlement of a claim against the deceased's estate. In that case the exemption on the death is reduced by the amount transferred by the exempt beneficiary. Thus if Paul agrees with a charity to leave them £100,000 in his will if the charity will then pay £50,000 to his mistress (who may have a claim against his estate), the effect of s.29A will be that only £50,000 of the gift to the charity will be exempt.

Family provision orders: s.146

A court has power, under the Inheritance (Provision for   **19–44**
Family and Dependants) Act 1975 to order that provision be made for the family and dependants of a deceased person out of his estate, and for this purpose to change the destination of

---

[27] Other exempt transfers covered are those to spouses, political parties, housing associations, maintenance funds and employee trusts.

property. When a court makes an order of this kind the property shall be treated for the purposes of inheritance tax as if it had on the deceased's death devolved in accordance with the order.[28]

Dispositions allowable for income tax or conferring retirement benefits: s.12

19–45   A disposition made by any person is not a transfer of value if it is allowable in computing that person's profits or gains for the purposes of income tax or corporation tax. It is difficult to think of a disposition which is allowable for income tax (or corporation tax) and yet which would need this section to protect it from inheritance tax; most commonly such a disposition would be a disposition for value and would consequently be excluded from inheritance tax by s.10 (no gratuitous intent). Perhaps certain kinds of business gifts would "fit the bill".

Contributions to approved retirement benefit schemes and approved personal pension schemes for employees and also dispositions to provide in some other way comparable benefits on or after retirement for an employee not connected with the disponer, or, after the death of the employee, for a widow, widower, civil partner or dependants, are not transfers of value.

Dispositions by close company on trust for benefit of employees: s.13

19–46   A disposition of property made to trustees by a close company whereby the property is to be held on certain trusts for the employees is not a transfer of value. The conditions of exemption are very strict and in practice not much use is made of this provision.

Waiver of remuneration: s.14

19–47   Sometimes an employee or, more commonly a director, waives (or repays) his remuneration for a period to his employer (company). If nothing were done about it, such waiver or repayment would be a chargeable transfer by the employee or director. Section 14 declares that the waiver or repayment shall not be a transfer of value provided that it is brought into charge in computing the profits or gains of the employer for income tax or corporation tax.

---

[28] In Scotland, the equivalent protection for families, etc. is the doctrine of *legitim*. The position with regard to IHT and that doctrine is set out in s.147.

Waiver of dividends: s.15

A person who waives any dividend on shares of a company   19–48
within 12 months *before* any right to the dividend has accrued
does not by reason of the waiver make a transfer of value.

Grant of an agricultural tenancy: s.16

A grant of an agricultural tenancy is not a transfer of value if   19–49
it is made for full consideration in money or money's worth.
Otherwise the almost inevitable reduction in the value of the
property (such leases have controlled rents) would lead to a
charge.

CHAPTER 20

COMPUTATION

Introduction

20–01 Inheritance tax is charged on any lifetime transfer of value which is a chargeable transfer, and also on the deemed transfer of value made by a deceased person immediately before his death. (The charges on settled property are discussed in the next chapter.) Remember that a PET becomes a chargeable transfer on the death of the transferor within seven years and that a gift subject to a reservation still in existence at death is part of the deceased's estate. If the reservation has ceased before then the gift becomes a PET at that time so that if the reservation ceases more than seven years before the death the gift is exempt. As we shall see, the existence of PETs complicates the computation rules.

In the case of a lifetime transfer the charge is on the value transferred. In the case of a deemed transfer on death the charge is on the value of the deceased's estate. Section 3 declares that: "... a transfer of value is a disposition made by a person (the transferor) as a result of which the value of his estate is less than it would be but for the disposition; and the amount by which it is less is the value transferred by the transfer." So for a lifetime transfer, one has to compare the value of the transferor's estate (remember that "estate" can refer to a living person's wealth, as well as to a dead person's) before the transfer with its value after the transfer. For a discussion as to how that comparison is to be made see para.18–03 above. For a death transfer this comparison does not arise.

Rates of Tax

Nil-rate and chargeable bands

20–02 As we have already seen, the rates of inheritance tax are applied on a cumulative basis so that in essence each chargeable lifetime transfer is charged at the appropriate rate taking into account previous chargeable transfers within the last seven years. This principle is applied equally on a death so that the rate takes into account the chargeable transfers made seven years prior to the death. Only if the transferor lives for more than seven years after making a transfer will it be taken out of the calculation. The effect of the transferor dying within seven years of making a chargeable transfer or a PET is discussed below.

The current rates for inheritance tax are very much simplified from those originally introduced. Schedule 1 currently (in 2008) provides that for a charge on a death the rate for the first £312,000 of cumulative transfers is nil. That figure is scheduled to rise to £350,000 by 2010. For all cumulative transfers above that amount the rate is 40 per cent. Section 7 provides that for a lifetime transfer the rates are half those on a death, i.e. nil and 20 per cent. For peace of mind it is better to regard the band up to £312,000 as being charged at a nil rate rather than as being exempt.

£325k

EXAMPLES   Thus if Fred, having made immediately charge-   20–03
able transfers of £312,000 in the previous seven years, makes another one of £100,000, that transfer will be charged at 20 per cent, since he will have exceeded the nil rate band. If his cumulative total had been £262,000, the £100,000 transfer would then have been chargeable at £50,000 × nil per cent and £50,000 × 20 per cent. In effect, therefore, Fred can make up to £312,000 of chargeable transfers in each seven year period without actually having to pay any tax. The position would have been the same if Fred, with a cumulative total of £312,000, had died and left an estate of £100,000, except that that estate would then have been taxed at 40 per cent. The fact that lifetime rates are half those on death is counterbalanced by the fact that capital gains tax may well be payable on a lifetime transfer whereas it does not apply on a death.

The nil-rate band: spouses and civil partners—transferable nil-rate band

The amounts of the nil-rate band for the years to 2010 have   20–04
already been set. In 2009/10 it will be £325,000 and in 2010/11 it will be £350,000. These figures, which in effect fix the inheritance tax threshold on death for most taxpayers for the year in question, became a very political issue in 2007. There was significant evidence that the increase in the threshold had not kept pace with the increase in housing values, thus extending the scope of the tax to many more estates than previously. Remember that there is no private residence exemption as there is for capital gains tax.

Although transfers between spouses and civil partners were

exempt, most couples did not take advantage of their two separate, individual nil-rate bands. Thus suppose a couple, A and B, own a house worth say £500,000 and they have modest savings, say of £100,000. A dies leaving all his property to B. There is no charge to tax as that is an exempt transfer. B then dies later that year, leaving all her property (including her inherited share of the house) to the children. B's estate is now worth £600,000. But only £312,000 of that is within the nil-rate band. The children would have had to pay 40 per cent tax on the other £288,000, some £115,000. In effect, none of A's nil-band rate has been utilised.

20–05   TRANSFER OF PROPORTION OF UNUSED BAND   Prudent couples could take steps to avoid this trap by using discretionary trusts in their wills, but in his pre-budget report on October 9, 2007, the Chancellor announced that as from that date *the percentage* of any unused nil-rate band on a person's death may be transferred to a surviving spouse or civil partner. This is now in ss.8A and 8B. The add-on is activated by a claim by the survivor's personal representatives that the unused percentage be added onto the survivor's nil-rate band on their death. Thus in the example above, on B's death (in the same year) she would have a nil-rate band of £624,000 (£312,000 + 100 per cent of A's £312,000); her estate would thus pass to her children tax free. The claim must be made within two years of the second death (or, if later, three months after the personal representatives start to act as such).

If, however, B survived for two more years, when the nil-rate band is set to be £350,000, her nil-rate band at death would be £700,000. That is her own £350,000 plus 100 per cent of A's nil-rate band *calculated at the then current figure* of £350,000 (and not the figure of £312,000 as at A's death). If, say, 50 per cent of A's nil-rate band had been used on his death (because he had left some chargeable legacies) then B would have been entitled to add £175,000 to her nil-rate band (i.e. 50 per cent of £350,000).

20–06   CUMULATIVE SURVIVORS   Where a person has survived more than one spouse or civil partner, the maximum additional nil-rate band which can be accumulated on their death is 100 per cent of the nil-rate band for the year of the survivor's death. Thus if B has survived both A and C, her former spouses, and then dies in 2010, she can only add £350,000 onto her own nil-rate band, even if she was entitled to 100 per cent proportion in respect of both A and C. This maximum also applies where B dies having survived her spouse A, who in turn survived his former spouse, C, etc. In such consecutive cases, where the personal representatives of A did not claim any unused nil rate band from C's death, B's personal representatives may do so so as to reach the 100 per cent limit.

None of this largesse, however, extends to co-habiting couples who are neither spouses nor civil partners, e.g. two sisters sharing a house. That anomaly was unsuccessfully challenged as being a breach of human rights in *Burden v UK* (2008).

The effect of a death on chargeable transfers and PETs made within the previous seven years—taper relief

CHARGEABLE TRANSFERS To avoid taxpayers making immediately chargeable transfers shortly before death so as to attract the lower rate of tax, s.7(4) provides that where the transferor dies within seven years of making a chargeable transfer the rates applicable on a death will be retrospectively imposed on that transfer. Since the transfer will have already borne tax at the lifetime rate there is in effect an additional charge to tax (on the transferee) based on the original value of the transfer. That additional charge is computed by working out what the amount of tax would be if the current death rate had applied and deducting from that the tax already paid on the original transfer. However, in making this calculation, if the transferor has survived more than three years after making the transfer, only a percentage of the death rate will be used. This is known as taper relief. Thus if the transferor survives for six years only 20 per cent of the death rate will be used; for five years, 40 per cent; for four years, 60 per cent; and for three years, 80 per cent.

20–07

To take an example:

Suppose that George having already made chargeable transfers of £312,000 in the previous seven years makes a gift of £20,000 (gross) to a company. Since that is an immediately chargeable transfer, tax at 20 per cent will be payable, i.e. £4,000. If George dies two years later the Revenue will claim extra tax from the company. The full death rate will be applied to give a figure of £8,000 tax (at 40 per cent) and the company will have to pay the extra £4,000. If George had survived for four years only 60 per cent of the death rate tax would be used to give a figure of £4,800 tax so that the company would only be liable to find an extra £800 tax.

Sometimes the application of taper relief means that no extra tax is payable on the death (e.g. if George had lived for more than five years in the above example, the recalculation at 40 per cent of the death rate would give a total of £3,200, which is less than the £4,000 already paid). There is no refund of any of the original tax, however. Section 131 provides that if the gift has fallen in value between the gift and the subsequent death, the additional tax is calculated on that reduced value,[1] but the original value remains as part of the transferor's cumulative total for the purposes of calculating the rate applicable to the transfer of his death estate.

20–08   PETs   The position is slightly more complicated where the transferor dies within seven years of making a PET (including a gift with reservation where that reservation has ceased within seven years of the death). As we have seen the PET will then become chargeable (on the transferee) in accordance with the transferor's cumulative total at the time when the PET was made, on the value then transferred (unless it has since fallen in value, when that lower value can be used). The rate of tax will, however, be the death rate applicable at the date of death (unless the rates have increased in which case the rates at the time of the transfer are used). Once again taper relief, calculated as above, will be available to lower the amount payable but of course there is no deduction for tax already paid since none was payable at the time. Thus, in the example above, if the gift had been made to Harry instead of a company, no tax would have been payable at the time. On George's death, Harry would have become liable to tax at £8,000 in the first scenario and £4,800 in the second.

20–09   EFFECT ON CUMULATIVE TOTAL   But this activating of the charge has another effect. Since the transfer is no longer a PET it will be treated as if the transferor had always made a chargeable transfer at that time. Thus although it was not originally included in the transferor's cumulative total it will have to be so included retrospectively. Accordingly the tax payable on previous chargeable transfers may have to be recalculated on that basis.

To take a simple example:

Ian, having made no previous chargeable transfers, makes a

---

[1]   This does not apply to wasting assets, i.e. those which are inevitably going to decrease in value.

PET of £200,000 to John. The next year he makes an immediately chargeable transfer to trustees of £200,000. Ian's cumulative total prior to that (at that time) is nil so that the chargeable transfer is within the nil band. If Ian dies within seven years the PET becomes chargeable so that Ian's cumulative total at the time of the transfer to the trustees is recalculated at £200,000 and that transfer will now fall as to £112,000 into the nil band and £88,000 into the taxable band (the tapered death rate applies as it was within seven years of the death).

Where the transferor has made a combination of PETs and chargeable transfers within seven years of his death the recalculations are almost endless.

Transfers of more than one property

It is provided by s.265 that where the value transferred by a chargeable transfer is determined by reference to the values of more than one property the tax chargeable on the value transferred shall be attributed to the respective values in the proportions which they bear to their aggregate. This is subject to any provision reducing the amount of tax attributable to the value of any particular property.   **20–10**

The "But subject" part of the subsection means that if, for example, on death X leaves a farm to Y and shares in Unilever Plc to Z, Z does not enjoy any part of the agricultural property relief. The main part of the subsection means that, for example, if A leaves property worth £60,000 to B and property worth £40,000 to C, the tax is spread evenly over the whole value transferred. The gift to B bears 60 per cent of the tax bill and the gift to C bears 40 per cent.

Transfers on the same day

Lifetime transfers on the same day by the same transferor present some difficulty. The basic principle is stated in s.266(1): where the value transferred by more than one chargeable transfer made by the same person on the same day depends on the order in which the transfers are made, they shall be treated as made in the order which results in the lowest value chargeable. For example, if on the same day A makes a chargeable transfer to B (A paying the tax) and a separate chargeable transfer to C (C paying the tax), the gift to B will have to be grossed up, (see para.20–15 below), whereas the gift to C will not. So it is "cheaper" in tax terms to count the gift to B before the gift to C, because the grossing up will come at a point lower   **20–11**

363

down the scale. The legislation permits that. Then, the order of the gifts having been established, s.266(2) declares that there shall be an "effective rate," namely the tax which would have been charged if the transfers had been a single transfer. So A pays tax on the gift to B and C pays tax on the gift to himself, both at the same rate.

Transfers reported late

20–12   This is dealt with by s.264. Where an earlier transfer is not notified to the Revenue (see Ch.23, below) until after the tax has been paid on a later transfer, the position depends upon the gap between the transfers. If the gap is seven years or more there is no problem since they would not be cumulated together anyway and so tax plus interest is payable on the earlier transfer at the rates then applying. If the gap is less than seven years the earlier (unreported) transfer is charged at the rate then applying and the extra tax which should have been collected on the second transfer (because of cumulation) is now charged on the first one (plus interest).

Liabilities

20–13   In considering this topic it is necessary to distinguish between liabilities resulting from a chargeable transfer and other liabilities.

Liabilities resulting from a chargeable transfer

20–14   One has to remember that the value transferred on a lifetime transfer is the amount by which the transferor's estate immediately after the disposition is less than it would be if the disposition had not been made.

A chargeable transfer may give rise to inheritance tax and at the same time to two other taxes—capital gains tax and sometimes stamp duty. Also there may be incidental costs of the transfer, such as conveyancing fees. All these items, if paid by the transferor, will diminish the value of his estate immediately after the transfer. So, in the absence of any provision to the contrary, they would all increase the amount of the "value transferred" and so increase the amount of tax payable.

To some extent, the Act does make provisions to the contrary. Section 5(4) provides that in determining the value of the transferor's estate immediately after the transfer, his liability to inheritance tax on the value transferred shall be taken into account, but not his liability for any other tax or duty. And by s.164 the incidental expenses, if borne by the transferor, shall be left out of account and, if borne by the transferee, shall reduce the value transferred.

The great point to grasp is that when one is considering liabilities immediately *after* the transfer, the effect of taking a liability into account is to increase the diminution in value of the transferor's estate and so increase the value transferred and so increase the inheritance tax. Conversely, the effect of leaving a liability out of account is that that liability (e.g. liability to capital gains tax or liability to pay conveyancing fees to one's solicitor) does not increase the inheritance tax.

And if the capital gains tax is borne by the transferee, that is treated (for inheritance tax) as actually reducing the value transferred: s.165.

There are special rules about debts due to foreign residents (s.162(5)).

Grossing up—lifetime transfers

LOSS TO THE ESTATE The principle of grossing up a lifetime transfer is embedded in s.5. As we have just seen, if the transferor is to pay the inheritance tax, his liability to the tax is to be taken into account in calculating the diminution in his estate caused by the transfer. Thus the loss to his estate is both the transferred amount and the tax on that amount, and tax is charged on that total amount, i.e. tax is charged on tax—that is grossing up. If A makes a chargeable transfer to B of £x in cash or of property worth £x (tax free), A's estate is diminished by £x plus the relevant inheritance tax. So £x must be grossed up to find what sum must be paid by A to the Revenue to put £x into the hands of B free from any liability to the tax. If one calls that additional sum £y, A must pay £x to B and £y to the Revenue.

20–15

EXCEPTIONS If A makes a transfer to B, stipulating that B must pay the inheritance tax on it, no grossing up arises. This is because A's estate is not diminished by inheritance tax, since he is not going to pay any of it. Since most lifetime transfers are now PETs, any tax which becomes chargeable will only be due after the transferor's death on the transferee so that no grossing up occurs.

20–16

In a general sense there is no grossing up either in the case of a transfer on death. This is because grossing up is, in effect, built into the situation since it is only the sums net of tax which will reach the beneficiaries. However, where a specific gift is left by will "tax-free" a kind of grossing up has to take place to determine the entitlements of other beneficiaries: see Ch.22 below, under the heading "Incidence".

20–17   Computations   With regard to the actual process of grossing up, in principle it is just like grossing up for income tax. If A wants to put into the hands of B £40,000, one has to work out what sum, after deduction of tax, will leave £40,000 clear. But in practice it is often very much more complicated than is the income tax process. This is because (a) the tax on any particular transfer has to take account of the transferor's previous tax history under the principle of cumulation and (b) the particular gift itself may cross the rate bands.

The principle of grossing up is perhaps best explained as follows:

If A makes a net chargeable transfer (i.e. after tax) of £100,000 to B Ltd the tax is calculated in the following way: tax payable on £100,000 = £x. The loss to A's estate is therefore £100,000 + £x. The tax actually payable is therefore the tax on (£100,000 + £x) = £y. A's cumulative total carried forward for the next transfer is thus £100,000 + £y. £y in effect represents an element of tax on tax (£x).

If, however, A makes a gross chargeable transfer of £100,000 to B Ltd, he will actually pay to B Ltd £100,000 less £x (the tax element of the £100,000). The loss to A's estate will thus only be £100,000 and that will be his cumulative total for future transfers.

20–18   Effect of grossing up   The effects of grossing up are therefore to increase both the tax payable on the individual transfer and the cumulative total of the transferor. On the other hand the transferee will receive a set amount, in our example £100,000 and not an amount variable according to the tax payable. As we have seen, however, this concept has been reduced in importance by the introduction of PETs. It is limited to those lifetime transfers which are not PETs.

Other liabilities

20–19   What we are talking about here is liabilities other than those which result from a chargeable transfer. The importance of the topic is that it is clearly relevant to the comparison which has to be made in the case of lifetime transfers between the value of a person's estate before and after the transfer (its relevance is to the "before" part) and it is clearly relevant to reduce the valuation of a person's estate on death.[2]

RELEVANT LIABILITIES A liability is not taken into account unless it is a liability imposed by law or it was incurred by the transferor for a consideration in money or money's worth: s.5(5). Thus an outstanding mortgage on a house would be deductible but not a voluntary covenant. In *Curnock v IRC* (2003), where the bank agreed to pay a cheque drawn on the deceased's account but not cleared until after his death, it could not be regarded as a liability against the deceased's estate, since the cheque was regarded as part of the administration of the estate and so was not incurred for a consideration in money or money's worth.

20–20

ARTIFICIAL DEBTS In establishing the value of an estate on death, s.5(5) is supplemented by s.103 of the Finance Act 1986. This section disallows what are known as "artificial debts". These are defined as debts for which the consideration was either directly derived from the deceased[3] or provided by another person to whose resources the deceased contributed. In the latter case there must be a causal link between the contribution of the deceased and the debt transaction. A simple example of this section applying is where Jane gives away a valuable asset to Kate and three years later she buys it back for full market value but leaves the debt outstanding until the date of her death five years later. The gift to Kate will not be taxable since it was a PET made more than seven years before her death and the debt owed to Kate, having been made for full consideration, would be deductible under s.5(5). But since the consideration for the debt, the asset, derived from Jane's estate it would not be allowable under s.103 of the 1986 Act.

20–21

Where an artificial debt is paid off during the deceased's lifetime, the repayment is treated as a PET: s.103(5) of the 1986 Act. Thus if Jane repaid Kate a year before her death it would become a chargeable transfer on her death. This will probably not apply, however, if Jane pays Kate the full amount immediately on buying the asset back—no debt has been incurred.

---

[2] Liabilities which reduce a person's free estate to below zero cannot be transferred to settled property which is deemed to belong to the deceased: *St Barbe Green v IRC* (2005).
[3] Unless it was a transfer of value. See *Phizackerley v HMRC* Sp Comm (2007).

20–22 SUMMARY Before we leave liabilities, notice this general point about them: if it is a question of valuing an estate *before* a transfer (or immediately before death) it is advantageous to the taxpayer if a liability can be taken into account: if it is a question of valuing an estate *after* a transfer it is disadvantageous if a liability is to be taken into account.

Relief Against Double Charges

20–23 Section 104 of the Finance Act 1986 allows regulations to be made to prevent double charges to inheritance tax applying in certain situations. The Inheritance Tax (Double Charges Relief) Regulations 1987 (SI 1987/1130) and 2005 (SI 2005/3441) apply such a relief in five situations.

PET and transfer back
20–24 Where A makes a PET of some property to B, B transfers the property back to A (e.g. in his will), and A then dies within seven years of the PET. The double charge arises because the property would be chargeable on the gift to B (the PET has become chargeable) and also on A's death (it forms part of his estate). The solution is to either charge the property as part of A's estate at his death and ignore the PET or to tax the PET and ignore the value of the property on A's death, whichever produces the lower amount of tax.

Chargeable transfer and gift with reservation
20–25 Where A makes a gift subject to a reservation which is also a chargeable transfer, e.g. a gift of his house to a company but he continues to live in it, and he dies still enjoying that reservation (or did so within seven years of his death). Since tax will have been paid on the chargeable transfer and the house will still form part of his estate on his death (or will be a chargeable PET) there is again the potential for a double charge. The solution again is to take the lower of charging the house as part of A's estate at death and to ignore the gift or to tax the gift and ignore the house as part of A's estate (or as a chargeable PET).

Transfer and loan back
20–26 Where A makes a chargeable transfer (or chargeable PET) of money to B and B lends an equivalent sum back to A. A then dies with the loan to B outstanding. The double charge here arises because the debt would not be allowed under s.103 of the Finance Act 1986 as an artificial debt (see above). Thus the money given is chargeable on the transfer and as part of A's

estate on death. The regulations provide that the tax payable is to be the lower of taxing the transfer and allowing the debt against the estate or ignoring the transfer and disallowing the debt.

Transfer and transfer back

Where A makes a chargeable transfer (but not a PET) and the **20–27** transferee returns the property to A, which is beneficially owned by A on his death within seven years of the original transfer. The double charge in this case is the additional tax which will be payable on the original transfer because of A's death within seven years and the tax payable on the property as part of A's estate at his death. Again either the original transfer or the value of the property on A's death is to be ignored, although there is no relief for the tax already paid on the transfer.

Transfer of property and debt

Suppose A enters into arrangements whereby he transfers **20–28** both property (relevant property) and a debt owed to A. The debt is then written off. If on A's death the relevant property and the death are chargeable to inheritance tax, two separate amounts must be calculated. The first is the tax chargeable on A's death disregarding the value transferred by the relevant property. The second is the amount so chargeable disregarding the value transferred by the debt. The tax chargeable is then reduced to the greater of those two amounts.

Valuation

Open market value

The basic principle of valuation is stated in s.160. Except as **20–29** otherwise provided the value at any time of any property shall be the price which the property might reasonably be expected to fetch if sold in the open market at that time. This is generally called "open market value" and takes us into the realms of a hypothetical sale.

The subsection then goes on to say (perhaps rather inconsistently) that the price shall not be assumed to be reduced on the ground that the whole property is to be, hypothetically, placed on the market at one and the same time. So if A owns 100,000 shares in XYZ Ltd the shares are valued (in the absence of an actual sale) without any reduction for the fact that if such a parcel of shares were put on the market at one time the price would be depressed.

20–30 ② ESTATE DUTY PRINCIPLES The definition of open market value continues the valuation rule which existed for estate duty purposes. The general judicial definition is that it is the best price available from a hypothetical purchaser in the market and not necessarily the highest price.[4] If there are a range of prices which competent valuers would consider as open market values then the highest is no more likely than the lower. It seems that some account may be taken of the existence of a special purchaser, e.g. the owner of adjoining land, who might pay "over the odds" to acquire the property.[5]

20–31 ④ RESTRICTIONS ON SALE If there is no open market, e.g. there are restrictions on sale, the property is to be valued under what is known as the *Crossman* principle on the assumption that a hypothetical purchaser buys freely in a hypothetical market but, having bought it, becomes subject to the restrictions.[6] This is particularly the case with private company shares which usually have some form of restriction attached to them. Section 168 provides that in such a case the hypothetical purchaser buying in the hypothetical market must be assumed to know all the information which a prudent prospective purchaser might reasonably require to know if he were buying from a willing vendor at arms length.[7] This is in itself an exception to the basic rule that it is the market value of the property and not its intrinsic value which counts, e.g. a painting will be valued at its then market value even if it later turns out to be a forgery.

20–32 ⑤ OTHER LIABILITIES The *Crossman* principle has also been applied where the property is subject to some form of liability other than a restriction on sale. This was the decision of the Court of Appeal in *Alexander v IRC* (1991). The property was a flat in which the deceased had acquired a leasehold interest at a discount under a statutory scheme. Under the lease the tenant had to repay that discount to the landlord if the lease was sold within five years. The tenant died within the first year. What was the value of the lease? The Court of Appeal held first that the obligation to repay was an incumbrance on the property incurred for a consideration and so fell to be taken into account in valuing the property. They then held that the value of the flat

---

[4] *Re Hayes W.T.* (1971); cf. *Ellesmere v IRC* (1918).
[5] *IRC v Clay* (1914); cf. *IRC v Crossman* (1937).
[6] *IRC v Crossman* (1937); *Re Lynall* (1972).
[7] e.g. whether the company's profits are increasing. The whole concept has a touch of Lewis Carroll about it.

for inheritance tax purposes was what a hypothetical purchaser would pay to acquire the lease subject to the obligation to repay the discount if there was a sale within five years but disregarding the fact that his own (hypothetical) purchase would have given rise to such a liability.

In *Walton v IRC* (1996) the deceased owned an interest in a tenancy (as a partnership asset). The other interest was held by one of his sons and the landlords were the deceased and his two sons. The court upheld a valuation of that interest on the basis that since it could not be assigned without the landlord's consent and that might be withheld, it could not take into account the value of the land as if the lease and reversion were merged. The intentions of the actual landlords could be taken into account; there was no requirement to use a hypothetical landlord.

Restriction on freedom to dispose: s.163

The rule referred to above on restrictions on sale could lead to abuse. To avoid this there is a complex provision which is best understood if we take one particular kind of restriction on freedom to dispose, namely an option. Suppose A grants to B an option to purchase a house. If the option price is the same as the then market price, say £50,000, there is no transfer of value. If the option price, say £35,000, is less than the then market price there is a transfer of value unless B pays for the option a sum (£15,000) equal to the difference between the prices. If, later, B exercises his option and buys the house for £35,000 when it is worth £60,000, the amount of the "value transferred" depends on how much consideration B gave for the option. If B gave no consideration, the "value transferred" by the sale is £25,000 (the gratuitous element). If B gave £15,000 for the option, the "value transferred" by the sale (assuming B pays the tax) is £45,000 (£60,000 – £15,000) less £35,000 = £10,000.

20–33

Valuation of related property: s.161

The concept of "related property" is an important one. Property is related to the property comprised in a person's estate if (a) it is in the estate of his spouse or civil partner, or (b) it is (or has been within the preceding five years) the property of a charity, political party, etc., and became so on an exempt transfer made by him or his spouse.

Where the value of any property *would be* less than the appropriate portion of the value of the aggregate of that and any related property, it *shall be* the appropriate portion of the value of that aggregate. That is the rather obscure wording of s.161(1). We have italicised "would be" and "shall be" in the

20–34

hope of making it a bit clearer. But it needs an example. The background is that the enactment is intended to stop up a tax-avoidance device. Suppose A owns 70 of the 100 issued shares in XYZ Ltd. Mrs A owns none. A transfers 30 shares to his wife. Controlling shares are worth say £10 each; non-controlling shares are worth say £6 each. The transfer to Mrs A is exempt. The legislation ensures that after the transfer A's holding is valued (e.g. on his subsequent death) as being worth not merely $40 \times £6$ (i.e. £240), but $\frac{40}{70}$ of the value of the combined (controlling) holding. The combined value is £700, so A's holding is valued at £400, and Mrs A's holding is valued at £300.

A relief is provided (by s.176) where property was valued on death on the related property basis and is subsequently (within three years of the death) sold for a lesser amount to those who inherited the property on the death on an arm's length sale.

Value of lessor's interest: s.170

20–35   In a settlement, sometimes the life tenant is treated as owning the whole settled property and the holder of the reversionary interest is treated as owning nothing, because his interest is "excluded property" (see Ch.21). In addition a lease for life, if the lease was not granted for full consideration, is treated (see s.43) as a settlement, but with the modification that the lessor's interest is not excluded property. This present section (s.170) provides that the value of the lessor's interest in the property shall be taken to be such part of the value of the property as bears to it the same proportion as the value of the consideration, at the time the lease was granted, bore to what would then have been the value of a full consideration. So, if L grants a lease for life to T at 75 per cent of full consideration, L's interest in the property is taken to be 75 per cent of the value of the property. (And, as we shall see, T's interest is taken by s.50(6) to be 25 per cent of that value.)

Value of life policies, etc.: s.167

20–36   This section provides that the value of certain life policies and contracts for deferred annuities shall be treated as not less than the total of premiums paid (minus any surrender value paid, e.g. on a partial surrender) where that would be higher that its market value at the time of a lifetime transfer. This does not apply on a death.

Value transferred on death

20–37   Inheritance tax is charged on the death of a person as if, immediately before his death, he had made a transfer of value and the value transferred by it had been equal to the value of his estate immediately before his death: s.4.[8] His estate does not include "excluded property": s.5(1). It does include property over which he had a general power to appoint or dispose, settled property in which he had a life interest (except, in certain circumstances, where the property reverts on the death to the settlor or the settlor's spouse) and his share in a joint tenancy.[9]

OPEN MARKET VALUE: LOTTING On a death, therefore, the whole of the deceased's estate must be valued on the open market basis on the assumption of a hypothetical sale of all the estate immediately before the death. The methods of ascertaining such a value are the same as for lifetime transfers (see para.20-29 above). One rule which is peculiar to ascertaining the market value on a death, however, is that where by taking a number of items together a higher price could be obtained that must be done, e.g. by valuing a set of Hepplewhite dining chairs as a single unit rather than by reference to each chair. (The related property rules, above, prevent this being avoided by transfers of part of such a set to a spouse and part to another). This is known as the process of "lotting"[10]. In *Gray v IRC* (1994), this approach was applied by the Court of Appeal to aggregate the deceased's partnership interest in a farming business, including a lease of the land farmed, with the deceased's freehold reversionary interest in that land. The fact that taking the two together did not form a natural unit of property was irrelevant. The only question was whether a prudent hypothetical vendor would have adopted this course of action in order to obtain the most favourable price without undue expenditure of time and effort. 20-38

OTHER RULES The Act also lays down some detailed rules, as follows. 20-39

(i) An allowance shall be made for reasonable funeral expenses (s.172).
(ii) Certain changes (whether increases or decreases) in the

---

[8] In *Curnock v IRC* (2003), the deceased's attorney wrote a cheque for X a day before the deceased died. The cheque, for £6,000 was intended to use up the available lifetime transfer exemption. The cheque was not cleared until after the deceased's death. Since, until then, there was no complete gift, the money was part of the deceased's estate under s.4.
[9] Which is still in existence the moment before death.
[10] That phrase had been used in the House of Lords case which established this principle: *Buccleuch v IRC* (1967).

value of the estate which occur *by reason of* the death are treated as having occurred before the death. An example of an increase would be the proceeds of a life insurance policy; these proceeds count as part of the estate. An example of a decrease would occur if a restaurant business lost value through the death of its successful proprietor; this fact is to be taken into account in valuing the business as part of the deceased's estate (s.171). An allowance is also made for the extra expense of administering or realising foreign property (s.173).

(iii) Sections 178 to 189 provide some relief where "qualifying investments" (notably quoted shares and holdings in an authorised unit trust) are sold within the 12 months following the death for less than the value at the date of death. In that case the sale proceeds can be substituted for that value.

(iv) Sections 190 to 198 provide a similar relief where land (which may include buildings) is sold within three years of the death for less than the value at death. To claim this relief legal title to the land must have been conveyed. A mere exchange of contracts, although a sale in equity, is not sufficient.[11]

---

[11] *Jones v IRC* (1997).

CHAPTER 21

SETTLED PROPERTY

Development of the charges on settled property

The original intention in taxing settled property was said to be   **21–01**
to ensure that property within settlements bore the same level of
taxation in the longer term as unsettled property. To achieve this
therefore required a charge amounting to the equivalent of at
least a charge on the death of each generation (trusts as such
don't die) and on any property exiting the settlement in the
meantime. The solution until 2006 was to tax the two generic
types of settled property in different ways and to implement a
special regime for specially favoured trusts.

Fixed interest trusts

Fixed interest trusts (where there was someone entitled to a   **21–02**
beneficial interest in possession, i.e. to the income as it arose)
were taxed as if the whole settled property belonged to the
holder of that interest. Thus on his or her death it formed part of
their estate and tax was calculated (and paid by the trust)
accordingly. Any lifetime charges (such as the ending of the
interest otherwise than on a death), including creating the settlement, were PETS.

Discretionary and other non-fixed interest trusts

Other trusts without such a beneficial interest in possession,   **21–03**
usually discretionary trusts, were taxed as separate entities with
their own cumulative total etc. (They could not, by definition, be
linked to a specific beneficiary so as to link into the tax in that
way.) Charges were made on the whole settled property every
ten years and on property exiting from the trust. None of the
charges, including setting up the trust, were PETS.

Specially favoured trusts

A group of trusts were treated separately for social and   **21–04**
political reasons. These included charitable trusts, trusts for a
disabled person and an accumulation and maintenance trust (for
a beneficiary under 25). They were generally exempt from all

charges unless the criteria for exemption was lost, in which case a charge arose based on how long the trust had been so exempt.

The 2006 revolution

21–05   With no prior consultation or warning, the Finance Act 2006 instituted a major change in the way that settled property became subject to inheritance tax. In effect, most fixed interest trusts ceased to be taxed by reference to the beneficiary with an interest in possession. They were subsumed into the independent tax regime formerly applied only to discretionary trusts. Only a few exceptions were made and only two and a half years was allowed for taxpayers to amend their affairs. In addition the favourable regime for accumulation and maintenance trusts was substantially reduced.

The result is that, after March 22, 2006, most trusts have become subject to the ten year and exit charges and neither those nor the creation of such trusts are PETS. Before, creating a fixed interest trust and other charges on such trusts, except on a death, were PETS.

Settlement

21–06   "Settled property" is not separately defined; it is simply property comprised in a settlement. What, then, is a settlement, for the purposes of the Act? Section 43 states that it is a disposition or dispositions whereby property is for the time being:

(1)   held in trust for persons in succession; or
(2)   held in trust for any person subject to a contingency; or
(3)   held on discretionary trusts; or
(4)   held on trust to accumulate the income; or
(5)   charged (otherwise than for full consideration)[1] to pay an annuity; or
(6)   subject to a lease for life if the lease was not granted for full consideration.[2]

Property subject to provisions equivalent to heads (1) to (5) above under the law of a foreign country can constitute a

---

[1]   An annuity not charged on property (e.g. an annuity purchased from an insurance company) is not a settlement. Even an annuity which is charged on property is not a settlement if it is granted for full consideration. Hence (probably) an annuity granted by continuing (commercial) partners for a former partner or his dependants is not a settlement.
[2]   Presumably the point of this is to prevent a person from seeking to avoid the rules relating to settled property by granting a lease for life instead of a life tenancy.

"settlement." Foreign settled property is, however, excluded property unless the settlor was domiciled in the United Kingdom at the time the settlement was made.[3]

Neither a tenancy in common nor a joint tenancy therefore is as such a settlement, but either of them will be a settlement if it also falls under any of the heads enumerated above.

One or more settlements

Just as in capital gains tax (see para.14–64 above) it is sometimes necessary to decide whether a settlor has made one single settlement or more than one. This can arise (as in capital gains tax) where a power is exercised so as to transfer assets out of a settlement. The question for inheritance tax in such a case is whether the exercise of that power amounts to a disposition within s.43. In *Minden Trust (Cayman) Ltd v IRC* (1985), it was held that where the exercise of the power amounted to a transfer of the entire trust property into a sub-trust, that was a settlement within s.43. The question can also arise when the settlor creates a number of trusts around the same time, often in identical form—are they separate settlements or a single settlement?

This was the question in *Rysaffe Trustee Co (CI) Ltd v IRC* (2003). The settlor set up five identical discretionary trusts, different only in the date of creation. The Revenue argued that these constituted a single settlement under s.43 since that section allowed for a settlement to be created by a disposition or *dispositions*. The Court of Appeal and the judge rejected that argument. Whether there was one or more settlements was basically a matter for the law of trusts and s.43 did not alter that. Whether a settlor chose, say, to set up a single trust of £1m for 5 beneficiaries or 5 trusts of £200,000, 1 for each of the beneficiaries, was a matter for the settlor. The use of the plural *dispositions* in s.43 was there to cover the situation, e.g. where a settlor added property to an existing trust. On the facts these were five separate settlements.

21–07

Putting property into a settlement

Creating or adding to a settlement on a death is taxed as any other transfer on death under s.4. In the case of a lifetime transfer, however, it will be an immediately chargeable transfer and not a PET, unless it is either: (i) a gift into a trust with a disabled person's interest (see s.89B) or (ii) it occurs on the

21–08

---

[3] But not reversionary interests—see the end of this chapter. Domicile here has its extended meaning for inheritance tax purposes.

ending, inter vivos,[4] of *an immediate post-death interest*[5] where the property continues under the settlement to be held for a *bereaved minor*.[6]

Settlements still subject to the beneficiary-link principle—categorisation

Three types of beneficial interest in possession

21–09   After 2006, only trusts with one of three specific types of beneficial interest in possession (one transitional) are still subject to the former fixed-interest trust inheritance tax regime. That, as we shall see, in effect treats the whole settled property as part of the estate of the holder of that interest so as to impose the tax charges. These three are: an immediate post-death interest (an IPDI); a disabled person's interest; and a transitional serial interest (TSI).

Immediate post-death interest

21–10   An IPDI is defined in s.49A. This is a beneficial interest in possession in a settlement which: (i) was created on a death (by will or on intestacy); and (ii) whereby the owner of the interest became entitled to it on the death of the testator or intestate. An interest in a bereaved minor's trust and a disabled person's interest cannot be IPDIs. Thus a typical IPDI will be where A dies and leaves property to B for life and then to C for life and then to D. B will then have an IPDI. After B dies, C will not have an IPDI—condition (ii) will not be satisfied.

Disabled person's interest

21–11   Under s.89B a disabled person's interest is one held under the terms of s.89 (trust set up for a disabled person) or s.89A (self-settlement by a person with a condition expected to lead to a disability).

Transitional serial interest

21–12   A TSI which arises after October 5, 2008 is defined in s.49D.[7] It is a beneficial interest in possession in a settlement: (i) which

---

[4]   Such as the ending of a determinable interest or a surrender of the interest.
[5]   This is as defined in s.49A and para.21–10, below.
[6]   See s.71A and para.21–43, below.
[7]   Section 49C applied a wider definition to those arising before that date. Trustees were given a transitional period, originally to April 5, 2008, but extended until October 5, 2008, to rearrange pre-March 2006 trusts so that they contained a TSI, either for an existing or other (younger) beneficiary and so retain the beneficiary-link principle for some time.

was a fixed interest settlement prior to March 22, 2006, i.e., there was a prior beneficial interest in possession; (ii) that that prior interest ended on the death of the holder of that interest, being either the spouse or civil partner of the successor interest; and (iii) the holder of the successor interest became entitled to it at that time. This is therefore a very limited category of interest. It would apply, e.g., where a pre-March 2006 settlement left property to A for life, then to A's spouse, B, for life, remainder to C. If A dies, B will have a TSI.

Bereaved minor's trusts are excluded from TSIs, as are disabled person's interests (whether as the prior or successor interest).

Beneficial interest in possession

Each of the above only apply if they are beneficial interests in possession in the settled property. It is still necessary therefore to decide what that means in this context. The Revenue published a statement on February 12, 1976[8] setting out their understanding of the term "interest in possession." In particular they dealt with the position where a person is entitled to the income of the property subject to a power of revocation or appointment or a power of accumulation. It is accepted that, in general, it is entitlement to the income as it arises which indicates a beneficial interest in possession (e.g. s.50 defines the size of the interest by reference to the proportion of income received). The Revenue's point was that it must be immediate entitlement to the income, so that if there is a power to accumulate income there is no interest in possession, the trustees can withhold current income as it arises, whereas in the case of a power of revocation or appointment over, the trustees can only deprive the beneficiary of future income, thus leaving him with a beneficial interest in possession in the meantime.

21–13

PEARSON v IRC   This view was tested all the way up to the House of Lords in *Pearson v IRC* (1980). By a majority of three to two, overruling both a unanimous Court of Appeal and the judge below, the House of Lords upheld the Revenue's argument that a power to accumulate does prevent the person taking in default of accumulation from having a beneficial interest in possession. Lord Keith, in the majority, concluded that the daughter only had the right to a later payment if the trustees either by inaction or decision did not accumulate the income— she had no absolute right to the income as it accrued.

21–14

---

[8]   See, e.g. [1976] B.T.R. 418.

That majority decision, as Lord Russell (in the minority) implied, is based on two basic misconceptions: (1) as to the nature of a vested interest subject to defeasance; and (2) as to the difference between trusts and powers. The interest was an interest vested subject to defeasance, a perfectly acceptable form of beneficial interest in English law which gives the owner the right to the income until it is taken away. The obsession with it being an "absolute" interest is irrelevant. Powers of accumulation, like powers of revocation or appointment, are only powers, i.e. they must be exercised unanimously to take effect. If one trustee disagrees then the power will not apply and the income be paid under the underlying trust, in this case to the daughter. The reader is referred to the speech of Lord Russell for a perfect example of what the law ought to be.

It may be noted, however, that the decision was not all bad for taxpayers. It may be desirable to ensure that X receives all the income of a trust but does not have a beneficial interest in possession (to avoid the trust property being regarded as part of X's estate).[9] That should be possible by giving X a right to the income subject to a power of accumulation which is not intended to be exercised.

21-15   No income trusts   An interest in possession can also exist where the settled property does not produce an income, provided that the beneficiary has a present right to present possession of the settled property e.g. sole occupation of a house.[10]

21-16   Effect of powers   The effect of powers generally in relation to the use of income or the right to possession arising under the trust depends upon whether they are classified as administrative (thus not affecting the beneficiary's right to the income (or possession) as it arises) or dispositive (with the opposite effect). In *Miller v IRC* (1987) the Court of Session held that a power to use income to maintain the capital value of the fund was an administrative power so that there remained an interest in possession. The criterion was said to be that administrative powers are those relating to the prudent management in discharge of the trustees' duty to maintain the trust estate. A dispositive power is one which diverts income away from one beneficiary for the benefit of others.

---

[9]   See *Moore & Osbourne v IRC* (1985) and *Stenhouse's Trustees v Lord Advocate* (1984).
[10]   *IRC v Lloyds Private Banking Ltd* (1998).

Settlements Still Subject to the Beneficiary-Link Principle—Charging Provisions

Deemed Holder/entitled to all property

The basic point to grasp here is that the person holding the   **21–17**
IPDI[11] is treated "as beneficially entitled to the property in
which the interest subsists": s.49(1). So if A is entitled to an IPDI
in Blackacre he is treated for the purposes of the tax as though
he were the owner of Blackacre itself. And if B is entitled to an
IPDI in a settled fund worth £500,000 he is treated as though he
were the owner of £500,000. But if the holder is entitled to part
only of the income of settled property his interest is taken to
subsist in only a proportionate part of the capital. So, if B were
entitled to, say, half the income of the settled fund he would be
treated as the owner of £250,000 (s.50).

Reversionary interests

It follows that a reversionary interest is not an interest in   **21–18**
possession. A reversionary interest is defined in s.47 as "a future
interest under a settlement, whether it is vested or contingent
..." A future interest cannot be an interest in possession because
it is not "*in possession*". An interest in possession means an
immediate entitlement: a present right of present enjoyment.
There is a distinction in the general law between a reversionary
interest and a remainder interest, but the definition quoted
above makes no distinction of this kind—both are reversionary
interests. So, if property is held on trust for A for life with
remainder to B absolutely, A has an interest in possession and B
has a reversionary interest.

EXCLUDED PROPERTY   It was pointed out above that in this   **21–19**
situation A is treated as though he were the owner of the settled
property itself. If B were also to be treated as owning something
there would be some degree of double taxation. So the legislation treats B as owning nothing. This is achieved by declaring a
reversionary interest to be "excluded property": s.48(1). The
effect of this is most clearly seen in relation to a death. Section 5
provides that "the estate of a person immediately before his
death does not include excluded property". So, if property is
settled on trust for A for life with remainder to B, and B dies
while A is still alive. B's reversionary interest is not taxed on B's
death.

---

[11] References to IPDIs from here on will also apply to a disabled person's
interest and a TSI.

There are three (perfectly reasonable) exceptions to this principle. A reversionary interest is not excluded property if (1) it has at any time been acquired for consideration, or (2) it is one to which either the settlor or his spouse or civil partner is beneficially entitled or (3) it is the interest expectant on the determination of a lease for life which is treated as a settlement. The problem of purchased reversions is dealt with at para.21–54, towards the end of this chapter.

Charge on the death of the beneficial owner

21–20   Let us again take the simple case of a settlement by which property is settled on the death of the settlor on A for life with remainder to B. A, the holder of an IPDI, dies. A's life interest is part of his estate immediately before his death (s.5) and so is taxed under s.4, just as is his unsettled property. The only special point that arises (and it is one that has already been made) is that (under s.49) A is treated as owning the settled property itself. So, if the subject-matter of the trust is Blackacre, what falls to be valued on A's death is Blackacre itself, and not merely A's life interest in Blackacre. Apart from this (very important) valuation point, there is no difference on the occasion of death between an IPDI and any other kind of property (except that the tax is normally payable by the trustees out of the settled property).

We now turn to look at the two circumstances in which a PET may be made during the lifetime of the holder of an IPDI.

Termination of a relevant interest in possession

21–21   This circumstance is dealt with in s.52(1) as follows:

"Where at any time during the life of a person beneficially entitled to an [IPDI, disabled person's interest or TSI] his interest comes to an end, tax shall be charged ... as if at that time he had made a transfer of value and the value transferred had been equal to the value of the property in which his interest subsisted."

Notice the valuation point cropping up again in the last few words: what has to be valued is the property itself, not the value of the interest merely. There is no grossing up. The deemed transfer of value will be a PET. An example of an IPDI coming to an end during the lifetime of the holder would be a determinable interest such as where property is held on trust for X until she shall remarry and she does remarry. Another example would be where property is held on trust for Y for life with remainder to Z, and Y surrenders his life interest to Z. Y's interest has been extinguished by the surrender.

Disposal of a relevant interest in possession

This depends on s.51. Where a person beneficially entitled to **21–22**
an IPDI, disabled person's interest or TSI disposes of his interest,
the disposal is not a transfer of value but is treated as the coming
to an end of his interest. So if a s.51 situation arises, it is equated
with a s.52 situation: that is to say, disposing of the interest is
treated as a coming to an end of the interest. So, if A gives away
to X his IPDI in Blackacre, a tax charge arises just as if his
interest had come to an end. Consequently there is a PET by A
(without grossing up) on the whole value of Blackacre.

Extension of the termination and disposal rules

If the point were not dealt with in the legislation it would be **21–23**
very easy to minimise the tax by depreciating the value of settled
property by various transactions between the trustees and persons connected with the settlement.[12] The point is dealt with by
s.52(3). If such a transaction takes place there is a deemed
partial termination of the interest and so a PET arises. Thus, for
example, if the trustees let a house rent-free to the holder of an
IPDI on a lease a tax charge will arise. A depreciatory transaction by an individual is taxable on the ordinary principle that it
diminishes his estate. But trustees do not have an estate. That is
why it is necessary to have this express rule.

Qualifications to the termination and disposal rules

We now have to look at a number of qualifications to the **21–24**
disposal and termination rules.

NEW ENTITLEMENT   If A's IPDI terminates but he becomes **21–25**
on the same occasion entitled to the property or to another
interest in possession in the property, there is no PET unless the
later interest is of less value than the former, in which case there
is a deemed transfer of value equal to the difference: s.53(2) and
s.52(4). This exception is a logical consequence of the principle
that the holder of an interest in possession is treated as the
owner of the property.

DISPOSAL FOR A CONSIDERATION   If the holder of an IPDI **21–26**
disposes of his interest for a consideration (that is, sells it as
distinct from giving it away) the value transferred is reduced by
the amount of the consideration: s.52(2). So if A, the holder of
an IPDI in settled property worth £700,000, sells his interest for
£200,000, a PET arises not on the whole £700,000 but on

---

[12] See, e.g. *Macpherson v IRC* (1988).

£500,000. One might think that this provision would mean that no PET at all would arise if the holder of an IPDI were to sell his interest for its full market value. This is not really so because in practice a life interest (except in very rare circumstances) is always worth less than the property itself in which the interest subsists. The full market price of a life interest in Blackacre is almost certain to be less than the value of Blackacre itself. So if the life tenant sells his interest in Blackacre even for the full market price of the interest there may still be a PET of the difference on the disposal.

Relief for successive charges

21–27   There is "quick succession" relief for successive charges on relevant interests in possession under s.141 in the same way as on a death transfer. Thus if there is a charge on a settlement, by the activating of a PET, or the death of the holder of an IPDI, within five years of a previous chargeable transfer of the settled property (including the creation of the settlement), the tax payable on the second transfer is reduced by an amount equal to a percentage of the tax paid on the first, i.e. as a tax credit. If the period since the last chargeable transfer is one year or less that percentage is 100 per cent; if the period is not more than two years the reduction is 80 per cent; if the period is not more than three years the reduction is 60 per cent; if the period is not more than four years the reduction is 40 per cent; if the period is not more than five years the reduction is 20 per cent.

Close companies

21–28   We have seen (see para.18–35 above) that by ss.94 to 98 a transfer of value of unsettled property by a close company can be apportioned to the participators.

In addition, where a close company is itself entitled to an IPDI or TSI the participators are treated as being the persons beneficially entitled to that interest according to their respective rights and interests in the company: s.101. Again these transfers will not be PETS.

Other settlements—the independent tax regime

Relevant property

21–29   We turn now to look at the inheritance tax treatment of settlements other than those which have an IPDI, a disabled person's interest or TSI in them. We must also exclude those specially favoured settlements such as charitable trusts, which we deal with below. For the majority of settlements after

March 22, 2006, however, the charging provisions are in ss.58 to 85 of the Act. None of these charges are PETS.

The sections apply to "relevant property". Section 58 states that that means any settled property (which we have already defined) in which no *qualifying interest in possession* exists. Under s.59, a qualifying interest in possession is limited to IPDIs, disabled persons' interests and TSIs. Section 58 also excludes the specially favoured settlements from being relevant property.

The independent tax regime

The application of inheritance tax to relevant property is to divorce the settlement from any of its actual or potential beneficiaries and instead to treat it as a taxable entity in its own right. (This was necessary for discretionary trusts since there was no obvious beneficiary to link the trust to—it is of course not necessary for fixed interest trusts, that is therefore a matter of fiscal choice.) This independent tax system poses three questions. First, when will there be a charge to inheritance tax? The issue there is that each generation of beneficiary in the nature of things dies (and so would attract a charge) every 33 years or so. Trusts, on the other hand, do not die. Second, what property and at what value will actually be charged, and third, at what rate? There is after all no beneficiary into whose estate the property is deemed to fall and so whose cumulative total can be utilised for that purpose. 21–30

PRINCIPAL AND EXIT CHARGES The answer provided is, roughly, to charge the trust to tax every 10 years in such a way as to provide a charge on the whole settled property every 30 years or so, and to charge any property leaving the settlement in the meantime. The 10-year charge is known as the *principal charge*, the exit charges as *interim charges*. In relation to both types of charge the three questions above must be answered, but it is important to keep them separate in your mind. The rules, particularly as to the calculation of rates involved, are complex, and further difficulties arise because of the more generous treatment of discretionary trusts in existence before March 27, 1974, i.e. the date when the tax was introduced. This is because the tax regime for discretionary trusts was altered dramatically from that under estate duty law and it was thought unfair to apply the full rigour to such trusts. In general the basic difference is that a post March 26, 1974 settlement carries with it the cumulative total of the settlor at the date of the settlement whereas an earlier one does not. 21–31

It is now time to examine the charges.

The principal or 10-year charge

When will there be a charge?

21–32   Section 64 provides that on the tenth anniversary of the date on which the settlement commenced and on every subsequent 10-year anniversary, a principal charge to inheritance tax is to be levied. However, s.61 provides that no date prior to April 1, 1983 could be such an anniversary. It follows that settlements created prior to April 1, 1973 could not have a chargeable 10-year anniversary until after April 1, 1983. It therefore became something of a lottery as to how soon such a settlement (created before this tax was thought up) would be taxed. For example, a settlement created on April 1, 1973 will have been taxed on April 1, 1983 but a settlement created on March 31, 1973 would not have been taxed until March 31, 1993. What price tax planning?

It is obviously important therefore to decide when a settlement was created. Section 60 provides that this is when the property first becomes comprised in it, but for post March 22, 2006 settlements where a settlor, or his spouse or civil partner, has an IPDI or a disabled person's interest when the settlement is first created, the property is only treated as having become comprised in the settlement when neither the settlor nor his spouse or civil partner have such an interest (s.80).

What is subject to the charge?

21–33   A 10-year charge is levied on the value of the relevant property comprised in the settlement, valued at the date of the charge. Since the whole amount is being charged no question of grossing up can arise. It is important to remember that this is all that is being charged when grappling with the rules as to the calculation of the applicable rates.

What rate is to be charged?

21–34   Here one has to distinguish between pre-March 27, 1974 settlements and others.

21–35   SETTLEMENTS CREATED AFTER MARCH 26, 1974 The rate of tax is calculated according to s.66. It is three-tenths of the effective rate of tax payable on a *notional chargeable transfer* made by a *notional transferor* with a *notional cumulative total* charged at the lifetime rates.

The *notional chargeable transfer* consists of:

  (i) the relevant property which is actually being charged, valued now;
 (ii) other property comprised in the settlement which is not relevant property (e.g. in which there is an IPDI or which is a charitable trust), valued at the time it entered the settlement; and
(iii) property comprised in any related settlement (s.62 defines that as one made by the settlor on the same day as the settlement except a charitable trust). These should be avoided.

The *"transferor's" notional cumulative* total is:

  (i) the settlor's seven-year cumulative total of chargeable transfers at the date of the creation of the settlement; and
 (ii) the full amount charged to interim charges (see below) in the 10 years prior to the anniversary.

ADDITIONS There is an additional sting in the tail. If the   21–36
settlor has added property during the 10-year period his cumulative total at that time will be used if it is higher than his total at the time of the creation of the settlement. Conversely, however, if property is comprised in the settlement but has ceased during the 10-year period to be relevant property the amount upon which an exit charge has been made can be deducted from the cumulative ladder (s.67).

In an attempt to display these rules in a different way it may be helpful to give an example.

X, with a cumulative total of previous chargeable transfers of   21–37
£312,000, created a settlement on December 1, 1998, of £100,000. On the same day he made a charitable settlement (not relevant property) worth £50,000.

The 10-year charge will arise on December 1, 2008. Let us suppose that the settlement is then worth £200,000.
The notional transfer will be
£200,000 (chargeable relevant property)
 £50,000 (value of related accumulative and maintenance settlement at date of settlement)
_____
£250,000

387

The notional cumulative total, since there have been no exit charges, is that of the settlor at the date of creation of the settlement, viz. £312,000

therefore calculate the notional tax at lifetime rates on such a transfer of £250,000
i.e. tax on £562,000
less tax on £312,000
= £X

Next, express £X as a percentage of £250,000 to give the effective rate of tax on the notional transfer, i.e. Y per cent. (Under the current simplified rates this is relatively easy.)

The rate chargeable is then $\frac{3}{10}$ Y per cent.

Remember that rate is then only charged on £200,000, i.e. the value of the relevant property at the anniversary.

21–38   REDUCTIONS   Under s.66(2) in applying this rate to the relevant property, if part of that property has not been subject to the trust for the whole 10-year period (e.g. additions to the property) the tax payable on that part of the relevant property is to be reduced by one-fortieth for each completed quarter of a year prior to its becoming comprised in the settlement.

Thus if a settlement of £500,000 is subject to a 10-year charge of £30,000 under the rules above, but £100,000 was only added two years (or 8 quarters) prior to that charge, the tax payable on that £100,000 is reduced as follows:

the tax payable on that part is $\frac{£100,000}{£500,000} \times £30,000 =$ £6,000; and

that figure (£6,000) is reduced by $\frac{32}{40}$, i.e. reduced to £1,200.

21–39   SETTLEMENTS CREATED PRIOR TO MARCH 27, 1974   Section 66(6) amends the above rules for settlements in existence at the introduction of what is now inheritance tax. The basic concept is, however, the same. i.e. three-tenths of the effective rate on a notional chargeable transfer made by a "transferor" with a notional cumulative total.

In this case, however, the notional transfer consists only of the chargeable relevant property and no account is taken of either other property in the settlement or related settlements.

Further, the notional cumulative total consists only of the

amount subject to exit charges during the 10-year period. The settlor's prior total is ignored unless he has made an addition to the property after the March 1982, in which case his cumulative total then will be included.

In the first example given above therefore the notional transfer would be £200,000 and the notional cumulative total nil. The nil band would therefore apply.

The interim or exit charges

When will there be a charge?

Section 65(1) provides that there will be a charge to inheritance tax if either (a) any part of the property ceases to be relevant property (e.g. on an advance of capital to a beneficiary) or (b) the trustees carry out a depreciatory value-shifting transaction which has the effect of reducing the value of the settled property, e.g. a loan to a beneficiary at a low rate of interest, etc.

21–40

The donative intent exception in s.10 applies to the second of these charges, as in effect does s.3(3), omission to exercise a right being regarded as equivalent to a transaction.[13]

There is no charge in the first quarter after either the creation of the settlement or a 10-year charge,[14] for trustees' costs and expenses, or for income distributions (i.e. income in the hands of the recipient). Nor is there a charge if the property ceases to be relevant property because it becomes comprised in a charitable trust (s.76).

What is subject to the charge?

Section 65(2) provides that the interim charges are to be levied on the amount by which the relevant property after the event is less than it would be but for the event. This is the standard measure for inheritance tax, in effect the loss to the settlement's estate. It follows that unless the tax is paid by the beneficiary (i.e. it is a gross transfer) the transfer will have to be grossed up for tax purposes.

21–41

What rate is charged?

In this case it is necessary to distinguish between whether there has been a 10-year principal charge or not. With regard to exit charges prior to the first 10-year charge there was a dis-

21–42

---

[13] The associated operations provisions also apply. See *MacPherson v IRC* (1988).
[14] For an unexpected consequence of this see *Frankland v IRC* (1997), CA.

tinction between pre-March 27, 1974 settlements and others. The former have by now all had a 10-year charge and so those provisions are redundant.

21–43   ALL SETTLEMENTS PRIOR TO THE FIRST 10-YEAR CHARGE
Section 68 requires us to apply the *appropriate fraction* of the effective rate of tax on a *notional chargeable transfer* made by a "transferor" with a *notional cumulative total*.

The appropriate fraction is:

$$\frac{\text{number of quarters since the settlement commenced}}{40}$$

except for property which has not been in the settlement for the whole of that time, in which case for that property one uses only the number of quarters since it became relevant property.

The *notional transfer* consists of:

(i) the value of the settled property at the commencement of the settlement;
(ii) the value of any related settlement;
(iii) the value of any addition to the property, valued at the date of entry.

The *notional cumulative total* is the settlor's cumulative total at the date of the settlement, ignoring any transfers made on that day.

To take an example:

A set up a £200,000 discretionary trust on January 4, 2003. He had previously made chargeable transfers of £500,000. Also on January 4, 2003 he set up a £70,000 trust for charity. On February 10, 2009 the trustees advanced £30,000 to F absolutely.

There is an interim charge on the £30,000 (ceases to be relevant property). There has been no previous 10-year charge.

To find the rate:
notional transfer

= £200,000 (value of settled property in 2003)
+   £70,000 (related settlement)
   £270,000

notional cumulative total = £500,000 (settlor's total in 2003)

therefore calculate tax on £770,000
less tax on £500,000
= £x

express £x as a percentage of £270,000 to give effective rate = y per cent.

The appropriate fraction is

$^3/_{10} \times {}^{24}/_{40}$ (no. of quarters since 2003) = $^9/_{50}$
so the rate chargeable on £30,000 is $^9/_{50}$ of y per cent.

ALL SETTLEMENTS AFTER THE FIRST 10-YEAR CHARGES In **21–44** such cases s.69 provides a simpler way of calculating the rates on an interim charge. It is simply the appropriate fraction of the rate charged on the last 10-year charge (ignoring any deduction for added property). We can for once dispense with notional transfer and the like.

The appropriate fraction is:

$$\frac{\text{number of quarters completed since the last 10-year charge}}{40}$$

The only complication is if at the time of the interim charge the settlement includes relevant property which was not there at the 10-year charge. In that case the 10-year charge has to be recalculated to include the added property, valued at the time it becomes relevant property.

Special Kinds of Settlement

As we have said before, some special types of settlement are **21–45** not relevant property and as such are not liable to the interim and principal charges even though there is no beneficial interest in possession. However, if the property ceases to be held on the specified trusts there is a flat rate charge which increases according to the length of time the property has been exempt and so avoided the 10-year charge (see s.70). This is subject to a maximum of 30 per cent and no period prior to March 13, 1975 will be counted.

The list of these trusts can be found in s.58(1). These include trusts for the benefit of employees, superannuation schemes, charitable trusts, and protective trusts.

Pre-2006 accumulation and maintenance trusts

Until March 22, 2006 a similar favourable regime applied to **21–46** accumulation and maintenance trusts. Under s.71 these only required (in general terms) that a beneficiary would, on or before the age of 25, acquire an interest in possession, the income in the meantime to be either applied for his or her maintenance or accumulated, and that the beneficiaries are or were the grandchildren of a common grandparent. Section 71 no longer applies to trusts created after March 22, 2006. Existing trusts could either simply lapse into the relevant property regime (although that in itself was not a chargeable event) or convert, by April 2008, into one of the two replacement categories: trusts for bereaved minors and age 18-25 trusts.

Trusts for bereaved minors

21-47   Under ss.71A and 71B, favourable treatment is given to a trust created either by the will, or on the intestacy, of a *parent* for the benefit of a *bereaved minor*. This also applies to any such trust established under the Criminal Injuries Compensation Scheme. A *bereaved minor* under s.71C means anyone under 18 who has lost at least one parent. Under s.71H, a *parent* in this context means anyone with parental responsibility as defined in the Children Act 1989.[15]

21-48   THE CONDITIONS To receive the favourable treatment, the trust must satisfy three conditions (s.71A(3)):

(i)   that the minor will on or before the age of 18 become absolutely entitled to the settled property, the income then arising and any accumulated income;
(ii) that until then, any income arising must be applied, if at all, for the minor's benefit; and
(iii) that until then, the minor is beneficially entitled to all the income arising, which may not be used for the benefit of any other person.

21-49   TAX ADVANTAGES There will be no charge on such a trust where the bereaved minor becomes absolutely entitled to the property on or before the age of 18. Nor where he or she dies under that age, or where property is advanced to him or her (thus avoiding a partial exit charge).

21-50   TAX CHARGES Where the trust ceases to continue to comply with any of the conditions in para.21-44 above or the trustees involve themselves in a depreciatory value-shifting transaction

---

[15] Or the Children (Scotland) Act 1995, or the Children (Northern Ireland) Act 1995, as appropriate.

there will be a charge to inheritance tax either on the whole of, or the reduction in the value of, the settled property, respectively.

The charge, which applies to all specially favoured trusts in similar circumstances, is a tapering charge based on the number of quarters of a year from the time when the conditions were first fulfilled to the date of charge. It is a flat rate charge on the scale set out in s.70:   **21–51**

0.25 per cent for each of the first 40 quarters (10 years—10 per cent).

0.20 per cent for each of the next 40 quarters (11–20 years—further 8 per cent).

0.15 per cent for each of the next 40 quarters (21–30 years—further 6 per cent).

0.10 per cent for each of the next 40 quarters (31–40 years—further 4 per cent).

0.05 per cent for each of the next 40 quarters (41–50 years—further 2 per cent).

Thus if the time lapse is 15 years the rate is 14 per cent.

Age 18-25 trusts

Under s.71D an age 18-25 trust is any settlement established by the will of a *parent*[16] or under the Criminal Injuries Compensation scheme, whereby the property is held on trust for the benefit of a person under the age of 25, one of whose parents has died. It does not apply where the trust is one for a bereaved minor (above) or where there is a pre-March 22, 2006 interest in possession, an IPDI, TSI or a disabled person's interest in the settled property.   **21–52**

CONDITIONS To receive favourable treatment, the trust must comply with the same three conditions as apply to a trust for a bereaved minor with the substitution of age 25 for age 18 (see para.21-44, above).   **21–53**

TAX ADVANTAGES UP TO AGE 18 Under s.71E, there is no charge to inheritance tax if the beneficiary becomes absolutely entitled to the property on or before the age of 18 (not 25 as under s.70). Nor is there a charge if he or she dies under that age, or if part of the property is advanced before that age, or if it becomes a trust for a bereaved minor.   **21–54**

---

[16] As defined in s.71H. See para.21–43, above.

21–55   TAX CHARGE AGE 18-25   Under s.71F, there is a charge to inheritance tax, similar to an interim charge on relevant property, if the beneficiary dies, becomes absolutely entitled to the trust property or receives an advancement of trust property after he or she has reached 18. In effect therefore the tax shelter only applies up to the age of 18.

The charge is calculated as: the *chargeable amount* × the *relevant fraction* × the *settlement rate*. The *chargeable amount* is the loss to the settled property. The *relevant fraction* is 3/10 of the number of complete quarters since the beneficiary attained 18 (or, if later, when the settlement was created) over 40. The *settlement rate* is that which would have been paid on a transfer of the whole settled property (valued at creation) + any related settlements + any subsequent additions to the property (valued then), by a transferor with the settlor's cumulative total as at the date of the settlement.

21–56   OTHER TAX CHARGES   Under s.71G, if the settlement ceases to comply with the conditions required for it to be an 18-25 trust, or there is a depreciatory transaction by the trustees, the usual flat rate charges will apply as set out in para.21–51, above.

The Purchase of a Reversionary Interest

21–57   We have noted that except in certain circumstances a reversionary interest in settled property in the United Kingdom is excluded property. This was originally based on the now much reduced principle that for inheritance tax purposes the life tenant owned the whole settled fund and the reversioner owned nothing. Now, since most trusts are now relevant property, it is the trust (and trustees) and not individual interests of any kind which form the taxable unit for inheritance tax purposes.

There are a number of special provisions in the legislation, however, some of which are designed to prevent over-charging in respect of reversionary interests and some of which are designed to prevent tax avoidance.

Purchased revisions
21–58   The most important provision is that a purchased reversion is not excluded property: s.48(1)(a). This is to prevent an obvious form of avoidance. Suppose that £400,000 is settled on A for life, remainder to B. C purchases B's remainder for £90,000, which is its market value. This is not a chargeable transfer since there will be no loss to C's estate and in any event no donative

intent by B (protected by s.10). C has depleted his free estate by £90,000 and gained the reversion. If he could thus give the reversion to D as excluded property he would in effect have given D £90,000 free of inheritance tax. Thus there is a charge on the gift to D since a reversion, once purchased is not excluded property.

Settlement powers

In order to avoid the continued success of avoidance schemes such as that upheld by the Court of Appeal in *Melville v IRC* (2001), what are called settlement powers[17] are no longer regarded as being property for inheritance tax purposes (s.272, as amended). A settlement power is defined in s.47A as any power over, or exercisable (whether directly or indirectly) in relation to, settled property or a settlement. These would include both a power to direct the trustees to distribute trust assets and those in issue in *Melville*.

21–59

Purchased powers

Since such powers are not property they could be purchased for market value (which would not be a transfer of value not least as a result of the donative intent rule) and then transferred on by the purchaser free of any charge to the tax, who will thereby have disposed of the purchase price free of any inheritance tax consequences. Accordingly, s.55A provides that where a settlement power is purchased for money or money's worth, the purchaser is to be treated as having made a transfer of value of the amount paid for the power. The donative intent provision in s.10 is disapplied as are the spouse, charities and public benefit exemptions.

21–60

Thus if X buys such a power from Y for £200,000 he will make a transfer of value of that amount. Conversely if X then gives the power to Z there can be no charge since the power is not property so there can be no loss to his estate. The position is the same therefore as with a purchased reversion by someone with a prior interest in the trust (charge on acquisition but not

---

[17] In essence, a settlor creates a settlement but gives himself a power to recall the property after a certain time and a veto over any dispositive powers of the trustees. The case decided that those powers were property and so part of the settlor's estate after the transfer, thus drastically reducing the loss to his estate on the transfer.

subsequent disposition) rather than the simple purchased reversion (no charge on acquisition but charge on subsequent disposition).

CHAPTER 22

LIABILITY AND INCIDENCE

Introduction

In this chapter we deal with two matters which are separate   22–01
but related, namely liability and incidence.

Liability is concerned with who is to pay the tax to the Revenue. Incidence is concerned with who is ultimately to bear the burden of the tax. So, for example, an executor may be under a duty to pay the tax to the Revenue. He then looks to the rules of incidence to see against what beneficial interests under the will he is to charge it.

Liability

The following persons may, in various circumstances, be   22–02
liable to pay the tax: transferor, transferee, trustee, beneficiary, settlor, personal representative. Does anyone feel left out?

The details are set out Part VII, ss.199 to 214, of the 1984 Act.

Chargeable lifetime transfers

For *chargeable*[1] *lifetime transfers of unsettled property* the   22–03
persons liable are: (a) primarily the transferor and then the transferee; and (b) so far as the tax is attributable to the value of any particular property, any person in whom the property is vested (whether beneficially or otherwise) at any time after the transfer or who at any such time is beneficially entitled to an interest in possession in the property; and (c) where by the chargeable transfer any property becomes comprised in a settlement, any person for whose benefit any of the property or income from it is applied.

---

[1] There rules are modified for PETs which become chargeable transfers on the transferor's death within seven years and for any additional "death rate" payable on such a death. See below.

Settled property

22–04   For *chargeable transfers of settled property* the persons liable are: (a) primarily the trustees of the settlement; and (b) any person entitled (whether beneficially or not) to an interest in possession in the settled property; and (c) any person for whose benefit any of the settled property or income from it is applied; and (d) where the chargeable transfer is made during the life of the settlor and the trustees are not for the time being resident in the United Kingdom, the settlor.

Death

22–05   For *transfers on death* the persons liable are: (a) in respect of unsettled property and in respect of settled property being land in the United Kingdom which devolves upon them, the deceased's personal representatives[2]; (b) in respect of settled property, the trustees; (c) so far as the tax is attributable to the value of any particular property, any person in whom the property is vested (whether beneficially or otherwise) at any time after the death or who at any such time is beneficially entitled to an interest in possession in the property; and (d) so far as the tax is attributable to the value of any property which, immediately before the death, was comprised in a settlement, any person for whose benefit any of the property or income from it is applied after the death.[3]

Death within seven years of transfer

22–06   *Where the transferor dies within seven years* of making a chargeable transfer the additional tax which becomes payable (i.e. the difference between the lifetime rates and the death rates) is principally the liability of the transferee. Similar rules apply where the transferor dies within seven years of making a PET and the transfer becomes chargeable. But if, for example, the transferee does not pay within 12 months the personal representatives are liable. All concerned are advised to take out insurance against such a contingent liability.

In any circumstances where two or more persons are liable for the same tax, each is liable to the Revenue for the whole of it. But, of course, the Revenue cannot get more tax than is due.

---

[2]   This liability is a personal liability of the personal representatives and not a liability of the deceased which they assume. See *IRC v Stannard* (1984).

[3]   Liability also extends to anyone who interferes or "intermeddles" in the estate to become an *executor de son tort*. See *IRC v Stype Investments (Jersey) Ltd* (1982).

Property

References in the above contexts to any property include references to any property directly or indirectly representing it. So one does not escape the tax charge merely by selling the original property and investing the proceeds in some other property. (For the tax position of the purchaser, see para.22–09 below.)

22–07

Transfers between spouses and civil partners

Where a transferor is liable for any tax and by another transfer of value made by him any property becomes the property of a person who at the time of both transfers was his spouse or civil partner, that spouse or civil partner is liable for so much of the tax as does not exceed the value of the property at the time of the transfer to him or her. See s.203, which is designed to stop up a rather crude avoidance device—namely, make a transfer of value to someone overseas and make also an exempt transfer of the rest of one's estate to one's spouse or civil partner, and leave the Revenue to whistle for their money.

22–08

Exception of purchaser from liability

A purchaser of property is not liable for tax attributable to the value of the property purchased, unless the property is subject to an Inland Revenue charge (on which see para.23–07, below): s.199(3).

22–09

Limitations of liability

There are limitations on the extent to which a person is liable for the tax. For instance, a personal representative is liable only to the extent of the assets he has received or might have received but for his own neglect or default. Somewhat similar limitations apply to trustees, beneficiaries and transferees: see s.204.

22–10

Incidence

We now come to the question of who is to bear the ultimate burden of the tax, bearing in mind that the person, from the list above, who pays the tax may not be the person on whom the burden should ultimately fall.

22–11

Problems of incidence are most acute in relation to tax arising on death. In the case of lifetime transfers it is a matter between the parties as to who bears the tax. The main effect, as we have seen, will be as to whether "grossing up" is necessary.

Testamentary expenses—charge on residue

22–12   Whilst prima facie each item of property comprised in a person's estate at death carries its own burden of tax this general principle is largely reversed by s.211. Tax attributable to the value of property in the United Kingdom which vests in the deceased's personal representatives and which was not, immediately before the death, comprised in a settlement, is to be treated as part of the general testamentary and administration expenses of the deceased, unless the will provides to the contrary. This of course means that, apart from any jointly owned property passing by survivorship which will not vest in the personal representatives, the tax attributed to the bulk of the average testator's estate will be treated as part of the general testamentary and administration expenses of the deceased for it is only in exceptional circumstances that the average estate includes overseas property. The incidence of tax for the average testator is therefore to be determined by s.34 and Part II of Sch.I to the Administration of Estates Act 1925. The rule is that where the deceased has left a will effectively disposing of the residue of his estate the burden will be thrown on that residue.

Legacies etc. free of tax

22–13   This process is reinforced by the tendency of testators to include in their wills directions that particular gifts should be paid free of inheritance tax. As we shall see in a moment, such a direction does, however, have another potential effect on the incidence rules on death. There is one exception to this power of testators to make tax free gifts. Suppose a testator gives his residue equally to his wife and his mother, with a direction that the mother's share is to be free of inheritance tax. The gift to the spouse is exempt, whilst that to the mother is chargeable. Section 41 provides that such a chargeable residuary gift must bear its own tax so that the direction that such tax shall be borne by the exempt gift of residue to the spouse is void.

This means that the net share actually received by the mother will be less than that received by the spouse since the former will be reduced by the tax payable on it. If the testator actually wishes the spouse and mother to receive equal net shares (i.e. after tax has been paid) this can be achieved if the will makes it clear that the mother's share of the residue, before tax, is to be enlarged by an amount which will ensure that when the tax is deducted from it her net share is equal to that of the spouse.[4] But this must be very clearly expressed and the courts will not infer

---

[4]   Re Benham's Will Trusts (1995).

it simply because the more likely explanation that the executors were intended to pay the tax due as a testamentary expense out of the gross residue before the shares were divided is prohibited by s.41.[5]

Estate rate

It is important on a death to calculate the estate rate, i.e. the   **22–14** rate of tax which applies to the whole estate, taking into account the nil band. Thus if A dies, having made no previous chargeable transfers, leaving a chargeable estate (ignoring exempt transfers) of £412,000, tax will currently be chargeable at nil on £312,000 and at 40 per cent on £100,000. Thus the tax bill will be £40,000. Applied across all the assets this gives an average rate of 10.3 per cent. That rate will then be deducted from any legacies which have to bear their own tax before the money is paid over to the legatee. Tax-free legacies will be paid in full with the tax coming out of residue. This apparently simple calculation is, however, as in many areas of tax law, not always quite so simple.

Partially exempt transfers on death

In many cases the rule that inheritance tax is a testamentary   **22–15** expense to be paid out of residue causes no problems. Thus where all the legacies are both chargeable and tax free and the residue is also chargeable, the whole tax bill (at the estate rate) is charged on the residue. Similarly, if the legacies are either all exempt, or are to bear their own tax under the terms of the will, the residue and the tax-bearing legacies will simply bear their own tax at the estate rate. But problems arise in three not uncommon cases. These problems are the subject of ss.36 to 42. The following is an outline of the effect of these sections, which in practice involve many complex calculations:

(i) Where the testator leaves a legacy free of tax[6] and an   **22–16** exempt gift of residue; e.g. £200,000 to my daughter, free of tax, residue to my wife. In this case, in order to work out how much tax should be charged on the legacy (i.e. the estate rate since the residue is exempt) it must be grossed up (in the same way as a net lifetime transfer). The tax then payable on that grossed up legacy is deducted from the residuary gift and the daughter will receive the net £200,000.

---

[5] *Re Ratcliffe* (1999).
[6] Remember this will be the case unless the will provides to the contrary.

22–17   (ii) Where the testator makes both tax-free legacies and those which must bear their own tax, together with an exempt gift of residue. Grossing up only the tax-free legacies would not be enough (since there are other legacies involved in assessing the tax liability) but grossing up all the legacies would be too much (since those bearing their own tax are not required to be grossed up, just as with a gross lifetime transfer). The solution is to gross up the tax-free legacies at a rate of tax applicable to a hypothetical transfer of the total of the grossed-up tax-free legacies and those bearing their own tax. This is known as "double grossing up".

In essence, the tax-free legacies are first grossed-up in the normal way, then the rate for grossing up a second time is calculated on a transfer of the total of that grossed-up figure plus the tax-bearing legacies (say 20 per cent). The tax-free legacies are then grossed-up again at that rate. The estate rate of tax is then calculated on the total of those doubly grossed up legacies and the tax bearing legacies (say 25 per cent). That rate will then be deducted from the residue in respect of the tax-free legacies and from the tax-bearing legacies in respect of their own tax.

22–18   (iii) Where the testator leaves both tax-free and tax-bearing legacies, as above, but the residue is partly chargeable and partly exempt. In this case, the tax-free gifts are again subject to a double grossing-up, but the second grossing up must be at a rate calculated on a hypothetical transfer of the total of the grossed up tax-free legacies, the tax-bearing legacies and the chargeable part of the residue (divided after deducting the single grossed up tax-free legacies and the tax-bearing legacies). After the tax-free legacies have been so doubly grossed-up, the estate rate is calculated on the total of the doubly grossed-up legacies, the tax-bearing legacies and the chargeable part of the residue (now divided after deducting the doubly grossed-up legacies and the tax-bearing legacies). That rate is then charged on the residue as a whole in respect of the tax-free legacies. Only after that will the residue be divided and the estate rate applied to the chargeable part. That rate will also be deducted from those legacies bearing their own tax.

CHAPTER 23

ADMINISTRATION AND COLLECTION

Introduction

Section 215 of the 1984 Act announces that inheritance tax   **23–01**
"shall be under the care and management of the Board" (i.e. Her
Majesty's Commissioners of Revenue and Customs). Part VIII of
the 1984 Act (ss.215 to 261) provides detailed rules concerning
the administration and collection of the tax.

Delivery of an account: s.216

Subject to certain exceptions, the personal representatives of a   **23–02**
deceased person are under a duty to deliver an account to the
Revenue specifying to the best of their knowledge and belief all
appropriate property[1] and its value. And a similar duty rests on
a transferor and a trustee[2] of a settlement concerning any lifetime transfer which is not a PET, which since 2006, now include
creating settlements inter vivos. The transferee must also deliver
an account in respect of a PET if the transferor dies within seven
years and the personal representatives must also deliver an
account of any PETs made by the deceased in the seven years
prior to the death, again to the best of their knowledge and
belief.

If there are no personal representatives appointed within 12
months of the death the duty to account falls on those beneficially entitled to the property or an interest in the property
(including certain discretionary beneficiaries). The phrase "best
of their knowledge and belief" means the personal knowledge of
the individual. This includes documents in his possession or
custody but he is not required to be an information gatherer.[3] If,
after making the fullest, practical enquiries, the personal representatives are unable to ascertain the exact value of any

---

[1] Including any interests in possession or general powers of appointment held
by the deceased.
[2] This includes a foreign trustee of a foreign trust made by a UK settlor: *Re
Clore (dec'd) (No. 3) (1985).*
[3] *Re Clore (dec'd) (No. 3) (1985).*

property, a provisional value can be given, pending a later exact valuation.

23–03   TIME LIMITS   Personal representatives must deliver their account within 12 months from the end of the month in which the death occurs or within three months of the time when they first acted (if this period expires later).

Any other person must deliver his account within 12 months from the end of the month in which the transfer took place, or (if it expires later) the period of three months from the date on which he first became liable for tax. (There are special rules about conditionally exempt works of art, etc. and about timber.) There are penalties in default both initially and for continuing default, and for providing incorrect information unless there is a reasonable excuse (s.245).

Exceptions

23–04   There are a number of automatic types of exception to the obligation to deliver a formal inheritance tax account.

EXCEPTED ESTATES ON DEATH   There are currently three types of excepted estate where the personal representatives do not have to file an account. The first is where the total of the gross estate (before business or agricultural relief) and certain "specified" lifetime transfers by the deceased, is less than the relevant nil rate band. In addition, of that property, not more than £150,000 must be settled property, the value of any property outside the UK must be less than £100,000, any chargeable transfers in the past seven years must be of cash, shares or land and less than £150,000 in total.

The second category is where the gross value of the estate and specified lifetime transfers by the deceased does not exceed £1 million and after the deduction of any spouse, civil partner or charity transfers (all exempt), the net figure is less than the relevant nil rate band.

The third category is where the deceased was never domiciled in the UK and the estate in the UK consists only of cash or listed shares or securities with a gross value of less than £150,000.[4]

23–05   EXCEPTIONS FOR TRANSFERORS AND TRUSTEES   With regard to immediately chargeable transfers (including creating a

---

[4]   See the Inheritance Tax (Delivery of Accounts) (Excepted Estates) Regulations 2004 SI 2004/2543, as amended by the Inheritance Tax (Delivery of Accounts) (Excepted Estates) (Amendment) Regulations 2006 SI 2006/2141.

settlement), if the property transferred is quoted securities or cash no account need be filed if the total, including the chargeable transfers made by the transferor in the last seven years, does not exceed the current nil-rate band. For transfers of other property, the threshold is 80 per cent of the nil-rate band. Similar rules apply in the few cases where a life tenant is still regarded as owning the settled property for IHT purposes and his interest comes to an end inter vivos.[5]

Where there is a chargeable transfer of relevant property in a settlement (the ten year and exit charges under most settlements), if certain conditions are met, there is no obligation on the trustees to file an account if the notional aggregated transfer does not exceed 80 per cent of the nil-rate band. The conditions are: (i) the settlor is and has at all material times been domiciled in the UK; (ii) the trustees are resident in the UK; and (iii) there are no related settlements.[6]

Probate

Personal representatives cannot get probate until they have paid the tax, and they cannot sell any of the estate assets (so as to get cash with which to pay the tax) until they have got probate. That looks like a vicious circle. But the problem can be overcome. The personal representatives can submit a provisional account and pay tax on that, then get probate, then sell off some of the estate assets, then submit a corrective or supplementary account and pay tax on that.   23–06

Returns by certain persons acting for settlors: s.218

There is a special provision concerning overseas settlements. Where any person, in the course of a trade or profession (other than the profession of a barrister) has been concerned with the making of a settlement and knows or has reason to believe that the settlor was domiciled in the United Kingdom and that the trustees of the settlement are not or will not be resident in the United Kingdom, he must within three months of the making of the settlement make a return to HMRC stating the names and addresses of the settlor and of the trustees of the settlement. This requirement does not apply to a settlement made by will nor to any other settlement if such a return has already been made by   23–07

---

[5] See the Inheritance Tax (Delivery of Accounts) (Excepted Transfers and Excepted Terminations) Regulations 2008 SI 2008/605.

[6] See the Inheritance Tax (Delivery of Accounts) (Excepted Settlements) Regulations 2008 SI 2008/606.

another person or if an account has been delivered in relation to it. The provision applies to (amongst others) solicitors and accountants and there are penalties in default (s.245A).

Returns following a variation of a disposition taking effect on death causing extra tax to be payable

23–08   Where there is an effective instrument varying a disposition taking effect on death made under s.142 (see para.19–34, above) and, as a consequence, additional tax has become payable, the parties to the instrument and the personal representatives (if they hold sufficient assets to discharge that liability) must deliver a copy of the instrument and notify the Revenue of the additional tax. Notification by one discharges the others. If no additional tax becomes payable there is no need to inform the Revenue.

Power to require information and inspect property: ss.219, 219A, 219B, 220 and 220A

23–09   The Commissioners of Revenue and Customs, with the consent of a Special Commissioner, may by notice in writing require any person to furnish them within such time, not being less than 30 days, as may be specified in the notice with such information as the Commissioner may require for the purposes of inheritance tax. The notice may be combined with a notice relating to income tax. Legal professional privilege is protected except that a solicitor (not a barrister) can be required to disclose the name and address of his client and (in certain circumstances relating to an overseas client) the names and addresses of his client's clients in the United Kingdom.

In addition, an officer of the Revenue and Customs may call by written notice for any documents, accounts or particulars from anyone liable to deliver an account. There is no requirement for the consent of a Special Commissioner but there is an appeal to such a person by the recipient of the notice. There is no further right of appeal by either side. The power is limited to the purpose of determining whether an account is incorrect or incomplete.

If the Commissioners authorise any person to inspect any property for the purpose of ascertaining its value for the purposes of inheritance tax the person having the custody or possession of that property shall permit him to inspect it at such reasonable times as they may consider necessary.

There is also provision for bilateral exchange of information with foreign governments relating to inheritance tax and its foreign equivalent. Where such an agreement with a foreign government is in force, the power to require information for inheritance tax purposes applies to information relating to the foreign tax charge.

Determination and appeals: ss.221 to 225

Instead of the word "assessment" which is the technical term applying to income tax, capital gains tax and corporation tax, the term used in relation to inheritance tax is "determination". The Commissioners make a determination and then serve a notice of determination.

23–10

Appeals (which must be made within 30 days of service of notice of determination) go to the Special Commissioners except in two cases as follows: (1) where it is so agreed between the appellant and the Commissioners, or where the High Court (on an application made by the appellant) is satisfied that the matters to be decided are likely to be substantially confined to questions of law and gives leave, the appeal goes to the High Court direct, thus cutting out the Special Commissioner stage; (2) any question as to the value of land in the United Kingdom must be determined by the appropriate Lands Tribunal.

Payment of tax: ss.226 to 236

In general, inheritance tax becomes due six months after the end of the month in which the chargeable transfer was made or, in the case of a transfer made after April 5 and before October 1 in any year otherwise than on death, at the end of April in the next year. So in many instances tax is due before the account is due. Tax on PETs is due six months after the death which activates the charge. So is the additional tax payable on the death of the transfers of a chargeable transfer within seven years.

23–11

Tax which is due and unpaid attracts interest at prescribed rates and there is no income tax relief for the interest payments. Where there has been an overpayment of tax the repayment by the Revenue carries interest (at the same rates as above) from the date on which the overpayment was made, and this interest is not subject to income tax.

Payment by instalments

23-12   In certain circumstances the tax can be paid by instalments. This facility applies only where the tax is attributable to certain kinds of property: land, controlling shares or securities; other shares or securities which are unquoted and in respect of which certain detailed conditions are satisfied; and a business or an interest in a business to the extent of its net value (as defined).[7]

The instalment provisions apply to transfers on death. They also apply, with certain modifications, to lifetime transfers but only if either (a) the tax is borne by the person benefiting from the transfer or (b) the property is settled property and remains in the settlement after the transfer.

Interest on land is payable in instalments from the date on which the first instalment fell due, but in other cases interest only runs if an instalment is in arrears so that there can be interest-free instalments.

Repayments

23-13   Where dispositions by the deceased are subsequently set aside, the liability to inheritance tax may be reduced and a repayment of tax paid fall due. If the dispositions were void then interest is payable from the date of payment of the tax (s.235). If, however, they were voidable, interest only accrues from the date of the claim for repayment (s.236(3)). Dispositions set aside by equity for mistake fall into the latter category.[8]

Inland Revenue charge for unpaid tax: ss.237 and 238

23-14   The word "charge" in this context is being used in the same sense in which a mortgage is a charge. Section 237 automatically imposes an Inland Revenue charge on all property included in a chargeable transfer[9] and, in the case of settled property, on any property included in the settlement. The holder of the property can thus be liable for the tax. On a transfer on death, however, the charge does not apply to personal[10] or movable property in

---

[7]   Rather special instalment provisions apply to timber in certain circumstances.
[8]   *Re Griffiths.*
[9]   It also applies to the various chargeable events connected with conditionally exempt heritage property.
[10]   Until 1999 leaseholds counted as personal property for this purpose.

the United Kingdom comprised in the free estate of the deceased. A purchaser of land where the charge is not registered and a bona fide purchaser of personal property without notice is not subject to the charge; where this is the case the charge attaches to the proceeds of sale.

PART FIVE

VALUE ADDED TAX

CHAPTER 24

THE CHARGE TO VAT

Introduction

Value added tax is almost always known as VAT. Even the VAT   **24–01**
Act calls it that. So shall we. Not only does it save time, it also
avoids awkward questions about whether we have the name
right! We call it "value added tax", but the Irish call it "value-
added tax", and are probably correct. Why? Because the name is
a direct translation from the French *taxe sur la valeur ajoutée*—
tax on added value. Somewhere we turned the noun "value"
into an adjective.

VAT has turned from a foreign idea into Britain's second
biggest tax in one generation. Why? There are two main reasons: a legal reason and a practical reason. The legal reason is
that VAT is the only permissible general sales tax in the European Union. When we joined the EC in 1973, we were obliged
to adopt the tax. As we see below, virtually all of the basic legal
concepts of the tax are increasingly a matter of the construction
of European law.

The practical reason is that the EU is, in fiscal terms, a customs
union. For many centuries much English, then British, government revenue was earned from customs duties. Now the UK
government gets precisely nothing from customs duties—they
are a European tax, and cannot be imposed between the Member States of the EU. We can only tax goods from other
European countries to the same extent as we tax domestic production. So we tax both equally—and that is the heart of VAT.

VAT is a charge on:

- domestic supplies of goods and services;
- cross-border acquisitions from other states in the EU; and
- imports from states outside the EU.

Each of these three charges is a distinct but related part of the
tax. However, in this and the following chapters, we shall deal
with the tax on the assumption that all relevant aspects of
taxable transactions take place in the United Kingdom.

The importance of the European Union

The directives

24-02   The United Kingdom adopted VAT as part of its Treaty obligations on joining the EC. Article 93 of the EC Treaty provides for the harmonisation of "turnover" taxes in the EC This has been effected by the successive introduction of a number of EC Directives on VAT.

The principles of the EC VAT were laid down in 1967 in the First VAT Directive (Directive 27/227). Four further directives followed over the next ten years and EC VAT law was consolidated into the Sixth VAT Directive in 1977 (Directive 77/388). That Directive was itself subsequently amended and added to by a succession of directives until the relevant EC law was again consolidated in 2006 into what is called the Recast VAT Directive (Directive 2006/112). That Directive has been operative throughout the 27 Member States of the EU[1] as from January 1, 2007. From now on we shall refer to this latest directive as "the Directive" in the text.

24-03   IMPORTANCE OF EU LAW   The importance of the Directive and EU law in general in VAT cannot be over-emphasised. Not only does it trump national law when there is a difference, but principles of EU law have to be applied in interpreting the Directive. EU law also governs the vexed questions of VAT abuse and avoidance. We must look at each of these issues in turn.

24-04   CONSEQUENCES OF DIRECT EFFECT   The primary reason for the Directive's pre-eminence in VAT law is that it has long been held by the European Court of Justice (ECJ) to have direct effect.[2] In extreme cases, this means that a provision of national law which is incompatible with the Directive is disapplied as against certain individuals affected by it. In *Fleming* v *HMRC* (2008), the House of Lords accepted that the failure by the UK law to provide a transitional period for the introduction of a three year time limit for certain repayment claims was simply contrary to the Directive. Accordingly the time limit was disapplied as against the claimants whose claim predated the introduction of the three year limit in 1997. There was some disagreement as to how long that disapplication should last. The

---

[1]   This includes the Isle of Man but not the Channel Islands for this purpose.
[2]   See e.g. *Finanzamt Munchen III* v *Mosche* (1997) ECJ.

2008 Finance Act duly introduced a transitional period of a year to March 2009 for claims which accrued before 1997.

But in most cases, the idiosyncratic UK concept of zero-rating apart (see para.25–07 below), direct effect means that the relevant national provision must be construed so as to give effect to the Directive for all purposes. In practical terms it is therefore very common now for a dispute before a United Kingdom court as to the effect of a provision in a United Kingdom statute on VAT to be argued in terms of whether it complies with the relevant article of the Directive and we shall come across many such examples as we look at the tax. The ECJ has in fact ruled that in certain cases national courts should refer the issue to it, even if the parties have not asked for a reference.[3] It follows that the basic framework of VAT is also derived from the Directive, e.g. as to what exemptions are permitted[4] or in what circumstances illegal transactions are taxable.[5]

IMPLEMENTING THE DIRECTIVE As with all directives, 24–05 transposing the Directive into national law requires Member States to comply with the general principles of Community Law, including that of equality of treatment.[6] Failure by the UK authorities to implement the Directive properly can lead to the EC Commission asking the ECJ to order the UK to correct its error and, if it has charged less VAT than it should have done, it may have to account to the EU (in its budget contribution) as if it had properly implemented the Directive.[7]

OTHER AREAS The Directive is not exhaustive, however. In 24–06 particular, it does not lay down any procedural rules relating to the operation of VAT. Thus it is for Member States to provide safeguards for rights (e.g. as to payment and repayment of the tax) conferred by Community Law. But, in *Marks and Spencer Plc v CEC* (2002),[8] the ECJ ruled that (i) the fact that a directive has been properly implemented does not affect an individual's right to ensure full application of the rights conferred under it,

[3] *Fazenda Publica v Camara Municipal do Porto* (2001)
[4] See e.g. *Norbury Developments Ltd v CEC* (1999).
[5] *Fischer v Finanzamt Donaueschingen* (1998).
[6] *Idéal Tourisme SA v Belgian State* (2001)
[7] *Fazenda Publica v Camara Municipal do Porto* (2001)
[8] This decision was applied to the facts by the CA (2004). See also the decision in *Local Authorities Mutual Investment Trust v CEC* (2004) on the validity of time limits on the claiming of input tax. These principles do not apply if there is no Community right involved, e.g. a claim by CEC for repayment of money wrongly repaid to the taxable person: *R. v CEC, Ex p Building Societies Ombudsman Co Ltd* (2000).

provided they are sufficiently precise and unconditional; e.g., as in that case, the right to recover wrongly paid tax based on a misinterpretation by the HMRC of the directive; (ii) whilst the rules for collection and repayment of overpaid tax were a matter for domestic law, the general principles of Community law would be applied to them.

Thus national rules could not distinguish between repayment claims based on community rights and purely domestic rights (*principle of equality of treatment*). Further, they could not make it impossible nor excessively difficult to exercise those rights (*principle of effectiveness*) nor must they go further than is necessary to achieve their object (*principle of proportionality*). Thus, whilst a time limit for making repayment claims was not as such incompatible with Community law, the scheme in the case was. The period allowed for claims had to be both reasonable and allow for transitional arrangements for pre-existing claims—the UK, by imposing limitation periods for claims retrospectively, was in clear breach of the principle of effectiveness. Finally, the ECJ held (iii) that retrospective withdrawal of a Community right such as the right in this case was also a breach of the *principle of legitimate expectation*.

In *Marks & Spencer Plc v HMRC* (2008), it was held by the ECJ that whilst there was no enforceable Community right with regard to zero-rating, the principles of Community law applied to the consequences of the national court misinterpreting the national legislation. Fiscal neutrality and equal treatment had to be applied.

Application of principles of community law

24–07   It is therefore not just in the wording of the Directive itself that the influence of Community law is felt. In applying the terms of the Directive[9] the United Kingdom courts are obliged to apply those broader Community law principles of construction. This was recognised very early by Nolan J. in *Yoga for Health Foundation v CEC* (1984). Thus many decisions are based upon EC principles such as equal treatment, legitimate expectation, legal certainty, proportionality, non-discrimination, equivalence and effectiveness.

---

[9]   Including any decision to implement one of the derogations allowed by the directive: *Finanzamt Bergisch Gladbach v Skripalle* (1997). But see *Belgocodex SA v Belgium* (2000) on the rights of Member States to revoke such derogations. See also the comments of Lindsay J. in *HMRC v Weald Leasing Ltd* (2008) at [31].

FISCAL NEUTRALITY There is a particular stress on the principle of fiscal neutrality, i.e. that economic operators carrying on the same business should be taxed the same. Thus the ECJ was able to find that the Directive made no distinction between a nursing home run by a company and one run by a partnership.[10]   24–08

That principle also requires that there be no distinction between lawful and unlawful activities unless there is no possibility of competition between the lawful and unlawful sectors.[11] Thus in *CEC v Polak*,[12] VAT was applied to the activities of an escort agency. It was not clear that the activities of the agency were unlawful throughout the Community. Unlike narcotics or forgery, prostitution was not itself illegal. The Court also applied the principle of *proximity* so that the time spent by the escorts which was a separate and legitimate activity of the agency could be separated from the activities of the escorts and their clients.

In *Marks & Spencer Plc v HMRC* (2008), the ECJ considered that on a claim for repayment of wrongly charged VAT, the defence of unjust enrichment was not an automatic breach of the fiscal neutrality principle. The taxpayer, it was argued, had passed on most of the VAT to its customers. The Court also said the fiscal neutrality could be impaired if a trader's turnover was affected by the error.

CORE OF THE PRINCIPLE In *Lex Services Plc v CEC* (2004), Lord Walker, without referring the matter to the ECJ, considered that the principle of fiscal neutrality had a core, which he described as "whether goods purchased by the final consumer have been through the hands of a dozen different traders at successive stages of their manufacture, distribution and marketing or are the product of a single manufacturer who is also the retailer the VAT system should ... produce the same end result" (and similar for services).[13] But he also considered that the principle was qualified by that of legal certainty and does not require that transactions, which have the same economic or business effect, should for that reason be treated alike for VAT   24–09

---

[10]   *Gregg v CEC* (1999).
[11]   *Staatsesecretaris van Financiën v Coffeeshop Siberië vof* (1999).
[12]   (2002).
[13]   (2004) at para.26.

purposes,[14] thus, in that case distinguishing between a car dealer who gives a discount on the list price of a new car and one who gives a generous part exchange allowance on the customer's old car, even though the net price paid by the customer is the same in both cases.

Fraud, evasion, abusive practices and avoidance

24-10   As we shall see, VAT basically has two financial components. A makes a taxable supply to B. A must account to the HMRC for VAT on that supply (output tax). B may then (unless he is the final consumer) claim that back from HMRC as input tax (but of course will himself have to account for ouput tax on supplies from him, say to C, and so on). It is in the order of things that suppliers will seek both to minimise their accountability for output tax and maximise their claims for input tax. Apart from using actually fraudulent figures, which of course can be rectified (and prosecuted on), these may take the form of a fully-disclosed tax planning scheme, be part of a complex series of transactions designed to achieve an evasion of the tax (e.g. the so-called carousel fraud) or somewhere in between.

It is also in the nature of things that the HMRC will seek to counter these activities. But unlike other UK taxes, if it uses the statutory scheme for recovery it can only do this within an EU framework and the ECJ has laid down some pretty clear guidance as to the parameters within which the UK authorities must work.

24-11   OBJECTIVE NATURE OF THE TAX   In the case of fraud or evasion, the ECJ held in *Teleos Plc* v *CEC* (2008) that although the HMRC are entitled under EU law to take measures to counter the actual fraud or evasion, they must not offend the principle of proportionality; i.e. they must not render the obtaining of a Community right impossible or excessively difficult. In *JP Commodities Ltd v HMRC* (2008) it was held that a simple requirement to include the VAT registration number of the recipient of an intra EC supply by an exporter seeking to claim that it was a zero-rated export supply, was proportionate. It was a small thing to ask (unless of course the recipient did not have one, which was the whole purpose of the exercise).

It has been held, however, by the House of Lords in *HMRC v*

---

[14] "The principle of the neutrality of VAT does not mean that a taxable person with a choice between two transactions may choose one of them and avail himself of the effects of the other." *CEC v Cantor Fitzgerald International* (2001) at para.33. See [2004] BTR 99.

Total Network SL (2008), that in default of using that statutory recovery scheme, HMRC does have the ability to bring a civil claim for damages for the tort of conspiracy based on harm intentionally inflicted by persons combining for that purpose, whether or not it would be actionable against any one individually.

But the HMRC has also sought to set transactions aside on the basis that, although they were themselves between innocent parties, they were part of an overall fraudulent scheme designed to allow input tax to be improperly reclaimed. This equates to attacking avoidance schemes in direct tax law. That approach was firmly rejected by the ECJ in *Optigen Ltd v CEC* (2006).[15] The various concepts relating to what amounts to a taxable supply etc in the Directive are wholly objective and questions of motive are irrelevant in determining whether there has been a supply leading to a claim for repayment of input tax. The right to deduct input tax is an integral part of VAT. Thus any supply which constitutes a taxable supply under the Directive remains a supply even if carried out with the sole object of obtaining a tax advantage (as opposed to fraud or evasion etc). Thus the recipient of a supply of goods who does not and could not know that it was linked to a fraud by the seller, is entitled to a deduction of input tax so paid. That was held by the ECJ in *Kittel v Belgium* (2008).

AVOIDANCE—ABUSIVE PRACTICES But these decisions on the   **24–12** objective nature of non-fraudulent supplies is subject to one major limitation, laid down by the ECJ in *Halifax Plc v CEC* (2006) and confirmed by them in *Kittel v Belgium* (2008). It is subject to the principle that Community Law cannot be relied on for abusive or fraudulent ends. But the ECJ also stressed that there is a need for legal certainty in the system of VAT and there is certainly no requirement that a supplier should structure its business so as to attract the highest possible tax. As a result it set out two requirements for a practice to be regarded as an abusive practice for VAT:

> (i) after applying the relevant national and EC rules, a tax advantage (e.g. a repayment claim[16]) accrues which would be contrary to the purpose of the directive; and

---

[15] See also *University of Huddersfield Higher Education Corporation v* CEC (2006) where the ECJ rejected a similar attack on a non-fraudulent domestic VAT tax planning scheme.

[16] Most of the cases have involved these, but the CA in *Debenhams Retail Ltd v CEC* (2005) (para.52) considered that it would equally apply to a claim to lower output tax.

(ii) the essential[17] aim of the transaction concerned is to obtain that advantage.

If there are other commercial explanations then the doctrine will not apply.

The ECJ added that any such finding of an abusive practice would not lead to any criminal sanctions. Instead the transaction would have to be *redefined*. This would entail establishing the situation which would have obtained in the absence of the transaction constituting such a practice. This could involve the payment or repayment of the tax and any third party rights.

24–13   APPLYING THE TESTS   In the *Halifax* case, the ECJ stated that in applying these difficult tests as to advantage and essential aim, national courts must work on objective factors and determine the real substance and significance of the relevant transaction(s). They could, however, have regard to the purely artificial nature of a transaction and any links of a legal, economic and/or personal nature between the operators involved in a tax reduction scheme.

In *HMRC v Weald Leasing Ltd* (2008), Lindsay J. rejected the Commissioners' argument that it would be sufficient to show that in a case where the essential aim of a series of transactions was to obtain a tax advantage, with no commercial motive, the transactions were not part of normal commercial operations. There had, in addition, to be something which was contrary to the purposes of the directive. In that case, simply being able to deduct a greater amount of input tax than would have been available without it, could not be so described.

But, in *WHA Ltd v HMRC* (2007) the Court of Appeal applied the ECJ's abusive practices tests to an avoidance scheme, the effect of which was that an insurer seemed to be able to claim repayment of input tax in relation to non-taxable supplies (i.e. where no corresponding output tax had been paid). The Court looked at the scheme as a whole and not just each transaction in isolation (as required by the ECJ). They then determined that the scheme was contrary to the VAT principle (test (i)) that only taxable supplies can create an input tax claim. Then they considered the artificial aspects of the scheme and found that overall it was objectively "commercially pointless" (test (ii)). They also held that the fact that this was a UK only case and so did not depend as such on EC law was irrelevant. Finally they said that redefinition was pointless since there were

---

[17] They also used the word "sole" aim.

no third parties involved, the tax due had been paid and had not been overpaid.

VAT in the United Kingdom

In the United Kingdom, VAT is imposed by the Value Added   **24–14**
Tax Act 1994, a consolidation measure, together with significant provisions in delegated legislation. Partly as a result of a series of cases brought against the United Kingdom Government by taxpayers and by the European Commission, many of the differences that used to exist between the EC VAT and its United Kingdom version have been removed.

VAT law is a curious mix of broad principles and considerable amounts of detail. This is because of the nature of the tax. In principle it is a very broad-based tax, much broader than income tax or corporation tax. Potentially it applies to any economic transaction under which anyone adds value to any business activity; that is, under which anyone recovers not only the cost of materials used in a transaction, but also the cost of his or her own labour (or that of employees) or a profit. Of course, both are usually the aim. VAT therefore can apply to any economic activity. Further, it applies directly to those activities, not at one remove in the way corporation tax or income tax do. We must in every case establish not who makes the money, but who makes the supply, to whom, and of what. Easy? No, because what appear to be even straight forward everyday transactions need careful analysis to establish the VAT consequences.

Sources of VAT law

At the same time, therefore, United Kingdom VAT law has to   **24–15**
follow a European paradigm and deal with considerable detail. Both make the traditional pattern of imposition by means only of primary legislation inappropriate. In practice, there are four tiers of operative legislation. The top tier, as we have seen, is formed by the European Directive. The next tier is the VAT Act and amending Finance Acts. Below that are a considerable number of orders in Council and other delegated legislation. Then comes the fourth layer: official Notices. These Notices are issued by the Revenue and Customs Commissioners and, unusually, have, at least in part, legislative status. Taxpayers to whom the Notices are issued are obliged to follow their contents. By this multiple means, the law is imposed. Supported both by considerable use of the appeals process, and also by agreements with trade organisations, extra-statutory conces-

sions, parliamentary questions, press releases, and information sheets and notes, those who need to do so can find out at least what the local VAT offices think they should be doing. Of this wealth of material, you may find it useful to obtain one Notice in particular. Notice No. 700, *The VAT Guide*, is an excellent summary, with worked examples, of the tax for those who have to operate it. It is available free from your local VAT office.

Administration and appeals

24–16   VAT administration is the task of Her Majesty's Commissioners of Revenue and Customs. Before its fusion with the Inland Revenue, VAT was under the control of HM Customs and Excise, the oldest British government department. Day to day administration is still undertaken by a local VAT office responsible for overseeing registration and collection of the tax which usually works on an invoice basis.[18] There are both civil and criminal penalties for, e.g., failing to register[19] or making returns.

24–17   APPEALS   Appeals are currently heard by the VAT and duties appeal tribunal (VADT). Originally set up only to hear VAT appeals, this tribunal now deals with all aspects of the indirect taxes or, in effect, appeals from decisions of HMRC. The VADT has the power to deal with any question of law, procedure or fact in an appeal. Appeals can only be made on a point of law. This right is part of the general right to appeal to the High Court from a tribunal granted by s.11 of the Tribunals and Inquiries Act 1992. For proposed reforms, see para.1–26.

VAT in Scotland is exactly the same as in England, save that appeals from the VADT lie to the Scottish courts rather than the English courts. There are, however, not one but two common lines of appeal on Scottish cases and English cases. The first is to the House of Lords. The second, as we have seen, is to the European Court of Justice in Luxembourg.[20]

How VAT works

24–18   As we shall see, VAT is charged on a supply of goods and services by the supplier. It is an indirect tax in the sense that it is

---

[18] See *Elliniko Dimosio v Karageorgou* (2006) ECJ.

[19] See *Khan v CEC* (2006).

[20] See para.24–02, above. There will be no reference to the ECJ, however, if the matter has been resolved or is clear. In other cases a reference will usually be made, and must be by the House of Lords. See e.g. *Town and Country Factors Ltd v CEC* (1998).

charged as part of the purchase price for those goods and services and accounted for by the recipient of that consideration. The tax operates as a *value-added* tax. This requires an examination of the way VAT works from the viewpoint of a trader rather than on a transaction-by-transaction basis.

EXAMPLE   Alan owns a forest. He sells planks of wood cut   24–19
from the trees. Beech buys the planks and turns them into chair frames. Caitlin buys the chair frames from Beech, upholsters them, and turns them into chairs. Den buys the chairs from Caitlin, and sells them to customers in his shop. Six of the chairs are bought by Eka for £200 each. How does VAT apply to this series of transactions? Let us assume that A, B, C, and D are all registered for VAT.

A sells the planks from which the parts are made for £10 to B. To this must be added VAT at 17.5 per cent (the standard rate). B therefore pays A £11.75. A keeps the £10, but pays the £1.75 to the local VAT office. B sells the chair frames to C for £30, again plus VAT. B therefore charges C £30 plus the VAT, a total of £35.25. Of the £5.25 VAT he receives, B sets off the £1.75 paid out to A, and hands £3.50 to the VAT office. B's profit is therefore £20. Similarly D pays C £100 plus VAT for the chairs, a total of £117.50. C recoups the £5.25 from the £17.50, handing over £12.25, and keeping a profit of £70.

E pays D £200. VAT is not added to this price, so must be included in it. E is therefore treated as paying D £170.21 plus £29.79 VAT. D keeps £17.50 of the £29.79 VAT, handing the balance of £12.29 over to the VAT office. D's profit is £70.21.

E has therefore paid VAT at the standard rate of 17.5 per cent on the full purchase price paid, the £29.79. VAT has been paid at this rate at each of the four stages of manufacture and sale of the chairs and their components. But at each stage, the seller has kept back the VAT incurred by her or him. The local VAT office has therefore collected only £29.79. A paid in £1.75, B adding £3.50, C adding a further £12.25 and D the final £12.29. This reflects the profits of A (£10), B (£20), C (£70), and D (£70.21). In other words, each has paid VAT on the value-added at that stage of production.

INPUTS AND OUTPUTS   As this example shows, the tax is   24–20
turned into a value-added tax by allowing each taxable person to collect VAT on the full sale price, but deduct from it any VAT paid out in making the sales. In VAT terms, the VAT collected by a trader is known as the *output tax* (or tax on outputs). The VAT incurred by the trader is *input tax* (or tax on inputs to the

business). The VAT payable to the VAT office is the balance of output tax less input tax.

This position is complicated by the fact that there are exempt and zero-rated supplies. We shall deal with those in the next chapter. The detailed rules as to the collection and computation of the tax are dealt with in Ch.26. We must now turn to when the tax will be charged.

When VAT Applies

24–21   The three key questions to be answered in determining the structure of VAT are: who are the taxpayers? on what are they taxed? when, and how much, tax is paid?

Taxpayers and taxable persons
24–22   In a practical sense, the taxpayers of VAT are the final consumers who buy the goods and services subject to the tax. The legal obligation to account for the tax, however, is not placed on them, but on those that supply them. These are called not taxpayers but *taxable persons* in the VAT legislation. This helps us keep in mind that the tax is imposed on transactions rather than persons, although the taxable persons are those required to collect the tax. Who are taxable persons? Section 3(1) of the VAT Act tells us that "a person is a taxable person for the purposes of this Act while he is, or is required to be, registered under this Act." We will explore later who is in these two categories.

Scope of the tax
24–23   What is subject to VAT? Section 4(1) of the Act says that "VAT shall be charged on any supply of goods or services made in the United Kingdom, where it is a taxable supply made by a taxable person in the course or furtherance of any business carried on by him"; while s.4(2) adds that a "taxable supply is a supply of goods or services made in the United Kingdom other than an exempt supply." We must add to this helpful definition the further guidance that *supply* includes all forms of supply, but not anything done otherwise than for a consideration, and that anything which is not a supply of goods but is done for a consideration (including, if so done, the granting, assignment or surrender of any right) is a supply of services (s.5(2)).

24–24   THE DIRECTIVE   But wait a minute. VAT is a European tax. Has the British legislation carried out the requirements of European law? The key provision is art.2 of the VAT Directive. This provides that "The following transactions shall be subject to value added tax: 1. the supply of goods [or services] effected for consideration within the territory of the Member State by a taxable person acting as such..."

To this we must add art.9 of the Directive: "Taxable person" shall mean any person who independently carries out in any place any economic activity including those specified, whatever the purpose or results of that activity.

Despite the differences in wording, the structure of the British VAT is that required in EC law. We should therefore read the British charging provisions in the light of the European provisions—with two cautions. The same words may appear in the two texts, but with different meanings. For example, we shall see that *taxable person* in the European text does not have the same meaning as *taxable person* in the British text. The second warning is that words in the European text may appear to be ordinary English words when they are not. *Consideration* is an example of this, as again we see below. One reason for this is that the European text exists in several equally authoritative language versions.

Subject to those warnings that—as in any tax law—we must always remember precisely what each word means, we can use the two sets of provisions to state the key structure of the VAT as it applies to supplies internal to the United Kingdom.

The Charge to VAT

VAT on domestic supplies applies to: 24–25

- supplies;
- of goods and services;
- for consideration;
- other than exempt supplies;
- in the United Kingdom;
- by a taxable person;
- as part of the economic activities of that person.

Each of these elements must be present, or be deemed to be present, before the tax operates on a supply. A supply made when one or more of the elements of the tax are missing is said to be outside the scope of the tax. It is a criminal offence deliberately to charge VAT on a supply that is outside the scope of the tax. These seven elements are therefore the necessary criteria for the operation of the tax. They are not sufficient to determine tax liability in full, but we shall examine these key issues first, then deal with the other provisions.

Supplies

24–26   The phrase *supplies of goods and services for consideration* should seem familiar to a student of commercial law, and who should therefore have heard of the Supply of Goods and Services Act 1982. Unfortunately, the analogy is not valid. None of the words in that phrase bear the same meaning as in English contract and commercial law, although there is a large area of overlap between the two sets of rules in practice. This is both because VAT is a European tax, and cannot be confined by the commercial rules of any one country, and also because the aim of VAT is different. It is to ensure that the tax is collected regardless of the legal niceties of a particular transaction. See, for example, the early case of *CEC v Oliver* (1980). The High Court had to decide whether a sale through a car auction that was later established to be a void contract was a "supply". Under commercial law principles it was not, but the judge rejected the analogy and found it was a supply.

24–27   UNLAWFUL TRANSACTIONS   On that basis, the ECJ has made it clear that the principle of fiscal neutrality requires that there be no general distinction between lawful and unlawful transactions. If VAT were not levied on the latter then the unlawful trader would in effect receive a tax subsidy as against the lawful trader making a similar supply. Only trades which are per se illegal and so cannot be performed lawfully such as illegal drugs, are outside the neutrality principle.[21] A straightforward theft is not however a supply by the victim to the thief.[22]

24–28   SELF-SUPPLIES   VAT is a tax on trading transactions, and the main base of the tax is commercial sales. More broadly, the tax operates when someone does something that realises value to that person from some other person. The word used for this is *supply*. I supply you with, say, buttered toast or a musical performance, and you pay me. But I cannot, in the ordinary sense, supply myself with the buttered toast. Nor do I supply myself with the butter or the loaf that I use to make the meal. In other words, self-supply is not a supply. Where, for example, a manufacturer makes bolts that are then used by that manufacturer in making windows to sell to others, the manufacturer

---

[21] *Staastssecretaris van Financiën v Coffeeshop Siberië vof* (1999) ECJ.
[22] *British American Tobacco International Ltd v Belgian State* (2006) ECJ.

supplies windows, not bolts. There must be a customer for there to be a supply.

Exceptions to this general rule exist to avoid distortion of competition in certain market sectors. The exceptions are limited, and in the United Kingdom they are confined to: self-supplies of motor vehicles by vehicle manufacturers, self-supplies of commercial buildings by building developers in certain circumstances, and self-supplies of printed stationery.

DEFINING A SUPPLY   Neither British nor EC VAT laws define   24–29
supply, beyond the vague guidance in the VAT Act that "supply ... includes all forms of supply". Nor is a general definition possible. This is because the English term *supply*, useful and concise though it is, is a term untranslatable into many western European languages. There is therefore no equivalent of it in the French original EC text, or the German, Spanish or other official texts. Any attempt at defining supply must therefore be made in the context of the kind of supply, of goods or of services.

PASSING OF TITLE   Despite the warning set out above, law-   24–30
yers looking at the concept of a supply of goods will be tempted to turn to the commercial law of their own systems to establish when the goods transfer from supplier to customer. Under commercial law rules, that usually occurs when ownership, title, or risk transfers. Of course, if there is title reservation, then ownership does not transfer, although risk may. Is there a supply when goods are handed over, but the ownership is not, and is it relevant that risk passes? For VAT purposes, there are two issues here. First, a supply of the use of goods (for example, equipment leasing) is not a supply of goods at all—it is a supply of services. Secondly, a supply of goods does not always take place if and when the local commercial laws determine that title has transferred. This is because supply is a European concept. The Directive, having refrained from defining supply, defines instead *supply of goods* as *the transfer of the right to dispose of tangible property as owner* (Art.14). Following this, the ECJ has ruled that in the case of a supply of goods it is not relevant whether title to the goods has passed under the national law: *Staatssecretaris van Financiën v SAFE BV* (1991).

IDENTITY OF SUPPLIER   Similarly, although the identity of the   24–31
supplier is usually simply a matter of contract law, where VAT is concerned the position must be looked at from an EU perspective—has there been a transfer of tangible property by X so as to empower Y to dispose of it as if he were the owner. If so,

then the fact that there is no contract between X and Y, because X is simply carrying out Z's contractual obligations to Y, will not affect the issue. There is still a supply by Z to Y. But if the contract between Z and Y is partially novated so as to create a contract between X and Y, then there will be a supply to Y by X and not by Z.[23]

24–32   TAX ON CONSUMPTION   VAT is in essence a tax on consumption. In *Parker Hale Ltd v CEC* (2000) this was held to include the voluntary handing-in of handguns in return for compensation from the Government. A supply of goods would give rise to consumption wherever a right was acquired to dispose of those goods as owner. In that context the fact that the Government intended to destroy the handguns was irrelevant. That case was followed by the Court of Appeal in *Stewart v CEC* (2002)—a supply included the transfer of the whole property in the goods and consumption could be presumed irrespective of the motives or intentions of the recipient.

24–33   SERVICES   The definition of *supply* in the context of a supply of services is even more difficult to establish. It is intertwined with two other definitions, that of services, and that of consideration. This is clear from the British law itself: "anything which is not a supply of goods but is done for a consideration (including, if so done, the granting, assignment or surrender of any right) is a supply of services" (s.5(2)). In *Trinity Mirror Plc v CEC* (2002), it was accepted by the Court of Appeal, upholding the decision of the judge below, that there were six characteristics of a supply of services. In addition to it not being a supply of goods (see the next paragraph) and being done for consideration, the characteristics are: that it must have constituted a transaction; that something must have been done by the supplier; that which was done must have been capable of being used by and for the benefit of an identified recipient; and that benefit must be regarded as a cost component of the activity of another person in the commercial chain.

There was no requirement that the activity had to be part of the company's turnover, as in income or corporation tax. Thus issuing shares to raise funds was a supply of services by the company.[24]

---

[23] See the analysis in *Telewest Communications Plc v CEC* (2005) CA.

[24] But not raising money by borrowing—in that case the supply was made to the company. Remember it is always essential to identify the exact nature of the supply.

Goods and services

There is no general definition in the United Kingdom VAT legislation of *goods*. Instead, we must turn to Sch.4 to the VAT Act. There we are told (in para.1) that a transfer of the whole property in goods is a supply of goods, but anything less is a supply of services. Likewise, the transfer of possession as part of an agreement for sale is a supply of goods, as is transfer of possession where a sale expressly contemplated. A credit sale or hire-purchase is therefore a supply of goods. Equipment leasing, where a sale might occur, is not.

24–34

The main point to grasp is that "goods and services" for VAT purposes can mean whatever the Treasury want them to mean. They can by order treat any transaction as a supply of goods, or of services, or as neither (s.5).

LAND ETC Land is an example of this. Land cannot be moved, so it cannot be goods. But neither is it a service. What, then, do we make of the provision that the supply of a major interest in land is a supply of goods (para.3). For VAT purposes, land has to be deemed to be goods or services. This is because, as we have seen, anything which is not goods is a service. In the binary world of VAT, a sale of land, or of a lease of more than 21 years (a major interest: s.96) is a supply of goods. All else to do with land is a supply of services.

24–35

The same is true of other forms of property that do not naturally fit into the deliberately simplified framework of VAT. Supplies of intellectual property, and of the right to use that property are alike treated as supplies of services, even when title is transferred. (This is implied by para.1 of Sch.5.) Supplies of electricity and similar intangibles are supplies of goods (Sch.4, para.3).

GOODS AND SERVICES Tricky problems also occur where a supply is both goods and services. For example, the supply of buttered toast is a supply of the butter, the bread, and the effort of toasting and buttering the bread. Is that goods or services or both? The practical answer may be that it does not matter. The difference between goods and services is only of importance if it changes the amount of tax due, or when the tax is due. The only general difference between goods and service lies in the timing rules about when supplies occur. Otherwise, the problem is the more detailed one of whether a particular supply is charged at one rate of VAT or another. In our example, the tax rate on buttered toast is different to the tax rate on a loaf of bread, so

24–36

the detail is important. We return to it when we deal with tax rates.

Consideration

24–37   A supply is only subject to VAT if it is made *for consideration*, or is deemed to be made for consideration. The idea behind this requirement is an economic one. To be taxable, a transaction must be one that adds value. Consequently, unless in some way value is realised from a supply, there is nothing to tax. In practice, value is realised if the supplier gets paid for the supply. If nobody pays, there is no added value. It is in this way that the rule has been interpreted by the European Court, in a case which nicely illustrates the clash between traditional English thinking and the more general approach required for VAT.

24–38   EUROPEAN MEANING In *Apple and Pear Development Council v CEC (1988)*, the Council carried out two groups of activities. The first group was of ordinary trading activities. The second group comprised activities financed by a statutory levy, and required by the law establishing the Council. The Council claimed that all its activities were for consideration. Much of the argument about this was framed in terms of the English law of contract. Was the statutory levy consideration for the supplies made to those who paid the levy of the statutory services? The case was argued in this way until it came to the House of Lords. The House noted that the point was one of European law, not English law, and found a reference to the ECJ was necessary.

The European Court noted that the question was a general one. Based on a linguistic analysis of the multilingual forms of the texts of the directives, the court laid down the test that there must be a payment for a supply, and that the payment and supply must be directly linked. In accordance with practice, the European Court left it for the national court to determine whether there was a direct link on the facts of the particular case.

24–39   DIRECT LINK The direct link test means that not all supplies for which payments are made are supplies for consideration (or against payment). There must be a legal relationship between the parties,[25] reciprocal performance and the remuneration received must constitute the value actually given by the provider.

---

[25] This was established in *Stewart v CEC (2002)*, because once the scheme (handing in of hand guns) had been promulgated and acted upon, the owner could insist on its being carried out.

The European Court itself has ruled in several cases that there was no such direct link; e.g. donations to a street musician[26] payments to a farmer in return for not using land,[27] and the provision of free transport by an employer for its employees.[28]

But there is no need for the supplier to be legally bound to provide all the services, e.g. in a "spot the ball" competition where payment of the prize money was not legally enforceable. There was reciprocity and the amount paid related directly to the services.[29]

USING NON-TAXABLE AGENTS   In the United Kingdom the issue has arisen originally mainly in connection with supplies by clothing and other companies through "hostesses" holding parties in their own homes. Thus in *Rosgill Group Ltd v CEC* (1997)[30] at such a party sufficient goods were sold to entitle the hostess either to take a cash commission of £2.89 or to obtain a discount on a blouse of £7.23. She chose the latter, thus paying some £20 for a blouse priced at £28. The Court of Appeal held that the consideration for the supply of the blouse by the company to the hostess was not only the cash she paid but also the holding of the party. There was a direct link between the latter and the supply of the blouse, both contractually (she was entitled to the discount) and causatively (without the party there would have been no supply of the blouse at the reduced price).   24-40

DISCOUNT OR CONSIDERATION   The question in such cases is whether the price reduction or cash commission received by the agents is simply a discount on the single transaction (e.g. of the sale of the blouse) or whether the agents have provided some form of consideration, usually in the form of services, for that reduction, so that there is in effect additional consideration provided by the agent for the supply (e.g. of the blouse) to him or her by the main supplier. In that latter case, as we shall see (in Ch.26), there is no discount for VAT purposes at all. In *CEC v Littlewoods Organisation Plc* (2001), the Court of Appeal held on the facts that there was no direct link between the agent's right to take commission on sales made by him or her in the form of a reduction in the price of goods supplied to the agent and any services provided by the agent to Littlewoods. This was   24-41

---

[26] *Tolsma v Inspecteur der Omzetbelasting Leenwarden* (1994).
[27] *Landboden-Agrardienste GmbH & Co KG v Finanzamt Calau* (1998).
[28] *Julius Fillibeck Söhne GmbH & Co KG v Finanzamt Neustadt* (1998).
[29] *Town and Country Factors Ltd v CEC* (2002).
[30] See also *Naturally Yours Cosmetics Ltd v CEC* (1988).

in the main because it was impossible to tell whether that commission had been earned in respect of purchases by the agent on his or her own account or on purchases negotiated by the agent by third parties—the right to the commission was simply triggered by a payment of money by the agent to Littlewoods.

24–42   NON-CASH CONSIDERATION   But if it is clear that the right to the commission is linked to the supply of goods or services to a third party, negotiated by the agent, then it seems that there will be a direct link between the supply of those services by the agent to the main supplier and the commission. It follows that if that is taken in the form of discounted goods[31] it will amount to the provision of non-cash consideration by the agent for those goods as in *Rosgill*.[32] This distinction can produce some strange results which seem difficult at times to reconcile with the principle of fiscal neutrality.[33] We shall return to it again in Ch.26 when we consider the actual value of a supply—at this stage we are merely identifying what the supply is made in return for. In *CEC v Euphony Communications Ltd* (2004), Hart J. took a different route by regarding the supply of services by the agent (in introducing a new customer) as a separate supply by the agent so that the consideration for that supply (the commission in the form of a price reduction on goods) could not be a discount.

24–43   PART EXCHANGE DEALS   The same Court of Appeal in *Littlewoods* also heard the cases of *Lex Services Plc v CEC* and *CEC v Bugeja* which involved part exchange deals. They upheld the principle that the goods tendered in part exchange must form part of the consideration for the supply. The *Lex Services* case has since been upheld by the House of Lords (2004). The question which then arises is what value is to be attributed to those goods. Again we will come back to that in Ch.26.

Specific problems concerning supplies of goods or services

24–44   The basic requirement of a supply of goods or services for a consideration has led to a number of specific problems for the courts to deal with. Three of these are sufficiently fundamental to VAT as to require some consideration at this point.

---

[31] If taken purely in the form of a cash payment then there is no supply of goods or services to the agent for which it can form consideration.

[32] See e.g. *Bertelsmann AG v Finanzamt Wiedenbruck* (2001).

[33] See [2002] BTR 179.

IDENTIFYING WHAT IS SUPPLIED AND TO WHOM VAT **24–45**
depends upon a supply to fix upon for there to be a charge.
Sometimes identifying exactly who is supplying what and to
whom is far from straightforward, but by doing so the VAT
position is thereby clarified. In *CEC v Diners Club Ltd* (1989)
an everyday cash card transaction whereby the card holder used
his card to buy goods from a retailer so that there was an
assignment of the debt by the retailer to the card company and
the payment of that debt by the company less commission, was
held to constitute a supply of financial services by the card
company to the retailer, in addition to the supply by the retailer
to the card company.

THIRD PARTY SUPPLIES In *Trustees of Nell Gwyn House* **24–46**
Maintenance Fund v CEC (1999) the trustees of a maintenance
fund for a block of flats were required and did employ staff to
provide maintenance, etc. of the building. The House of Lords
held that they were supplying the whole services of the staff to
the tenants (i.e. the total cost of the operation) and not just the
act of arranging for the staff to work (i.e. the organisation costs
only). There is a clear distinction between A paying B for services to be provided by B, and A putting B in funds so that B
could arrange for C to provide the services. This was clearly the
former.

Similarly, if A supplies goods to B for a sum, out of which A **24–47**
will have to pay C for services rendered to A, A will have to
account for VAT on the whole amount received from B. Only if
the services were provided by C to B will the amount paid to C
be deductible from the supply by A. This distinction was applied
in *Debenhams Retail Plc v CEC* (2005).[34] Debenhams sold say a
coat for £100 but purported to say, in their till receipt, that if
this was a store card purchase, that £97.50 was paid to
Debenhams for the coat and £2.50 to DRS, an independent
Debenhams company, for the provision of financial services (an
exempt supply). The CA held that on the facts there was only
one contract and one supply, by Debenhams for £100. Thus
output tax had to be accounted for on the full amount. But, even
on the assumption that there had been two contracts, the consideration for the supply by Debenhams would still have been
£100.

THE PLANTIFLOR CASE This distinction was central to the **24–48**
decision in *CEC v Plantiflor Ltd* (2002). The company supplied

---

[34] See [2006] BTR 54.

plants to customers partly by mail order. Delivery, if requested, was by Parcelforce and £2.50 was charged for postage and packing of which £1.63 related to the charge by Parcelforce. The Court of Appeal held that there were three supplies. The first was of the goods by Plantiflor to the customer; the second was of the service of arranging delivery of the goods and packaging the goods, also by Plantiflor to the customer; and the third was of the actual delivery which was supplied by Parcelforce to the customer. There was no fourth supply of services by Parcelforce to Plantiflor. On that analysis the consideration for the supply by Plantiflor to the customer could not include the £1.63 since it was the consideration for the supply by Parcelforce to the customer and to hold otherwise would be to impose VAT twice on the same consideration (although in that case the supply by Parcelforce was in fact an exempt supply).

The House of Lords came to a different conclusion, however, which had also been favoured by the judge but not the Tribunal. By a majority (4 to 1) they considered that the delivery to the customer by Parcelforce was made solely under a contract with Plantiflor acting as principal and not as an agent for the customer. It followed that the only supply of the delivery of the goods for a consideration was made by Parcelforce to Plantiflor (i.e. there *was* a fourth supply). The £1.63 was paid by the customer to Plantiflor not for delivery of the goods but for the supply of the benefit of its arrangement with Parcelforce to deliver goods to them free of any charge to the customer (who was never under any obligation to pay Parcelforce anything). It was therefore part of the consideration paid for that supply by Plantiflor. In effect, Plantiflor were supplying the delivery services of Parcelforce as part of their overall supply to the customer in the same way as the trustees in the *Nell Gwyn* case were supplying the maintenance services.

24–49   PARALLEL OR SIMULTANEOUS SUPPLIES   The case of *Loyalty Management UK Ltd v HMRC* (2007) raised the issue as to whether A could in a single transaction make two supplies, one of goods to B (the final consumer of the goods) and one of services to C (a trader). C had made a payment to A and was claiming an input tax credit on that payment. The company (C) operated the Nectar rewards card scheme. The collector (B) using the scheme, accumulated points by shopping at certain stores and garages, which could then be used to redeem goods from one of a list of specified suppliers (A). The example used in the case was where B had accumulated 20,000 points and was thus, by redeeming them, able to obtain a television worth £100 from A. A was then reimbursed £80 by C (the difference being part of C's profits). C now claimed that there had been a supply of services by A to C (that being the redemption of C's obligations to B under the scheme). The judge refused to allow the claim, regarding the payment by C as simply providing third party consideration for the (sole) supply of the goods to B.

The Court of Appeal disagreed. Whilst it was true that there could be no parallel supply of goods to C in those circumstances, since C was never entitled to the goods (e.g. the television, above) at all,[35] it was clear law that there could be a parallel supply of services to C.[36] The House of Lords had earlier held that there could be parallel supplies of services by A to both B and C, in circumstances such as the present case; i.e. where B was the final consumer and C made a payment and claimed input tax credit. All that was needed was a payment by C to B, which represented consideration for services supplied to C by B, and the use of those services in the course of C's business. All those features were present. C did receive value in return for the payment. The claim was therefore allowed, there being no difference simply because one of the parallel supplies was one of goods.

A similar analysis was made by the Court of Appeal in *Baxi Group Ltd v HMRC* (2008) concerning the payment by the sponsoring company to the scheme operator in respect of goods supplied by the latter to the customer. Such payments were for services, including the discharge of the company's obligations to the customer.

SINGLE TRANSACTION—MULTIPLE OR SEPARATE SUPPLIES   24–50

What is the position when in return for a single consideration a person receives several benefits? Are these separate supplies, (so that some might be exempt or taxed at different rates) or can they be taken together to form a single supply? If the answer is the latter then a second question is whether that multiple supply is one of goods or one of services or exempt, or zero-rated, etc.

This problem has arisen several times. In *British Airways Plc v CEC* (1990)[37] the Court of Appeal held that a supply of in-flight catering on a domestic flight was integral to the flight itself and so was not a separate supply. In *CEC v United Biscuits (UK) Ltd*

---

[35] Following the ECJ's decision in *Auto Lease Holland BV v Bundesamt für Finanzen* (2005).

[36] Applying the analysis in *CEC v Redrow Group Plc* (1999) HL. See [2008] BTR 17 and Ch.26, below.

[37] See also *Virgin Atlantic Airways Ltd v CEC* (1995).

(1992) the Court of Session in deciding that a supply of biscuits in a decorative tin was a supply of biscuits which happened to be in such a container and not a separate supply of the biscuits and container, said that the test was whether one supply was either an integral part of the other or incidental to it. In *CEC v Wellington Hospital* (1997) the Court of Appeal said that in applying this test it was not appropriate to look at the whole transaction and see whether one part of it was ancillary to the whole, but rather to ask whether one element was so dominated by another that it lost its separate identity for tax purposes.

24–51 PRINCIPAL/ANCILLARY TEST The situation was initially clarified by the ECJ in *Card Protection Plan Ltd v CEC* (1999). It is essential to identify the essential features of the transaction. In particular there will be a single supply if one or more elements can be regarded as the principal supply and others can be regarded as ancillary. "Ancillary" in the context of services means that it does not constitute an aim in itself but only a means for customers of better enjoying the principal service supplied. Itemising the different services in price terms might be significant, but is not conclusive.

That principal/ancillary test i.e. (a) is one part of a supply of services really ancillary to another part, and (b) ancillary for that purpose meaning that it does not constitute an aim in itself but is only a means of better enjoying the principal service supplied, was adopted in relation to supplies of services by the courts on several subsequent occasions. The House of Lords itself, having originally referred the matter to the ECJ, had to apply that Court's test to the facts of *Card Protection* itself. That company insured credit card holders against loss but also kept a register of the cards and notified the credit companies if they were lost or stolen. The House of Lords ruled that it was important to determine the essential element of the supply, which in that case was the insurance. The other elements were mainly administrative and so ancillary to that element. Their Lordships stressed that the question should be answered from an economic point of view and courts should refrain from making over zealous or artificial divisions.[38]

---

[38] See also *CEC v BT Plc* (1999) in relation to a delivery charge on the purchase of a new car; *Pilgrims Language Course Ltd v CEC* (1999), accommodation on residential educational courses; *Peugeot Motor Co Plc v CEC* (2003), free car insurance on a new car.

THE ARTIFICIAL TO SPLIT TEST In two cases, however, the **24–52**
House of Lords extended the test from that originally derived
from the *Card Protection* case. The principal/ancillary test was
said to be only appropriate to certain cases.[39] There were many
cases where although one aspect of the supply was in no way
ancillary to the other, there would still a single supply. Referring
back to the *Card Protection* decision, their Lordships applied a
second, alternative test, which might be called the "artificial to
split test". The ECJ in *Card Protection* had emphasised that the
normal rule was that every supply was to be regarded as a
separate and distinct supply but that supplies which constituted
a single service from an economic point of view should not be
artificially split, as that would distort the system of VAT.

Applying that test, their Lordships held in *Dr Beynon and
Partners v CEC* (2005) that although diagnosing and then pre-
scribing medicines were in no way ancillary to their
administration, the whole was from an economic point of view a
single supply of medical services. Similarly it was held in *College
of Estate Management v CEC* (2005) that although course
materials provided in a distance-learning package (amounting to
94 per cent of the costs) could not be said to be ancillary to the
teaching element, there was, from an economic point of view, a
single supply of educational services and not a separate supply
of the materials. To achieve these results, their Lordships said
that the analysis should seek to achieve "a level of generality,
consistent with economic and social reality." In both cases they
overruled the Court of Appeal who had instead asked whether
from the purchaser's point of view each supply was capable of
being a separate independent supply.[40]

Applying this test is a matter of law and the courts may disagree
with the Tribunal. In *Weight Watchers (UK) Ltd v HMRC*
(2008), the judge upheld the decision of the Tribunal that at the
initial meeting of Weight Watchers a client was given separate
supplies of literature and weight reducing services, but reversed
their decision that the same applied to subsequent meetings
attended by the client. On the artificial to split test that was a
single supply of weight reducing services. The Court of Appeal
agreed with him on subsequent meetings, but reversed him on the
initial meeting point. In *Birkdale School Sheffield v HMRC*
(2008), the judge disagreed with the Tribunal and held that a

---

[39] See also *Kimberley-Clark Ltd* v CEC (2004) as to the application of the test to
a composite supply of goods rather than goods and services and the need to
distinguish between the supply to the retailer and then to the customer.
[40] See [2005] BTR 190; [2006] BTR 54.

separately costed scheme which allowed parents to obtain a partial refund of school fees if their child was absent ill from school, was simply a part of the overall provision of educational services to the parents. The fact of a separate payment was not conclusive. In those cases, however, both judges thought that the same result would have been obtained by applying the principal/ancillary test.

This test has also been applied where the customer pays for the right to a number of services, e.g. to the use of various leisure facilities provided by the supplier. Where there is no specific allocation of each service, it is not possible to itemise the supply by reference to subsequent use by the customer. There is a single supply at the time of the contract of the right to use the various services. This was the decision of the Court of Session in *Highland Council v HMRC* (2008). It is different if the supply is of the right to a single service (at say a reduction), as in *British Railways Board v CEC* (1977).

24–53   CATEGORISING THE SINGLE SUPPLY   If the decision is that there is a single composite supply, it is of course necessary to categorise that supply for the purposes of applying VAT to it (e.g. is it an exempt or zero-rated supply). This will be done by identifying, in the economic and reality context set out above, the predominant elements of the supply.[41]

24–54   TWO SUPPLIERS   The Court of Appeal, in *Telewest Communications Plc v CEC* (2005) held that there can be no single supply if the two supplies are actually made by separate suppliers—fiscal neutrality should not be confused with economic reality.

24–55   LIMITATIONS ON EFFECT OF FINDING A SINGLE COMPOSITE SUPPLY   In *Talacre Beach Caravan Sales Ltd v CEC* (2006), a question arose as to what the position would be if a composite supply consisting of elements A (caravan) and B (certain fittings) was found to be a single supply, with supply A being the predominant supply, if that supply was within a zero-rated category, but B was expressly excluded from that category by the legislation. Could the single supply categorisation take B into the zero-rated category and so in effect override the legislation. The ECJ was clear that it could not and that the same would also apply to the categories of exempt supply.[42]

---

[41]   *Levob Verzekeringen BV v Staatssecrataris van Financiën* (2006) ECJ; *Byrom v HMRC* (2006).
[42]   See [2007] BTR 17 as to the possible consequences of this decision, and *Hartwell v CEC* (2003).

Where there are two supplies to different customers but only one payment of consideration by one customer

This problem arises because just as in income tax, and for similar reasons, VAT has a rule that where a business makes a supply of business assets otherwise than for a consideration then there is a deemed supply at the cost to the supplier (Sch.4, para.5).[43] In *CEC v Telemed Ltd* (1992), Telemed produced medical videos which it distributed free to doctors. The videos contained advertisements for drug companies for which it charged a fee. It was argued that the company was therefore making two supplies, one of the services to the drug companies for a fee and one of the videos to the doctors which were caught by para.5. This was rejected by the judge on the basis that the company only supplied the videos as part of its contractual obligation to the advertisers. This approach was followed by the House of Lords in *CEC v Professional Footballers Association* (1993) in deciding that trophies presented at an annual dinner and met out of the cost of tickets for the dinner were not separate supplies under para.5. There was a direct link between the consideration paid for the tickets and the awards.

24–56

Taxable supplies and exempt supplies

All supplies within the scope of the tax are taxable supplies unless they are exempt supplies (VAT Act, s.4 (2)). A supply is exempt if, and only if, it is one of the kinds of supply listed in Schedule 9 to the 1994 Act. This copies into the United Kingdom law directly operative provisions of EC law. Exemption covers some major kinds of economic activity such as financial supplies and many kinds of health, education and welfare activity. Some UK supplies are taxable but at zero-rate. We will examine some of these in the next chapter.

24–57

In the United Kingdom

The Directive contains a number of provisions to establish where a supply of goods (arts 31–42) and services (arts 43–61) takes place. These raise many complex issues which are outside the scope of this book. The basic rules are that a supply of goods takes place where the goods are located at the time of the supply or where they are located prior to dispatch to the customer. For

24–58

---

[43] Such as gifts given by petrol companies to customers who have collected vouchers: *Kuwait Petroleum GB Ltd v CEC* (1999). Whether there has been a supply for no consideration requires an analysis of what the parties thought they were agreeing to. See *Kuwait Petroleum GB Ltd v CEC* (2001) and *Peugeot Motor Company Ltd v CEC* (2003).

services it is the place where the supplier has his business or establishment or, failing that, his usual residential address. There are many special rules, however.

Taxable persons

24–59   The structure of European VAT is such that anyone making a taxable supply for consideration can be regarded as a taxable person. United Kingdom VAT does not work this way. Instead, it sets a threshold of activity before the imposition is necessary. Anyone whose level of activities is at or above the level of the threshold is required to register with the VAT office for the locality, and to impose VAT on all taxable supplies made. If there is a failure to register, VAT will be deemed to have been charged by the taxpayer. Those not required to register may, however do so on a voluntary basis. A person who has the intention, confirmed by objective evidence, to commence independently an economic activity and who has incurred the first investment expenditure for that purpose is a taxable person and so able to claim input tax even without a formal registration.[44]

24–60   CHARITIES, PUBLIC BODIES   For VAT purposes, a *person* is any individual or any body of persons with separate legal personality (such as a company or limited liability partnership) that is engaged in economic activities. This includes non-profit organisations that do not pay income tax or corporation tax such as charities and clubs as well as companies. Article 13 of the Directive provides that national and local government bodies, and others "governed by public law" are taxable persons for a limited number of purposes and where their treatment as non-taxable persons would lead to a significant distortion of competition. But otherwise they are not to be taxable persons "in respect of the activities in which they engage as public authorities" and, even better, in respect of certain exempt supplies they are better off if they are so regarded. There are often difficult questions as to whether a body is so operating as a public authority and the courts are wary of laying down binding rules.[45]

24–61   PARTNERSHIPS   In addition, a partnership despite its lack of legal personality is also treated as a separate person (unlike the income tax approach). A partnership is therefore separate from the individual partners and is registered as the taxable person.

---

[44] *Finanzamt Goslar* v *Breitsohl* (2001).
[45] See e.g. *Edinburgh Telford College v HMRC* (2006) CS (IH) and cases discussed there.

The liability for VAT remains a partnership debt, however, so that all apparent partners remain liable, even if they have ceased to be partners, until HMRC has either been informed of the change or the partnership has been de-registered.[46] An individual partner may have a separate registration for other business activities, including making supplies to the firm.[47]

GROUPS ETC. Companies and other large organisations can **24–62**
register divisions or separate parts of the organisation separately. For example, if only part of an organisation is making supplies to which VAT applies, that part can register separately from any other part. This excludes those other parts from the requirements of VAT, but it also means that any supplies made by that part of the organisation to the other parts are subject to VAT.

By contrast, a group of companies can make a common registration for VAT in the name of one of the companies. Where this happens, supplies between companies within the group are outside the scope of the tax. It is only supplies by the group to others that are caught. For this purpose, two companies are in a group if both are based in the United Kingdom and one controls the other or both are controlled by the same third person (VAT Act, s.43A).[48] Each of the companies must be involved in an economic activity, so that a company that is purely a holding company has to be left out (*Polsar Investments* (1993)). This sensible idea of grouping has been abused widely. The result is that anti-avoidance provisions were introduced by the Finance Acts 1996 and 1999 designed to counteract the spurious use of grouping. Even these failed to prevent abuses and the Finance Act 2004 allowed for further criteria to be introduced in limited circumstances, in the form of targets. No company can be in two VAT groups at the same time.

REGISTRATION THRESHOLDS A person (in the sense just **24–63**
described) is required to register for VAT if the total turnover from taxable supplies in any period of 12 months is currently £67,000 or more or if there are reasonable grounds to believe that the rates of taxable supplies in the next 30 days will exceed £67,000. (These are the 2008 figures—they are adjusted every year.) Any exempt supplies or supplies outside the scope of VAT are excluded from the total. The total is calculated on the

---

[46] *CEC v Jamieson* (2002).
[47] *Staatssecretaris van Financiën v Heerma* (2001).
[48] Group registration, once obtained, is only lost where either the company as the CEC takes formal steps: *CEC v Barclays Bank Plc* (2001).

assumption that no VAT is charged on the supplies. Note that the amount is for turnover, not profit. It is irrelevant that the person is making a loss, or is not in business to make a profit. It also applies to persons, not to businesses. If I run two businesses, one as a farmer, and one as a sports journalist, I must account for total turnover from both my activities even though they may be treated separately for income tax purposes. The test is applied each month on a rolling basis. However, if the person can show that supplies for the current year are below £65,000 (in 2008), then the requirement to register does not apply. There is some scope for abuse of this provision by dividing turnover between different legal persons to ensure each is below the limit. Where that happens, the VAT office has the right to impose a group registration to bring all the associated avoiders into the tax net.

24-64   VOLUNTARY REGISTRATION   A person not required to register under any of these provisions has the right to register on a voluntary basis. Why should anyone want to become a taxpayer voluntarily? In the case of a tax like income tax, there are few, if any, good reasons. VAT is not a tax like income tax. As we shall see later, a VAT payer may actually receive money from the government, rather than pay it. Few businesses can resist a government handout!

A further reason is that those who are registered for VAT usually prefer to buy from others who are registered—it is cheaper. Someone who expects to have to register a business in any event may find it advantageous to register before being compelled to do so. Not all traders that could ask for voluntary registration do so. Some refrain from registering in order to avoid VAT. The irony is that they end up paying more VAT by doing so. We see why in the next chapters.

Economic activities

24–65   The final element in the structure of VAT is that activities are only relevant if they are economic activities of the taxable person (in art.9 of the Directive) or, in the United Kingdom text, *in the course or furtherance of a business carried on by him*. In this phrase, business is defined as including any trade profession or vocation (s.94). In practice, although the United Kingdom legislation has continued to use the reference to business, it is more accurate to think of the more general, and broader, European phrase. In part, this is because it is clear that VAT is wider than the implicit reference in s.94 to the income taxation of trading etc. income might imply.

BUSINESS The early cases, using the UK text, concentrated **24–66** on the meaning of a "business". Thus in *CEC v Royal Exchange Theatre Trust* (1979) the raising of money by a charitable trust to convert the Manchester Corn Exchange into a theatre and the subsequent gift of the theatre was held not to be a business. Similarly a charity that supplied goods to beneficiaries without payment, or for a token fee, was not acting as a business: *Whitechapel Art Gallery v CEC* (1986), where the running of an art gallery to which free admission was granted was accepted as outside the scope of VAT. An interesting example of a marginal case is the decision in *Lord Fisher v CEC* (1981), which established that shooting (and equally hunting and fishing) one's own land with one's own friends contributing to one's costs is not always a business.

ECONOMIC ACTIVITY Modern cases are now argued on the **24–67** basis of the "economic activities" test in the Directive. The House of Lords in *ICAEW v CEC* (1999) had to decide whether the regulatory services provide by the Institute of Chartered Accountants on behalf of the Government in respect of insolvency practitioners, licensed auditors, etc., fell within VAT. After reviewing the decisions of the ECJ, they held that the Institute was not carrying on an economic activity. It was not enough that it was making supplies for a consideration, there was no element of commercial activity. What was needed were activities of an economic nature.[49]

EXPLOITATION OF PROPERTY The Directive includes the **24–68** exploitation of property within the definition of an economic activity. The ECJ has stated that exploitation in that context refers to all transactions by which it is sought to obtain income from the property on a continuing basis. But it has held that the activity by governments of allocating frequencies and then licences for mobile phone operators was not such an activity. It was a precondition to the carrying on of an economic activity by the telephone companies.[50]

OBJECTIVE CONCEPT The ECJ in *Optigen Ltd v CEC* (2006) **24–69** made it clear that whether an activity is an economic activity has

---

[49] See also *University of Southampton v HMRC* (2006), as to publicly funded research undertaken by the university.

[50] *T-Mobile Austria GmbH v Republic of Austria* [2008] S.T.C. 184 ECJ; *Hutchinson 3G UK Ltd v HMRC* [2008] S.T.C. 218 ECJ. In both cases the Advocate General came to the opposite, and it would seem more logical, conclusion that this was the exploitation of intangible property.

to be decided on purely objective grounds. The motive of the person making it is irrelevant. Thus a transaction which is not itself in any way fraudulent and fulfils the objective criteria of commerciality, is an economic activity even though it forms part of an overall fraudulent or tax avoidance scheme. Further, if the trade is lawful, there is an economic activity irrespective of whether any trader is acting fraudulently or not: see *R. v Hashash* (2008), applying decisions of the ECJ.

24–70   SERVICES   Article 9 of the Directive states that an economic activity includes all activities of producers, traders or persons supplying services, and in particular the exploitation of tangible or intangible property for the purpose of obtaining income therefrom on a continuing basis. This has been widely defined but it does not include the mere acquisition, holding and transfer of shares in a company. A private shareholder as such is not a taxable person. This also applies to any purely financial holding in any undertaking.[51] Most recently it has been held to exclude the entry of a partner into a partnership in return for a payment of capital.[52]

24–71   ACTING AS SUCH   The tax applies to economic activities of taxable persons *acting as such*. An individual buying a house to live in, or buying a car for private use, is not engaging in an economic activity but a private activity. This is true also when the house or car is sold. There is a complication here to which we must return. If a private person sells a car, there is no VAT on the sale. If a car dealer sells it, there is VAT. The same thing applies to antiques, and to horses and ponies. Whether VAT applies therefore partly depends on the identity of the seller, not the kind of goods. This can cause problems, and special rules apply to these occasional or secondhand goods.

Agents and employees

Employees

24–72   VAT only applies to a person carrying on an economic activity or business. The most important group of people excluded from VAT by this rule are employees. An employee is carrying on the employer's business as agent, and is not in business by himself or herself. VAT therefore does not apply to the payment of earnings by employer to employee. If the employee's services are supplied to some third party, any VAT is

---

[51] See *Harnas & Helm CV v Staatssecretaris van Financiën* (1997) ECJ; *Wellcome Trust Ltd v CEC* (1996) ECJ.

[52] *KapHagRenditefonds 35 Spreecenter Berlin-Hellersdorf 3. Tranche GbR v Finanzamt Charlottenburg* (2005) ECJ.

applied to the charge made by the employer to the third party for those services. The effect of this important exclusion is that the added value on which someone is charged includes the total of all payments to employees.

The rule applies to office holders such as company directors as well, unless the office holder is holding that' office as part of a separate business. For example, a partner in a firm of solicitors may act as a director of a client's business in order to advise the client. Fees paid to the director, or the partnership, should be subject to VAT (s.94(4)).

Commercial agents

The position is more complex for other agents. By definition, **24–73** an agent is someone making supplies on behalf of someone else. If the person is an agent rather than an independent contractor, the supply is not made by the agent but by the agent's principal. It is therefore important to decide whether a person is making a supply on their own behalf or on behalf of a principal. This is mainly because of the registration threshold. If the supplies are made as agents then they will be counted towards the principal's total (who may well be registered for VAT anyway)—so VAT would be chargeable and accounted for by the principal. But taken individually, the suppliers, if acting as independent contractors, may well not reach the registration threshold and so no VAT would be chargeable. The latest colourful case on this involved dancers in a lap-dance club. They were held to be independent contractors and not agents for the club, which was not therefore liable to account for VAT in respect of their charges to the clients.[53]

UNDISCLOSED AGENCY There is a complication where the **24–74** identity of the principal is unknown to the buyer. Take the case of an auctioneer. The auctioned goods are not owned by the auctioneer, but the buyer usually does not know the identity of the seller. The buyer of, say, antique furniture has therefore no way of knowing if the seller is a registered person for VAT purposes, or whether the sale is an economic activity within the scope of VAT. At the same time, the only activity on which an auctioneer is liable for VAT as an agent is the service as an agent. To avoid complications, auctioneers and other agents where the agency is not disclosed are treated as making the supplies themselves. If the agency is disclosed, the VAT is imposed by the principal.

---

[53] *Spearmint Rhino Ventures (UK) Ltd v CRC* [2007] S.T.C. 1252.

CHAPTER 25

VAT RATES AND EXEMPTIONS

Introduction

25–01   If the British VAT were a simple form of value-added tax with a single rate, the previous chapter would have covered most of the problems. It is not, and it does not. In this chapter therefore we discuss the rate structure of the tax and the extensive way in which exemptions apply to the tax. In the next chapter we discuss the surprisingly complex problem as to how the value of a taxable supply is found and the rules as to the payment of the tax, including how input tax is deducted.

The VAT rate structure

25–02   The simplest form of VAT would have one rate of VAT applying equally to all goods and services. But the United Kingdom structure is far more complex.

The structure under the Directive

25–03   The Directive, in art.97, requires every Member State to have a standard rate of VAT of not less than 15 per cent. In addition, arts 98 and 99 allow for the use of one or even two reduced rate bands of VAT, of not less than 5 per cent, on certain specified supplies (listed in Annex III to the Directive). There are also special provisions (e.g. for supplies of gas and electricity) and a considerable number of "temporary" variations, often specific to a particular Member State. One of these allows the UK to maintain its anomalous zero-rated list of supplies.[1] The Directive (in Title IX) also lists those supplies which are exempt from the tax altogether and so cannot amount to taxable supplies. That list is mandatory.

The structure in the United Kingdom

25–04   The UK rate structure is as follows:

---

[1]   These are described in the Directive (art.110) as supplies with deductibility of the VAT paid at the preceding stage.

 (i) a standard rate of 17.5 per cent
 (ii) a reduced rate of 5 per cent on certain specified types of supply
 (iii) zero-rate (0 per cent) on another group of specified supplies
 (iv) special rates for special regimes such as the 4 per cent flat rate scheme for farmers
 (v) a general flat rate scheme for small businesses.

There are also the categories of exempt supply as required by the Directive.

ZERO-RATING AS A SUBSIDY   As a result, the United Kingdom   25–05
has one of the most complex rate structures for VAT in the developed world. The structure, particularly zero rating, gives scope for many disputes and distortions to competition. The United Kingdom is the only major system to use its VAT in this way as a subsidy for certain kinds of domestic activity. Why? The zero-rates reflect the exemptions that used to apply to taxes before VAT. However, the zero-rate in VAT is not the same thing as a zero sales tax. It is in reality a subsidy resulting in regular repayments of tax to those who sell zero-rated goods because since they are still making taxable supplies, they will have no output tax (zero-rated) but will be able to reclaim their input tax. Add to the predictable consumers' resistance at a rate increase, the pressure to retain the monthly tax rebate paid to those who are zero-rated, and we see why the lobby for the status quo is a strong one. This is so although it makes the British VAT one of the most inefficient around. We see a similar situation in the lower rate of VAT on domestic fuel supplies. The debate over the attempt to increase the VAT on domestic fuel to the standard rate from a zero-rate resulted in a government defeat in the Commons and the original compromise of 8 per cent has since been reduced to 5 per cent. It is precisely because of all this that we must spend some time looking at the rate structure.

APPLYING THE RATES   There is a strict order for determining   25–06
at what rate, if any, VAT applies to a supply:

1. Exclude any supply that is outside the scope of the tax, or deemed not to be a supply of goods or services. If it is not excluded:
2. See if the supply is exempt. If it is not exempt:

3. See if the supply is one of those listed as zero-rated. If it is not listed:
4. See if any special tax regime or reduced rate applies. If it does not:
5. Apply the standard rate.

The order is important because it means that anything to which a special category does not apply is to be taxed at the standard rate, without exception. The flat rate scheme for small business does not effect the actual rate applied to the supply, it relates, rather to the accountability of the supplier to HMRC. We noted the scope of the tax in the last chapter. We must now explore zero-rating, the reduced rate categories, exempt supplies, the special regimes and the flat rate scheme.

Zero-rated supplies

25–07 A supply is zero-rated if it is listed in Sch.8 to the 1994 Act. The Schedule is divided into (currently) 15 groups[2], several of which are of considerable complexity.

The policy of zero-rating

25–08 Several themes run through the Schedule. The first is of international supplies: see Group 7 (international services), Group 8 (transport), Group 10 (gold) and Group 13 (imports, exports, etc.) for the main relevant groups. The policy here is to ensure that no British VAT gets hidden in the cost of any goods or services offered on the international market. Any VAT imposed on a supply or its inputs in the United Kingdom before export is therefore rebated in full, and no VAT is applied on export. The purpose is to keep British goods and services as competitive as possible.

A second theme is that of supplies of a social or community nature. These include: Group 1 (food), Group 2 (domestic sewerage and water supplies), Group 3 (books), Group 4 (talking books for the blind), Group 5 (construction of homes and some other buildings), Group 6 (listed buildings), Group 8 (transport), Group 9 (houseboats and caravans used as homes), Group 12 (medicines), Group 15 (charities), and Group 16 (children's clothes and protective clothing).

25–09 THE UK'S FREEDOM OF ACTION The European Commission has always been opposed to this concept on the basis that it distorts the application of the tax. But the concept was sanc-

---

[2] Confusingly numbered 1–16. Gp.14 was repealed in 1999.

tioned by the ECJ in *EC Commission v UK* (1988) and is allowed as a "temporary measure" in art.110 of the Directive. It is referred to there (not entirely accurately) as supplies with refund of tax paid at the preceding stage. An attack based on the concept of direct effect failed before the Court of Appeal in *Marks and Spencer Plc v CEC* (2000).

The current status of zero-rating was discussed by the ECJ in *Talacre Beach Caravan Sales Ltd v CEC* (2006). The ECJ pointed out that it was a derogation from the obligation to charge the standard rate and that, as such, must not only be strictly construed (as are the categories of exempt supply) but is also subject to a number of conditions. These are principally that the categories must have been in force on January 1, 1991, and that they can only be allowed for clearly defined social reasons, for the benefit of the final consumer[3] and in accordance with Community Law. Thus the current list of zero-rated supplies is finite and can only be reduced by the UK Parliament. In the *Talacre* case itself, the ECJ held that the composite supply principle could not be used to zero-rate a supply which was expressly excluded by the Act.[4] As to other possible consequences of that decision see [2007] BTR 17.

Another anomaly thrown up by zero-rating is the decision in *HMRC v EB Central Services Ltd* (2008) that the words of Sch.8 are not to be interpreted in line with the Directive but as national law provisions. This is because they are by definition a derogation from the harmonised provisions of the Directive. In *Marks & Spencer Plc v HMRC* (2008), the ECJ further held that zero-rating confessed no Community rights, although the consequences of the misinterpretation of the national law were subject to the principle of equal treatment.

Food

One result of the attractiveness to suppliers of zero-rating is that Sch.8 is now of considerable complexity. Each group contains a detailed list of what exactly amounts to a zero-rated supply. This is especially true of Group 1 which is headed "Food". This is defined as any supply within four categories of which the most important is food of a kind used for human consumption. But that general class is subject to no less than seven lists of excepted items, which are therefore standard rated, unless they fall within a further seven lists of items overriding

25–10

---

[3] This means a non-business consumer. Thus, e.g. water supplies to industry (Gp 2) are not zero-rated.

[4] See para.24–55, above.

those excepted items, in which case they become zero-rated again.

25–11   Biscuits and cakes etc.   The intention is, we assume, to charge non-basic foodstuffs but to zero-rate the essentials of life. Thus zero-rating does not apply for example to confectionery but it does apply to cakes and biscuits "other than biscuits wholly or partly covered with chocolate or some product similar in taste and appearance". This means that, for reasons which are not entirely clear, chocolate cakes are zero-rated but chocolate biscuits are standard-rated. That in turn leads to disputes as to whether a particular product is a cake or a biscuit or neither.[5]

Another of the excepted items lists: "ice cream, frozen ices, frozen yoghurt or other frozen products." This particular list raised the question as to the position of frozen soft yoghurt which only freezes at −5°C and is sold above that temperature but below zero °C. It was decided that "frozen" in the list meant yoghurt sold on or below zero °C and not whether the product itself was frozen.[6]

25–12   Catering   There is also a general exception to zero-rating for a supply "in the course of catering". That in turn is defined as including a supply of food for consumption on the premises on which it is supplied (i.e. food eaten in a restaurant or café) and any supply of *hot* food for consumption off the premises.[7] Because that definition is inclusive only, it follows that even cold food supplied in the course of catering will be standard rated. In *CEC v Safeway Stores Plc* (1997), Keane J. regarded the test as to what is in the course of catering as being an objective one. Would an ordinary person regard it as being such a supply. It could include the delivery of food to a house if there was more, such as table service etc. But he stressed that no one factor was conclusive. He held that where customers bought "party trays", which had been pre-ordered, from the delicatessen counter of a supermarket, that was not a supply since most people would regard the host/hostess and not the supermarket as doing the catering.

That approach was approved by a majority of the Court of

---

[5]   See e.g. *CEC v Ferrero UK Ltd* (1997) as to the position of wafer products. Other disputes have centred around bagels, dips and jelly products, and even as to the nature of "sweetness" in confectionery. The issue of chocolate tea cakes sparked off the Marks & Spencer Plc litigation.

[6]   *Meschia's Frozen Foods v CEC* (2001).

[7]   Whether it is on or off the premises is a question of fact: *HMRC v Compass Contract Services UK Ltd* (2006).

Appeal in *HMRC v Compass Contract Services UK Ltd* (2006). In that case, the BBC Television Centre had outsourced the provision of food to its employees and visitors to the taxpayers who sold sandwiches and salads. That was held not to be a supply in the course of catering; nor was it on the premises. Apart from the contract with the employer, there was no difference between this and a high street sandwich shop.[8] Why should a contract with an employer affect the liability of the customer to pay VAT?

HOT FOOD What is meant by hot food in this context is further defined as food which has been heated "for the purposes of enabling it to be consumed at a temperature above the ambient air temperature" and at the time of the supply is above that temperature. Such detailed statutory wording has inevitably led to disputes as to how it is to be applied in practice. In *John Pimblett and Sons Ltd v CEC* (1988), the Court of Appeal, no less, were faced with the situation of a retail baker who sold fresh pies for consumption off the premises. Fresh pies are of necessity hot. The Court of Appeal held that the predominant purpose of the baker was to supply fresh and not hot pies so that they did not fall within the definition.[9]

25–13

ANIMAL FEEDING STUFFS Another major category zero-rated under Group 1 is animal feeding stuffs, animal to include birds, fish, crustaceans and molluscs. This has been interpreted as meaning substances supplied for the purpose of feeding and growing animals and not just substances which are nutritional to animals. Thus the sale of maggots to fishermen for bait was held not to be zero-rated; they were supplied only for the purpose of enticing the fish onto hooks.[10]

25–14

Other groups
Other groups have also led to litigation. Thus in Group 3 (Books, etc.), we have legal definitions as to what amounts to books[11] and newspapers[12] and in Group 8 (Transport) detailed reasons as to why a roller coaster could not be included as being the transport of twelve or more passengers.[13] In general zero-

25–15

---

8 See e.g. *R v CEC, Ex p. Sims* (1988).
9 See also *Malik v CEC* (1998) on the position of food which was cooked and then kept hot before delivery.
10 *Fluff Ltd v CEC* (2001).
11 *Odhams Leisure Group Ltd v CEC* (1992); *CEC v Colour Offset Ltd* (1995).
12 *Geoffrey E Snushall Ltd v CEC* (1982).
13 *CEC v Blackpool Pleasure Beach Co* (1974).

rating for transport only applies to vehicles, ship or aircraft designed or adapted to carry ten or more passengers. In *Cirdan Sailing Trust v CEC* (2006), a boat with nine berths but which could carry 14 passengers was held not to fall within that category. The design, layout and use of the boat all pointed to nine being the correct number to apply in this context.

Group 16 (children's clothing) raises difficult questions as to size and style since it excludes those suitable for older persons (over 13). In *H & M Hennes Ltd v CEC* (2005) the distinction was held to be one of age rather than of physical development and then adjudicated on questions of height.

Reduced rate supplies

25–16   There are a number of specified supplies which attract a reduced rate of VAT, currently 5 per cent which is the minimum allowed by art.98 of the Directive. These can be found in Sch.7A to the 1994 Act. Originally designed to avoid the political fall-out from taxing domestic fuel consumption, the current selection can be seen as an eclectic and subjective list, chosen from the list of permitted such supplies in Annex III to the Directive.[14]

25–17   THE CURRENT GROUPS   There are currently eleven groups of reduced rate supplies.[15] These are: supplies of domestic fuel or power (Group 1); installation of energy-saving materials (Group 2); grant-funded installation of heating equipment or security goods or connection of gas safety (Group 3); women's sanitary products (Group 4); children's car seats (Group 5); residential conversions (Group 6); residential renovations and alterations (Group 7); certain contraceptive products (Group 8); welfare advice or information given by a charity or a state-regulated welfare institution or agency (Group 9); supplying and servicing mobility aids in private dwellings (Group 10); and smoking cessation products (Group 11). Looking at the Schedule will show you not only how detailed some of these groups are but may also extend your knowledge—see, for example, the concept of a "booster seat" in relation to children's car seats.

Exempt supplies

25–18   A supply is exempt if it is within the terms of one of the groups in Sch.9. The Schedule presents a similar but not identical exercise to Sch.8, and again contains several themes. The

---

[14] There are 18 categories in the list.
[15] Groups are added by SI almost annually it seems. See e.g. the VAT (Reduced Rate) Orders 2006 and 2007, SIs 2006/1472 and 2007/1601.

chief difference is that behind Sch.9 are detailed provisions in arts 131 to 166 of the Directive. The details of this Schedule are therefore decided by direct reference to terms of the Directive, as interpreted by the ECJ. Where the United Kingdom provision is wider than the Directive it is not open to the Revenue and Customs to rely on the Directive although, of course, the UK wording will have to be changed.[16] Unlike zero rating which is limited only by EC law, exemption is entirely a matter of EC law which is mandatory.[17]

STRICT INTERPRETATION   Given this need for the UK Schedule to comply with the Directive, the UK courts have struggled to decide how they should construe the relevant legislation. It has often been said that, since these are exemptions, the words must be construed strictly. But Chadwick L.J. in *Expert Witness Institute v CEC* (2002) said that that did not mean the most restricted or most narrow meaning—strict should not be equated with restricted. The task of the court was to give the exempting words a meaning which they could fairly and properly bear in the context in which they were used. In *CEC v Electronic Data Systems Ltd* (2003), Jonathan Parker L.J., pointed out the inherent tension between this need for a strict construction and the need to adopt the purposive approach to EC legislation in the Directive. His solution was to interpret the exemption in a way which did not have the effect of extending its scope beyond its fair meaning, as ascertained by adopting a purposive approach.

25–19

TYPES OF SUPPLY   One group of exemptions deals with supplies where it has proved extremely difficult to apply VAT. The main group of this kind is Group 5 (financial services), and linked with it is Group 2 (insurance). The chief problem is isolating the value-added in a financial supply such as a loan, or under insurance against a risk. There are also complexities in some kinds of supplies of land (Group 1), and in betting (Group 4). In practice, it can prove easier to put excise taxes on these kinds of supply, and leave them excluded from VAT. This happens in most European countries (including the United Kingdom) with insurance and betting and with many land transactions. The question of VAT on financial supplies also causes a direct overlap with income tax.

25–20

A second group of supplies are those made to individuals

[16] See *CEC v Civil Service Motoring Association Ltd* (1998), per Mummery L.J.
[17] See *EC Commission v UK* (1988).

rather than for commercial purposes, and left out for social reasons. These include education (Group 6), health and welfare (Group 7), burials (Group 8), cultural services (Group 13), sports events (Group 10) and charity fund-raising (Group 12). The oddments include postal services (Group 3). Why add VAT to stamps when the state runs the postal service? Another is works of art (if there is an IHT or CGT exemption applying).

25–21   QUESTIONS OF INTERPRETATION—EDUCATION   As with zero-rating, the individual groups have given rise to a substantial body of interpretative litigation. To take an example,[18] Group 6 on education sets out six different items, of which item 1 is the provision by an *eligible body* of education, research (where supplied to an eligible body) or vocational training and item 4 covers the supply of any goods or services which are closely related to a supply within item 1, by or to the body making that item 1 supply. An eligible body is widely defined but includes schools, universities and colleges. Thus, top up fees for Universities do not attract VAT.

In *CEC v University of Leicester Students' Union* (2001), it was held that since the students' union was not itself an eligible body nor under its constitution was it part of the University which was such a body, it was not making exempt supplies. In *EC Commission v Germany* (2002) the ECJ declared that a provision of German law which exempted research done by universities for a consideration was contrary to the Directive. The purpose of the exemption was not to hinder education by making the cost of it subject to VAT, but if a university charged VAT on its commercial research that would not increase the cost of university education. Further, contrary to current UK government thinking, the ECJ held that although such projects might be of assistance to university education, they were not essential to the objectives of teaching students to enable them to carry out a profession. Such projects were therefore not closely related to university education.

Zero-rating and exemption compared
25–22   The reason for zero-rating rather than exempting certain favoured supplies is the need to impose tax on supplies that cannot be exempted under EC law. Ironically, however, zero-

---

[18] Group 13 (cultural services) has also led to some detailed litigation in the ECJ on the purpose of the Directive and the UK implementation: see *CEC v Zoological Society of London* (2002). See also on Group 9 (subscriptions) *Expert Witness Institute v CEC* (2002).

rating is more advantageous than exemption, so the effect in the United Kingdom of the European rule is the reverse of that intended.

Advantages of zero-rating

The advantages of zero-rating and the disadvantages of 25–23 exemption were the reasons for the dispute in *Royal Bank of Scotland Group Plc v CEC* (2002). The bank issued its own bank notes (zero-rated), but it also issued them through its cash machines to customers of other banks on a reciprocal basis in return for a fee. In respect of that fee the bank was held to be providing financial services to the other banks (an exempt supply) and not issuing its own bank notes.

Zero-rating, as we have seen, is known in EC circles as exemption with credit. They intend this to emphasise the fact that those making zero-rated supplies can claim refunds for input tax incurred for the purpose of those supplies. This is because they are technically taxable supplies, although no new tax will be paid. By contrast, an exempt supply is one for which no input tax credit is possible. The comparative effect of these categories depends on the identities both of suppliers and those being supplied.

Input tax

It is largely a matter of indifference to taxable persons 25–24 receiving inputs whether the inputs are taxed at the standard rate or at a zero-rate. The only difference is one of cash-flow. They must pay the input tax on the standard-rated supply before reclaiming it. By contrast, an exempt supply to a taxable person is more expensive. This is because the supplier will probably pass on any input tax as part of the non-taxable price for the supply. The recipient therefore pays for that VAT, but cannot reclaim it. In other words, a taxable person would rather buy supplies taxed at the standard rate than exempt supplies. This also explains why taxable persons may prefer to deal with a registered supplier rather than a supplier that chooses to remain unregistered when under the compulsory limit for registration.

An ordinary consumer cannot claim back any VAT. Nor can a claim be made by someone who makes only exempt supplies, or who is not registered for VAT. In each case, they have to bear the cost of VAT whether it is express or hidden. For them, therefore, zero-rated supplies are better than exempt supplies, because there is less total VAT. For them exempt supplies *are* in effect taxed supplies, while zero-rate taxable supplies are not.

Partial exemption

25-25   A problem arises for those who make both taxable supplies and exempt supplies, whether or not they are mixed. The supplier, if registered, is entitled to an input tax credit for input tax incurred for the purpose of taxable supplies. It is not entitled to a tax credit in respect of input tax for exempt supplies. Anyone in this position must therefore take steps to identify which inputs relate to the taxable supplies, and which relate to the exempt supplies. The ECJ has ruled in *Midland Bank Plc v CEC* (2000) that there must be an immediate and direct link between a particular input transaction and a taxable rather than an exempt output transaction for the input tax to be deductible. It must also be a cost component of it. Some of the complexities of this are discussed in para.26–33 below. In practice many input supplies are linked to both exempt and taxable output supplies, e.g. electricity used by a shop which sells both taxable and exempt goods. Many such traders agree a percentage with their local VAT offices so that, for example, they can claim 60 per cent of the input tax as a fair share of total inputs. The flat rate scheme for small businesses may also simplify the position.

Special regimes

25-26   VAT also lends itself to the development of a multiplicity of special schemes. As with the schedules on zero-rating and exemption, we derive little benefit from a detailed study of these schemes, but they do solve some tricky practical problems.

One series of special schemes (provided for in official Notices in the 727 series) is that for retailers. These are designed to deal with the problems of those selling a mixture of goods that are taxed at different rates, or are exempt. Examples are the supermarket, high-street retailers and even the corner shop. They can agree with the local VAT office to avoid having to make separate calculations of VAT on every sale, or having to separate zero-rated goods from standard-rated goods.

Another set of special schemes are those dealing with goods sold by dealers but bought by them from private customers. For example, if I sell my private car to a dealer, I add no VAT to it. But I bought my car from a garage and paid VAT when I did so. If the dealer charges VAT on the whole price of the car when selling it to another customer, it is being double taxed. To avoid this, a *margin scheme* operates. In effect, the dealer has to account for VAT only on the difference between the price paid to me and the price for which the car is sold. Similar regimes apply to antiques.

A further group who get special attention are farmers. The

problem here is the assumed aversion of farmers from keeping accounts. Yet someone buying from a farmer wants an input tax credit for any supply, on which the farmer would charge VAT. The compromise, made at European level, is a deemed input tax equal to 4 per cent of the output.

The flat rate scheme for small businesses

Under s.26B of the 1994 Act small businesses may use a flat rate scheme in calculating their VAT. This does not strictly vary the rate of VAT charged by the supplier, it relates to the accountability of the supplier to the CEC, but it is more convenient to deal with it here than in the next chapter. The scheme is currently available to businesses making no more than £150,000 taxable supplies annually (which includes zero-rated supplies) and which has no more than £187,500 tax exclusive annual business income (which would include exempt supplies). Such businesses may choose to operate the flat rate scheme rather than become involved in keeping detailed records of its outputs and inputs. Instead the VAT payable will be calculated by applying a flat rate percentage to the supplier's total tax inclusive business turnover (i.e. all its business income). The relevant percentage depends upon which trade sector the business, or main business, falls under. These percentages were lowered in December 2003 and vary from 2 per cent (retailing food, confectionery, tobacco, newspapers or children's clothing) to 13.5 per cent (laundry and dry cleaning services)—see Information Sheet 17/03, December 10, 2003. Such businesses will therefore lose the right to claim any input tax credits but will still be able to issue tax invoices (and so collect output tax) at the appropriate (normal) rate, be it standard, reduced or zero-rated.

25–27

CHAPTER 26

VAT COMPUTATION AND ACCOUNTABILITY

Introduction

26–01   Having established that there is a charge to VAT and what the appropriate rate is, the final questions for domestic supplies are: what is the value of the supply so that the amount can be calculated? When is that tax charged? And how is it actually accounted for to the Revenue and Customs?

Valuation

Everything which constitutes the consideration

26–02   On how much do we impose the VAT? Section 19 of the 1994 Act provides that where the consideration for a supply is in monetary form, the value is the amount that, when the VAT is added, equals the consideration. For example, if the price I pay for a supply is £117.50, the VAT rate being 17.5 per cent, then the value of the supply for VAT purposes is £100. Similarly, if the price I pay is £100, then the value of the supply is £85.10, with VAT of £14.90 i.e. 17.5 per cent of £85.50 payable. This suggests that if we offer you a price for a product, the price is VAT-inclusive, rather than VAT-exclusive.

Section 19 is the United Kingdom's implementation of arts 73 to 80 of the Directive, which have direct effect. As originally enacted the section was found to be inconsistent with some of the provisions of the Directive and it was amended in 1992 to provide only the general rule set out above. The Directive is in fact far more detailed and so all the recent disputes as to valuation of a supply have in fact been decided by reference to that rather than the Act.

Article 73 provides that the taxable amount of a supply is "everything which constitutes the consideration which has been or is to be obtained by the purchaser, the customer or a third party for the supply, including subsidies directly linked to the price of such supplies".

SUPPLIES FREE OF CHARGE In the case of goods supplied free **26–03**
of charge but caught by para.5 of Sch.4 (see para.24–56), art.74
provides that the consideration is their purchase or cost price. In
Kuwait Petroleum (GB) Ltd v CEC (2001), this was applied to
"free" gifts purchased and provided by Kuwait in return for
coupons given by the company on the sale of petrol. It was not
there decided whether such gifts could amount to a post-supply
discount in relation to the petrol (see para.26–14 below).

INCIDENTAL EXPENSES Article 78 provides that this is to **26–04**
include any incidental expenses and taxes other than VAT itself.
What is an incidental expense depends upon first deciding
exactly what the supply amounts to. If the supply, properly
ascertained, consists of two elements, X and Y, it is not then
permissible to use art.78 to argue that X is an incidental expense
of Y for the purpose of whether there is a single supply in which
X is subsumed into Y. Article 73 applies only therefore to
determine the value of the consideration so ascertained (i.e. X
and Y). Thus in *CEC v BT Plc* (1999) where the House of Lords
held that the supply was a composite supply both of a new car
and its delivery direct to the customer, it could not be said that
the delivery costs were incidental expenses of the supply of the
car under art.78.

SUBSIDIES Since art.73 includes subsidies directly linked to **26–05**
the price of the supply as part of the consideration, such subsidies will only include those which constitute the whole or part
of the consideration.[1] But in *Keeping Newcastle Warm v CEC*
(2002), on the other hand, there was no dispute that a flat rate
£10 subsidy, paid under a Government scheme for assisting
energy savings, formed part of the consideration for the supply
of energy saving advice by the suppliers. But it was argued that
since this subsidy was not linked to the price of the supplies it
did not fall to be included in the value of the supply since it was
not within the specific wording of art.73. The ECJ ruled that
since it formed part of the consideration for the supply, the
subsidy fell within the general wording of art.73 and formed
part of the taxable amount.

IDENTIFYING THE CONSIDERATION The value of a supply is **26–06**
therefore inextricably linked to the consideration for the supply,
which as we have seen means what is received as a direct link for
the supply; e.g. the fact of the hostess holding a party in return

---

[1] *Office des Produits Wallons ASBL v Belgium* (2003).

for a discounted blouse in *Rosgill Group v CEC* (1997), which we discussed in Ch.24. It is important to stress again that it is necessary first to decide precisely what the supply is, and what the consideration for it is, before applying any part of the valuation provisions. Those provisions (including the permitted deductions set out below) cannot be used in that process; they are concerned only with the value of the consideration of that supply once ascertained. Thus in the *Trustees of Nell Gwyn House Maintenance Fund v CEC* (1999) where, as we have seen, it was held that the trustees were supplying to the tenants of a block of flats not only the maintenance staff but also the whole costs of the maintenance of the block, it was not permissible to then argue that the payments for the staff were received from the tenants as repayment for expenses paid out on their behalf under art.79, discussed below.

Non-cash consideration

26–07   Where there is an element of non-cash consideration involved in the supply, the question is of course what monetary value to give it. There have been many European and United Kingdom cases on which formula is to be used.

26–08   MONETARY EQUIVALENT   The generally accepted analysis of these cases was set out by Chadwick L.J. in *CEC v Littlewoods Organisation Plc* (2001). The consideration must be capable of being expressed in money or a monetary equivalent and the basis of the assessment is the subjective value of the consideration. By subjective, he meant not the traditional UK meaning of the word "subjective", but the consideration actually received for the goods or services actually supplied, as distinct from some "objective" value which is independent of the actual transaction—it is therefore the value which the parties must have adopted for themselves for the purposes of the transaction which applies.[2] Only if it is impossible to ascertain such a value will the amount be the cost to the supplier.

26–09   "SUBJECTIVE VALUE"   In many cases this subjective value is relatively easy to ascertain, especially where the supply is of an item at a reduced price from its catalogue or retail price. Thus, in the *Rosgill* case the value of the consideration was the £8 reduction in the catalogue price paid by the hostess for the blouse. That was the value the parties had implicitly attributed

---

[2]   As opposed to what they think they adopted as the value—that would be the UK meaning of subjective.

to her holding the party.[3] This cannot happen, however, if the goods have no catalogue or retail price as was the case in *Empire Stores Ltd v CEC* (1994) where "free" goods provided to an agent as commission for sales from their catalogue to third parties had no market value which could have been attributed by the parties to them. The cost to the supplier was therefore used.

ATTRIBUTION It follows that the key question is whether the parties have attributed a value to the non-cash consideration. **26–10**

In *CEC v Westmorland Motorway Services Ltd* (1998) a coach driver was provided by the motorway service station with a free meal if he took a coach party of 20 or more people there and remained there for at least half an hour. Clearly there was a supply of a meal to the driver for a consideration but what was its monetary value? There were two possible cash valuations: what it cost the service station to provide the meal (cost price) or some other (higher) value attributed to it by the parties (i.e. in this case what it would have cost the driver to buy the meal—the retail price). The Court of Appeal held that on the facts the parties had impliedly attributed the latter value.

NOT EXTRINSIC VALUE A variation on this accepted approach was taken by Carnwath J. in *CEC v Bugeja* (2000). The case concerned the supply of videos which were sold for £20 each or £10 plus the return of a previously bought video. The judge held that since it was shown that the actual replacement cost of a video to the supplier was £3 that was the subjective value of a returned video, making the consideration for the supply of the second video £13. Goods, unlike services in cases such as *Westmorland*, could have a value established by extrinsic evidence. That decision was, however, reversed by the same Court of Appeal as in the *Littlewoods* case (2001), applying Chadwick L.J.'s principles. There could be no valid distinction drawn between goods and services and there was no difficulty in discovering the "subjective" value of the returned video, i.e. the £10 reduction in the purchase price of the second video. That was the value placed on it by the parties in respect of the second purchase transaction and not simply the value placed on it by one party for the purposes of a different transaction (buying a replacement). **26–11**

---

[3] See also *e.g. CEC v Euphony Communications Ltd* (2004).

26–12   Part-exchange value   That same Court of Appeal (2001) also approved the decision of Arden J. in *Lex Services Plc v CEC* (2000). This case demonstrates very clearly the difference between the subjective and objective value as described by Chadwick L.J. It was the everyday situation where a customer trades in his used car in part exchange for a new car. Rather than give the customer a reduction on the list price of the new car (which was frowned on by the manufacturers), to expedite a sale the salesman would give the customer a part exchange price in excess of the used car's trade value. The latter was used, however, as quantifying the repayment to the buyer if the deal fell through. The value to be attributed to the used car as part consideration for the new car was the inflated value as agreed between the parties. Thus VAT was in effect chargeable on the full list price of the new car even though in practice the garage received less than that amount (i.e. reduced by the inflated part of the part exchange allowance). The logic of this approach when compared with the VAT treatment of a simple discount off the list price is discussed below at para.26–07. Nevertheless, the Court of Appeal's decision was upheld in identical terms by the House of Lords (2004).

26–13   Zero value   In one case the subjective value of the part exchanged goods was held to be zero. In *CEC v Ping (Europe) Ltd* (2002) the company sold a new golf club to a customer for £22 plus the return of an old club which had been declared illegal under the rules of golf. In those unusual circumstances the value attributed by the parties to the returned club was nil—it was worthless. There were no normal rules of trade relevant to this transaction.

Allowable deductions

26–14   Article 73 is subject to art.79 which allows certain items to be deducted from the consideration. These are (a) price reductions for early payment; (b) price discounts and rebates allowed at the time of the supply; and (c) amounts received by the supplier from a customer as repayment for expenses paid out on behalf of the customer to a third party.

With regard to such expenses under paragraph (c), there is a clear distinction between expenses paid to a third party C which have been incurred by A in the course of making his own supply of services to B and as part of the whole of the services rendered to him by B, which would not be deductible by A under para.(c); and where specific services have been supplied by C to B (not A) and A has merely acted as B's known and authorised representative in paying C, which would be so deductible. In *CEC v Plantiflor Ltd* (2002) the company (A) sent plants by mail order to customers (B) and charged B the costs required by Parcelforce (C) to deliver the plants. The House of Lords, having found that the delivery was part of the services provided by A to B (there being a separate supply by C to B) refused to allow that amount as an expense with regard to the consideration for the supply by A to B.[4]

Discounts

Price rebates and discounts at the point of sale are thus allowed under art.79.

These will reduce the value of the supply accordingly. Price reductions made *after* the time of the supply are allowable under art.90 at the time of the reduction by way of a repayment of VAT already paid by the supplier. The interaction of these two Articles on contemporary and post-supply discounts, was considered by the ECJ in *Freemans Plc v CEC* (2001). The company sold goods through agents selling either to themselves or others from a catalogue. Every time an agent made a payment to the company, 10 per cent of that amount was credited to a separate account in the name of the agent. The agent could either take that amount in cash or reduce the balance owed for goods already purchased, but it could not be used to reduce the catalogue price of goods at the time of purchase. The ECJ held that art.79 could not apply since no reduction was given against the actual purchase—the 10 per cent credit in effect gave the agent a right to a future discount against the purchase. That fell within art.90 which would apply when the credit was actually used to reduce the balance owed. In effect it was a post-supply discount on the original order and not a pre-sale discount on a subsequent order.

CASH COMMISSION A similar decision was made by the Court of Appeal in *Littlewoods Organisation Plc v CEC* (2001). In this case the agents selling through a catalogue and who either bought goods for themselves or for others (referred to as the primary goods) were entitled to take either a 10 per cent cash commission or a 12.5 per cent discount on a future purchase (of secondary goods). The Court of Appeal was only concerned with the VAT situation arising in the context of goods purchased by the agents for themselves. They held that the cash

26–15

26–16

---

[4] See also *Debenhams Retail Plc v CEC* (2005), where the services were actually supplied by C to A.

commission operated as a post-supply discount on the primary goods under art.79—it was only payable after the sale; the non-cash commission was, however, allowable as a discount under art.90 against the value of the secondary goods as a discount at the point of supply of those goods. The non-cash commission which arose from goods ordered by the agents for third parties would have raised another question—was that not a discount but a recognition of the consideration provided by the agents to the company in selling goods on their behalf, as in the *Rossgill* case? We will return to that issue at para.26–20.

Vouchers

26–17   SAME SUPPLIER   The issue of consideration/discount was also at the centre of the initial dispute when a supplier provides a coupon or voucher on a first supply which can be used to obtain a reduction on the price of a second supply from the *same* supplier. The issue was resolved by the ECJ in *Boots Co Ltd v CEC* (1990) when it held that the customer had not provided any consideration for the voucher, which in any event had no monetary value as such. It was instead merely an undertaking by Boots to give a discount on the second purchase to which art.79 would apply. This approach was followed by the Court of Appeal in *Tesco Plc v CEC* (2003) in relation to its "club card" scheme. Under that scheme when a person purchased goods at Tescos and presented a clubcard at the checkout, he or she was awarded points based on the amount spent. Those points could then be used to reduce the purchase price of subsequent goods purchased in the supermarket. Again there was no consideration provided by the customer for the award of those points which operated as a simple discount on the second purchase. The major factor was that on the first purchase a customer paid the same amount whether or not a card was presented.

In *Hartwell Plc v CEC* (2003) a different Court of Appeal considered that the issue of a "purchase plus" voucher by a garage which took the form of a discount note which could be used against the price of a new car (inflating the part exchange value having proved a failure in VAT terms in the *Lex Services* case). They decided that the voucher did form part of the consideration for the supply of the new car rather than simply effecting a discount, but that it had no monetary value. The effect was of course the same as giving a discount.

26–18   VOUCHERS REDEEMABLE DOWN THE SUPPLY CHAIN   The position is more complex if the person providing the voucher and the person making the supply at which it can be used to effect a reduction are not the same. The usual situation is where the reduction is made further down the supply chain of the same goods. Two issues commonly arise. The first is what is the value of a retail supply where, e.g. the money off coupon is provided by the manufacturer (A) to the customer (C), say in a magazine. (A) supplies the relevant goods directly to the retailer (B), who then takes the coupon as part of the price of the supply to (C). (A) then reimburses (B) the amount of the coupon. In *Yorkshire Co-operatives Ltd v CEC* (2003), the ECJ held that insofar as the supply from (B) to (C) was concerned the consideration provided by (C) was the cash and the coupon, the face vale of which was the value of that consideration. (B) got full value for the supply since it was reimbursed by (A).

VOUCHERS IN SAME SUPPLY CHAIN AS A POST SUPPLY   26–19
DISCOUNT   The second issue, in that situation, is what is the knock-on effect if any on the supply by (A) to (B)—is (A)'s reimbursement of (B) in effect a post supply discount under art.90? That question came before the ECJ in *EC Commission v Germany* (2003). The situation was more complex in that the voucher was issued by the manufacturer (A) who supplied the goods to a wholesaler (B). (B) in turn supplied the goods to the retailer (C), who then supplied the goods to the customer (D), taking the coupon as part consideration. (A) then reimbursed (C) direct. It was argued that to allow this reimbursement from (A) to (C) to operate as a post-supply discount on the supply from (A) to (B) (there was no supply from (A) to (C)) would distort the system of VAT since it would be rewriting a supply which had not been affected by the reimbursement. The ECJ held that art.90 did apply to the supply from (A) to (B) since there was the overriding principle of fiscal neutrality. (A) should not have to account for VAT on more than it actually received by way of consideration. The position would be even clearer if there had been a direct supply from (A) to (C) (i.e. cutting out the wholesaler) as in the *Yorkshire* case above.

VOUCHERS OUTSIDE THE CHAIN OF SUPPLY (THIRD PARTY   26–20
VOUCHERS) AS A POST-SUPPLY DISCOUNT   The position is different if the supplier provides vouchers which are exchangeable not for the supplier's goods either directly (as in *Boots*) or further down the supply chain (as in *EC Comm v Germany*), but for goods from other retail outlets. We have already seen in *Kuwait Petroleum (GB) Ltd v CEC* (1999), that if the supplier obtains the goods from the third parties and then provides them

to the customer, those goods are deemed to have been supplied at market value under para.4 of Sch.5. But that case did not decide whether the cost to the supplier of redeeming those vouchers could be deducted from the value of the primary supply as a post-supply discount under art.90. The position is even more acute where the vouchers are exchangeable with the third parties for goods. Those third parties then being reimbursed by the supplier. After all, just as in the cases above, the supplier in these cases ultimately receives less consideration for the primary supply because of having to fund the voucher scheme (i.e. by buying the goods or reimbursing the retailers who redeem the vouchers).

The issue was, however, directly in point in *HMRC v Total UK Ltd* (2008). The Court of Appeal held that there was no such art.90 discount. They adopted the wording of the Advocate General in *EC Comm v Germany* that it was not like a normal discount or rebate scheme. This scheme involved the supplier supplying more goods (petrol and vouchers for the redemption goods) at the same price, rather than supplying the same goods (petrol) at a lower price. In the supply chain cases only one set of goods was involved and the reduction was given on those goods, albeit down the line.

The Court of Appeal also dismissed an argument based on fiscal neutrality. That point is dealt with next below. There is a related point as to the VAT implications when such (third party) vouchers are redeemed by the customer and the goods are supplied by the retailer, who is then reimbursed by the issuer of the vouchers. That was dealt with in the case of *Loyalty Management UK Ltd v HMRC* (2007) as described in para.24–48. above and [2008] BTR 17.

Limited to amount paid

26–21   Underlying the test that in valuing non-cash consideration it is the amount received by the supplier which matters, is the principle that it would be unjust to tax a supplier on a figure which is in excess of what the customer actually pays, however many steps there are in the supply chain. This limited principle was set out by the ECJ in *Elida Gibbs Ltd v CEC* (1996). A good example is *Argos Distributors Ltd v CEC* (1996). Argos sold vouchers redeemable at its shops, only for goods to the value shown on the vouchers, to employers, who then gave them to their employees as incentives. Argos sold the vouchers to the employers at 95 per cent of their face value. Thus, for example suppose Argos sold a voucher with a face value of £100 to Fred for £95. Fred gave that voucher to his employee Sid, who bought goods worth £100 from Argos with it. What was the value of the supply by Argos to Sid? The ECJ held that it was the amount actually received by Argos for those goods, i.e. £95. That was the amount which Argos actually received for the goods and fiscal neutrality required that VAT be charged on no higher figure.[5]

TRI-PARTITE AGREEMENTS This principle has its limits, 26–22 however, and has not been applied where there is a tri-partite situation. In *Kingfisher Plc v CEC* (2000), P supplied vouchers to its customers (usually on credit) which could then be used to buy goods from W using the face value of the vouchers for the shelf price of the goods. W then invoiced P for the vouchers redeemed by it and P paid W 90 per cent of that value. The judge held that the supply by W to the customer was the full shelf price and not the 90 per cent eventually received from P. There were separate supplies by W to the customer, by P to the customer and by P to W (of financial services). W was getting the benefit of those services provided by P—in *Argos* there was no such agreement, the company gave its own discount. This approach was upheld by the ECJ in *CEC v Primback Ltd* (2001). X sold furniture on interest free terms to its customers. They borrowed the full list price from Y, the finance company. The customer over time repaid that full amount to Y but Y paid X less than the full price up front. Again the value of the supply by X to its customers was held to be at the full list price and not the amount received from Y. Here the price agreed between X and a customer and the price paid by the customer were the same—that was not true of the arrangement between Argos and the purchasers of its vouchers.

Discounts or consideration—limited value of fiscal neutrality
In *Elida Gibbs Ltd v CEC* (1996), the ECJ put forward the 26–23 following explanation of fiscal neutrality as applied to VAT:

> "The basic principle of the VAT system is that it is intended to tax only the final consumer. Consequently the taxable amount serving as a basis for the VAT to be collected by the tax authorities cannot exceed the consideration actually paid by the final consumer which is the basis for calculating the VAT ultimately borne by him."

---

[5] The Advocate General in that case thought that the 5% could not be a discount under art.79 since it was not given to the customer (Sid) at the point of sale. The Court did not express any views on that point.

An examination of the various cases just discussed in relation to the various aspects of valuation reveals that in fact the VAT position is very different depending upon the analysis by the Courts as to what the transaction involves, even though in wider economic terms, especially from the point of view of the consumer, the consequences are identical.[6]

To reiterate two examples. A buys a car from B with a list price of £10,000 and B takes in part exchange A's old car which has a trade value of £2,000. If B allows A £2,000 on the traded-in car but gives A a £500 discount on the list price, the value of the supply of the new car to A will be £9,500 (the £500 being a discount under art.97). But if instead B allows A £2,500 on the part-exchanged car and then charges the full list price on the new car, the value of the supply by B to A is £10,000 (*Lex Services* case). Again, if B allows only £2,000 on the part exchange and charges A the full list price, but gives A a purchase plus voucher worth £500 which B will accept as part consideration for the new car, the value of the supply of the new car is only £9,500 (*Hartwell*). Yet in all three cases A has handed over his old car and £7,500.

26–24   NEUTRALITY OR CERTAINTY   The reason for the disparity is that in situations (i) and (iii) the £500 is treated as being either a discount or as part of the consideration with no monetary value, and the value of the non-cash consideration (the old car) is agreed at £2,000, whereas in (ii) the agreed subjective value of that car is £2,500 and that must form part of the consideration. When this issue was put to the House of Lords in the *Lex Services* case, Lord Walker rejected any argument based on a wider application of the principal of fiscal neutrality on the basis of applying the principle of legal certainty. The principle, he said, does not require that transactions which have the same economic or business effect should for that reason be treated alike for VAT purposes. If a taxable person has a choice between two transactions he may not choose one of them and avail himself of the VAT effects of the other. There is no doctrine of commercial reality.

26–25   POST-SUPPLY DISCOUNTS AND FISCAL NEUTRALITY   This restrictive approach to the principle of fiscal neutrality was also applied by the CA in *Total UK Ltd v HMRC* (2008). In that case, Total offered vouchers to customers buying petrol. These

---

[6]   See [2002] BTR 179, [2003] BTR 153 and [2004] BTR 99 for detailed analyses of this problem.

vouchers could then be redeemed for goods at third party retailers such as Marks & Spencer. Total were not allowed to deduct the costs of reimbursing the retailers for the goods supplied in return for the vouchers as a post-supply discount on the price of the petrol. In analytical terms, more goods were supplied at the same cost and not the same goods at a lower cost. Total then argued that this result in fact infringed the principle in *Elida Gibbs* of fiscal neutrality. They were having to account for output tax (on the petrol) on an amount which was in fact greater than the net amount they actually received. Had they simply allowed the vouchers to be redeemed against future purchases of petrol or given cash-back the deduction would have been allowed. That could not be correct. Although the judge had agreed with this, the Court of Appeal was very dismissive of the neutrality argument on the basis that the *Elida Gibbs* case was no authority for such a general proposition[7] and specifically only applied to same vouchers applicable to goods in the same supply chain. Nothing in that case altered the fact that this was not a price discount scheme and so could not reduce the amount of the supply.

SEPARATE SUPPLIES   A different method of avoiding the principle of fiscal neutrality was used by Hart J. in *CEC v Euphony Communications Ltd* (2004). There the judge drew a distinction between cash commission earned by agents in respect of their becoming a customer and using the supplier's services (regarded as a post-supply discount under art.90 on the services supplied to them) and that earned by introducing new customers to the supplier. That was the subjective value of the consideration for the supply of services by the agent to the supplier. The judge decided that the principle of fiscal neutrality could not apply where there was a separate supply by the agent to the supplier in addition to the supply by the supplier to the agent— even though the amount received by the supplier was in reality the same in both cases. It is clear that so far as the UK is concerned, the principle of fiscal neutrality in this area has a rather limited role.

26–26

---

7   Citing *Primback* and *Kingfisher* as authority (see para.26–21, above). The value of the supply is based on the tax paid by the consumer and not on that collected by the supplier. See [2008] BTR 17.

Accounting for VAT

26–27   As we have seen the VAT payable to the VAT office is the balance (if positive) of output tax less input tax. If the balance is negative then a claim for repayment can be made. This balance requires accounting rules to determine when VAT is to be collected and returned to the VAT office, and what input tax can be deducted from the output tax. VAT laws have a special language for this as well:

- *Tax periods* are the periods for which taxable person must make returns to the VAT office.
- A *tax invoice* is the formal document required when a supply is made.
- *The tax point* is the time when VAT has to be charged on a supply, and therefore determines the tax period in which output tax on a supply must be returned.
- The *tax credit* is the amount of input tax that can be set against output tax for each tax period.

Tax periods

26–28   All registered persons must make regular returns to the VAT office and there are provisions for assessments in default. In the case of larger traders, this is done on a quarterly basis so that it is received by the VAT office within a month of the end of the quarter. For smaller traders, annual accounting is possible. Under this scheme returns are only made once a year and arrangements are made for instalments payments of VAT, monthly or quarterly, depending on the size of turnover, throughout the year on an estimated basis. Some traders are allowed to make monthly returns. These include exporters because, as we shall see, their returns amount to requests for refunds of tax, and so involve a payment by the VAT office to them. Very large traders, on the other hand, are required to make monthly payments on account.

Each return requires that the trader total up the output tax on all outputs made in the period covered by the return. A tax credit can then be claimed for all input tax incurred during the period, provided that the input tax is claimable as part of the credit.

In each case, the trader must have documentary evidence to substantiate the amounts returned which must be kept for six years. These are open to inspection by the VAT office who may make retrospective assessments. In the case of most transactions, the required evidence is a *tax invoice*. The actual amount payable is based on these invoices, although small traders may pay on a cash basis, i.e. the difference between output tax collected and input tax paid in any particular period.

Tax invoices

Each taxable supply must be documented in the required way.   26–29
In most cases, this is by the issue of a special invoice recording the transaction, called a tax invoice. A taxable person supplying goods or services to another taxable person must issue the latter with an invoice recording the key details of the supply. These include the VAT registration details of the supplier (including the VAT number that all registered persons are given on registration), names and addresses, the amount payable for the supply, and the amount of VAT on the supply. In this way, documentary evidence is recorded of the precise details of the transaction, including both the person who should be paying the VAT to the local VAT office, and the person who will be reclaiming that amount as input tax. This is one of the secret efficiencies of VAT: if the purchaser does not have a tax invoice, no input tax can be claimed. If the purchaser produces the tax invoice, the VAT office has the information to check that the supplier has paid in the VAT.

Tax points

Tax point is the VAT term for the time of supply. Article 63 of   26–30
the Directive states that VAT becomes chargeable when the goods or services are supplied. When then does a supply occur? The answer cannot be defined in terms of passing of title. Instead, the rule must be completely practical—it has to be applied by the sales assistant or bookkeeper recording the transaction. In addition, revenue protection requires that the tax point is something that cannot be postponed or avoided.

The solution, as allowed by the Directive and adopted by s.6, is a two-tier one. The formal time of supply of goods is either when the goods are delivered (or made available) to the customer, or when payment is made for the supply, whichever is earlier.[8] In the case of services the alternative to earlier payment is when the supplies are rendered. In practice, however, the tax point is usually the time when the tax invoice is issued. To tie the two together, the law requires that the tax invoice be issued not later than 14 days after the formal time of supply, in which case the date of the invoice will become the tax point. Normal

---

[8] See e.g. *CEC v Richmond Theatre Management Ltd* (1995).

practice with sales of goods is to issue the tax invoice at the same time as the sale and payment, but the rules give a little flexibility. Goods sold on "sale or return" are taxed when there is known to be a sale or after 12 months, if earlier.

26–31   PAYMENTS ON ACCOUNT   Article 65 of the Directive provides that where a payment is made on account (e.g. a deposit) before the goods and services are supplied (the tax point), VAT becomes chargeable on the amount of such a payment on receipt. In *BUPA Hospitals Ltd* v *CEC* (2006), the ECJ held that could not apply unless all the relevant information about the future chargeable supply (e.g. as to future delivery or future performance) was already known. Payments on account of supplies which had not been clearly identified could not be subject to VAT.

26–32   INTERNET SALES   *HMRC* v *Robertson's Electrical Ltd* (2006), involved a common form of selling goods over the internet. Goods ordered online were paid for by the customers recording their credit or debit card details on the website. The invoice was prepared either at the date of dispatch or within seven days of the date of delivery. As required by consumer law[9] all goods not faulty or misdescribed could be returned within seven days of receipt. The taxpayers argued that as a result the goods were sold on a sale or return basis and the tax point was therefore the date when the customer no longer had the right to return perfect goods. The Inner House of the Court of Session disagreed. There was an outright sale at the date when the goods were ordered and paid for and that was the tax point. It was in effect a sale subject to a condition subsequent.

26–33   TAX RETURNS   All taxable persons must include in their tax returns all supplies where the tax point is within the period covered by the tax return, whether or not the payment has actually been made. They will also want to claim a tax credit for all input tax where the tax point is in that period.

Tax credits—input tax

Right to reclaim income tax

26–34   A taxable person[10] can claim a tax credit for all input tax incurred in a tax period in making taxable outputs. The United

---

[9]   The Consumer Protection (Distant Selling) Regulations 2000.
[10]   See *Finanzamt Goslar v Breitsohl* (2001).

Kingdom system is contained in ss.24 to 26B which mirror, but which have largely been ignored in legal disputes in favour of the wording of the Directive. The two key conditions are that the claimant holds tax invoices for the sum of input tax claimed (art.178),[11] and that there was an immediate and direct link between the input tax transaction and a particular taxable output transaction the input tax was incurred *for the purposes of* the taxed transaction (art.168).

FOR THE PURPOSES OF THE TAXED TRANSACTION There is therefore no right to deduct input tax if the relevant supply was made not to the taxable person but e.g. directly to one of its employees, albeit in a business context, e.g. legal defence costs of an employee, paid by the employer, charged with dangerous driving in a company car in the course of business.[12] On the other hand, where the input transaction was incurred in the course of the business, e.g. a lease of premises for a restaurant, input tax may still be claimed even after the business has ceased but only so far as is necessary to wind up the business.[13] Where the taxable person uses the inputs for the purpose of a business but the outputs are to be disregarded, there must be an apportionment: *HMRC v Gracechurch Management Services Ltd* [2008] S.T.C. 795. We shall return to the other test of an immediate and direct link shortly.

26–35

DISALLOWED INPUTS The treasury has power to disallow some kinds of input tax regardless of the reason for it is incurred (s.26). This power is allowed by European law under art.176. The British rules disallow expenditure on a number of inputs, in particular on private cars (with exceptions such as the purchase of cars for resale),[14] most forms of business entertainment,[15] and expenditure on accommodation provided for staff. Further, under s.26A, any taxable person who has made a claim for a tax credit but has not actually paid the supplier within six months of the supply, will be required to repay the credit claimed.

26–36

---

[11] This includes any document regarded by a Member State as an invoice and allows Member States to require additional evidence under national rules for the prevention of fraud: *Reisdorf v Finanzampt Köln-West* (1997).

[12] *HMRC v Jeancharm Ltd* (2005) CA.

[13] *I/S Fini H v Skatteministeriet* (2005) ECJ.

[14] This exclusion is valid even though cars are essential tools in the business concerned or could not be used for private purposes: *Royscot Leasing Ltd v CEC* (1999).

[15] As to what this amounts to see e.g. *BMW (GB) Ltd v CEC* (1997) and *CEC v Kilroy Television Co Ltd* (1997).

26–37   Policy considerations There is an inherent policy conflict in these rules. The tax authorities are concerned to
maximise tax revenues. From their viewpoint, input tax is lost
tax, and is therefore to be discouraged. But VAT is a tax on
value-added, that is, a tax on the differences between inputs and
outputs. Any attempt to reduce the entitlement to input tax so as
to tax more than the value added is wrong in principle. The
dilemma is heightened by the natural temptation of taxpayers to
claim as much input tax as possible. I may say that the new
power boat I purchased was bought directly for the purpose of
my (taxable) business. The tax authorities, watching me cruising
down the river on a Sunday afternoon, may not be entirely
convinced that I am doing it to impress my customers. They see
an age-old variant of the battle over deductible expenses turning
up in a new guise.

Of course, if the input tax invoices are shams then they will be
discounted. In *HMRC v Dempster* (2008), it was said that a
sham for this purpose was whether the rights and obligations for
VAT purposes expressed in the invoice were different from those
which the parties intended to create. Alternatively, knowledge
or wilful blindness to the fact that they were part of a tax fraud
would suffice.

Direct and immediate link

26-38   There is an early decision, entirely on the wording of the UK
statute and not the Directive, that the test is essentially a subjective one. In *Ian Flockton Developments Ltd v CEC* (1987),
an engineering company successfully claimed input tax credit
arising from the costs of maintain and running a racehorse. The
court said that where there was no obvious connection between
the expenditure and the business it was for the trader to show a
link, but its subjective intention was paramount. The issue is
however, one of mixed law and fact.

But since then the matter has been taken up by the ECJ. In
Midland Bank v CEC (2000), that Court said that the diversity
of commercial and professional transactions makes it impossible
to set out a single method of determining the necessary relationship between input and output transactions in order for
input tax to become deductible. It is for the national courts to
decide how to apply the direct and immediate link test of the
facts of each case, taking into account all the surrounding circumstances.

26-39   The basic test—taxable supplies only If a trader is
making taxable supplies only then the issue is whether the input

supplies are used for the purpose of those taxable supplies. Or to put in another way, is there an immediate and direct link between the input transactions and the trader's business? Guidance on applying this test in such a context was given by the House of Lords in *CEC v Redrow Group Plc* (1999). The company built and sold new houses. As part of a marketing scheme they paid prospective purchasers' estate agents' fees on selling their own houses. The company instructed the estate agents and monitored their activities. These expenses were not payable if the sale of the new house fell through. The House of Lords held that the input tax attributable to those fees was deductible. It was not necessary to show that there was a direct link between the payment of the input tax and the specific supply of houses by the taxpayers to the purchasers (output tax). The test was whether the input supply was received in connection with the business for the purpose of being incorporated within its economic activities. The fact that a third party benefited was irrelevant. On the facts, once it was found that there was a supply of services by the estate agents to Redrow input tax could be deducted.[16]

TAXABLE AND EXEMPT SUPPLIES There is, however, a clear **26–40** need to make such direct links if the trader is making both taxable and exempt supplies since there is no input tax credit in relation to supplies to the trader which are used for the purposes of exempt supplies. The solution in the VAT (General) Regulations 1995 is to identify input supplies which are used exclusively for the business of making taxable or exempt supplies as appropriate[17] and then to apportion those supplies which are not exclusively used for one such set of supplies (e.g. the cost of office equipment) according to the ratio of taxable to exempt supplies. Further if an input is initially related to a taxable supply but is actually used in relation to an exempt supply, no deduction is allowed.[18]

IDENTIFYING THE LINK In deciding in such cases whether **26–41** there is an immediate and direct link between the whole or part

---

[16] That "input reasoning" was also applied in *WHA Ltd v CEC* (2003) where a garage charged an insurance company in respect of repairs to cars owned by those insured by the company. The "supply reasoning" was followed in *Loyalty Management Ltd v HMRC* (2007) CA: see para.24–49, above.

[17] See e.g. *CEC v Harpcombe Ltd* (1996).

[18] *Tremerton Ltd v CEC* (1999). This may not be so if the reason for the change is beyond the trader's control or the taxable supplies never materialised: *Midland Bank v CEC* (2000).

of an input supply and a taxable activity for the purposes of attribution, the basic test was set out by the ECJ in *BLP Group Plc v CEC* (1995) and is known as the *BLP* test. Sometimes this test has been formulated as to whether the input supply is part of the cost component of the taxable activity or essential to it. It is not enough that it is a consequence of that activity. Nor is it permissible to look beyond that purpose to some ultimate aim, or to apply a "but for" test. That is not enough. Thus the costs of legal services given to a bank after it had advised on a take-over were not so directly attributable to that advice (a taxable activity as opposed to general banking which is exempt)—it was a consequence of it; nor was it enough that it would not have been incurred but for the taxable activity.[19]

26–42   CONSEQUENCES OF TOTAL ATTRIBUTION   Under reg.101 of the 1995 General Regulations, if the whole of the input supply can be so attributed to a taxable activity, it is reclaimable in full. If none of it so relates, then none can be reclaimed. But if only part of it can be so attributed, then the question of apportionment arises.

26–43   CONSEQUENCES OF PARTIAL ATTRIBUTION   The effect of reg.101, where part of an input transaction can be identified with a taxable activity, is that the proportion of input tax which is allowed as a credit is equal to the ratio of the trader's exempt supplies to taxable supplies and not the part identified as applicable to a taxable activity. This may produce a surprising result. In *Mayflower Theatre Trust Ltd v HMRC* (2007), the trust paid production companies to put on plays etc at the theatre. Those were taxable supplies and the Trust incurred substantial input tax on them. Its problem was that 80 per cent of its output supplies were the sales of tickets which were exempt supplies. The other 20 per cent, however, were taxable supplies of theatre programmes, catering etc. Applying the *BLP* test, the CA held that there was an immediate and direct link between the payments to the production companies and the sale of the programmes. The subject matter of the productions formed part of the raw material used in the programmes and that objective link was sufficient to satisfy the test. Further, although there was no such link with the other taxable supplies, the effect of the 1995 General Regulations was that a full 20 per

---

[19] *Midland Bank Plc v CEC* (2000) ECJ. See also *Dial-a-Phone Ltd v CEC* (2004) CA.

cent of the input tax was recoverable and not just the percentage attributable to the programmes.

THE OVERHEADS EXCEPTION There is an exception to the **26–44** *BLP* test of specifically attributing an input supply to taxable and/or exempt supplies for the purposes of attribution. A taxpayer who makes both taxable and exempt supplies may deduct the relevant percentage of any input tax which is attributable to the *overheads* of the business.[20] These are the costs of goods and services which are properly incurred in the course of the business but which cannot be linked with any specific goods or services supplied by the taxpayer. Examples would be the cost of office carpets or audit fees. All that is needed is a direct and immediate link with the whole economic activity of the taxpayer. Thus, although the legal fees could not be attributed to any taxable supply in the *Midland Bank* case, they were attributed to overheads and so partly allowable.

Although this is a different methodology from that of attributing inputs to both specific exempt and taxable supplies as in the *Mayflower* case above, the appropriate proportion in the case of overheads is also based on the ratio of the taxpayer's taxable and exempt supplies and so the result would have been the same in that case even if the overheads approach had been used. It was said in *Abbey National Plc v CEC* (2001), ECJ, that if the input supplies could be attributed to the overheads of the taxable activities they would be fully deducible even though they might not attach to any specific supply.[21] That accords with the *BLP* test that it is the taxable activity with which the connection must be made and not necessarily with any specific supply.

Bad debt relief

Since liability to account for VAT arises at the tax point there **26–45** would be a problem for a trader who has issued a tax invoice in one quarter, and so accounted for the output tax on that invoice, if the customer subsequently defaults on payment so that the trader never actually receives that tax. From 1990 onwards therefore there has been an allowance for such bad debts. Section 36 currently provides that any supply on which a taxpayer has accounted for VAT to HMRC, and on which there is a debt

---

[20] *Abbey National Plc v CEC* (2001) ECJ; *Kretztechnik AG v Finanzampt Linz* (2005) ECJ. This is based on the need for fiscal neutrality and the ability to deduct relevant inputs to preserve the sanctity of the system.

[21] And so not at all, if fully attributable to the overheads of the exempt supplies only.

(whether in cash or in kind) which is more than six months old and which has been written off in the trader's books is eligible for such relief (i.e. the output tax paid can be reclaimed). Repayment of the relief is required if the debt is subsequently repaid or if the debt has been assigned to a person connected with the trader and payment is made to that person.

INDEX

487